Beaches, Bays, and Barrens

Beaches, Bays, and Barrens

A Natural History of the Jersey Shore

Eric G. Bolen

Rutgers University Press
New Brunswick, Camden, and Newark, New Jersey
London and Oxford

Rutgers University Press is a department of Rutgers, The State University of New Jersey, one of the leading public research universities in the nation. By publishing worldwide, it furthers the University's mission of dedication to excellence in teaching, scholarship, research, and clinical care.

Library of Congress Cataloging-in-Publication Data

Names: Bolen, Eric G., author. | Burger, Joanna, author of foreword.
Title: Beaches, bays, and barrens : a natural history of the Jersey Shore / Eric G. Bolen ;
foreword by Joanna Burger.
Description: New Brunswick : Rutgers University Press, [2024] | Includes bibliographical references and index.
Identifiers: LCCN 2023040120 | ISBN 9781978836181 (paperback) | ISBN 9781978836198 (hardcover) |
ISBN 9781978836204 (epub) | ISBN 9781978836211 (pdf)
Subjects: LCSH: Natural history—New Jersey—Atlantic Coast. | Estuarine ecology—
New Jersey—Atlantic Coast. | Coastal ecology—New Jersey—Atlantic Coast. | Atlantic
Coast (N.J.) | BISAC: NATURE / Ecosystems & Habitats / Coastal Regions & Shorelines |
NATURE / Ecology
Classification: LCC QH105.N5 B65 2024 | DDC 577.09749/09146—dc23/eng/20231221
LC record available at https://lccn.loc.gov/2023040120

For those naturalists, the few among many, who do so much to protect the biological and physical wonders of the Jersey Shore

Contents

Foreword

I HAVE FOLLOWED Eric Bolen's research career for decades, sometimes up close and sometimes from afar, and it has been remarkable and fun. I know of few others who have had such incredibly varied and daringly distinguished careers, while still retaining a naturalist's flare for mentoring students and scientists alike. He has written important papers and books on waterfowl, wildlife, and wilderness, about human-dominated ecosystems and those that have so far escaped much of our human imprint. In all his writing, whether that for a few who delve into very esoteric scientific journals or his books on natural history, he never ceases to intrigue and fascinate us. His love of nature and the intricacies of complex ecosystems shines through his writings, enabling us to see the natural world through new eyes and mindsets. It is truly an art to be able to weave together information and experiences from vastly different species and ecosystems to create a world we can imagine we are walking through with him.

Bolen brings alive the Jersey shores—the Atlantic coast, the Delaware Bay shore, and the Pine Barrens in between. It took decades for scientists to recognize that the New Jersey Pinelands is part of both coasts, a bridge between them, and integral to the complex coastal system that is New Jersey. Although he resides elsewhere, Bolen was born in New Jersey, hunted and fished there, and, perhaps more importantly, fell in love with the rich and contrasting ecosystems that make up our shores. New Jersey is a state in contrast; some see it only as the urban sprawl along the New Jersey Turnpike, identifying every place by its exit number, or, more recently, the Garden State Parkway. They understand the pull of the Jersey Shore but remain unaware of the mysteries and magic of Delaware Bay and the Pinelands.

People who have not visited Delaware Bay or the Pinelands are in for an amazing treat in this book. I had the pleasure of reading it before nearly anyone else, and even though I have worked on wildlife in Barnegat Bay, along the Atlantic and Delaware Bay, and in the Pinelands, I found the book enthralling and fascinating. Bolen weaves together tales of biology, ecology, evolution, conservation, and culture in a manner that is accurate, exciting, and breathtaking. His writing is so sharp and passionate that I hated each chapter to end—I wanted more.

Bolen brings a wealth of knowledge, experiences, and feelings to the vast array of different topics he weaves together in the book. He creates a tapestry of history, archaeology, biology, ecology, and toxicology, always with a backdrop of the changes people have wrought. The Jersey Shore was largely ignored, and the shoreline was changed only by the natural forces of wind and tides. Following the Second World War and the advent of insecticides to control mosquitos, there was a rapid increase in the human population living along the Jersey Shore. He seamlessly connects our own history with that of the plants and animals that make New Jersey their home. Whether he is writing about the naturalists who first explored New Jersey or the unbelievable harm caused by DDT and other contaminants in the 1950 and 1960s, he carries readers on a journey that places us within the natural world of the Jersey Shore.

To Bolen, the Jersey Shore is a matrix of ecosystems that includes the Atlantic coast, Cape May, and the Delaware, including the Pine Barrens in between that link them all. He captures the web of life from the small fiddler crabs scurrying along the mudflats to the endangered piping plover chicks searching for food, and from the beachgoers pursued by gulls in the summer to the waterfowl hunters in the late fall. He conveys the delicate balance protecting people from frequent fires and the fires required to maintain the pygmy pine forest, and between the need for retirement communities and the habitat destruction required to build them. We can almost hear the surf pounding the shore and picture the female pine snakes digging nests in open patches within the Pine Barrens. Bolen treats them as one intricate and interesting ecosystem of wind, waves, surf, mudflat, back bays, and sand that harbors a myriad of creatures that live complex lives that are intertwined. It is a book I started reading on my computer and then printed so I could experience it in a comfortable lounger, well into the night. For someone who has worked in all of these habitats for fifty years, I was amazed how much I learned and enjoyed the read.

Today, many scientists fail to understand that simply studying their species or population in the field, or their "question" in a laboratory or the field, is no longer enough. We have a responsibility as scientists to communicate both our findings and the importance of our findings not only to other scientists but to our broader human community. We are facing some of the greatest global challenges imaginable—habitat loss, species extinction, climate change, and sea level rises. These stressors not only affect us, in terms of food insecurity, wars, famine, and overpopulation, but have devastating effects on the species and ecosystems around us. This book brings together information on the diverse disciplines and topics needed to understand and appreciate New Jersey's coasts, including their associated terrestrial systems. Bolen's breadth of knowledge is amazing, his prose is captivating, and his ability to interweave human history, natural history, and culture is charming. This book represents a rare gem of information, insights, and inspiration.

JOANNA BURGER

Distinguished Professor of Biology

Rutgers, The State University of New Jersey

Naturalist and author of *A Naturalist along the Jersey Shore, Whispers in the Pines, Twenty-Five Nature Spectacles in New Jersey, Life along the Delaware Bay,* and *The Parrot Who Owns Me*

Preface

THIS BOOK is designed for the lay public—tourists, day-trippers, birders, summer renters, local residents and citizen scientists—in short, just about anyone with a curious interest in the Jersey Shore. I hope, of course, that others will find it engaging, especially teachers and their students, and perhaps even a professional biologist might find a nugget or two of new information tucked away in its pages.

My effort has been a long time coming. I started collecting information at least twenty years ago, and even did a bit of writing, but other things—all remarkably trivial in retrospect—took over and the project languished. When I recently finished my share of work on a similar book about Texas, I decided that it was time to deal with what I had postponed for far too long—a tour of the Jersey Shore that would similarly mix some highlights about its biological treasures with a few historical nuggets. Texas had been my home for more than twenty-five years and North Carolina for a like amount, but New Jersey was my birthright and where I first experienced nature while hunting and fishing. My outdoor experiences also included some clamming in Barnegat Bay, and as this book suggests, the bay's clinging mud has yet to wash completely away. Now, a lifetime later, when I perch on a dune at Mantoloking and watch the endless parade of breaking waves, I think of the eternal magic of this and beaches everywhere.

Repeated scans of two wonderful and hard-to-find books in my library helped stir me into action. Bayard Randolph Kraft's *Under Barnegat's Beam* and Charles Edgar Nash's *The Lure of Long Beach* both offer ecological as well as historical insights into yesteryear on the Jersey Shore. These rich volumes tell of the gothic stands of cedars once covering parts of Long Beach Island—long since cut, the stump of one goliath boasted no fewer than 1,080 annual growth rings—or of the waterfowl fatally attracted to the light of Old Barney. More recent publications, Kent Mountford's *Closed Sea: A History of Barnegat Bay*, John Lloyd Baily's *Six Miles at Sea*, and Robert Jahn's *Down Barnegat Bay: A Nor'easter Midnight Reader*, further fueled my desire to complete a long-stalled project. Readers will want to peruse two other books about the natural history of New Jersey, each authored or coauthored by Joanna Burger—her memoir, *A Naturalist along the Jersey Shore*, and (with Michael Gochfeld) an informative guide, *Twenty-Five Nature Spectacles in New Jersey*. I find it hard to imagine any biologist with a greater knowledge of the state's natural history than that amassed by Joanna Burger, and I have frequently extracted findings from these and her legion of research papers to gird my own writing. To that end, I am honored that she agreed to write the foreword for this book.

Not long ago, I visited the Carranza Memorial deep in the Pine Barrens, which reinforced my intention to complement my focus on natural history with a bit of traditional history. Standing alone in the pines surrounding the monument honoring a courageous pilot only deepened my appreciation for the quiet sanctity of an ecological wonderland that was heralded a century ago by naturalists Witmer Stone and, especially, John Harshberger. From there I went to the bird-rich marshes protected by the Forsythe National Wildlife Refuge. The skyline of Atlantic City provided the backdrop, which cemented the realization that New Jersey, despite its advanced urbanization, still has much to offer to those who, like Aldo Leopold, cannot "live without wild things."

My lunches with the late Elizabeth Morgan were special events during this book's formative stages. For dessert, we took field trips to a few of the historical and ecological haunts she knew so well, which for me was a welcome swap of unneeded calories for some helpful background. Even a brief stop at the cottage once occupied by John Harshberger when he was investigating the Pine Barrens offered a landmark in my efforts to learn more about that unique area of New Jersey. I peppered her with questions, and on those rare occasions when she had no answers, she always knew of someone who did—Elizabeth was a living Rolodex for sources familiar with the natural history of the Jersey Shore, and I wish she had lived to see the result of her tutelage in print.

The book's plan is straightforward. In the introduction I present a quick review of early naturalists and their visits to New Jersey, which is followed by some thoughts, as I have emphasized elsewhere, about the rationale of saving endangered species and the values of natural history as a bona fide component of the biological sciences. Thereafter, we visit—chapter by chapter—what I think represent easily recognizable landforms, each with distinctive ecological components and historical highlights. Our journey begins in the ankle-deep swirl of the swash zone and continues across the beach and into the dunes—taking pause en route to rummage through the storybook debris of the wrack line. That done, we explore salt marshes and their sea of grasses, fiddler crabs, and mummichogs, then move on to an extensive tour of the eelgrass meadows in Barnegat Bay. Next comes a visit to Cape May, whose peninsula each fall collects and funnels birds and insects southward on their remarkable rite of passage. On the leeward side of the peninsula we wander along New Jersey's "Other Shore," where each spring horseshoe crabs and famished shorebirds unite in one of nature's more notable spectacles. Our journey ends in the Pine Barrens, which I suppose is not really the Jersey Shore in the sense of wide beaches and pounding surf, but this unique environment of pygmy pines and dark bogs surely justifies a bit of ecological gerrymandering.

Finally, after completing our literary fieldtrip from beaches to barrens, an afterword considers ways to protect and perhaps enhance the biological integrity of natural areas and wild things on the Jersey Shore. Although hardly complete, the choices offer several levels of action, from participating in hands-on, sometimes muddy, projects to championing conservation in the public square. All of this is a handoff to you, the reader, to get off the sofa and make New Jersey a better place to live.

Beaches, Bays, and Barrens

FIGURE 1.1. Island Beach State Park showcases a rare area of essentially undeveloped beach and coastal wetlands still remaining on the Jersey Shore. Photo credit: Pernille Ruhalter.

1

Background and Other Thoughts

[T]he call of the Jersey Shore is still strong and overpowering.
—JOANNA BURGER, *A NATURALIST ALONG THE JERSEY SHORE*

NEW JERSEY, at least in places, is a land dominated by factories, industrial parks, closely packed housing, and traffic jams accompanied by a population density akin to that of India. But elsewhere, spacious farmland, forests, and wetlands offer treasures well removed from smokestacks, malls, and warehouses. The beaches and dunes at Island Beach State Park and remote Pine Barrens are among these, but so too are the marshes and waters of Barnegat Bay and the shoreline of Delaware Bay (fig. 1.1). Migrating birds and butterflies, wintering waterfowl, dwarfed forests of pines and oaks, and fiddler crabs represent just part of a much larger trove of things wild and wonderful. Decoy carvers, blueberry husbandry, nor'easters, and the tragedy of a plane crash and horror of shark attacks flavor the mix. This is the essence of a special slice of New Jersey—the Jersey Shore—featured in this book.

New Jersey: The Big Picture in Brief

Guided by geology, geographers partition New Jersey into four physiographic provinces (fig. 1.2). The smallest of these is the Ridge and Valley Province, tucked into the northwest corner of the state. For some, the Delaware Water Gap or High Point State Park provide iconic features of this region, whereas others might think

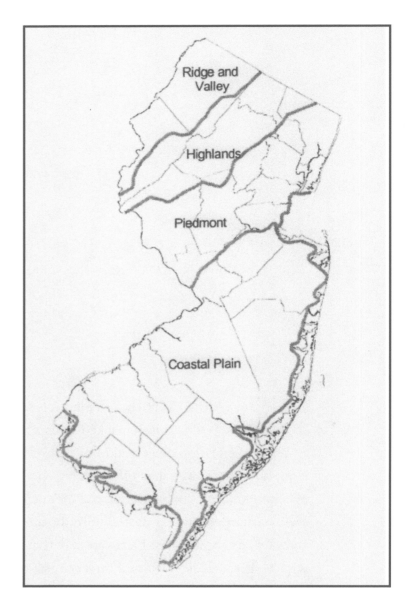

FIGURE 1.2. Four physiographic provinces characterize the topography of New Jersey, each sloping along a northeast-southwest axis—a feature that influences the movements of birds, especially hawks, during their fall migration (see chapter 5). Map prepared by, and used with the permission of, the Department of Environmental Protection, New Jersey Geological and Water Survey.

of hawks coursing southward each fall between the mountains or perhaps envision an enclave of timber rattlesnakes denning in the rocky slopes.

Just to the south lies the Highlands, a province of rolling hills and lakes and streams, many the longtime favorites of anglers. Among these, the Lake Hopatcong basin serves as a reminder of the glaciers that shaped the terrain of northern New Jersey. Some areas in the Highlands, so far escaping the axe and saw, still wear a woodland cloak of oak, hickory, and beech. In sheltered spots, often along a stream, the forest includes dark glens of majestic eastern hemlocks—a visit to Ken Lockwood Gorge Wildlife Management Area near Califon will reveal just such a place.

Next in line is the Piedmont, where eons of relentless erosion steadily lowered the elevation in comparison to the adjacent Highlands—the former consisting of shales and other soft rocks, the latter with a foundation of harder gneiss. In places, however, the gently rolling terrain gives way to a few high points, among them the Palisades along the Hudson River and the three ridges forming the Watchung Mountains. These heights, formed of lava, resist erosion and thus stand above the surrounding landscape. Chimney Rock lies at the convergence of two of the Watchung ridges and serves as a prime lookout point for migrating hawks. At the end of the Wisconsin Ice Age, the Watchungs penned in Lake Passaic, a huge lake that formed from glacial melt water. In time, the moraine that contained the lake gave way, and the outpour of rushing water cut the channel of what is today the Passaic River. The Great Swamp, now a national wildlife refuge, and Troy Meadows are remnants of the ancient lake basin.

The Coastal Plain, the fourth and largest physiographic province, covers about 60 percent of New Jersey and is subdivided into two regions based on soil differences. Cretaceous deposits underlie the Inner Coastal Plain, whereas younger Tertiary deposits distinguish the Outer Coastal Plain. Interglacial deposits from the Pleistocene cover both regions, but the fertility of the clay-rich soils in the Inner region exceeds that of the sandier Outer area. A belt of hills—formally known as cuestas—extending along a southwest-northeast axis further separates the two regions. West of these hills water drains into the Delaware River or north to Raritan Bay. On the east side, surface water flows to the ocean or southwest to Delaware Bay.

With this brief journey across New Jersey, we have arrived at our destination. If the coast is the frontier between land and sea, it is nowhere more prominent than "Down the Jersey Shore." On a summer day, throngs of visitors enjoy the lure of the sand and waves—the ingredients for a pleasing tan, a vigorous round of beach volleyball, or a swim in the Atlantic's agreeable waters—and commonly a combination of these. But in a more ethereal way, the Jersey Shore also offers opportunities to sense—by touch, smell, sound, as well as by sight—some of nature's best works.

Shore Note 1.1 Island Beach State Park: A Taste of What Used to Be

A visit to Island Beach State Park comes close to touching nature as it existed centuries ago on the Jersey Shore. To be sure, a central road serves as the park's major artery and a few buildings rise above the sand, but for the naturalist, this is a good as it gets to experience a beach unfettered by summer homes and boardwalks.

The park protects nearly 10 miles of an undeveloped barrier beach that separates the Atlantic Ocean from Barnegat Bay. Once a true island, the site became a peninsula when an inlet filled in more than two centuries ago, as further described in chapter 2. Native Americans camped and foraged on the island long before Europeans arrived, but formal ownership began in 1635 when it was included in a land grant awarded by Charles I to the first Earl of Stirling. The beach remained undeveloped for centuries but eventually attracted anglers who built makeshift shacks. In response to frequent shipwrecks, the U.S. Life Saving Service opened three stations on the beach in 1849; these buildings today house the park's nature center, office, and maintenance equipment. After the railroad reached the coast, the influx of hunters and anglers increased, which spurred the construction of two hotels on the island, but both are now just memories.

Steel tycoon Henry Phipps Jr. acquired the property in 1926 with the intention of developing an upscale seaside resort. He built three large homes, but his dream ended with the crash of the stock market in 1929. Phipps died in 1930, but the beach remained in the care of his estate foreman, Francis Freeman, who with his wife and a local Coast Guard officer formed the Borough of Island Beach. Freeman issued rules to all comers: "Leave things be. Don't trample the sand dunes, don't pick the flowers, and don't annoy the osprey."

Island Beach, except for the Freemans and a Coast Guard patrol, was evacuated during World War II; because of its isolated location, the beach served as a testing site for military rockets. Once considered as a candidate for the National Park System, but short-circuited by inadequate funding, Island Beach was instead acquired in 1953—for $2.7 million—by the New Jersey government and opened as a state park in 1959. With its preservation ensured, Island Beach will provide future generations with a unique sample of the past—pristine beaches, healthy dunes, and unblemished scenery.

To accomplish its goals of preservation, education, and recreation, the park is divided into three management zones: two natural areas lie astride a central recreation area. In particular, naturalists will profit from visiting the Sedge Islands Marine Conservation Zone. Signs indicate the activities allowed in each zone, but the dunes remain off-limits throughout the park. In addition to the nature center, the interpretive program includes a seasonal schedule of walking tours, kayak trips, and other activities. Birds occur everywhere from shore to shore across the island, but the bayshore generally offers a greater variety. The vegetation, which developed in several distinctive communities, includes more than 200 species of native plants.

First Europeans on the Scene

Henry Hudson (ca. 1565–1611), on his third voyage to the New World, sailed along the New Jersey coast in 1609 and during his explorations came upon what is today known as Barnegat Bay. The log of the *Half Moon*, kept by first mate Robert Juen, notes that this "great lake of water" was part of "a good land to fall in with, and a pleasant land to see." Juen also recorded the sea breaking in the shoal-filled "mouth" of the lake—an apt description of the treacherous tidal flow racing through Barnegat Inlet—but made no mention of the area's natural resources. Juen did, however, record a "great fire" on shore and, without too much imagination, likely was a conflagration arising in the Pine Barrens (chapter 7). Two years later, on his fourth voyage across the Atlantic, Hudson perished when his mutinous crew set him adrift on the icy waters of a northern sea, today's Hudson Bay. (Earlier, in 1524, Giovanni da Verrazzano [1485–1528] also cruised northward along the New Jersey coastline but somehow failed to notice either Delaware Bay or Barnegat Bay, although he did sail into New York Harbor, an event honored today by a bridge bearing his name.)

On at least one of his several voyages along the mid-Atlantic coastline between 1614 and 1624, mariner Cornelius Jacobsen Mey (ca. 1580–post-1624) also encountered the tumultuous "mouth" of Juen's "great lake." Impressed, he warned that it was a breaking inlet, or *barende-gat* in Dutch, thus establishing the origin of "Barnegat." Mey continued southward along the coast, where he found an inlet that his ship could safely enter. There a large bay awaited, as did the noisy rookeries of nesting waterbirds—herons, egrets, gulls, and terns—thick on the adjacent shores. Thousands of nests contained tens of thousands of eggs and nestlings, prompting Mey to name the site "Eyer Haven," today's Little Egg Harbor. A bit to the south, Mey and his mariners encountered yet another bay and nesting area, this one now known as Great Egg Harbor. Sailing for the Dutch West India Company, Mey later explored the Delaware Bay area and traded for furs with Native Americans in the region. Furs were a valuable commodity in Holland, and he undoubtedly gained some insight about this and other natural resources utilized by his trading partners. Mey's legacy, of course, endures in several well-known locations in New Jersey, not the least of which is the Cape May Peninsula (chapter 5).

About a decade after Mey's voyages, another Dutch explorer, David Pieterzen de Vries (ca. 1593–1655), sailed into Little Egg Harbor and continued inland up

Shore Note 1.2 Whales and Whaling in New Jersey

In 1690, a small band of mariners established the first permanent whaling station on the New Jersey coast on Long Beach Island at what is today Harvey Cedars. The station remained in operation until at least 1823. A tall pole outfitted with climbing pegs and topped by a crow's nest served as a spotting tower. However, the first record of whaling along the New Jersey coast occurred when a ship under the command of David Pieterzen de Vries (ca. 1593–1655) chanced upon a large pod in 1632; 17 whales were "speared," but only 7 of these were landed. Word of such bounty spread quickly and soon attracted whalers from ports in New England. Enterprising businessmen obtained charters that granted them exclusive whaling rights, one for all waters between Barnegat Bay and Sandy Hook and another extending from Little Egg Harbor to Cape May. In 1683, while searching for a place to settle, William Penn observed that "mighty whales roll upon the coast near the mouth of the Bay of Delaware," adding, "We justly hope a considerable profit by whalery. They being so numerous and the shore so suitable." By 1692, a whaling settlement known as Town Bank had sprouted on a sandy bluff on Delaware Bay, about three miles north of Cape May Point. The original town later succumbed to beach erosion and now lies underwater offshore.

Unlike the long seagoing voyages of New England whalers, New Jersey whalers hunted from skiffs launched from shore and manned by six hardy souls. Once harpooned, the whale dragged the skiff on a "Nantucket sleigh ride" until it succumbed from exhaustion and additional harpoon thrusts. The whalers then faced the arduous task of towing the whale ashore, where the blubber was rendered into oil in huge cast iron cauldrons. One such site, Spermaceti Cove at Sandy Hook, earned its name from the sperm whales landed there by early settlers. Smaller whales were hauled into the surf zone with block and tackle, then flensed at low tide. Larger whales were difficult to beach, however, and these were towed through inlets and flensed while floating in quiet waters. This procedure enabled access to blubber on the whale's downside that otherwise would have been inaccessible and wasted.

Stranding data compiled by NOAA for 40 whales that were examined or entangled in nets on the coasts of Monmouth, Ocean, Atlantic, or Cape May county between 1988 and 2016 may approximate the current composition of the whales migrating along the Jersey Shore. Of these,

the Mullica River. In the woodlands beyond the coast, he marveled at the abundance of a single species—the trees were alive with passenger pigeons. Whether de Vries and his crew enjoyed a meal of pigeons remains unknown, but if they did, their gunshots heralded the beginning of the end for what was once the most abundant bird in North America and possibly the world. More than two centu-

humpback whales represented the majority (40 percent), followed by minke (35 percent) and fin (20 percent) whales, with the remaining 5 percent split equally between North Atlantic right and sperm whales. Except for sperm whales, the largest of the toothed whales, all of the others sieve their food from sea water using the fringes of keratin plates (baleen, or "whale bone") that hang like curtains in their huge mouths. The blubber from all of these species yields oil that once fueled lamps and lighthouses, and baleen provided the material for corset and collar stays, umbrella ribs, whips, brushes, skirt hoops, brooms, and even carriage springs. Sperm whales also produce an especially fine grade of oil ("spermaceti") in their head cavities as well as ambergris, an intestinal secretion valued in the manufacture of perfumes. Although unconfirmed, some believe that the indigestible beaks of squid—the favored food of sperm whales—trigger the secretion when they block the intestinal tract.

Of the whales traveling along the New Jersey coast, the North Atlantic right whale is by far the most endangered. Whalers preferred the species because the carcasses floated and the blubber yielded large amounts of oil—hence it was the "right" whale to hunt. Moreover, their migration was predictable and occurred nearshore, which facilitated overexploitation of a vulnerable population.[1] In 1935, the United States banned further hunting of North Atlantic right whales in its territorial waters; the species also was among the first listed as endangered under the provisions of the Endangered Species Act of 1973. Nevertheless, collisions with ships (now somewhat lessened by speed restrictions) and entanglements with fishing gear continued to reduce the population. By 2022, so few North Atlantic right whales remained—about 340, of which just 72 were reproductively active females—that the conservation value of each animal became obvious. Indeed, preventing the death of just two adult females per year will maintain the growth rate of the population at its replacement level. Lacking that, northern right whales will continue inching toward extinction.

---

[1] Gray whales likewise migrated nearshore along the Atlantic coastline and, by the early eighteenth century, they had been overhunted, never to recover. Fortunately, the Pacific population of gray whales survived a similar calamity and, after gaining legal protection in 1949, have returned to their former numbers.

ries of wanton exploitation followed, reaching its peak in the 1880s, then faded as the birds became too few to hunt. "Martha," the last passenger pigeon, died in 1914, alone in a cage in the Cincinnati Zoo. De Vries also can be credited as being the first to harpoon whales on the New Jersey coast, which likewise began an era that ended with most of the commercially viable species becoming endangered.

Natural History in New Jersey: The Early Days

Philadelphia served as the intellectual capital of the American colonies and remained so in the decades following the Revolutionary War. Because of residents such as Benjamin Franklin, Charles Willson Peale, Benjamin Rush, John Bartram and his son William, and Benjamin Smith Barton, Philadelphia became the hub of the American Enlightenment. Such a pool of talent led to the founding of both the American Philosophical Society in 1743 and the Academy of Natural Sciences of Philadelphia in 1812, both of which remain active (the latter become the Academy of Natural Sciences of Drexel University in 2011). The Philadelphia Linnaean Society, founded in 1806 but later disbanded, also contributed to the fervor of the period. Note here that Benjamin Smith Barton (1766–1815) exerted substantial influence on science in early America, in part by aiding Jefferson plan the Lewis and Clark Expedition. Indeed, the explorers carried with them the first edition (of three) of his *Elements of Botany*. In 1807, Barton published *A Discourse on Some of the Principal Desiderata in Natural History, and on the Best Means of Promoting the Study of Science in the United States*, which became a catalyst for decades of scientific pursuits.

Not surprisingly, Philadelphia's collection of brains and facilities became a powerful magnet for like-minded visitors. New Jersey, of course, lies just across the Delaware River and, germane to our theme, offered beaches, bays, and pine forests awaiting exploration and discovery. For visitors and residents alike, a bumpy ride in a stage coach or teamster's wagon to the Pine Barrens or on to Tuckerton became a journey well-taken to the Jersey Shore.

John Bartram (1699–1777), heralded as America's first native-born botanist, lacked a formal education but nonetheless gained prominence with naturalists both in Europe, including acclaim from the renowned taxonomist Carl Linnaeus, and in the American colonies. Born into a farming family near Philadelphia, he developed an interest in medicinal plants, which became a feature in the garden at his own homestead on the Schuylkill River. He supplemented his farm income by selling seeds of American plants to clients in Europe. Bartram traveled widely to collect stock for his garden; these included trips to northern locations such as Lake Ontario as well as to Florida in the Deep South. Likewise, the flora of the New Jersey Pine Barrens—to him, "the desert"—provided ample rewards for his enterprise; seeds from Atlantic white cedar, laurels, hollies, pines, and oaks were among those he sent to Europe. He traveled to New Jersey often, including three trips in 1739, followed by "4 prety [*sic*] long Journeys in Jersey & three times in ye desert" in 1740. In 1742, he collected pine cones near Egg Harbor for the Duke of Norfolk. Pehr Kalm, a Swedish botanist associated with Linnaeus, occasionally traveled with Bartram in southern New Jersey.

Bartram also described the landscape, noting a plain covered with a "strang kind of dwarf pine" growing with "dwarf oaks about brest high full of acorns." He also perceived that the cones borne by pitch pine remained closed until fire stimulated their opening for seed dispersal. In 1765, George III appointed Bartram as the king's botanist for North America. Bartram's garden emerged as a gathering point for important figures, among them George Washington, James Madison, and Alexander Hamilton, as well as for a parade of naturalists such as André Michaux and Henry Muhlenberg. Today, the 46-acre site still serves as an active center for natural history; in 1960, the National Park Service selected Bartram's Garden as a National Historic Landmark.

John's son, William (1739–1823), continued in his father's footsteps—quite literally, in fact, when he traveled to Florida in 1773. He described this four-year trip in a book familiarly known as *Bartram's Travels* in lieu of its exceptionally long title. William knew birds and other animals almost as well as he did plants, and his book accordingly includes many observations of the fauna as well as flora he encountered along the way. Insights about Native Americans also enrich his book (a Seminole chief dubbed William "Puc Puggy," or Flower Hunter, because of his quest for new and interesting plants). *Bartram's Travels* became—and remains—an American classic as one of the foremost books on natural history.

An artist of considerable talent, William began drawing birds at 14, later followed by illustrations of turtles, shells, and plants, some of which appeared in British publications. More famously, he illustrated plants he or his father discovered. One of these, popularly known as Franklin's Lost Tree, later completely disappeared from its native habitat. Fortunately, the seeds collected by the Bartrams saved the species from extinction, and the trees survive today in gardens and arboretums in both Europe and America. American lotus, the subject of another of his well-known illustrations,[1] was drawn from plants collected in New Jersey—likely from

----

[1] American lotus, superficially similar but unrelated to waterlilies, bears round leaves two feet or more in diameter that, along with its flowers, rise well above the water's surface; the stems originate from tuberous

FIGURE 1.3. American lotus, shown here in a New Jersey wetland bordering Delaware Bay, captured the interest of John and William Bartram, a father-and-son team of botanists active during America's colonial period. In 1767, William sketched the species, here represented in part by a facsimile drawn by Elizabeth Bolen (inset); the original work is housed in London's Natural History Museum. Photo credits: Joel Fry, Bartram's Garden; Dale Lockwood (inset).

marshes at the mouth of the Salem River—and, after several failed attempts, eventually propagated in his father's famous garden (fig. 1.3). Like his father

---

rhizomes in wetlands three to six feet deep. Its yellow to white flowers produce large seeds housed in woody structures shaped like showerheads, which break off, float, and distribute the seeds. Bartram's drawing, critically analyzed by art historian Elizabeth Athens, also included a small vignette of a heron and Venus flytrap.

FIGURE 1.4. Curly grass ferns, perhaps the most notable plant in the flora of New Jersey, were discovered in the Pine Barrens near Quaker Bridge on the Batsto River; like the plants shown here, these unique ferns may emerge in the herbaceous understory of Atlantic white cedar communities. Note the coiled fronds at the base of the plants, whereas comb-like structures tip the erect fronds, but only the latter are fertile. Photo credit: Kevin Knutsen.

before him, William shared his knowledge with visitors, often becoming a mentor for aspiring naturalists—one of these, as we shall see, was a young Scot with an interest in birds. Another was Thomas Say, now regarded as America's "father" of entomology. For years William kept a journal in which he recorded the flowering dates for the plants in his garden as well as the seasonal presence of birds.

Frederick T. Pursh (1774–1820) also collected plants in the Pine Barrens, but on occasion he suffered from ethical lapses, one of which involved his "discovery" of curly grass fern, a standout in the flora of New Jersey (fig. 1.4). In fact, Dr. W. C. Eddy found the plant; he was among a group of naturalists, Pursh included, that stopped at Quaker's Bridge on the Batsto River circa 1805. However, Pursh claimed sole credit when he later published a description of the new species, a circumstance he repeated on other occasions. Another such lapse occurred when Benjamin Smith Barton hired Pursh to work on the plants collected by Lewis and Clark. But Pursh did little and eventually left for his native Germany, taking with him some of the treasured specimens, which he then described in his own publication.

Thomas Nuttall (1786–1859), who succeeded Pursh in the service of Barton, collected plants along the New Jersey coast in 1809. He established the first state record for eastern glasswort, which he found in the salt marshes at Great Egg Harbor. The plant, once considered quite rare in the regional flora, later turned up in other areas, among them on the sandy shoreline of Barnegat Bay between Mantoloking and Chadwick in Ocean County and along the Bayshore in Salem County. At the latter locations, eastern glasswort develops as a turf in the tidal zone on mud banks anchored by bulrushes and cordgrass. Unfortunately, the erosion currently degrading much of the New Jersey Bayshore almost certainly bodes ill for this small and uncommon plant.

His discoveries aside, all did not go well for Nuttall during his trip to New Jersey. Mosquitoes all but drove him back to Philadelphia and, adding injury to insult, infected him with malaria—an experience that no doubt fueled his characterization of New Jersey as an "arduous" place for fieldwork. His distinguished career, highlighted by collecting trips across much of North America, included managing the plant collections at the Academy of Natural Sciences. In addition to botany, Nuttall's endeavors included ornithology, geology, and other areas of natural history.

In 1818, chemist turned botanist John Torrey (1796–1873) also visited the Pine Barrens, doing so again in 1820 in the company of Nuttall. On one of these trips, Torrey collected curly grass fern at Quaker's Bridge, the same location where Pursh had made his "discovery" in 1805. Torrey later emerged as one of America's premier botanists. He is honored in the name of the Torrey Botanical Club (now Society), which is the oldest organization of its genre in the United States.

Meanwhile, the avifauna on the Jersey Shore did not go unnoticed. Alexander Wilson (1766–1813), widely regarded as the father of American ornithology, got into a bit of trouble in his native Scotland, enough so that he sailed for America in 1794. He taught school near Philadelphia, where he came under the influence of William Bartram, who encouraged Wilson to combine his artistic talents with his budding interest in ornithology. Thus began Wilson's mission to find, describe, and paint the birds of eastern North America. Among his extensive travels, he visited the coast of what is today Cape May County on six occasions between 1810 and 1813, most often seeking new subjects near Great Egg Harbor (see shore note 5.1).

Whooping cranes were among the species Wilson observed at Cape May, especially in the marshes at Egg Island where the stately birds stopped during their fall migration. Others included great blue herons, long-billed curlews, and a variety of waterfowl. The latter included American wigeon, which he cited as a common winter resident on the bays of Egg Harbor and Cape May. Wilson likely was the first to describe the thievery of hungry wigeon. Wigeon relish many of the same aquatic plants, notably wild celery, that canvasbacks readily dive to obtain for themselves. However, wigeon, which do not dive, await at the surface, where they snatch the plants from the canvasbacks' bills when they emerge. These circumstances, Wilson noted, cause the two ducks to "live in a state of perpetual contention." Wilson also described how wheat from a ship wrecked at the mouth of Great Egg Harbor temporarily stalled the southward migration of a large number of canvasbacks. Local gunners reacted quickly and shot as many as 240 canvasbacks in a single day during a spree that lasted for three weeks. Some of the birds sold locally for 25 cents a pair, but those going to market in Philadelphia commanded up to six times as much (where Wilson himself bought two that he described as unsurpassed for their "excellence of flesh").

Wildlife managers currently place heavy emphasis on the welfare of the black duck population, prompted by a significant reduction in their numbers in recent decades. In Wilson's day, however, black ducks—then sometimes known as "dusky" ducks—were the "most numerous" of all waterfowl in New Jersey's salt marshes during the winter. Wary birds, they rose from the marshes in "prodigious numbers" from a far-off report of a hunter's gun. Wilson suggested there were at least ten black ducks, and likely more, for every goose or brant in the area. Today, any of the state or federal wildlife refuges in New Jersey would be proud to claim a ratio half as large.

Wilson displayed a flair for ingenuity when "some humane person" (who was likely Wilson himself) submitted anonymous newspaper notices warning that American robins, because their diet included certain berries, were unfit and even dangerous to eat. At the time, market hunters shot hundreds of robins for sale as table fare—indeed, Wilson cited one instance in which two gunners together killed "30 dozen" for just such a purpose. Wilson's ploy worked, and demand for the birds "ceased almost instantly" after the notices appeared—the warnings had accomplished what pleas to halt the slaughter had failed to effect.

John James Audubon (1785–1851) also painted birds on the New Jersey coast. On a June night in 1829, he bumped across the Pine Barrens in a caravan of wagons driven by "fisherman gunners"—his term for purveyors of fish and fowl—arriving at Great Egg Harbor the next morning. He spent the following three weeks collecting specimens to illustrate in his celebrated folios of American birds. One of these, and among his finest, was a drawing of an osprey clutching a large weakfish. In the first volume of his *Ornithological Biography*, Audubon marveled at the abundance of the birds on the New Jersey coast: "I have seen upwards of 50 of their nests in the course of a day's walk."

A century and a half later, however, the osprey population of New Jersey (and elsewhere) was just hanging on. Runoff from years of pesticide applications, mainly DDT and its sister compounds, had accumulated and concentrated in aquatic food chains to levels where they impaired apex predators. Few individuals died outright, but for ospreys and other fish-eating birds the toxins thwarted the deposition of normal eggshells. As a result, the birds produced thin-shelled eggs that were crushed during incubation or, in extreme cases, eggs with virtually no shells at all. By 1974, a census revealed only 53 osprey nests on the entire New Jersey coast. Meanwhile, developments on barrier islands and the adjacent mainland deprived ospreys of trees large enough to support their heavy nests. The long road to recovery began when DDT was banned and federal, state, and private conservation organizations erected, maintained, and monitored nesting platforms (fig. 1.5). By 2016, ospreys again nested along the New Jersey coast in numbers equal to or even exceeding those of Audubon's day.

In 1824, three years before the first of his famous folios appeared, Audubon drew a bird for an engraver in Philadelphia. The engraving—of a heath hen—was to appear on a New Jersey banknote, but no record survives to confirm that any bills bearing his drawing were actually printed (a bank in Trenton, likely the intended source for the bills, failed at about this time). Instead, the engraving turned up in the designs for bank notes elsewhere, among them for a three-dollar bill for a bank in Ohio, but these, too, were never issued. Still, the engraving marks a milestone

FIGURE 1.5. Osprey populations in New Jersey and elsewhere plummeted in the pesticide era that followed World War II. The species experienced a strong recovery after DDT and related pesticides were banned in the early 1970s. Nesting platforms atop poles about 16 feet in length, which replaced the loss of large trees, also contributed significantly to the recovery of ospreys. Today these fish-eating birds may be even more numerous than when Audubon visited the Jersey Shore in 1829. Photo credit: Kevin Knutsen.

in Audubon's young career, and it seems probable that his selection of a heath hen resulted from encounters with the birds in the New Jersey Pine Barrens.

We end this brief survey with Charles Willson Peale (1741–1827). While still a humble apprentice saddle maker, Peale began painting and soon developed into a masterful portraitist, a pursuit that would become the cornerstone in his multi-faceted career. Indeed, he painted portraits of virtually all of the prominent figures of the day, among them George Washington, Thomas Jefferson, Henry Clay, John Adams, Benjamin Franklin, Meriwether Lewis, and William Clark, as well as fellow naturalists such as Thomas Say and William Bartram. Ever restless, he opened a natural history museum in Philadelphia in 1784—yet another institution of the American Enlightenment—which quickly became a well-known attraction. One of the displays in Peale's Museum was a mastodon skeleton he excavated from a bog near Newburgh, New York. With private assistance and help from the Jefferson administration, this was the nation's first organized scientific expedition, which Peale famously captured on canvas.

Peale, an accomplished taxidermist, also traveled to the Jersey Shore to collect specimens for his museum. One such trip (to Cape May in 1799) was in search of wading birds in full breeding plumage. On this occasion, Peale brought along five guns, plenty of ammunition, and a supply of spirits but, taking a cue from his teetotaling host, he converted on the spot to total abstinence. Whether this sudden reformation improved his marksmanship remains unknown, but he did record that he could thereafter digest fat pork and bacon without a complaining stomach. Peale also collected rattlesnakes in the Pine Barrens at sites along the Maurice River. He and his companions wisely looked for their quarry in February when the snakes were hibernating. They searched in swampy areas where the snakes found shelter under the roots of large trees and stumps, as noted more fully in chapter 7. Peale, aware of the snakes' lethargy at that time of year, did not hesitate to handle those they encountered. The party located eight rattlesnakes in a den close to running water and visited another site where 75 had been discovered three weeks earlier.

Peale also obtained fossils from New Jersey. One of these was apparently presented to Peale by Benjamin Franklin, then the president of the American Philosophical Society. After some false starts, the specimen was eventually identified as a foot bone from a duck-billed dinosaur discovered in Gloucester County. Many of the fossils in Peale's collection were transferred to the Academy of Natural Sciences when his own museum, then run by one of his sons, closed its doors in 1849. But many other curiosities so assiduously collected by Peale were acquired by another showman extraordinaire, P. T. Barnum.

Two Titans of the Twentieth Century

John William Harshberger (1869–1929), characterized in a biographical sketch as Friend of the Pine Barrens, had indeed befriended New Jersey's fabled Pine Barrens not only as a special place to study but also as a unique ecosystem deserving lasting protection from abuse and exploitation. The results of his research in the sandy pinelands, published in 1916, became a benchmark for its era as one of the first ecologically based studies of a distinctive landscape (see chapter 7).

Harshberger's interests in botany began early—at seven, he had already established a small herbarium stocked with plants representing the flora near his home in Philadelphia. The embryonic collection marked the beginning of a career distinguished by its breadth and mastery of numerous areas in the field of botany. A partial listing of the subjects covered in his published works clearly indicates the intellectual sweep of his interests: ecology and geographical distribution (91), biography and history (24), gardening and landscape work (24), trees and forestry (20), plant morphology (17), wild flower preservation and conservation (16), mycology and plant pathology (11), plant physiology (10), teaching botany (9), nomenclature and terminology (7), plant genetics (6), and economic botany (5), among others. In 1886, Harshberger notably coined the term "ethnobotany"—the subject of an additional 11 papers—a discipline that examines how people of a particular culture or region use indigenous plants for medicines, food, or other applications. In all, his publications number well over 300.

In what must be judged as an academic feat then and now, Harshberger earned a bachelor's degree in 1893 at the University of Pennsylvania while concurrently working toward a doctorate, awarded just a year later. He investigated the botanical and economic aspects of maize for his doctoral research, which concluded that the ancestor of corn evolved from a Mexican grass, teosinte, a theory still widely recognized. He immediately began teaching botany, biology, and zoology at Penn, rising through the ranks to full professor, the position he held for the remainder of his life. Harshberger complemented his lifelong affiliation with Penn by directing the ecology courses taught at the Marine Biology Laboratory at Cold Spring Harbor and by teaching nature studies at the Pocono Pines Assembly. He also traveled widely, collecting and studying plants in Mexico, the West Indies, Europe, South America, and northern Africa, in addition to field trips throughout most of the United States.

The Vegetation of the New Jersey Pine Barrens ranks among his major works, accompanied by *A Textbook of Mycology and Plant Pathology* and *A Phytogeographic Survey of North America*. The latter, a monumental accomplishment, attempted to classify and map all of the plant communities in North America. Because of his interest in fungi, he was among the first to forecast the looming threat of chestnut blight, a disaster sometimes compared with the extinction of the passenger pigeon. He was a member of more than 25 societies, including the Ecological Society of America, of which he was a cofounder and president.

Harshberger's interest in the vegetation of New Jersey no doubt blossomed during his brief tenure (in 1892) as an assistant botany instructor at a marine laboratory run by the University of Pennsylvania at Sea Isle City in Cape May County. Years later, he would conclude his monograph on the Pine Barrens with "the State should take over large blocks of the forest for the future use and pleasure of its people"—a hope realized in 1978 with the formation of the 1.1-million-acre Pinelands National Reserve, administered by the National Park Service. The following year New Jersey became a partner with the enactment of the Pinelands Protection Act and subsequent creation of the Pinelands Commission. In 1983, the United Nations designated the Pinelands as an International Biosphere Reserve. Harshberger did not live to celebrate these events—he died suddenly in 1929—but to the end he remained a true Friend of the Pine Barrens.

Witmer Stone (1866–1939) represents one of the best—and certainly one of the last—of America's old school naturalists (fig. 1.6). Few scientists achieve the stature of Stone in one field, let alone three: ornithology, mammalogy, and botany. Although a lifelong Philadelphian, he maintained close ties with New Jersey, notably devoting his fieldwork to the flora and fauna of the southern counties as well as vacationing at Cape May (chapter 5). Stone's career took shape as a boy roaming the woods and fields in Chester County, Pennsylvania, collecting plants, insects, minerals, and the skins and eggs of birds. This exposure promoted a broad interest in nature that was bolstered by his association with boyhood pals—the brothers Amos and Stewardson Brown—who would later establish careers in, respectively, geology and botany.

Stone completed an undergraduate degree in 1887 at the University of Pennsylvania, where he would subsequently earn a master's degree in 1891 and, still later, an honorary doctorate. In 1888, the Academy of Natural Sciences of Philadelphia—the oldest institution of its kind in America—appointed him as a Jessup Fund Student, a position that allowed him access to the collections. The latter included a long-neglected, dusty collection of some 25,000 birds, but still considered one of the finest in the world; in keeping with the standards of the early nineteenth century, these were mounted on stands for display but nonetheless represented valuable research material (e.g., type specimens, those described to formally rec-

FIGURE 1.6. Witmer Stone stands at the pinnacle of "old-time naturalists" working in New Jersey. His monumental *Bird Studies of Old Cape May* remains a classic still available as a reprint of the 1937 original two-volume treatise. From the Collections of the University Archives, University of Pennsylvania.

ognize a new species). Stone accordingly began transforming these specimens into study skins that could be stored and protected in tight cases. Pertinent data for these specimens appeared on the bottoms of the stands—many in the handwriting of Audubon and other pioneering ornithologists of the period—which had to be transcribed onto labels and into museum catalogs. With these labors, Stone, almost single-handedly, had ushered the academy's bird collection into the twentieth century and a new era of museum management; he would do likewise for other zoological taxa in the years ahead (e.g., the reptile collection of famed paleontologist Edward Drinker Cope). His tenure at the Academy of Natural Sciences lasted for 51 years, during which he held positions, among others, as curator of vertebrates, curator of North American birds, director of the museum, and vice president of the academy.

In 1890, he helped found the Delaware Valley Ornithological Club, which remains active today. In recognition of Stone's energies and abilities, the club authorized him to prepare *The Birds of Eastern Pennsylvania and New Jersey*, a major work and baseline for later surveys of the regional avifauna. His professional affiliations included the American Ornithologists' Union,[2] in which he served as president and, remarkably, as editor of the society's journal, *The Auk*, for 25 years. In addition to his own work, he published some 1,500 book reviews in *The Auk* and chaired the society's Committee on Bird Protection at a time when plume hunters slaughtered egrets and other birds for their plumage. Stone and his colleagues proved a potent force in securing legislation that ended this needless exploitation.

A man for all seasons, Stone maintained an active interest in mammalogy and published on topics ranging from pumas to the statewide treatment of mammals in New Jersey. He remains one of only two scientists to be elected as president of both the American Society of Mammalogists and the American Ornithologists' Union. Stone also produced a score of botanical publications, including his seminal *The Plants of Southern New Jersey*, which remains a standard work for the Pine Barrens. He also amassed a large collection of insects, which he bequeathed to the academy, and had a working knowledge of reptiles, crustaceans, and mollusks. Still, ornithology remained foremost among Stone's interests, and he produced hundreds of publications dealing with birds, including *The Birds of New Jersey, Their Nests and Eggs*. But *Bird Studies at Old Cape May*, a two-volume treatise, stands alone as a monument to Stone's career, for which he posthumously received the Brewster Medal from the American Ornithologists' Union. The work, written with considerable charm at a time when declining health limited his physical activities, was gleaned from years of field notes and, in the words of a colleague, presented "Stone at his best, both as a naturalist and writer." Stone recognized the importance of the peninsula as a point of convergence for migratory birds as well as its

---

[2] Now the American Ornithological Society.

attraction for species seldom seen elsewhere in New Jersey. In short, Witmer Stone, born a naturalist, remained a naturalist to the end of his days.

When history honors the foremost naturalists of our day, the roster will surely include the names of Joanna Burger, Pete Dunne, David E. Fairbrothers, Larry Niles, Amanda Dey, Howard P. Boyd, P. D. "Pete" McLain, Jay Kelly, Emile DeVito, Robert T. Zappalorti, Clay and Pat Sutton, William "Willie" deCamp, Kenneth Able, and Paul Kerlinger. Because of their efforts, along with the contributions of many other dedicated naturalists, New Jersey's natural areas and native biota will remain a viable heritage for yet another generation.

Why Care about Endangered Species?

Unfortunately, far too many plants and animals in New Jersey appear on the state and federal lists of threatened and endangered species (fig. 1.7). Others fall into a somewhat less severe category—"species of concern." A few success stories, notably the recovery of bald eagles and ospreys, highlight the protection and management accruing from proactive legislation, although such measures were far too late to save passenger pigeons, heath hens, and Labrador ducks. Nevertheless, dedicated efforts continue for the benefit of piping plovers, swamp pink, and, yes, timber rattlesnakes in New Jersey.

But why should we trouble ourselves about species with skidding populations? To be sure, some such as whooping cranes and redwoods rally wide support because they inspire positive images of being "cuddly," "majestic," or "awesome." Charismatic species thus become an "easy sell" for protection and management, as witnessed by the global appeal of giant pandas—the icon of endangered species. But what about the others, the hundreds of distressed species of a humble or unappealing nature. A rare spider or minnow, for example, usually produces no more than a dismissive shrug, let alone instill a willingness to commit resources for its continued existence. Some even draw ire when they stymie a highway, airport, or other project deemed necessary for human progress. So why should we care about an imperiled mouse or obscure insect? A review of the lives and philosophies of three giants of conservation may suggest some answers.

FIGURE 1.7. Piping plovers breeding on the Atlantic coast, listed by New Jersey as endangered and federally as threatened, nest on undisturbed sandy beaches near clumps of sparse vegetation. The bird shown here was the first to nest (in 2016) at Island Beach State Park in 25 years (note partially visible egg). Others nest on barrier beach environments elsewhere, including the Holgate Unit of Edwin B. Forsythe National Wildlife Refuge. In all, about 110 pairs of piping plovers nest in New Jersey each year. Photo credit: Kevin Knutsen.

John Muir (1838–1914), after arriving in California, quickly fell under the spell of the Sierras and especially the magic of Yosemite Valley. However, the indiscriminate logging of redwoods deeply troubled Muir and triggered his campaign to end the ruinous exploitation of the magnificent trees. As noted by nature writer Kim Heacox, Muir emerged into the twentieth century as an "unapologetic preservationist [and] America's preeminent fang in the fight against irresponsible industry and runaway development"—a characterization underscored by Muir's own sardonic observation, "Nothing dollarable is safe." Thus began his crusade for wilderness preservation that gained even more momentum after he founded the Sierra Club in 1892. Two years before his death, Muir proposed a plan for a federal agency to protect natural areas—an idea realized in 1916 with the formation of the National Park Service.

Muir's concepts apply to endangered species as well as to wilderness. His insights were rooted in the philosophies of two well-known writers and thinkers of the mid-1800s—Ralph Waldo Emerson (1803–1882) and Henry David Thoreau (1817–1862). Together they founded what is formally known as the Romantic-Transcendental Preservation Ethic, the belief that communion with nature brings humans closer to their divine creator. In other words, nature is a sacred temple that only logging and other thoughtless intrusions of humans can tarnish. The harmony and beauty of nature form the cornerstones of transcendentalism, which Muir translated into preservation. In short, leave nature alone, thereby embracing the idea that species should be preserved simply because they represent God's wondrous creations. Muir's own words offer the best summary: "What creature of all that the Lord has taken the pains to make is not essential to the completeness of that unit—the cosmos?"

Next we turn to Gifford Pinchot (1865–1946) for quite another and highly pragmatic view of nature. History grants to Pinchot, a forester, the claim of coining the term "conservation," a concept that flourished when President Theodore Roosevelt named him (in 1905) as the first chief of the newly established U.S. Forest Service. He championed the protection of forests, watersheds, and other natural resources, but in his eyes their value was determined by the marketplace for timber, irrigation, and other uses. This view, however, values only those species for which a utilitarian value is already well established and thereby ignores future discoveries. For example, a compound derived from western yew—considered a forest "weed" in Pinchot's day—later became the basis for treating some forms of cancer. Nor does it recognize income derived from nonconsumptive values such as nature tours, outdoor photography, birding, and camping. Significantly, however, Pinchot recognized that natural resources could be renewed indefinitely by scientific management, and to that end he helped found the Yale School of Forestry. Thus grounded on economic values and proactive management, Pinchot established the Resource Conservation Ethic.

Muir and Pinchot each viewed nature from the standpoint of human welfare, but from opposite ends of the spectrum. Muir stressed spiritual enlightenment, whereas Pinchot emphasized the economic importance of species. Neither, however, recognized that nature held its own intrinsic value as a complex community of species and their interactions in a physical environment. For that view, we visit the last of our trio of eminent "movers and shakers."

Aldo Leopold (1887–1948), the American "father" of wildlife management, graduated from the Yale School of Forestry in 1909 and began a career with the U.S. Forest Service in New Mexico and Arizona. Leopold's interests, however, extended well beyond timber production—he became an advocate for wilderness preservation. Because of his pioneering efforts, the Gila Wilderness Area became a reality and the first of its kind in the national forest system. In 1927, Leopold moved to the Forest Products Laboratory in Madison, Wisconsin, but he soon left to begin private consulting work. In 1933, he published *Game Management*, the first textbook on the subject, and began teaching at the University of Wisconsin. Along the way, Leopold helped found The Wilderness Society and The Wildlife Society.

Leopold also wrote *A Sand County Almanac*, which was published posthumously in 1949 and remains at the core of conservation philosophy. One chapter, "Thinking Like a Mountain," poignantly underscores his realization that predators play vital roles as part of a healthy community—a point reinforced years later when wolves again roamed in Yellowstone National Park. He wrote much of the book at his "shack," a hideaway on an abandoned farm where the worn-out soil reflected years of abuse. In this setting, he developed—and practiced—the concept of what was to become known as the Evolutionary-Ecological Land Ethic. In this view, nature consists of interlocking parts—species—that have evolved into a functioning, interdependent system in the same way that mountaineers tether themselves to each other when scaling a cliff. Each species, he believed, bore its own intrinsic value, not as a commodity but as a part of a complex jigsaw puzzle of which humans are just one of many components. In some cases, certain species represent keystones that, if removed, diminish or destroy entire communities, although we seldom recognize these relationships until after the damage is done. A healthy environment thus includes all of its original components. Leopold captured the importance of species, whether cuddly or not, when he wrote in his journal, "To keep every cog and wheel is the first precaution of intelligent tinkering"—an awareness realized decades later in the Endangered Species Act.

Someone once observed that losing a species is like burning a book before we read it, which might be expanded to compare a destroyed ecosystem with a burned-out library. So, whether we favor the spiritual reverence of Muir, the hard-dollar values of Pinchot, or the ecological web of Leopold (or some combination of the three), silent inaction becomes unconscionable whenever another species spirals toward extinction. As John Sawmill, a former president of The Nature Conservancy, observed, "In the end, our society will be defined not only by what we create, but by what we refuse to destroy." Well said.

Natural History Today

A few words about the current state of natural history seem relevant here, as suggested by the concerns expressed by some prominent naturalists; their insights shape the following paragraphs.

Natural history, as practiced by Witmer Stone and others noted earlier, faded into a jaded and somewhat unfashionable calling in the decades following World War II. It was replaced in large measure by a focus on the so-called hard sciences spawned at first by the global conflict itself, then by the Cold War that followed, and driven by the quest for ever-better military hardware. Chemistry and physics, in particular, emerged as the jewels in the crown of science, a perception furthered even more when *Sputnik* soared into the heavens in 1957. That feat added mind-boggling mathematics (at least for many of us) and microtechnology to the family of hard sciences. Studies of nature, by comparison, withered into a "soft" sideshow that lingered as a relic from a bygone era of pickled fish, pinned insects, and pressed plants. Meanwhile, biology moved indoors into sterile laboratories in search of medicines and molecules.

These changes did not go unnoticed by students with interests in science, nor did universities ignore the lure of large research grants and advancement for faculty who obtained such funding. In short, biology had marched headlong into the cell and molecule and out of the prairie and forest. As the naturalist-philosopher Aldo Leopold observed, "Education, I fear, is learning to see one thing by going blind to another. One thing most of us have gone blind to is the quality of marshes."

Many universities also rid themselves of valuable plant and animal collections that once served as an integral part of teaching and research—the bulky specimen cases took up too much space and perhaps represented a Victorian image of science best forgotten. Fortunately, however, public and private museums steadfastly husband their natural history collections, some of which include large numbers of eggs (e.g., upward of 60,000 at Chicago's Field Museum of Natural History). Most of these eggs were collected prior to World War II, which enabled comparisons with eggs laid during the DDT era that followed the war. The evidence clearly indicated that the postwar shells of several species, particularly those of raptors, were so thinned by pesticides that few could hatch—and became the "smoking gun" that helped ban the harmful chemicals from further use in the United States. Similarly, analyses of feathers from seabird skins housed in museums traced a 150-year tale of mercury accumulations in certain parts of the Atlantic Ocean. More recently, a comparison between current laying dates for the eggs of 72 species of birds with those collected over a 143-year period demonstrated the influence of climate change. Overall, the laying dates advanced by about 10 days during this period, with a third of the species—primarily migrants—showing an average advance of 25 days. In another example, scientists compared the flowering times of herbarium specimens dating to the last century with those of living plants of the same species to highlight the march of climate change—the results revealed progressively earlier flowering times. Herbarium specimens have also linked climate change with increased insect herbivory and by disclosing the influence of ocean upwellings on Pacific sardine populations, as determined by the levels of nitrogen isotopes in red algae collected as far back as 1878.

The lesson: seemingly outmoded plant and animal collections harbor a trove of modern information, and if we wish to foresee how our tampering might shape nature, then it becomes prudent to maintain such collections as vouchers for what nature once was—and can still tell us. Moreover, plant and animal taxonomy stands at the core of natural history, yet today few university curricula include these essential foundations and seldom replace retiring professors with taxonomic skills with faculty with similar interests. Some universities no longer offer field trips and instead rely on computer simulations to connect students with nature. Taken together, these events initiate a downward spiral—with fewer openings available, fewer students seek careers in natural history and the discipline withers for want of faculty and students.

All of these events paralleled the rapid growth of cities and suburbs, which separated a large segment of America's population from regular contact with nature. For many, the outdoors had become a concrete landscape interspersed with lawns, a few trees, and, perhaps, a manicured park. In such an environment, computer screens and TV sets emerged as part of a lifestyle that precluded contact with nature. In particular, children no longer experienced nature in ways that might stimulate their curiosity about the natural world. Indeed, an average American boy or girl currently spends some seven hours a day in front of a screen but only thirty minutes or less per day in outdoor activities. The result is an alienation of children from the natural world, or an aptly named "nature-deficit disorder."

Nonetheless, some bright spots exist. To some degree, natural history has returned to the limelight because of concerns for biodiversity and endangered species. In particular, conservation biology, a discipline dedicated to saving and restoring distressed species and communities, has gained considerable traction within the broader spectrum of science. This thrust also widened the breadth of subject matter by including more than just the popular groups of vertebrates and charismatic species. Mollusks, insects, and other invertebrates as well as plants today command the attention of conservation agencies, which seek college graduates equipped to deal with species at or nearing "the brink." Additionally, the life history and ecological role remains unknown for many species already described, and discoveries of new species and communities add to this backlog. Not long ago, for example, a new realm for natural history opened up when biologists probed the unique life isolated in forest canopies.

In *How to Raise a Wild Child*, paleontologist Scott D. Sampson urges that parents—to which I add grandparents—accompany their children outdoors as mentors and catalysts for connecting with the environment. In short, the oldsters become coadventurers with the youngsters in sampling nature. Renowned writer-naturalist Rachel Carson championed this thought decades ago in an essay, "Help Your Child to Wonder." Nature can then be experienced in backyards, gardens, and empty lots as well as in state or national parks, forests, and remote beaches. These visits are not structured exercises but instead should promote "hands-on" contact—which by no means excludes dirty fingernails and muddy feet—that develop in concert with the natural curiosity of children as they explore essentially unfettered. Outdoorsman Steven Rinella recently offered a guide for getting kids engaged with nature, including bloody hands. Fishing, for example, can be more than catching a trout or sunfish but also presents a chance to see what's in its stomach. He further suggests that such outdoor experiences, when accompanied by guidance on the what, how, and why of nature, will implant in children a lasting sense of stewardship of the natural world. Otherwise, families may be "trapped inside four walls where perhaps the biggest obstacle of all—technology—abounds."

As in the past, amateurs still provide useful contributions. Unfortunately, the term has been corrupted from its original meaning—"one who loves"—to imply a lesser degree of competence. Nonsense. Thousands of amateurs participate in the national Christmas Bird Count conducted each year by the National Audubon Society. These data reveal long-term trends in the distribution and populations of birds that would otherwise be unavailable. Others help with conservation activities ranging from rescuing overturned horseshoe crabs and replanting storm-ravaged dunes to serving as docents at nature centers or assisting children on field trips. Amateurs, often distinguished as "citizen scientists," also sustain research projects such as monitoring butterfly populations. In these and in so many other ways, the commitment of a dedicated corps of amateurs improves the health and knowledge of our natural world.

So what might be the overarching merits of natural history? In response, consider the thoughtful message framed by lepidopterist and environmental writer Robert M. Pyle: "It may be the naturalists who save us in the end by bringing us all back down to Earth."

Readings and References

General

Burger, J. 1996. A naturalist on the Jersey Shore. Rutgers University Press, New Brunswick, NJ.

New Jersey: The Big Picture in Brief

Harper, D. P. 2013. Roadside geology of New Jersey. Mountain Press, Sevierville, TN.
Kemble, W. 1964. The geology and geography of New Jersey. Van Nostrand, Princeton, NJ.
Owens, J. P., P. J. Sugarman, H. F. Sohl, et al. 1999. Bedrock geologic map of central and southern New Jersey. U. S. Geological Survey, Washington, D.C.
Stansfield, C. A. 1998. A geography of New Jersey, the city in the garden. Rutgers University Press, New Brunswick, NJ.

First Europeans on the Scene

Greenberg, J. 2014. A feathered river across the sky, the passenger pigeon's flight to extinction. Bloomsbury, New York.
Mountford, K. 2002. Closed sea: from Manasquan to the Mullica, a history of Barnegat Bay. Down the Shore Publishing, West Creek, NJ. [See chaps. 2 and 3.]

Pierce, A. D. 1957. Iron in the pines: the story of New Jersey's ghost towns and bog iron. Rutgers University Press, New Brunswick, NJ. [See pp. 55–57 regarding Pursh and Quaker's Bridge.]

Natural History in New Jersey: The Early Days

Athens, E. 2015. William Bartram's inimitable picture: representation as the pursuit of natural knowledge. Journal of Florida Studies 1(4):1–15.

Audubon, J. J. 1831. Ornithological biography 1:415–421. Biodiversity Heritage Library. [See for observations of ospreys at Great Egg Harbor, NJ.]

Berkeley, E., and D. S. Berkeley. 1982. The life and travels of John Bartram: from Lake Ontario to the River St. John. University Presses of Florida, Tallahassee.

———— (eds.). 1992. The correspondence of John Bartram 1734–1777. University Press of Florida, Gainesville.

Brewster, T. M. 1840. Wilson's American ornithology. Arno Press, New York (1970 reprint). [See p. 22 for Wilson's strategy to quell robin hunting; see also the respective species accounts for his other observations of birds in New Jersey.]

Burtt, E. H., Jr. 2016. Alexander Wilson, enlightened naturalist. Bucknell University Press, Lewisburg, PA.

————. 2017. The birds of Alexander Wilson—why the father of American ornithology? Wilson Journal of Ornithology 129:905–906. [Summarizes Wilson's contributions to the study of birds; for example, in the first volume of *American Ornithology* (1808) he introduced the binomial system—genus and species—of Linnaeus to America.]

Clark, K., and B. Wurst. 2017. The 2016 osprey project in New Jersey. New Jersey Division of Fish and Wildlife, Trenton, NJ, and Conserve Wildlife Foundation of New Jersey, Trenton, NJ. [Annual report of nesting activities.]

Fogg, J. M., Jr. 1934. *Lilaeopsis chinensis* in southern New Jersey. Bartonia 16:51–56.

Fry, J. T. 1997. The pond at Bartram's Garden. Bartram Broadside (summer):1–7. John Bartram Association, Philadelphia. [A detailed history of American lotus and other aquatic plants propagated by John and William Bartram.]

Gallagher, W. B. 1997. When dinosaurs roamed New Jersey. Rutgers University Press, New Brunswick, NJ. [See p. 28 regarding the fossil in Peale's museum.]

Graustein, J. E. 1967. Thomas Nuttall, naturalist: explorations in America, 1808–1841. Harvard University Press, Cambridge, MA.

Harper, F. (ed.). 1958. The travels of William Bartram, naturalist's edition. Yale University Press, New Haven, CT. [A reprint of Bartram's original 1791 book enhanced with commentaries and an annotated index.]

Miller, L. B. (ed.). 1988. The selected papers of Charles Willson Peale and his family. Vol. 2, pt. 2:168. [Account of rattlesnake hunt in New Jersey. See also p. 242 concerning Peale's trip to Cape May and his decision to no longer drink spirits.]

Noble, G. H. 2017. John James Audubon: the nature of the American woodsman. University of Pennsylvania Press, Philadelphia.

Peck, R. M., and E. P. Newman. 2010. Discovered! The first engraving of an Audubon bird. Journal of the Early Republic 30:443–461.

Rhodes, R. 2004. John James Audubon: the making of an American. Knopf, New York.

Rodgers, A. D. 1942. John Torrey—a study of North American botany. Princeton University Press, Princeton, NJ.

Sellers, C. C. 1980. Mr. Peale's museum: Charles Willson Peale and the first popular museum of natural science and art. Norton, New York.

Stone, W. 1913. Bird migration records of William Bartram, 1802–1822. Auk 30:325–358.

Stuart, D. C. 2002. The plants that shaped our gardens. Harvard University Press, Cambridge, MA. [See p. 88 regarding Nuttall's encounter with mosquitoes.]

Thompson, K. S. 1990. Benjamin Franklin's lost tree. American Scientist 78:203–206.

Two Titans of the Twentieth Century

Anonymous. 1929. John William Harshberger. Bartonia 11:451–455.

———. 1939. In memoriam: Witmer Stone (1866–1939). Proceedings of the Academy of Natural Sciences of Philadelphia 91:415–418.

Gershenowitz, H. 1982. John William Harshberger: friend of the Pine Barrens. Cape May County [New Jersey]. Magazine of History and Genealogy 8(2):126–128.

Harshberger, J. W. 1911. A phytogeographic survey of North America. G. E. Strehert, New York.

———. 1916. The vegetation of the New Jersey Pine-Barrens: an ecologic investigation. Christopher Sower, Philadelphia. [Reprinted in 1970 by Dover, New York.]

———. 1917. A textbook of mycology and plant pathology. P. Blakiston's Son, Philadelphia.

Huber, W. 1940. Witmer Stone (1866–1939). Journal of Mammalogy 21:1–4.

McConnell, S. 2015. Witmer Stone: the fascination of nature. Self-published.

Nichols, G. E. 1930. Obituary notice, John William Harshberger, 1869–1929. Ecology 11:443–444.

Pennell, F. W. 1938–1939. The botanical work of Witmer Stone. Bartonia 20:33–37,

Rehn, J. A. G. 1941. In memoriam: Witmer Stone. Auk 58:299–313.

Stone, W. 1899. The pumas of the western United States. Science 9:34–35.

———. 1908. The mammals of New Jersey. Pp. 33–110 in Annual report of the New Jersey State Museum for 1907, Trenton, NJ.

———. 1909. The birds of New Jersey, their nests and eggs. Pp. 11–347 in Annual report of the New Jersey State Museum for 1908, Trenton, NJ.

———. 1911. The plants of southern New Jersey, with special reference to the flora of the Pine Barrens and the geographic distribution of the species. Pp. 25–825 in Annual report of the New Jersey State Museum for 1910, Trenton, NJ.

———. 1937. Bird studies at Old Cape May: an ornithology of coastal New Jersey. 2 vols. Delaware Valley Ornithological Club, Philadelphia.

Why Care about Endangered Species?

Bolen, E. G. 2006. Why endangered species matter. Wildlife in North Carolina 70(11):26–31. [Source for much of what appears here in condensed form.]

Flader, S. L. 1974. Thinking like a mountain: Aldo Leopold and the evolution of an ecological attitude toward deer, wolves, and forests. University of Nebraska Press, Lincoln.

Heacox, K. 2014. John Muir and the ice that started a fire. Lyons Press, Guilford, CT. [Source for Muir's "dollarable" quote.]

Leopold, A. 1949. A sand county almanac and sketches here and there. Oxford University Press, New York. [This seminal work concludes with "Land Ethic."]

Leopold, L. B. 1953. Round river: from the journals of Aldo Leopold. Oxford University Press, New York. [See p. 147 for "tinkering" quote.]

Meine, C. 1988. Aldo Leopold: his life and work. University of Wisconsin Press, Madison.

Miller, C. 2001. Gifford Pinchot and the making of modern environmentalism. Island Press, Washington, DC.

Pinkett, H. T. 1970. Gifford Pinchot, private and public forester. University of Illinois Press, Urbana.

Ripple, W. J., and R. L. Beschta. 2012. Trophic cascades in Yellowstone: the first 15 years after wolf reintroduction. Biological Conservation 145:205–213.

Whelan, J. 2002. Targeted taxane therapy for cancer. Drug and Discovery Today 7:90–92.

Worster, D. 2008. A passion for nature: the life of John Muir. Oxford University Press, New York.

Natural History Today

Bates, J. M., M. Fidino, L. Nowak-Boyd, B. M. Strausberger, K. A. Schmidt, and C. J. Whelan. 2022. Climate change affects bird nest phenology: comparing contemporary field and historical museum nesting records. Journal of Animal Ecology 92(2):263–272.

Carson, R. 1956. Help your child to wonder. Woman's Home Companion 83(7):25–27, 46–48. [For an expanded version completed just before her death, see The sense of wonder. 1965. Harper & Row, New York.]

Chapman, B. R., and E. G. Bolen. 2018. The natural history of Texas. Texas A&M University Press, College Station. [Includes a discussion about the status of natural history.]

Enderson, J. H., and D. D. Berger. Pesticides: eggshell thinness and lowered production of young in prairie falcons. BioScience 20:355–356.

Futuyma, D. J. 1998. Wherefore and wither the naturalist? American Naturalist 151:1–6.

Grant, P. R. 2000. What does it mean to be a naturalist at the end of the twentieth century? American Naturalist 155:1–12.

Kemp, C. 2017. Collections matter. Natural History 125(9):38–39.

Leopold, A. 1949. A sand county almanac and sketches here and there. Oxford University Press, New York. [Quote about education appears on p. 158.]

Louv, B. 2006. Last child in the woods—saving our children from nature-deficit disorder. Algonquin Books, Chapel Hill, NC.

Lowman, M. D., and H. B. Rinker (eds.). 2004. Forest canopies. 2nd ed. Academic Press, Cambridge, MA. [See for discoveries in an unexplored realm.]

Meineke, E. K., A. T. Classen, N. J. Sanders, and T. J. Davies. 2019. Herbarium specimens reveal increasing herbivory over the past century. Journal of Ecology 107:105–117.

Meineke, E. K., C. C. Davis, and J. Davis. 2018. The unrealized potential of herbaria for global change biology. Ecological Monographs 88:505–525.

Miller, E. A., S. E. Lisin, C. M. Smith, and K. S. Van Houtan. 2020. Herbaria macroaglae as a proxy for historical upwellings in central California. Proceedings of the Royal Society B 287:20200732. doi:10.1098/rspb.2020.0732.

Noss, R. F. 1996. The naturalists are dying off. Conservation Biology 10:1–3.

Primack, D., C. Imbres, R. B. Primack, A. J. Miller-Rushing, and P. del Tredici. 2004. Herbarium specimens demonstrate earlier flowering times in response to warming in Boston. American Journal of Botany 91:1260–1264.

Pyle, R. M. 2001. The rise and fall of natural history. Orion (autumn):16–23. [This and other essays by the same author appear in The tangled bank: writings from Orion. 2012. Oregon State University Press, Corvallis.]

Rinella, S. 2022. Outdoor kids in an indoor world: getting your families out of the house and radically engaged with nature. Random House, New York.

Sampson, S. D. 2015. How to raise a wild child—the art and science of falling in love with nature. Houghton Mifflin Harcourt, Boston.

Schmidly, D. J. 2001. What it means to be a naturalist and the future of natural history at American universities. Journal of Mammalogy 86:449–456.

Thompson, D. R., R. W. Furness, and P. M. Walsh. 1992. Historical changes in mercury concentrations in the marine ecosystem of the north and northeast Atlantic Basin as indicated by seabird feathers. Journal of Applied Ecology 29:79–84.

Weigl, P. D. 2009. The natural history conundrum revisited: mammalogy begins at home. Journal of Mammalogy 90:265–269.

Wheeler, Q. D., P. H. Raven, and E. O. Wilson. 2004. Taxonomy: impediment or expedient? Science 303:285.

Wilcove, D. S., and T. Eisner. 2002. The impending extinction of natural history. Chronicle of Higher Education 47(3):B24.

Shore Note 1.1. Island Beach State Park: A Taste of What Used to Be

Anonymous. ND. History of Island Beach State Park, a self-guided history tour. Brochure, New Jersey State Park Service.

Martin, W. E. 1959. The vegetation of Island Beach State Park, New Jersey. Ecological Monographs 29:1–46.

Shore Note 1.2. Whales and Whaling in New Jersey

Fujiwara, M., and H. Caswell. 2001. Demography of the endangered North Atlantic right whale. Nature 414:537–541.

Johnson, A., G. Salvador, J. Kenney, et al. 2005. Fishing gear involved in entanglements of right whales and humpback whales. Marine Mammal Science 21:635–645.

Kemp, C. 2012. Floating gold: a natural (and unnatural) history of ambergris. University of Chicago Press, Chicago.

Kraus, S. D., R. D. Kenney, C. A. Mayo, et al. 2016. Recent scientific publications cast doubt on North Atlantic right whale future. Frontiers in Science 3: Article 137 doi:10.3389/fmars.2016.00137.

Methot, J. 1988. Up and down the beach. Whip Publishers, Navesink, NJ. [See chap. 3, Whaling.]

Mountford, K. 2002. Closed sea: from the Manasquan to the Mullica, a history of Barnegat Bay. Down the Shore Publishing, West Creek, NJ. [See pp. 119–122.]

NOAA. Whales stranded on the New Jersey coast. Raw data provided by the National Oceanographic and Atmospheric Administration.

Reed, J., L. New, P. Corkeron, and R. Harcourt. 2022. Multi-event modeling of true reproductive states of individual female right whales provides new insights into their decline. Frontiers in Marine Science 9. doi:10.3389/fmars.2022.994481.

Weiss, H. B. 1974. Whaling in New Jersey. New Jersey Agricultural Society, Trenton.

Whitt, A. D., K. Dudzinski, and J. R. Laliberte. 2013. North Atlantic right white distribution and seasonal occurrence in nearshore waters off New Jersey, USA, and implications for management. Endangered Species Research 20:59–69.

2

Shifting Sands

Beaches, Dunes, and Inlets

On the sands of the sea's edge, especially where they are broad and bordered by unbroken lines of wind-built dunes, there is a sense of antiquity that is missing from the young rock coast of New England.

—RACHEL CARSON, *THE EDGE OF THE SEA*

MOST VISIONS of New Jersey's beaches focus on throngs of humans enjoying the pounding surf and its parallel band of sun-warmed sand during the summer months. But there is even more life, some seasonal, some year-round, on the beaches—creatures, often overlooked but numbering in the hundreds of millions, dwell in these same environments. They form communities structured little differently than those in a forest, prairie, or lake, with predators, prey, herbivores, and scavengers, but lack much output of primary production from rooted plants. Instead, photosynthesis remains largely confined to the sparse cover of dune vegetation and the minute forms of algae—mostly diatoms—tucked away either singly or in chains in the interstitial space between the grains of sand in the zones where the waves break and wash ashore. The abundance of algae—the foundation for much of the food chain in these communities—is closely linked with grain size, with more chlorophyll-based energy originating from algae sheltered in sand no larger than sugar—a relationship based on the large amount of surface area per unit of volume of small objects. Hence, beaches with smaller grains of sand provide more habitat for algae than those formed of coarser sediments. Communities persisting on sandy beaches also receive metabolic energy from external sources (e.g., seagrass meadows and estuaries elsewhere along the coast). The physical environment itself is dynamic and subject to the timeless forces of tides, currents, winds, and storms, hence we begin where waves greet a sandy shore.

The Swash Zone

After a wave breaks, a turbulent, foamy lens of water continues rushing upward over the beach; when its energy is expended, the flow reverses direction and returns to the surf zone. The endless motion, with the rhythm of a pendulum, defines a zone of activity perhaps as old as life itself. Here the upwash and backwash of the dying waves shape the activities of creatures living within what is known as the swash zone. In terms of surficial geology, flow in the swash zone represents the prime means of relocating sand. When the prevailing wind changes direction across the beach, so too does the deposition of sand carried by the waves. Erosion, especially prevalent in winter, originates in the swash zone and commonly lessens the beachfront (i.e., the swash zone moves progressively inland); the "lost" sand usually settles on offshore bars where it will later refill the lost real estate.

Sea glass reflects the harsh and relentless force of abrasion on sandy shores. These are weathered fragments of bottles and other glass objects that have lost their sharp edges tossing about on the seafloor, ending their journey tumbling in the confusion of the swash zone. Highly collectable, most of the shards are brown, blue, clear, or various shades of green, with red and "black" (actually well-aged dark green) particularly prized. Today, beachcombers encounter much less sea glass and far more plastic debris, which regrettably litters shorelines and marine communities around the globe.

Despite the turmoil, coquina clams abound in the swash zones of undisturbed beaches; in fact, these thumbnail-size clams serve as biological indicators of a healthy shore (fig. 2.1, left). Coquina clams—only one species occurs on New Jersey coast—live in the upper inch of sand where they filter single-celled algae and detritus from the roiling water. They partly emerge when a wave washes ashore, taking in their nourishment during the backwash, then quickly retreat into the sand and repeat the cycle with each new wave. Coquinas move back and forth with the tidal cycle, thereby remaining in their niche within the boundaries of the swash zone. As might be expected, coquina populations do not fare well when dredges pump sand on eroded beaches—a process known as renourishment— although their numbers often recover about two years later. Under favorable con-

FIGURE 2.1. Small clams known as coquinas flourish at the lower edge of the swash zone (left). They rapidly dig into the sand if exposed by the receding wash of a spent wave, but with quick hands, beachgoers can capture enough to make a hearty chowder. Crustaceans known as sand fleas or mole crabs likewise dwell in this area and provide surf-fishing anglers with a readily available bait (right). Photo credits: Kevin Knutsen (left); Pernille Ruhalter (right).

ditions, they reach densities of several hundred or more per square yard, which in some areas (but not in New Jersey) resulted in the formation of coquina rock, a soft conglomerate of Pleistocene limestone cementing clusters of their shells. Coquinas, although small, provide the ingredients for a tasty broth or stew and food-savvy gourmands savor meals made from these colorful bivalves.

Coquinas often partner with a hydroid colony in a symbiotic relationship generally considered as an example of mutualism (i.e., both partners benefit from the interaction). Appearing as small brown brushes attached to the anterior end of coquina shells, the venom-bearing tentacles of the hydroid colony deter some predators, primarily shell-boring mollusks known as moon snails, although the sting poses no harm to humans. In turn, the coquinas provide the hydroids with a stabilized substrate on which they can anchor in an otherwise chaotic environment of swirling sand. Pebbles, broken shells, and other hard surfaces do not suffice for the shells of living coquinas. Because the coquinas move with the tides, so to do the hydroids, which prevents desiccation and overheating, while maintaining their constant exposure to food sources.

Crustaceans known as sand fleas, or by some as mole crabs, dwell just where the surf breaks and the swash zone begins (fig. 2.1, right). They, like coquinas, move in rhythm with the upwash and backwash as well as with the tidal cycle. No more than an inch in length, sand fleas rapidly disappear—in less than two seconds—into the sand when a wave retreats, only to emerge again when the next wave sweeps ashore. They move downward tail first, using their telsons ("tails") not only as efficient digging tools but also as anchors for secure lodging inside their burrows. When curled, the telson protects a sand flea's soft underbelly and shelters the egg masses attached to the abdomens of females. Sand fleas, despite their somewhat threatening appearance, lack claws on any of their five sets of legs, rendering them completely harmless. Their rear legs, however, function as paddles and enable sand fleas to swim even in the turbulence of a crashing wave. On firmer footing, they scamper backward.

Although buried, sand fleas give away their hidden position. To secure food, they capture phytoplankton and organic debris with two feathery antennae they unfurl and project above the sand as the backwash returns to the surf. However, the exposed antennae also produce a V-shaped wake in the receding water, tipping off shorebirds to the location of a good meal. Anglers find a handy source of good bait the same way.

Coquina clams and sand fleas offer examples of the macrofauna associated with the swash zone, but a meiofauna consisting not only of diatoms and other microalgae but also scores other species likewise dwell in miniature worlds hidden between the grains of sand. These include a plethora of minute marine worms, primarily polychaetes and nematodes, and equally diminutive crustaceans known as copepods, amphipods, and decapods. Small fishes also dart in the swash, gleaning from a cafeteria replenished with each new wave. Based on studies on a surf-washed beach at Avalon, minnow-like Atlantic silversides dominate the community of small fishes in the surf zone, with some of these venturing into the swash in search of food. The incoming waves often dislodge greenworms, a particularly abundant polychaete and choice food for predators in this narrow zone of habitat. They become available to silversides and other predators when incoming waves dislodge them from their tubular shelters; the survivors rapidly burrow into the sand as the waves recede. Somewhat curiously, the stomach contents of the silversides also contained insects, mostly beetles, entrapped by the swirling water; the presence of these terrestrial visitors adds even more diversity to the beachfront community and another link to what is otherwise a marine-based food chain.

Northeastern beach tiger beetles represent another dweller associated with the swash zone—or at least they were in the past. As adults, these handsome insects— distinguished by creamy white bodies and metallic green heads—forage on amphipods, flies, and other small arthropods in the swash zone and adjacent wrack, but also scavenge on the carcasses of dead fish and crabs. They spend most of their annual cycle, however, as larvae that hatch from eggs laid 10 to 14 days earlier in the top inch of sand, then spend two years developing in burrows located in the upper reaches of the swash zone or just beyond. High tides harmlessly cover many of the burrows, which range from about 4 to 12 inches in depth, with the deeper burrows occurring above the high tide line, presumably so the larvae maintain contact with moist sand; lacking a hard cuticle, the larvae remain susceptible to desiccation and may move at times in search of better conditions. The larvae plug their burrows during the day but become active at night when they ambush flies and other small insects. After developing through three stages, the larvae pupate in their burrows and emerge as adults in their third summer of life in an event apparently keyed to rainfall. The adults spend their six-week lifespan breeding, with the females laying three to four eggs per day.

Both larvae and adults prefer beaches undisturbed by human activities, which all but eliminates the shore of modern-day New Jersey as viable habitat. Human traffic, both pedestrian and vehicular, and modifications to the beachfront with groins, jetties, and bulkheads have essentially ended any chances for the continued presence of this fascinating shorefront insect. Prior to the 1940s, these insects occurred widely and abundantly from Cape Cod to central New Jersey and at a few sites on Chesapeake Bay. Today, however, northeastern beach tiger beetles hang on rather tenuously at a few locations in Massachusetts and Maryland but somewhat more widely in Virginia. Natural events such as nor'easters, hurricanes, beach erosion, and flood tides further threaten the already vulnerable beetle population.

Because of their precarious status, the beetles were formally listed as threatened in 1990, which triggered attempts to reestablish a population in New Jersey. Earlier trials translocated adult beetles to suitable habitat in Virginia, but these failed when they rapidly dispersed from the release sites. Hence beginning in 1994, a translocation effort in New Jersey concentrated on stocking beetle larvae. A beach at Sandy Hook in Gateway National Recreation Area was selected because it was already closed to the public to protect piping plovers, another threatened species. When released, the larvae readily burrowed, with most surviving the winter and emerging as adults the following summer; additional releases of larvae were made in subsequent years. The new population seemed well established, but their numbers plummeted after reaching a peak of 749 in 2001, dropping to just 6 in 2004 (more recently, a similar translocation at Cape Cod, Massachusetts, proved more successful). The cause of the crash remains uncertain, but it seems linked to heavy predation by gulls that flocked to sites where the adult beetles were emerging. Other factors may be involved, but the initial results nonetheless suggest that translocating larvae may be the best—and perhaps last—means of heading off the pending extinction of the northeastern beach tiger beetle.

Shorebirds remain the most obvious benefactors of the food-rich swash zone (fig. 2.2). Among these are sanderlings that behave like wind-up toys as they speed landward in advance of incoming waves, then turn about and follow the water as it retreats to the surf. The sanderlings thus rely on the backwash to dislodge and expose sand fleas, isopods, and other foods as a feeding strategy instead of probing with their relatively short bills. Conversely, dunlins feed on both sandy and muddy shores, where they probe with longer, droop-tipped bills in a motion often likened to the "stitching" of a sewing machine. Both dunlins and sanderlings migrate to nest in the far-off tundra of northern Canada after overwintering along much of the Atlantic shoreline.

The Wrack Line

A linear collection of marine vegetation and the tattered remains of various marine creatures known as the wrack line accumulates a few feet beyond the upper limits

FIGURE 2.2. Shorebirds of several species forage on the rich fauna of invertebrates living in the swash zone. As shown here, sanderlings hurry into the area exposed by a retreating wave, briefly feed, then scurry back when another wave washes ashore. Photo credit: Pat and Clay Sutton.

of the swash zone, tossed there by storm-driven waves (fig. 2.3). After tramping along the beaches of Cape Cod, Henry David Thoreau somewhat darkly likened this menagerie to a morgue where each tide turns and tucks the carcasses in fresh sand. Nonetheless, these materials provide a buffet for gulls and other scavengers and, as they decay, feed the beach with a limited source of otherwise absent nutrients. American sea rocket is among the few plants appearing in wrack lines.

The wrack line also invites the curious probes of beachcombers of all ages. Many delight in the weathered charm of driftwood, some of which may be the flotsam from a distant shipwreck or the gnarled limb of an exotic tree, but all cast ashore with a silent history. Whatever their origins, these well-traveled planks and logs morph into rustic habitat for some interesting marine creatures, not the least of

Shore Note 2.1 The Blues Are Running!

A torpedo with teeth aptly describes a prized game fish for anglers on the New Jersey coast. Sleek-bodied and blue-tinged silver in color, bluefish travel in schools of like-sized individuals whose appearance along the beachfront is often heralded by noisy gulls attracted to the scraps strewn by the slashing carnage occurring just below the surface. Thus alerted, anglers likewise flock to the beach for action-packed fishing as the school moves along the coast. "Snappers," those blues less than a foot in length, rarely reach 30 pounds when fully grown, and most anglers regard those half that size as trophies. The only living species in its family—related species are known only as fossils dating to bygone ages—bluefish occur in temperate and subtropical waters overlying many of the world's continental shelves, with the northern Pacific being a notable exception.

Blues mature at two years of age and spawn during the spring and summer along the outer edges of the continental shelf from North Carolina to New England before returning to the Florida coast for the winter. Their eggs and larval stages wander at the whim of the currents for up to two months—the Gulf Stream carries many northward and toward the shore—ending their hazardous journey along the New Jersey coast and beyond. Although bluefish were once thought to represent two breeding populations separated at Cape Hatteras, North Carolina, genetic studies later confirmed that these stocks represent a single population with two yearly peaks of spawning success. For reasons still unclear, bluefish populations follow a cyclic pattern that tops out about every 10 years.

For many, it's the frenzied and gregarious feeding behavior that distinguishes bluefish from all but a few of the ocean's other predators. Single rows of stout, sawlike teeth edge their upper and lower jaws, as unwary anglers soon find out when unhooking their catch. Indeed, teeth emerge in larval bluefish no more than three-sixteenths of an inch in length, and by the time the larvae grow to just over an inch, their diet switches from copepods and other soft-bodied prey to one dominated by fish. When grown, bluefish bite off pieces of their prey—as opposed to swallowing their victims whole—using large, dagger-like teeth set in deep sockets. They also feature rows of replacement teeth, with a greater number coming into use as the fish age. Bluefish in fact share some dental characteristics in common with barracudas.

Menhaden ("mossbunkers") are among the abundant baitfish favored by bluefish, although a wide variety of other prey, including crustaceans and marine worms, complement their diets. When encountered, the baitfish—typically moving in schools numbering in many tens of thousands—trigger a feeding frenzy known as a "bluefish blitz." The mayhem that ensues churns the water in a manner sometimes likened to a washing machine. In this state, bluefish will continue attacking well after sating their appetites, even to the point of striking bare hooks. At times, a bluefish blitz will force their terrified prey onto the shore, creating a row of flopping baitfish along the water's edge. Lacking dietary scruples, bluefish will dine on smaller members of their own species, which may explain why they normally assemble in schools of similarly sized fish. On occasion, anyone caught in the midst of a hungry school may experience some painful nips. So, on your next summer visit to the Jersey Shore, watch for a swirl of noisy birds and dancing water—sure signs that "the blues are running."

FIGURE 2.3. Wrack lines develop where storm-driven waves deposit various forms of marine life, drift wood, and assorted flotsam and jetsam at the high water mark on the beachfront. Accumulations of these materials provide an environment that attracts foraging birds such as the dunlin, shown here, as well as small mammals and foxes. Photo credit: Pat and Clay Sutton.

which are shipworms. Poorly named, shipworms in fact are uniquely adapted mollusks. Two shells, each like the unhinged half of a small clam, at the anterior end of their tubular bodies provide the boring tools that throughout history have damaged piers and, especially, the hulls of wooden ships. Some driftwood, although long barren of living shipworms, thus may be well riddled with their telltale tunnels. They reach lengths of a foot and feed primarily on the wood they excavate, aided by cellulose-digesting bacteria. Shipworms, in a twist of nature shared with relatively few other species, change their gender as they mature; they begin life as males, but after releasing sperm, transform into egg-producing females.

Barnacles likewise attach to driftwood (and, in modern times, also to plastic litter) still at sea. Rock or acorn barnacles, shaped like tiny volcanos, are the most common of these and, in addition to ending up on the stranded flotsam and jetsam in the wrack line, attach to other hard surfaces (e.g., jetties) where they align

Shore Note 2.2 A Tale of Two Wrecks

Centuries of shipwrecks earned the Jersey Shore the tag "Graveyard of the Atlantic." Many were three- or four-masted vessels that foundered in violent storms more than a century ago, but the toll also includes those merchantmen sent to the bottom by German torpedoes during World War II. Two wrecks, however, stand out in the seafaring chapter of New Jersey's history.

In February 1846, an exceptionally strong nor'easter claimed at least ten vessels coasting the Jersey Shore. Of these, the disaster befalling the packet ship *John Minturn* becomes a tale worth telling. She had sailed from New Orleans headed for New York with cargo and passengers, adding 20 more to the manifest by picking up a shipwrecked crew along the way. In all, 59 were aboard the doomed ship when it sailed headlong into the fury.

When the gale tore away the *Minturn*'s sails, the helpless ship slammed into an offshore bar at Mantoloking during the night of February 14. With the ship thus lodged, the pounding breakers relentlessly battered the vessel until its keel broke and slowly dismembered its hull. The passengers and crew huddled in the forecastle, awaiting dawn and rescue. Lifesaving crews, all volunteers, arrived before daybreak but faced the daunting task of launching lifeboats into the furious surf—an effort made worse by wind-whipped snow and sleet. Sadly, their heroics failed, and for 18 hours the freezing passengers and crew remained stranded as a growing crowd on shore maintained a death watch. Around 10 o'clock on the night of the 15th, the *Minturn* could take no more and broke apart, and the raging sea swept away everyone on board. Thirty-nine souls, including the captain and his family, perished that terrible night, whereas the thirteen survivors could tell and retell a chilling story for all to listen.

Triggered by the wrecks of the *Minturn* and other ships in what became known as the Great Storm of 1846—in all, 60 lives were lost—New Jersey representative William A. Newell requested funds for equipment for the "better protection of life and property on the coast of New Jersey." In 1848, a $10,000 appropriation thus established the Life-Saving Service with full-time seasonal (winter) employees. A series of stations also replaced the small boat sheds previously scattered on

in a horizontal band keyed to the amplitude of the local tidal cycle. Gooseneck barnacles occur less often in the wrack line, but they lie at the core of a medieval myth. Because of their long neck-like peduncles and feathery feeding structures, they seemed—at least to few imaginative English naturalists of old—like preformed geese ready to hatch and thereby explained the disappearance of the birds each spring. The geese, of course, actually migrated to their northern nesting grounds, but the fanciful association lingers in birds to this day identified as

the beaches between Sandy Hook and Little Egg Harbor. In 1915, the Life-Saving Service merged with the Revenue Cutter Service to form the U.S. Coast Guard, and so the tragedy of the *Minturn* came to some good purpose.

Nearly a century later, the burned-out hulk of the *Morro Castle*, a cruise ship with a weekly run between New York City and Havana, Cuba, beached at Asbury Park. Although the Great Depression gripped the nation in the 1930s, high-end rollers nonetheless enjoyed life in the fast lane, and the *Morro Castle* made it possible to do just that in Cuba. Moreover, with prohibition in force on shore, the cruise became a floating party for the 1,100-mile run each way. The 508-foot liner accommodated 489 passengers and a crew of 240.

Trouble for the *Morro Castle* began when the captain, complaining of a stomachache, suddenly died on the night of September 7, 1934, on the return to New York. It continued when the ship sailed into a developing nor'easter on the New Jersey coast the following day. Then, just before 3 A.M., a fire broke out as the storm-tossed ship passed Long Beach Island, but instead of changing course, it continued sailing into the wind. Thus fanned, the fire spread rapidly, aided by thick coats of paint on the interior walls. The electrical system failed, darkening the ship, and thick smoke further complicated efforts to quell the fire. Further, the acting captain did not promptly authorize SOS calls, and the rescue ships likewise responded slowly to the emergency. Only 6 of the ship's 12 lifeboats were launched, boarded by just 85 people (mostly crew) instead of the 408 they could have carried. Many passengers died when they jumped from the ship without properly deploying their life jackets. In all, 135 (some reports say 137) passengers and crew died.

The *Morro Castle* quickly became a popular tourist attraction at Asbury Park before it was towed off for salvage several months later. Intrigue persists about the cause of the fire, including arson, in which the radio operator remains a central figure. Like the *Minturn* disaster, the fate of the *Morro Castle* produced important safely improvements, including fire drills for passengers, ship-wide alarm systems, and fire-retardant construction materials. Lessons hard learned when the Graveyard of the Atlantic claimed two more ships.

barnacle geese. In the real world of the Jersey Shore, however, driftwood bearing clusters of gooseneck barnacles remains but another example of the wrack line's curiosities.

The debris and vegetation forming wrack lines become prime targets for what is known as beach grooming, which includes removing these materials with large rakes towed by tractors. Plastic trash and hazardous materials, of course, are unwanted, but many beachgoers also regard the windrows of seaweed as unsightly,

Shore Note 2.3 Jaws 1916 Style

July 1, 1916, was hot and Charles Vansant wanted to take a quick dip in the ocean before dinner. Born into a Main Line family in Philadelphia, the 25-year-old Vansant was spending a few days with his father and two sisters at an upscale hotel in Beach Haven, a resort town on the southern end of Long Beach Island. A friendly dog accompanied the young stockbroker into the chest-deep water just beyond the breakers, while on shore a lifeguard and former Olympic swimmer watched the two enjoy themselves. All seemed well until Vansant cried out—some bathers initially thought he was calling the dog—from a slick of blood-stained water. The lifeguard and a bystander rushed to help, hauling the stricken swimmer to the beach, apparently with the unyielding shark holding on for much of the way. In the hotel lobby, Vansant, with much of his left thigh stripped to the bone, bled to death stretched out on the hotel manager's desk. This was the first fatality of its kind ever recorded on the Eastern Seaboard of the United States—but more were coming, and soon. Shark attacks would terrorize the Jersey Shore for the next 12 days.

In Spring Lake, another plush resort town about 45 miles north of Beach Haven, a shark killed Charles Bruder on July 6. The 28-year-old Swiss bell captain, a strong swimmer, enjoyed the water during his lunch breaks. He was well offshore, perhaps 130 yards, when a shark severed both of his legs below the knee and gouged his abdomen in what were likely repeated assaults. Indeed, some witnesses claim he was tossed about during the attack. Because of so much bleeding, another witness thought a scuttled, red-hulled canoe lay just under the water's surface. Lifeguards rushed to the scene in a lifeboat, but Bruder died before they could return to the shore—the second shark victim of 1916.

Still farther up the New Jersey coast, a more or less typical tidewater stream meanders its way to Raritan Bay. Matawan Creek originates near its namesake, then a small town of shops and light

and these too are removed. Beach grooming, while increasing the visual aesthetics of recreational areas, diminishes the biodiversity and abundance of native plants and animals, shortens food chains, and further threatens highly vulnerable species (e.g., seabeach amaranth and piping plovers). In its various forms, beach grooming may increase the coarseness of the sand and destroy desirable features such as the embryonic stages of dune building. Beach grooming may also influence the resilience of beaches to erosion and increase the frequency of their renourishment, but these impacts remain undocumented.

New Jersey, by law, protects beaches, including their wrack lines, from raking, sand scraping, and nonemergency vehicular traffic at locations where the pres-

industries, including one where 11-year-old Lester Stillwell spent the summer assembling peach baskets. In his free time, Lester and his friends often went swimming in the creek at an abandoned wharf, as they did on the hot afternoon July 12. Suddenly, what the boys had thought was a sunken timber pulled Lester underwater. His friends sought help, which included an athletic 24-year-old tailor named W. Stanley Fisher, who dived in, located the boy's body, and started for shore. The shark again attacked, biting Fisher in full view of the gathered crowd and freeing his grip on the dead boy whose body would be not be recovered for two days. Like Vansant before him, Fisher bled to death from a severe thigh wound. About 30 minutes later and a half-mile downstream, a shark lacerated the leg of 12-year-old Joseph Dunn. The boy was rescued by his companions after a tug-of-war struggle with the shark; he recovered after spending weeks in a hospital.

Panic ensued along the Jersey Shore for the remainder of the summer. Wire nets, armed patrol boats, offers of bounties, and, in Matawan Creek, dynamite blasting were among the responses to the attacks. Sharks, it seemed, were everywhere, at least if the rush of sightings could be believed. But were the attacks made by one rogue or several sharks and of what species? Great white sharks head the list of "usual suspects," and two days after the attacks at Matawan, a fisherman caught a 7.5-footer in Raritan Bay not far from the creek's mouth. Its stomach contained flesh and bones later identified as human remains. Bull sharks, which frequent tidal creeks as well as beachfronts, offer another possibility. In any case, the bloody terror of 1916 ended at Matawan Creek, but it initiated the specter of man-eating sharks that still haunts the American psyche—an image significantly reinforced by Steven Spielberg's 1975 heart-pounding thriller. The good news: Americans face a greater risk of dying from lightning or fireworks than from a shark attack, so enjoy the beach and instead worry about thunderstorms and cherry bombs.

ence of threated and endangered species has been documented and declared a "No Rake Zone," but such sites remain protected only between May 15 and November 30. The statute allows beach grooming at any time on recreational beaches, defined as those within 100 yards of a staffed lifeguard stand. However, this restriction may not be rigorously enforced, despite documentation of the ecological damage grooming may inflict on New Jersey's (and other) beaches. Fortunately, compromises between maintaining clean beaches and protecting their ecological values can and have been achieved when all stakeholders act in good faith, yet many more sites want for the benefits of similar management.

The Backshore

A somewhat flatter area, a terrace known as the backshore (or berm), stretches across the beach from a usually well-defined edge lying near the upper edge of the swash zone landward to the foot of the dunes. This is the site where beachgoers pitch their chairs and blankets, hence human traffic may limit pioneering vegetation from gaining a foothold on public beaches. Natural conditions nonetheless impose their own rigorous limitations. The summer sun mercilessly bakes the backshore, leaving the sand in want of interstitial water and an austere bed for seed germination; in winter, the same aridity renders the sand bitterly cold. Moreover, winds turn the dry, loose sand into abrasive missiles and carry an invisible salt-laden aerosol across the beach. All told, the backshore remains rather barren and, lacking much primary production from either on-site or external sources, only a few short food chains persist. Unfortunately, human traffic—pedestrian or vehicular—places additional stresses on the sparse flora of the backshore.

Still, seabeach amaranth survives in this environment, producing spinach-like leaves born on fleshy red stems (fig. 2.4, bottom). Once established, the seedlings branch into clumps that accumulate and bind sand; the tips of the prostrate branches project upward. As annuals, the plants produce large numbers of seeds that likely retain their viability for long periods of time. Once abundant, the plant was first collected in New Jersey early in the nineteenth century, with a range later determined to extend from Massachusetts to South Carolina. Thereafter its numbers rapidly declined; a specimen collected at Island Beach State Park in 1913 marked the last time it was recorded in New Jersey. Seabeach amaranth accordingly appeared on the state's first list of endangered plants and was later added to the federal list of threatened species. Fortunately, some plants were discovered in 2000 on renourished beaches in Monmouth County, and surveys the following year revealed others in all of the four coastal counties. Even so, seabeach amaranth remains closely watched, given that the causes for its decline—habitat disturbances and modifications—remain all too prominent.

New Jersey likewise lists as endangered another occupant of this niche—seaside sandwort (fig. 2.4, top). Wind and water disperse the seeds of this succulent, but underground rootstocks also enable these perennial plants to spread across the sea-facing base of primary dunes. As an ecological pioneer, the species is one of the first to colonize even the most remote beaches, including Surtsey, the volcanic

FIGURE 2.4. Seaside sandwort (top), shown here in a clump arising from a common rootstock, and seabeach amaranth (bottom) both cope with beachfront environments lying between the high tide line and the toe of primary dunes. Regrettably, both species currently appear on New Jersey's list of endangered species. Photo credits: Jason Hafstad (top); Kevin Knutsen (bottom).

island that suddenly emerged from the sea near Iceland in 1963. Like some other species associated with beach and dune systems (see following), seaside sandwort helps capture and bind sand. The sexuality of the species is rather curious: the plants are subdioecious, which means the flowers of some individuals produce only seeds, whereas the flowers of others primarily generate pollen or yield a few seeds (i.e., some plants have only female flowers, but others have mostly male flowers as well as some female flowers). Because of its location on beachfronts, the species is vulnerable to human disturbances, even more so because it does not compete well with other plants (e.g., American beachgrass). New Jersey marks the southern boundary in the range of seaside sandwort in eastern North America, which suggests that rising global temperatures may push the species northward to the point where it no longer occurs in the state's flora.

American sea rocket also copes with the severe conditions of the backshore. Easily destroyed by storms, the plants grow beyond the reach of high water. Their distinctively lobed leaves are edible, which is no surprise given that the species is related to cabbages and other cultivated members for the mustard family. Remarkably, sea rocket can identify and respond to competing species such as seabeach amaranth. The proximity of a competitor stimulates additional root growth, presumably giving sea rocket the upper hand in the nutrient-poor and arid environment of the backshore. Conversely, this response does not occur when the neighboring plant is another sea rocket.

The sparse vegetation may include seaside spurge and a few others that also occur in the dunes that mark the end of backshore. The stems of these plants often develop in a thick growth that gives rise to seaside sandmat as an alternate name for the species. When damaged, seaside spurge secretes a milky substance that irritates the human skin in a manner similar to poison ivy. The plants attract insects, which likely play a key role as pollinators for this and other flowering species nearby.

A few creatures also call the backshore home. One of these, the ghost crab, lives in burrows near—or sometimes in—the dunes (fig. 2.5). The entrances to their burrows are about the size of a quarter and lead to a passage that extends downward for three to four feet to the water table, ending in a turnaround chamber. At night, ghost crabs forage in the wrack line before returning to the safety of their burrows at dawn, lest they fall prey to an ever-hungry gull. They also regularly visit the swash zone to wet their gills, a necessity that accommodates their other-

FIGURE 2.5. Ghost crabs scurry about on the drier, upper beachfront but must visit the surf several times daily to wet their gills. They thrive on undisturbed beaches but become scarce when and where human activities increase. Photo credit: Kevin Knutsen.

wise terrestrial lifestyle. For gravid females, the trip to the swash zone also wets their egg masses, and still later they return there to release their hatchlings. Ghost crabs overwinter in a state of torpor, surviving on oxygen stored in sacs near their gills that sustains them for as long as six weeks, after which they must again travel across the backshore to the swash zone

Otherwise protectively colored to match the sand, their claws are white and enlarged, but unlike fiddler crabs (to which they are related) male and female ghost crabs each bear one claw that is somewhat larger than the other. As part of their courtship ritual, adult males neatly pile excavated sand near the entrances to their burrows, which aids females to find and select their mates (the entrances to burrows occupied by females and immature ghost crabs lack such orderly architecture). The eyes of ghost crabs, mounted at the end of stalks, can swivel 360 degrees, a clear advantage for detecting predators. Additionally, they run quickly—clocked up to 10 miles per hour whether forward, backward, or sideways to avoid unhappy circumstances.

A few birds rely on backshores for nesting habitat. These include two species that nest in colonies, the least tern and black skimmer, and the piping plover, a solitary nester. The plovers separate into three geographic populations: the northern Great Plains, the largest, followed in size, respectively, by those associated with the Atlantic coast and Great Lakes. These populations overlap somewhat in their winter distribution, with those breeding on the Atlantic coast especially favoring the Bahamas. Piping plovers (fig. 1.7), state listed since 1984 as endangered, arrive in New Jersey in late March and early April and, after pairing, scrape shallow nest bowls in the sand and line the depressions with shell fragments; they commonly select sites near clumps of American beachgrass. They often nest within skimmer or tern colonies, thereby gaining additional protection from predators (see Coastal Colonies, chapter 4). Both parents incubate their well-camouflaged clutches of three to four speckled, sand-colored eggs. Piping plovers, adults and chicks alike, feed on small invertebrates including insect larvae, worms, and crustaceans occurring in the swash zone and other shoreline areas. Unfortunately, many of their nesting areas coincide with sites where human activities occur, stressing both the adults and their chicks to the point of lessening their foraging activities and likely their reproductive success as well.

Federal, state, and private agencies cooperate to protect the nesting sites for each of these three species, although locating the individual and well-concealed nests of piping plovers remains far more difficult than locating the busy colonies of black skimmers and least terns. Fortunately, many of the nesting areas for one or more of these species lie within the boundaries of beaches subject to federal jurisdiction, specifically Sandy Hook National Recreation Area and the Holgate Unit of the Edwin B. Forsythe National Wildlife Refuge. Fences surrounding active tern and skimmer colonies reduce human intrusions, whereas enclosures—some electrified—around plover nests inhibit predators (e.g., red foxes).

On beaches south of New Jersey (e.g., North Carolina), the backshore provides nesting terrain for sea turtles. New Jersey, however, lies to the north of the normal nesting range for any of the species occurring along the Atlantic coast of North America, although at least one loggerhead once attempted to nest at Island Beach State Park. Nonetheless, four species—Kemp's ridley, leatherback, green, and loggerhead—regularly cruise offshore and warrant the watchful eye of state and federal conservation agencies, largely to ensure that the nets of trawlers are outfitted with devices that allow entrapped sea turtles to escape drowning.

Dunes

Coastal dunes stand as sandy fortresses against the wrath of the sea. But unlike military fortifications, dunes can and do move across the landscape they defend. The harsh environmental conditions of the backshore continue into the dunes, and some of the same plants, among them American sea rocket, likewise gain a foothold at the foot of the sandy hills. However, the sand grains forming the dunes tend to be smaller, the result of sorting by the wind that carries the particles landward from the beachfront. The smaller grains in turn increase the water-holding capacity of the soils, which helps establish stands of American beachgrass (fig. 2.6). This species dominates the vegetation on undisturbed dunes forming along the

FIGURE 2.6. American beachgrass, essential for forming and maintaining the structure of dune systems in New Jersey, must be protected from human disturbances lest the dunes erode. Photo credit: Pernille Ruhalter.

coast north of Cape Hatteras in North Carolina, south of which sea oats occupy the same niche. Whereas burial threatens most species of plants that otherwise might occur on dunes, American beachgrass thrives on the steady buildup of sand, which in fact stimulates new growth that enables the stems and leaves to keep up with the accumulations of additional sand. Moreover, the arrival of fresh sand imports nutrients and, being sterilized by the ocean, lessens the incidence of pathogenic organisms. Root-knot nematodes are among the latter and attack the less vigorous stands of American beachgrass growing leeward of the foredunes (i.e., where fresh sand does not accumulate). Herbivorous insects, including aphids and grasshoppers, also become more prevalent as the distance from the oceanfront increases. In particular, a soft-scale insect severely damages the plants and, like the foregoing, appears in greater numbers behind the foredunes, in this case because their larvae gain protection from the abrasive action of wind-blown sand. All told, these factors help ensure the dominance of American beachgrass on the ocean-facing side of the primary dune system—a niche essentially free of competitors and pathogens—whereas the species fares poorly in the sheltered locations behind the foredunes where various limitations come into play.

At maturity, the stems and leaves of American beachgrass reach heights of 2 to 3 feet. Meanwhile, an extensive system of roots and rhizomes develops below-ground that may extend downward for 20 feet—an obvious adaptation for tapping into the miniature aquifers lying deep within the dunes. The network of roots may reach the same distance outward, which helps capture surface water from light rains. Recesses in the leaves shelter pores known as stomata, which lessen the loss of water, and the leaves themselves roll and fold in ways that reduce their exposure to the drying effects of coastal winds, strong sunlight, and intense heat. Mycorrhizal fungi help provide the plants with water and nutrients from the soil and in return receive organic materials, especially sugars, from the roots. Seed production is minimal, but their network of subsurface rhizomes enables the plants to spread 6 to 10 feet per year, producing up to 100 stems per clump.

The ecological significance of American beachgrass, of course, lies in its ability to intercept and hold blowing sand, thereby building and stabilizing dunes against erosion. Unfortunately, American beachgrass remains highly susceptible to human disturbances—and dunes inherently tend to attract visitors. A single run by an off-road vehicle kills both the mature plants and their rhizomes. Even light foot traffic takes a toll. Tests determined that just 200 passages in 45 days severely damage the plants—a disturbance equivalent to two people traveling through the vegetation twice a day during a short summer season. Interestingly, persons walking barefoot produce far less damage than those with footwear (as above) simply because they step between, not on, the plants in response to a greater sensory awareness of the flora. Blowouts may occur where the plants are damaged or killed and, unless replanted, endanger the integrity of the surrounding dune system. The implications are clear: permit no vehicular traffic in dunes and restrict high-volume pedestrian traffic to established paths, preferably those with boardwalks.

Although American beachgrass primarily reproduces by vegetative means, it nonetheless produces seeds, which provide winter food resources for birds, including Ipswich sparrows. DNA analyses determined these birds, once considered a separate species, represent one of at least 17 subspecies of the widely distributed savannah sparrow. Still, they remain unique, primarily because the entire population breeds only on Sable Island, a narrow crescent of dunes and heath lying 155 miles southeast of Nova Scotia. The birds are larger and paler in color than the other subspecies—traits that develop and persist because of philopatry (homing behavior), the return of each generation to breed at the same site. When this occurs at isolated locations, of which islands offer a prime example, the restricted gene pool typically produces a population with distinctive characteristics—a textbook case of reproductive isolation, which in this case fostered the rapid evolution of the birds' physical features. Ipswich sparrows also walk when searching for insects in summer and seeds in winter, whereas the other subspecies hop when foraging for these foods. Alexander Wilson was the first to note this "pale sparrow of the dunes" at the current site of Ocean City, but it was later "rediscovered" at Ipswich Beach in Massachusetts, hence establishing the name that still identifies this unique population.

Other dune plants include seaside goldenrod, which favors sites somewhat protected from the harsh conditions prevailing on the windward face of the foredunes (e.g., locations on the backside of primary dunes, low secondary dunes, and the edges of salt marshes). The plants, which reach heights of three to six feet, bloom in late summer and into October—their terminal spikes bear clusters of bright yellow flowers in an inflorescence that is the largest of all species of goldenrods (fig. 2.7, top). Exudates released from the roots of seaside goldenrod apparently limit the density of other plants growing in the immediate area—an example of allelopathy, the adverse effects on one plant by the chemical products of another plant.

FIGURE 2.7. Seaside goldenrod adds color to the dune vegetation (top), whereas beach pea adds protective cover as well as nitrogen to the nutrient-starved sands (bottom). Photo credit: Kevin Knutsen.

The stocky rhizomes of seaside goldenrod help control dune erosion, and sugar-rich nectar of the flowers provides a primary source of energy for monarch butterflies during their fall migration (see chapter 5). Several kinds of gall insects infest this and other species of goldenrod, with about half of these becoming winter food for chickadees and other small birds. Another insect, the goldenrod leaf beetle, uses its sense of smell to single out its host plants from other vegetation. Additionally, the breeding biology of these insects is geared to the development of goldenrod—the beetles produce only one generation per year even though the season is long enough for a second cycle (as occurs in other leaf beetles). The availability of tender leaves as food for the larvae may explain this relationship, likely because the foliage hardens and becomes unpalatable as the growing season advances, hence precluding nourishment for another generation of beetle larvae. Also, the beetles lay their eggs in the soil or on fallen leaves rather than on the foliage and thus hatch near a reliable food source the following spring. Otherwise, fall winds might carry dried, egg-bearing leaves to locales lacking goldenrod and thereby limit the survival of the newly hatched larvae. Yet another insect, the seaside goldenrod borer moth, in fact rarely visits dunes and instead seeks its namesake host plants at the edges of salt marshes well inland from the beachfront.

Entanglements of beach pea provide quilts of dense cover at some sites on the lee side of dune systems (fig. 2.7, bottom). The plants bear pinnately compound leaves, each with about five pairs of leaflets and terminating in a curling tendril; in season, five to ten purple flowers highlight the bright green foliage. Beach pea occurs globally in the coastal floras of Asia, Europe, and both North and South America—a circumpolar distribution that reflects its reproductive adaptations. The seeds remain viable in seawater for as long as five years, which allows time for them to drift great distances. They geminate when sand grinds away the seed coat in the turmoil of waves breaking on a beachfront—the same force that scours sea glass.

Plants belonging to two groups—yuccas and cacti—typically associated with western deserts and grasslands also dot the dunes along the New Jersey coast (fig. 2.8). Eastern prickly pear, long regarded as the only species of cactus native to the state, may grow singly or develop into expanding clumps.[1] The plants bear

---

[1] In September 2022, botanist Bob Cunningham identified a second species, dune prickly pear, growing in dispersed patches on the dunes near Ocean City. A storm likely conveyed viable parts of the plants or

FIGURE 2.8. Normally associated with the American Southwest, yuccas (left) and cactus (right) also occur in dune communities along the Jersey Shore. Photo credits: Pernille Ruhalter (left); Kevin Knutsen (right).

pads studded with prominent spines, although less obvious clusters of hair-like bristles called glochids prove far more painful. When embedded in a victim, barbs hold the tiny bristles in place and make it difficult to extract the source of an irritation that may fester for several days. Their striking yellow flowers, which sometimes become even more colorful with orange-red interiors, develop from buds on the rims of the pads. Although the flowers bloom for just one day, they nonetheless attract bees and, following pollination, produce pear-shaped fruits known as tunas. When ripe, the sweet red tunas furnish the ingredients for savory jams.

Adam's needle is just one of several names for a yucca whose native range extends from southern Virginia south to Florida and along the Gulf Coast to Louisiana.

---

their seeds to this relatively pristine site; the northernmost extent of the species otherwise ends along the coast of North Carolina.

Another, Spanish dagger, clearly reflects the long sword-shaped leaves that extend for 30 inches from a basal rosette. The stiff, pointed leaves of the species also underlie a more practical name, "sentry plant," which cautious fathers planted beneath their daughters' windows as guards against suiters with questionable intensions. Curly, tough fibers peel from the margins of the leaves, hence the species name *filamentosa*. Names aside, Adam's needle produces a central stalk five to eight feet high topped by a panicle of creamy-white bell-shaped flowers. Because of these showy inflorescences, and its hardiness to winter weather, the species became a desirable ornamental in northern states and, after escaping from yards, established itself along the coasts of New Jersey and other states lying beyond its original range (e.g., New England). The plants produce seeds encased in woody pods, but also spread vegetatively from fleshy taproots that, along with a deep network of lateral roots, help stabilize dune systems. Native Americans used yuccas for food, medicines, cordage, and soap.

This and other species of yuccas form half of a mutually beneficial relationship with moths that pollinate the plants that botanist George Engelmann (1809–1884) discovered in 1872. The female moths—those of a few species collectively known as yucca moths—visit the flowers and, using two tentacles near their mouths, roll a ball of pollen that they carry beneath their chins to the flowers of another yucca of the same species. There they lay their eggs inside the flower's developing ovary, then deposit the pollen balls on the stigmas, thereby ensuring production of seeds to later feed their larvae. Before leaving, they secrete pheromones that inform other females to look elsewhere for another flower—in effect, the scents proclaim "no vacancy," lest the flower's ovary become overloaded with moth eggs. After hatching, the larvae mature and depart before consuming all of the seeds, enough of which remain for the plants to reproduce another generation of seedlings. Even with the geographical expansion of Adam's needle, the moths managed to keep pace and follow the plants northward to New Jersey and beyond.

The silvery, wooly-felt foliage of dusty miller provides an attractive addition to the beach flora. In 1900, noted Harvard botanist Merritt L. Fernald (1873–1950) addressed the issue of the species' origin in North America. Whereas the plants flourished near coastal resorts ranging from Mount Desert Island in Maine to Sandy Hook in New Jersey, the species was not listed as part of the North American flora until 1877. Because the species was originally described from Kamchatka in the Russian Far East, botanists generally regarded the species as an introduced ornamental that later escaped. Still, doubts lingered, and the idea emerged that dusty miller had spread from Asia at the end of the "ice age" and thereafter remained overlooked because of its preference for remote beaches. Fernald, however, rejected these arguments, underscoring the popularity of dusty miller as a garden plant beginning in the 1870s. Moreover, even small parts of discarded plants easily propagate new growth. In sum, Fernald concluded that the sudden appearance of a popular and conspicuous garden plant on beaches near summer resorts and its omission from flora compiled prior to 1877 leave little doubt that dusty miller represents an introduced species now well established along the northeastern coast of North America.

Another introduced ornamental recently became the center of controversy on Seven Mile Beach, a barrier island in the Avalon area of southern New Jersey. Triggered by a major storm in March 1962, Japanese black pine became the species of choice for wind breaks, privacy screens, and ornamental plantings at beachfront properties as well as for stabilizing dunes on public lands (for patient gardeners the species also lends itself to bonsai culture). The trees cope well with wind-borne salt—more so, in fact, than any other species of pine—and at the time seemed resistant to disease and insect damage.

A half century later, however, the invasive nature of Japanese black pine became apparent at locations where the prolific trees formed crowded monocultures at the expense of native vegetation. The thick growth also accumulated blankets of needles, cones, and other tinder that presented a serious fire hazard, and the trees offered limited food or cover for wildlife. Moreover, several fatal pathogenic agents had emerged on the scene, among them blue stain fungus carried by black turpentine beetles and microscopic nematodes transported by pine sawyer beetles. Indeed, some refer to the latter as "deadly messengers" because of their role in spreading the nematodes. In short, the Japanese black pine—whether dead, dying, or still living—had become a problem.

In response, borough officials, cognizant of the ecological and economic values of stable dunes, opted to remove the pines on a tree-by-tree basis, leaving the stumps in place to hold the sand. The voids are filled with native plants, among them red cedar, bayberry, and beach plum, on sites subject to salt spray, whereas smooth sumac, American holly, black oak, and persimmon are planted on dunes farther inland. Still, the removal of the Japanese black pines ran contrary to the wishes of some residents who, aside from their genuine attachment to the groves,

FIGURE 2.9. Too often, blankets of the invasive Asiatic sand sedge overrun dunes, in the process replacing American beachgrass and other native vegetation, as shown here at Island Beach State Park. When mature, the plants stand about a foot tall and bear club-like flowering heads atop triangular stems (inset). Photo credits: Jason Hafstad; Helen Hamilton, National Park Service (inset).

felt the project benefited only a few property owners with a better view. A full assessment, however, suggests that the project bodes well for the future health of dune systems overwhelmed by Japanese black pine.

Yet another case of unintended consequences concerns Asiatic sand sedge, which arrived in North America at Island Beach circa 1929, probably when plants used as packing material were jettisoned from a ship carrying porcelain to New York (fig. 2.9). The species now ranges from Massachusetts to North Carolina, in part because it was propagated in the 1960s as an alternative to American beach-grass for stabilizing dunes. By the mid-1980s, however, the invasive nature of the plants was evident and they were withdrawn as nursery stock. Nonetheless, the plants continued invading beaches on the eastern coast on their own right, spreading by both vegetative (cord-like rhizomes) and sexual (seeds) means. Like many exotic species, Asiatic sand sedge remains unfettered in its new land and displaces native species, including seabeach amaranth and American beachgrass. It develops in dense stands, sometimes with more than 300 stems per square yard, which degrades nesting sites otherwise suitable for coastal birds such as piping plovers. Recent work, however, indicates that Asiatic sedge can better stabilize dunes when compared with American beachgrass. Hence, the role of this exotic species seems best suited for the short-term protection of vulnerable unvegetated dunes, later followed by the restoration of native vegetation. Superficially resembling a grass, Asiatic sand sedge can be identified by touch—small teeth edge its leaf margins— and, in season, by a spike of flowers borne atop triangular, not round, stalks. When mature, the flowers, produce seeds that develop individually in papery sacs.

Swales and Other Sandy Places

Depressions known as swales, also identified as slacks, lying between dune lines provide enough protection to establish communities less affected by the adversities of the beachfront environment. These include such plants as broomsedge and colonies of rose mallow as well as the widespread seaside goldenrod. Swales, along with the leeward sides of secondary dunes, also provide sites where woody vegetation can develop along the coastline. Bayberry and beach plum represent the latter— both help stabilize the sandy soils at these locations—which in later successional stages includes red cedar and black cherry (see Maritime Forests, following).

The fragrant BB-sized fruit of bayberries has long attracted humans. When separated by boiling, the coating on the berries provided settlers with highly scented but virtually smokeless wax for candles. The aromatic wax is still used for the same purpose, with about four pounds of berries required to produce one pound of wax. The waxy coating hinders digestion of the berries, but a few birds nonetheless thrive on the energy-rich fruit, notably yellow-rumped warblers and tree swallows (see chapter 5). This adaptation apparently explains why yellow-rumped warblers can winter farther north than closely related species that cannot assimilate saturated long-chain fatty acids. The blueish-gray berries, which develop in clusters, easily identify female plants. Bayberry shrubs, typically five to

FIGURE 2.10. In spring, the burst of beach plum blossoms heralds a fall crop of tart but edible fruit (inset). The shrubs help anchor secondary dunes, as shown here at Higbee Beach Wildlife Management Area at the tip of Cape May. Photo credits: Pat and Clay Sutton; Rutgers New Jersey Agricultural Experiment Station (inset).

eight feet in height, thrive on nutrient-starved soils largely because of nitrogen-fixing bacteria attached to their roots. Their leaves persist through much of the winter, hence they offer nearly year-round shelter for wildlife (the same feature makes bayberry boughs a favorite for concealing duck blinds).

Beach plum, a shrub typically 4 to 7 feet tall in dune environments, may reach heights of 14 to 18 feet farther inland. In spring, the plants produce showy blossoms that in fall yield fruit that, although variable in size, generally resembles large grapes (fig. 2.10). When ripe, the tough-skinned fruit varies in color—red to purple,

FIGURE 2.11. Swales may be moist enough at some locations to support wetland plants, as shown here by the green patch of common three-square bulrush (inset). The darkened sand in the swale, which contrasts with the sugar-white sand in the dunes, further indicates the wetter (mesic) conditions at this site. Photo credit: Bob Cunningham; Derek Tilley, USDA Natural Resources Conservation Service (inset).

or even black—with a white waxy residue. Regardless of their size or color, the plums abound with vitamin A and contain five times the minerals of cranberries. They make excellent jams and jellies that, because of their high pectin content, can be prepared simply by boiling the fruit or juice in water and sugar. A Beach Plum Festival is held annually at Island Beach State Park.

Wetland plants at times flourish in swales where freshwater temporarily accumulates, among them various sedges and rushes, as well as marsh fern and cattails (fig. 2.11). The leaflets on marsh ferns curl under at their edges, a feature that helps distinguish them from similar species. These ferns serve as the food source for the larvae of the aptly named marsh fern moth, although some evidence suggests that other species of ferns may fulfill the same role. Unfortunately, *Phragmites* often invades swales and overwhelms areas that otherwise could provide habitat for a diverse flora, including saltmarsh fleabane, slender sea purslane, and rare species such as Atlantic ladies' tresses (see shore note 6.1).

These interdunal wetland environments provide habitat for wildlife that might otherwise shun dune systems, including nesting birds such as black ducks and no doubt a few species of reptiles and amphibians. Likely candidates include the recently identified Atlantic coast leopard frog, Fowler's toad, eastern garter snake, and eastern mud turtle. The latter, just three to four inches long and weak swimmers, prefer sites with shallow water, including brackish wetlands. In some locations the interdunal fauna may well include species of special interest, as is the case with the Bethany Beach firefly, which dwells solely in swales containing freshwater along a 20-mile sliver of Delaware's coastline immediately south of Cape May. The expanse of Delaware Bay seemingly prevents the northward extension in the range of this highly vulnerable species into New Jersey. However, no obvious natural barrier limits the firefly's southward movements, which suggests that overdevelopment might have destroyed the insect's specialized habitat and thus confined its range to a dangerously small area.

Whereas much remains unknown about the swale fauna in New Jersey, studies of marshy swales at Island Beach State Park revealed the presence of three small mammals, with the meadow vole being the most abundant, followed by the meadow jumping mouse and less often by the white-footed mouse—each widely distributed across much of North America. Of these, meadow jumping mice catch our attention because of their disproportionately large feet that enable leaps of about three feet when the animals are disturbed (they otherwise hop for just a few inches). They also swim well, including underwater, and readily cross areas of open water. Seeds, fungi, and insects—especially moth larvae—form their diet. Meadow jumping mice hibernate below ground in nests constructed just for that purpose.

Except for the hibernating jumping mouse, these small mammals likely provide much of the food for the snowy owls that sometimes show up on the dunes in winter (fig. 2.12). The chunky meadow vole would seemingly offer a particularly rewarding meal, but only rarely can hungry predators be choosy when selecting their prey—opportunity, not preference, carries the day. Although an Arctic

FIGURE 2.12. The wintertime occurrence of snowy owls along the Jersey Shore provides birders with unique opportunities to see and photograph avian visitors from the Far North. Photo credit: Kevin Knutsen.

species, snowy owls appear somewhat irregularly as far south as North Carolina. Beaches resemble the treeless tundra where the owls normally occur, which likely explains why the birds favor coastal dunes when venturing beyond the Arctic. No clear reason explains their appearance, although many biologists believe food shortages may be involved. In the Arctic, lemmings dominate their diet—an adult snowy owl may eat 1,600 per year—but some owls nonetheless travel south even in years when lemmings, known for their huge swings in numbers, remain abundant in the Arctic. Still, most of the vagrant birds are juveniles, which seemingly reflects their limited hunting skills when competing with adults during food shortages. Reports of even one snowy owl on the New Jersey coast brings out numbers

FIGURE 2.13. Patches of beach heather often blanket back dunes and other undisturbed sites along the New Jersey shoreline. Photo credit: Pernille Ruhalter.

of anxious birders and photographers, but all should avoid trampling the vital vegetation that protects the dunes in quest of their prize.

Patches of beach heather carpet dry swales and other areas behind the dunes where the harmful effects of salt aerosol become diminished (fig. 2.13). The fine branches of this low-growing shrub, which stand just three to eight inches tall, bear scale-like leaves coated with soft, white, and wooly hair. In season, small but attractive flowers provide nectar for pollinating insects. In some locations elsewhere in its range, beach heather grows on with soils laden with cyanobacteria (also known as blue-green algae) that fix nitrogen, which may explain how the plants cope with nutrient-starved sands; this relationship, however, has not been confirmed for those growing in the coastal areas of New Jersey. Some evidence suggests that beach heather may produce compounds that reduce competition from other species—an example of allelopathy—as indicated where patches grow in relative isolation from other vegetation. As with other shoreline vegetation, beach heather suffers from trampling by either foot or vehicular traffic.

Maritime Forests

Maritime forests by definition develop along the coastline under the influence of a salty, windy, and storm-prone environment. The composition of these woodlands understandably varies between regions, with those south of Virginia (including the Gulf Coast) most commonly dominated by live oak interspersed with loblolly pine. These feature tightly knit, closed canopies whose windward edges slope roof-like toward the beachfront, sculpted by the relentless presence of salt spray (actually an aerosol). In New Jersey, however, maritime forests develop more variably in both their composition and structure. Trees as dissimilar from each other as post oak, holly, and eastern red cedar become important components of maritime forests along the Jersey Shore, and few of these produce closed, profoundly sculpted canopies. Instead, the profile slopes because the trees grow taller as the distance from the beachfront increases. Nonetheless, salt spray may still exert its influence and "burn" the buds on the windward side of shrubs and trees, whereas other buds experience relatively less damage (fig. 2.14). As a result, growth proceeds at an uneven rate, with those stems and leaves on the sheltered side outgrowing those facing the oceanfront.

Some maritime forests originate as thickets in swales beyond the reach of the more severe effects of wind-born salt (these are sometimes identified as "dune forests"). In some locations, particularly where organic matter accumulations foster richer soils, succession gradually replaces the shrubby thickets with stands of mature trees that once cloaked relatively large areas of New Jersey's barrier beaches. Sadly, however, only a few remnants of these forests remain, and most of these suffer from ills of various kinds (e.g., development, storm damage, and invasive species).

As indicated earlier, the composition of maritime forests varies by location. At one site on the barrier beach at Sandy Hook, for example, American holly plays a dominant role shared with, among others, black cherry, pitch pine, and

FIGURE 2.14. Plant succession along the shore culminates in maritime forests and thickets characterized by canopies sculpted on their windward edges by wind-borne salts. The community shown here at Island Beach State Park consists of black cherry, eastern red cedar, and bayberry. Stunted hollies in the maritime forest at Sandy Hook also develop salt-sculpted canopies (inset). Photo credits: Kathleen Strakosch Walz, New Jersey Department of Environmental Protection.

hackberry. Some of the larger hollies, perhaps 200 years old, exceed 18 inches in diameter. In contrast, eastern red cedar dominates the maritime forest surviving at Island Beach State Park, with the same species that occur at Sandy Hook assuming somewhat lesser prominence in the community. Other trees in the canopy at these and other locations include black gum, swamp magnolia, red maple, and a variety of oaks.

Sassafras also occurs as a prominent species in the maritime forest at some locations. The leaves on each tree develop in three shapes, some with no lobes, others with two lobes (shaped like a mitten, both right- and left-handed), and still others with three lobes. The spicy, aromatic bark is deeply furrowed and along with other parts of the tree yields teas and various home remedies, but these should be used with caution, if at all. The fragrant properties of sassafras attract spicebush swallowtails, butterflies that commonly favor the trees as hosts for their eggs and larvae. After hatching, the caterpillars lie along the midrib of a leaf and exude silk mats that contract, folding over the leaf in which they remain tucked away during the day to avoid predators. The larvae also gain protection by mimicry, with the younger caterpillars colored brown with a white underside that mimics a bird dropping. Later, they turn green and sport large dots that appear to be the eyes of a tree frog, lizard, or small snake. Like the larvae of other North American swallowtails, they also deploy osmeteria, fleshy defensive organs that remain inverted until needed. When a threat appears, the larvae rear up and evert their osmeteria, which appear to predators as the forked tongue of a snake. Together, these adaptations represent one of nature's more clever forms of deception. Still, there's more—the osmeteria secret chemical repellents that change in composition as the larvae mature, perhaps to counter threats from those predators that prefer older caterpillars. The adults also display mimicry, in this case by resembling a bitter-tasting relative, the pipevine swallowtail. Hence, when a bird or other predator catches—and quickly rejects—the latter species, it concurrently learns to avoid the lookalike but otherwise tasty spicebush swallowtail—an example of what biologists identify as Batesian mimicry.

A diverse shrub understory develops under the canopy of a maritime forest. In addition to a scattering of bayberry and beach plum, the more common shrubs include sweet pepperbush, arrowwood viburnum, highbush blueberry, and elderberry. Add to these various vines—trumpet creeper, greenbrier, Virginia creeper, and poison ivy—and one grasps the entangled nature of the understory. Birds seek the berries of Virginia creeper, which provide an energy-rich food for those migrating along the coast, and a reward of nectar awaits those hummers attracted to the flowers of trumpet creepers. In contrast with the shrub layer, however, herbaceous vegetation on the forest floor remains sparse and may feature only sphagnum moss or sometimes sundews in moist depressions.

Invasive species threaten the integrity of some maritime forests, including the forest at Cape May Point State Park. These gain footholds when windfalls create openings in the canopy and allow light to penetrate to the ground below. The troublesome species include Japanese honeysuckle and porcelain berry, however the aggressive and tenacious sweet-scented virgin's bower poses even greater concerns—it smoothers trees (thereby opening more of the canopy) and covers the forest floor to the point of excluding the growth of native species.

Inlets Come and Go, and So Do Islands

As years go, 1812 was rather eventful, not only for the beginning of a second war between England and the still-young United States but also for at least two geological changes. In that year, aftershocks continued from a huge earthquake that struck the region surrounding New Madrid, Missouri, whose tremors rang church bells as far away as Boston and for a short time reversed the flow of the Mississippi River. The event also isolated a large bend in the river's channel, creating Reelfoot Lake in nearby Tennessee, today the site for a state park and a national wildlife refuge.

In a second, though unrelated geological incident, a storm plugged Cranberry Inlet, which then separated Island Beach from the mainland to the north, thereby reforming a peninsula that now extends southward to Barnegat Inlet. The inlet originally cut through the stand sometime around 1750—accounts vary on the exact year—at the current site of Seaside Heights and, until 1812, provided a vital commercial route between Toms River on Barnegat Bay and the open Atlantic. The soggy swales between dunes bordering the former inlet became a haven for cranberries, which quickly provided a handy way to identify the channel. Because of the dynamic forces that periodically change the coastline, the once-common designations "new" or "old" were soon ill suited to identify inlets—what was once a new inlet became old whenever a newer inlet appeared. These are not isolated events, as when Hurricane Dorian alone ripped 54 new inlets in a fifty-six-mile stretch of barrier islands at Cape Lookout National Seashore, North Carolina, in 2019.

When the stormy hand of nature closed Cranberry Inlet, it dealt Toms River a serious financial setback. The once-busy harbor no longer bustled with ships, some built on-site, and those that still called at the port necessarily faced the difficulties of coursing the bay's shallow waters to access Barnegat Inlet some 12 miles distant. In response, Michael Ortley, for whom a beach town was named, attempted to dig a replacement channel a few miles north of the original Cranberry Inlet. After three years of toil, Ortley and his small crew succeeded in connecting the Atlantic with a new passage to Toms River—only to find that just one day later the incoming tide had stoppered the channel with a cork of sand. In 1847, a second effort by a small army of 200 to 300 over three days completed a channel at

Shore Note 2.4 Coastal Furies: Hurricanes and Nor'easters

Powerful storms relentlessly shape the Jersey Shore. Hurricanes develop where solar energy warms the ocean's surface and increases evaporation rates. In these unstable conditions, convection moves moist air upward and creates a low-pressure area known as a tropical depression—the first phase in what may become a hurricane. As the moist air rises, it condenses into clouds that produce thunderstorms. The updrafts continually strengthen as air is pulled into the core from the storm's edges, with the result that the clouds rise even higher and begin rotating in a counterclockwise motion. At this point, a tropical depression may dissipate or, if its winds exceed 39 miles per hour, strengthen into a tropical storm (and gain a name). A tropical storm becomes a hurricane if its surface winds exceed 74 miles per hour and circulate around a cloud-free eye. Meteorologists divide hurricanes into five categories, the weakest (1) with wind speeds of 74 to 95 miles per hour and the strongest (5) producing winds exceeding 157 miles per hour.

Landfall occurs when the eye reaches the shoreline, although the extended outer bands contact the coast much sooner. Hurricanes also spawn thunderstorms and tornadoes, often at considerable distances inland. Fortunately, high pressure systems and westerly winds guide some Atlantic hurricanes northward in an arc that carries the storms away from the coast. Others, however, cause significant wind damage and severe flooding. New Jersey has a long history with hurricanes, many of which were immensely destructive, but Superstorm Sandy (2012) ranks among the worst despite its low ranking (just below category 1). In this case, a powerful storm surge, not wind or excessive rainfall, caused immense property damage along most of the New Jersey coast and beyond. The surge washed away houses, commercial buildings, and municipal infrastructure, in places leaving behind a landscape of wreckage and sandy overwashes. Hurricanes of any size may inflect serious erosion of beaches and dunes, sometimes leaving behind steep cliffs in a process known as scarping. Some storm-wrought cliffs reach heights of 10 or more feet tall and, if not restored by humans, may take decades to recover their former profiles. As reported by The Press of Atlantic City, the remnants of Hurricane Ian produced scarping of this magnitude in 2022 at Stone Harbor, Avalon, and North Wildwood.

Biological damage, by comparison, is more difficult to assess but includes wind-damaged trees (and sometimes large areas of forest), vegetation burned by salt spray, uprooted seagrasses, beach and dune erosion, oil and sewage spills, and destroyed shorebird and terrapin nests. Remarkably, however, Superstorm Sandy did not significantly alter the species composition of saltmarsh vegetation as it swept across the northern coastline of New Jersey. Ironically, the storm actually produced some beneficial results when it flattened much of the dune system at the Holgate Unit of Edwin B. Forsythe National Wildlife Refuge and pushed the sand into the adjacent bay. The resulting overwash created prime nesting habitat for piping plovers, one of New Jersey's most endangered species, and improved the foraging area available to the chicks. By 2022, 49 pairs of piping plovers were nesting at Holgate, which represented a fourfold increase at the site since Sandy's destructive visit to the Jersey Shore.

Winter storms, familiarly known as nor'easters, move northward up the Atlantic Coast to New England and beyond. They normally develop between October and April, with most occurring in February. Named for the direction from which their winds blow, nor'easters circulate in a counterclockwise direction, but their wind speeds seldom reach hurricane strength. They commonly linger for several days, dropping large quantities of rain or snow during the course of their slow passage. Unlike hurricanes, which form over warm ocean water, nor'easters develop as cold-core systems that originate when a low-pressure system, often traveling eastward from areas well inland, encounters Arctic air in the jet stream, then runs headlong into moist, warm air that formed over the Caribbean Sea or Gulf of Mexico. This clash occurs along the mid-Atlantic coast (e.g., North Carolina), where it forms a nor'easter fueled by the sharp temperature differences between the warm and cold air masses—if this front occurs along the Gulf Stream, nor'easters may gain even greater strength. Meanwhile, the clockwise circulation of high-pressure systems lying to the north press nor'easters against the coastline.

The waves of nor'easters often reach greater heights than those of hurricanes but similarly erode beaches, overwash dunes, and cut new inlets. Additionally, damage from storm surges may be magnified because they extend across several tidal cycles. Whereas hurricanes typically damage relatively short stretches of coastline (i.e., 60 to 100 miles), nor'easters may devastate more than 900 miles of coastline. Some of the better-known nor'easters include the Blizzard of '88 (1888), the Ash Wednesday Storm (1962), and the Halloween Storm (1991). The latter produced waves more than 30 feet high. As a force of nature, winter storms have long enriched seafaring lore as well as art, notably in Winslow Homer's powerful painting *Northeaster,* and attracted the inquiring mind of Benjamin Franklin.

the site of the original Cranberry Inlet. Commerce temporarily resumed on the docks at Toms River, but once again the inlet closed, again dashing the town's lingering hopes to remain a seaport. Today Cranberry Inlet remains only as a memory of a landform obscured by a highly developed beachfront at Seaside Heights.

The sandy mutations of Tucker's Island also offer the prime example of coastal dynamics in the recorded history of the Jersey Shore. The earliest charts, circa the early 1600s, indicate that a five-mile-long barrier island later dubbed Short Beach once lay just to the south of Long Beach Island. In 1800, a storm cut an inlet through Short Beach Island, whose northern segment became known as Tucker's Beach, in recognition of Reuben Tucker who had bought the property years earlier (present-day Tuckerton honors his son, Ebenezer). In the years that followed, sand carried by longshore currents extended Long Beach Island southward, eventually closing the gap and uniting Tucker's Beach and Long Beach Island. Then, in 1920, yet another storm again changed the geography when it sliced an inlet through the southern end of Long Beach Island, creating what was thereafter identified as Tucker's Island. Beachfront erosion steadily nibbled at the edges of the new island, and by 1958 it was gone, taking with it (in 1927) the second lighthouse erected to mark the location. Still, the sands remain eternally restless, and Tucker's Island currently shows signs of reforming in what is today known as Little Egg Harbor Inlet.

The ecological significance of these low-profile islands was demonstrated when a sandy bank emerged on the southern edge of Little Egg Inlet near a unit of the Edwin B. Forsythe National Wildlife Refuge. Since its discovery in 2018, the shoal has grown slowly to its current size of about 100 acres, fed by sand carried by the southward-flowing longshore drift from Long Beach Island. By 2021, the elevation of the bank, dubbed Horseshoe Island for its distinctive shape, had reached a point where high tides no longer posed a threat to nesting birds, with the result that American oystercatchers, black skimmers, and terns established nesting colonies. As tallied by The Conserve Wildlife Foundation of New Jersey, the latter include the state's largest colony of least terns and the northernmost nesting colony of royal terns in the Western Hemisphere. Piping plovers and red knots, both at-risk species, also visit the new island, which is now under the joint protection of state and federal wildlife agencies. Similarly, Deveaux Bank, a sandy 215-acre strand with a history of playing hide and seek on the South Carolina coast, provides a previously overlooked roosting site for some 20,000 whimbrels, which represents almost half of the eastern population of the species. The whimbrels feed during the day in nearby salt marshes, where they gain fuel for the remainder of their northward migration, but at night they seek the safety on an offshore refuge where risks from predators remain relatively low. Over the ages, untold numbers of other sandy banks along the Atlantic coast have undoubtedly followed the same dynamic cycle as the two described here and, in doing so, provided shorebirds with valuable albeit ephemeral habitat.

One can only speculate at the number of similar circumstances that shaped and reshaped the Jersey Shore for millennia, but the power of these events became painfully evident when Superstorm Sandy slashed a destructive inlet near the Mantoloking Bridge in Brick Township. Roadways and houses disappeared overnight, and while these were rebuilt, scars remain in the hearts and minds of thousands of citizens. And so too should a lesson persist about the forces of nature and its place in our lives.

One final note. Jetties that today stabilize some inlets for marine traffic also provide naturalists with a welcome bonus. Like most of the eastern coast of North America, the Jersey Shore lacks a rocky edge with the ocean—one must visit New Hampshire or Maine to find extensive beaches of wave-lashed rocks and ledges. Nonetheless, the boulder-built jetties protecting Barnegat Inlet provide an analog of the New England coastline, including a microcosm of algae—so-called "seaweeds"—mollusks, and crustaceans that cling to the hard surfaces—features attractive to birds that largely shun sandy shorelines. One species, the harlequin duck, adds a palette of color to the local menagerie (fig. 2.15). A prize for birders, harlequins belong to a group of diverse waterfowl known as sea ducks, which include eiders and scoters, among others. Sea ducks feed primarily on animal life and nest in the Far North, some on lake edges in spruce-fir forests, others near tundra shorelines. Harlequins, however, breed near turbulent streams, only one of four species of waterfowl to do so (none of the others occur in North America). In winter, they prefer coastlines typical of those in New England, but fortunately some make their way each year to the Jersey Shore's "rocky coast," the length of which at Barnegat Inlet extends for 1.7 miles (i.e., combined lengths of the north and south jetties). Other birds associated with these jetties include long-tailed ducks, also a sea duck, and purple sandpipers.

FIGURE 2.15. Each winter a few harlequin ducks visit the "rocky coast" at Barnegat Inlet where long jetties mimic a type of shoreline otherwise absent on the Jersey Shore. Jetties at Manasquan and Avalon also create local habitat for birds associated with rocky shorelines. Photo credit: Eric Reuter.

Barrier Beaches on the Move

Erosion long ago erased most of the evidence of ancient shorelines in New Jersey, although remnants of a Pleistocene beachfront appear (at least to discerning eyes) in the Cape May Formation and an older (ca. 125,000 years ago) site that parallels Route 9 between Forked River and Waretown in Ocean County. These bench-like shorelines formed in bygone epochs when sea levels rose, then were stranded inland when the ocean retreated (i.e., times when glaciers tied up water); the present shoreline formed as the ocean again began rising.

Coastal formations known as barrier beaches—collectively including both islands and peninsulas—develop as narrow ribbons of sand that parallel the coastline (fig. 2.16). They form and move in response to changing sea levels, as noted above. When sea levels fall, water trapped behind these beaches forms shallow lagoons bordered with extensive marshes, of which Barnegat Bay offers the fore-

FIGURE 2.16. Barrier beaches parallel most of New Jersey's coastline. These include both islands and peninsulas that irregularly transform from one to the other in keeping with the effects of storms that fill in existing inlets or cut new ones. Shown here is the peninsula—once an island—occupied by Island Beach State Park. Barnegat Bay and the mainland shore appear in the upper left corner; the town of Seaside Park appears where the vegetation abruptly ends at the top center of the photo. Photo credit: Jay Kelly, Raritan Valley Community College.

most example in New Jersey. Conversely, when sea levels rise, the barrier beaches move landward in what can be described as storm-driven rollovers. In short, waves and high water pushed by storms transport sand from the oceanfront to the landward edges of a barrier beach. Sites known as washover passes—the beds of temporary streams laden with sand—offer clear evidence of this process; these breach the dunes en route to the marshes where the sand deposits form deltas (fig. 2.17). Note, too, that when a washover pass deepens into a larger and deeper channel, it cuts the beach into smaller segments. Hence, the ends of peninsulas become barrier islands and a single barrier island may divide into two. This process, as happened with Cranberry Inlet, may reverse so that a barrier island may again rejoin a peninsula. All told, the realm of barrier beaches belongs more to the sea than to the land.

FIGURE 2.17. Storms drive ocean water landward through the dunes on barrier islands, creating washover passes. The surge carries sand from the beachfront to the inner edges of the island, and in times of rising sea levels, an island gradually migrates toward the mainland. The washover pass shown here formed at the southern tip of Long Beach Island. Photo credit: Kevin Knutsen.

Over time, the sand at the front of the beach thus ends up at the backside, and, in such a manner, a barrier beach gradually creeps inland by rolling over itself. As more sand accumulates, it buries the marsh vegetation, which may appear centuries later as peat when the site emerges at what is by then the beachfront. In some cases, tree stumps or the shells of oysters once forming reefs in the bays also appear on the beachfront. Barrier beaches primarily develop on the Atlantic and Gulf coastlines because of the gentle contour of the continental shelf, whereas the shelf on the Pacific coastline of North America drops abruptly into deep water a short distance offshore (i.e., one coast abounds with sand, the other does not).

Currently, most barrier beaches are retreating in response to rising sea levels and what may be an increase in the intensity and perhaps frequency of storms and hurricanes. Although vulnerable to these forces, barrier beaches remain popular recreational spots for humans whose footprint often includes crowded rows of summer homes and boardwalk amusements. Nonetheless, local, state, and federal governments currently protect all or parts of some barrier beaches from additional development, of which Island Beach State Park reigns as New Jersey's crown jewel.

Trouble Offshore

The current era of viral infections, highlighted by COVID-19, also includes an epizootic—the equivalent of a human epidemic—that produced significant losses in bottlenose dolphins along the coast of New Jersey and elsewhere on the Atlantic coastline. Between 2013 and 2015, more than 1,600 dolphins died from the effects of a *Morbillivirus*, which infects at least 14 other species of cetaceans; the same genus includes the pathogens causing measles and canine distemper. The only census for these events originates from dead or dying dolphins washed up on the beaches of the Atlantic coastline, many of which were necropsied to determine the cause of their stranding. In New Jersey, for example, dolphin strandings averaged 15 per year between July 1 and March 1 during the five years preceding the epizootic but soared to 153 for the same period during the epizootic. Overall, estimates suggest that thousands more died undetected during the epizootic, and under provisions of the Marine Mammal Protection Act, the coastal population of dolphins has yet to fully recover. A 21-foot-long northern minke whale likewise afflicted with *Morbillivirus* washed ashore at Atlantic City during the same epizootic. An earlier *Morbillivirus* epizootic killed at least 742 dolphins in 1987 and 1988, which suggests that the disease might recur in a 25-year cycle (i.e., herd immunity may prevail between the epizootics). Fortunately, the disease poses no threat to humans, whether swimmers or those examining the carcasses.

The virus infects the lungs and brains of affected dolphins, which develop skin lesions as well. Moreover, it suppresses their immune systems, which increases the effects of other stresses (e.g., environmental contamination and opportunistic diseases). The infections spread from animal to animal primarily in the air they breathe, although the virus may also spread by direct physical contact. Dolphins surface to breathe in close proximity to each other, a practice accentuated by their play-like social nature. In doing so, they can exhale and inhale in synchrony, thus enhancing the exchange of the respiratory aerosol they create and enabling transmission of the virus. In particular, some males form close associations with other males, more so than do females, and may closely synchronize their emergence to breathe. As a result, the sex ratio of stranded dolphins infected with the virus favors males. Indeed, according to data compiled by NOAA for the strandings in New Jersey during the 2013–2015 epizootic, fully 74 (69 percent) of the 107 dolphins that could be sexed were males. Sadly, if the past offers insight for the future, a beloved and engaging marine mammal personified by Flipper may face yet another disastrous epizootic of the fatal virus in the years circa 2040.

Readings and References

General

Carson, R. 1955. The edge of the sea. Houghton Mifflin, Boston.

McLachlan, A., and T. Erasmus (eds.). 1983. Sandy beaches as ecosystems. Dr. W. Junk Publishers, The Hague, Netherlands.

Wootton, L., J. Miller, C. Miller, et al. 2016. Dune manual. New Jersey Sea Grant Consortium, Fort Hancock, NJ.

The Swash Zone

Adamkewicz, S. L., and M. G. Harasewych. 1996. Systematics and biogeography of the genus *Donax* (Bivalvia: Donacidae) in eastern North America. American Malacological Bulletin 13:97–103.

Cahoon, L. B., E. S. Carey, and J. E. Blum. 2012. Benthic microalgal biomass on ocean beaches: effects of sediment grain size and beach renourishment. Journal of Coastal Research 28:853–859.

Knisley, C. B., J. M. Hill, and A. M. Scherer. 2005. Translocation of threatened tiger beetle *Cicindela dorsalis dorsalis* (Coleoptera: Cicindelidae) to Sandy Hook, New Jersey. Annals of the Entomological Society of America 98:552–557.

Knisley, C. B., J. L. Luebke, and D. R. Beatty. 1987. Natural history and population decline of the coastal tiger beetle *Cicindela dorsalis dorsalis* Say (Coleoptera: Cicindelidae). Virginia Journal of Science 38:293–303.

Layman, C. A. 2000. Fish assemblage structure in the shallow ocean surf-zone on the Eastern Shore of Virginia Barrier Islands. Estuarine, Coastal, and Shelf Science 51:201–213.

McDermott, J. J. 1983. Food web in the surf zone of an exposed sandy beach in the mid-Atlantic coast of the United States. Pp. 529–538 in Sandy beaches as ecosystems (A. McLachlan and T. Erasmus, eds.). W. Junk, The Hague, Netherlands.

Russell, M. P., and J. R. Dougherty. 2005. The association between the coquina clam *Donax fossor* Say and its epibiotic hydroid *Lovenella gracilis* Clarke. Journal of Shellfish Research 24:35–46.

U.S. Fish and Wildlife Service. 2009. Northeastern beach tiger beetle (*Cicindela dorsalis dorsalis*): 5-year review, summary and evaluation. Virginia Field Office, Gloucester, VA.

The Wrack Line

Bondeson, J. 1999. The Freejee Mermaid and other essays in natural and unnatural history. Cornell University Press, Ithaca, NY. [See pp. 218–231 regarding the mythical origins of barnacle geese.]

Dugan, J. E., and D. M. Hubbard. 2010. The loss of coastal strand habitat in Southern California: role of beach grooming. Estuaries and Coasts 33:67–77.

Dugan, J. E., D. M. Hubbard, M. McCrary, and M. Pierson. 2003. The response of macrofaunal communities and shorebirds to macrophyte wrack communities on exposed beaches in Southern California. Estuarine, Coastal and Shelf Science 58:133–148.

Dugan, J. E., D. M. Hubbard, H. M. Page, and J. Schimel. 2011. Marine macrophyte wrack inputs and dissolved nutrients in beach sands. Estuary and Coasts 34:839–850.

Hurd, B. 2008. Walking the wrack line: on tidal shifts and what remains. University of Georgia Press, Athens. [Reflections stimulated by the miscellany collected in wrack lines around the world.]

Kelly, J. F. 2014. Effects of human activities (raking, scraping, and off-road vehicles) and natural resource protections on the spatial distribution of beach vegetation and related shoreline features in New Jersey. Journal of Coastal Conservation 18:383–398.

———. 2016. Assessing the spatial compatibility of recreational activities with beach vegetation and wrack in New Jersey: prospects for compromise management. Ocean & Coastal Management 123:9–17.

Richards, B. R., R. E. Hillman, and N. J. Maciolek. 1984. Shipworms. Pp. 201–225 in Ecology of Barnegat Bay, New Jersey (M. J. Kennish and R. A. Lutz, eds.). Springer-Verlag, New York.

Thoreau, H. D. 1998. Cape Cod. Heritage Press, New York. [A reprint of the original 1865 work published posthumously with an introduction by J. W. Krutch; see page 150 regarding the beach as a "morgue."]

The Backshore

Baillie, P. W. 2020. The perils of seabeach sandwort. Natural History 128(5):12–15.

Burger, J. 1987. Physical and social determinants of nest site selection in piping plover (*Charadrius melodus*) in New Jersey. Condor 89:811–818.

———. 1994. The effect of human disturbance on foraging behavior and habitat use in piping plover (*Charadrius melodus*). Estuaries 17:695–701.

Burger, J., and M. Gochfeld. 1990. The black skimmer: social dynamics of a colonial species. Columbia University Press, New York.

Dudley, S. A., and A. L. File. 2007. Kin recognition in an annual plant. Biology Letters 3:435–438.

Hancock, T. E., and P. E. Hosier. 2003. Ecology of the threatened species *Amaranthus pumilus* Rafinesque. Castanea 68:236–244.

Kelly, J. F. 2013. The status and distribution of *Amaranthus pumilus* Raf. (seabeach amaranth) and other rare beach plant species in New Jersey: field surveys and historical records. Bartonia 66:28–60.

McAtee, J. W., and D. L. Drawe. 1980. Human impact on beach and foredune vegetation of North Padre Island, Texas. Environmental Management 4:527–538.

Natural Lands Management. ND. Sea-beach amaranth. Fact sheet. Endangered plants of New Jersey. New Jersey Department of Environmental Protection, Trenton.

Safina, C., and J. Burger. 1983. Effects of human disturbance on reproductive success in the black skimmer. Condor 85:164–171.

Dunes

Anonymous. 2002. American beachgrass, *Ammophila breviligulata* Fern. Plant fact sheet. Natural Resources Conservation Service, Washington, DC.

Balduf, W. V. 1929. The life history of the goldenrod beetle, *Trirhabda canadensis* Kirby (Coleop.: Chrysomelidae). Entomological News 40:35–39.

Burkitt, J., and L. Wootton. 2011. Effects of disturbance and age of invasion on the impact of the invasive sand sedge, *Carex kobomugi*, on native dune plant populations in New Jersey's coastal dunes. Journal of Coastal Research 27:182–193.

Campbell, W. V., and E. A. Fuzy. 1972. Survey of the scale insect effect on American beachgrass. Shore and Beach 40:18–19.

Carbonneau, B. R., L. S. Wootton, J. P. Wnek, et al. 2017. A species effect on storm erosion: invasive sedge stabilized dunes more than native grass during Hurricane Sandy. Journal of Applied Ecology 54:1385–1394.

Cheplick, G. P., and M. Aliotta. 2009. The abundance and size of annual herbs in a coastal beach community is related to their distance from seaside goldenrod (*Solidago sempervirens*). Journal of the Torrey Botanical Society 136:102–109.

De Rooij-van der Goes, P. C. E. M., C. van Dijk, W. H. van der Putten, and P. D. Jungerius. 1997. Effects of sand movement by wind on nematodes and soil-borne fungi in coastal foredunes. Journal of Coastal Conservation 3:133–142.

Engelmann, G. 1872. The flower of yucca and its fertilization. Bulletin of the Torrey Botanical Club 3:33.

Fernald, M. L. 1900. Is *Artemisia stelleriana* a native of New England? Rhodora 2:38–40.

Godfrey, P. J., and M. M. Godfrey. 1980. Ecological effects of off-road vehicles on Cape Cod. Oceanus 23:56–67.

Immel, D. L. 2001. Adam's needle, *Yucca filamentosa* L. Plant guide. Natural Resources Conservation Service, Washington, DC.

Koske, R. E., J. N. Gemma, L. Corkidi, et al. 2004. Arbuscular mycorrhizas in coastal dunes. Pp. 173–187 in Coastal dunes, ecology and conservation (M. L. Martinez and N. P. Psuty, eds.). Springer-Verlag, New York.

Lea, C., and G. McLaughlin. 2005. Asiatic sand sedge, *Carex kobomugi*. Fact sheet. Plant Alien Plant Working Group, Plant Conservation Alliance, Washington, DC.

Maun, M. A. 2004. Burial of plants as a selective force in sand dunes. Pp. 119–135 in Coastal dunes, ecology and conservation (M. L. Martinez and N. P. Psuty, eds.). Springer-Verlag, New York.

Nickerson, N. H., and F. R. Thibodeau. 1983. Destruction of *Ammophila breviligulata* by pedestrian traffic: quantification and control. Biological Conservation 27:277–287.

Pellmyr, O. 2003. Yuccas, yucca moths, and coevolution: a review. Annals of the Missouri Botanical Garden 90:35–55.

Seliskar, D. M., and R. N. Huettel. 1993. Nematode involvement in the dieout of *Ammophila breviligulata* (Poaceae) on the mid-Atlantic coastal dunes of the United States. Journal of Coastal Research 9:97–103.

Sheahan, C. M. 2014. Seaside goldenrod, *Solidago sempeervirens*. Plant guide. Natural Resources Conservation Service, Cape May Plant Materials Center, Cape May, NJ.

Small, J. A. 1954. *Carex kobomugi* at Island Beach, New Jersey. Ecology 35:289–291.

Wootton, L. S., S. D. Halsey, K. Bevaart, et al. 2005. When invasive species have benefits as well as costs: managing *Carex kobomugi* (Asiatic sand sedge) in New Jersey's coastal dunes. Biological Invasions 7:1017–1027.

Zinc, R. M., J. D. Rising, S. Mockford, et al. 2005. Mitochondrial DNA variation, species limits, and rapid evolution of the plumage coloration and size in the savannah sparrow. Condor 107:21–28.

Swales and Other Sandy Places

Dickerson, J. 2002. Bayberry, *Morella pensylvanica* (Mirbel) Kartesz. Plant fact sheet. Natural Resources Conservation Service, Washington, DC.

Frazer, N. B., J. W. Gibbons, and J. L. Greene. 1991. Life history and demography of the common mud turtle, *Kinosternon subrubrum*, in South Carolina, USA. Ecology 72:2218–2231.

Heckscher, C. M., and C. R. Bartlett. 2004. Rediscovery and habitat association of *Photuris bethaniensis* McDermott (Coleoptera: Lamphyridae). Coleopterists Bulletin 58:349–353.

Kerlinger, P., M. R. Lein, and B. J. Sevick. 1985. Distribution and population fluctuations of wintering snowy owls (*Nyctea scandiaca*) in North America. Canadian Journal of Zoology 63:1829–1834. [Argues that the winter invasions of snowy owls occur independently of lemming numbers.]

Latham, R. 1953. *Fagitana littera* reared from larva. Journal of the Lepidopterists' Society 7:172. [Basis for suggesting that marsh ferns represent the obligate host for larvae of marsh fern moths.]

Murry, B. G., Jr. 1979. Fall migration of blackpoll and yellow-rumped warblers at Island Beach, New Jersey. Bird-banding 50:1–11.

Newman, C. E., J. A. Feinberg, L. J. Rissler, et al. 2012. A new species of leopard frog (Anura: Ranidae) from the urban northeastern US. Molecular Phylogenetics and Evolution 63:445–455. [Occupies a narrow coastal strip including New Jersey.]

Odum, W. E., and J. W. Harvey. 1988. Barrier island interdunal freshwater wetlands. Association of Southeastern Biologists Bulletin 35:149–155.

Pace, M. C. 2021. *Spiranthes bightensis* (Orchardaceae), a new and rare cryptic hybrid species endemic to the U.S. Mid-Atlantic coast. Phytotaxa 498:159–176.

Place, A. R., and E. W. Stiles. 1992. Living off the wax of the land: bayberries and yellow-rumped warblers. Auk 109:333–345.

Shure, D. J. 1970. Ecological relationships of small mammals in a New Jersey barrier beach habitat. Journal of Mammalogy 51:267–278.

Skaradek, W. B. 2009. Beach heather, *Hudsonia tomentosa* Nutt. Plant fact sheet. Natural Resources Conservation Service, Washington, DC.

Maritime Forests

Art, H. W., F. H. Bormann, and G. K. Voigt. 1974. Barrier island forest ecosystem: role of meteorologic nutrient inputs. Science 184:60–62.

Bellis, V. J. 1995. Ecology of maritime forests of the southern Atlantic coast: a community profile. Biological Report 30. National Biological Service, Washington, DC.

Bourdeau, P. F., and H. J. Oosting. 1959. The maritime live oak forest in North Carolina. Ecology 40:148–152.

Boyce, S. G. 1954. The salt spray community. Ecological Monographs 24:29–67.

Carter, M., P. Feeny, and M. Haribal. 1999. An oviposition stimulant for spicebush swallowtail butterfly, *Papilio troilus*, from leaves of *Sassafras albidum*. Journal of Chemical Ecology 25:1233–1245.

Hall, D. W., and J. F. Butler. 2015. Spicebush butterfly. Featured Creatures, Publication EENY-636. Entomology and Nematology Department, University of Florida, Gainesville.

Miller, C. F., and M. Pelligrine. 2009. Cape May Point State Park—a case study for improving the maritime forests. Pp. 110–113 in Invasive species in coastal dunes and maritime forests (L. Wootton and P. Rowe, eds.). Georgian Court College, Lakewood, NJ.

Omura, H., K. Honda, and P. Feeny. 2006. From terpenoids to aliphatic acids: further evidence for late-instar switch in osmeterial defense as a characteristic trait in swallowtail butterflies in the tribe Papilonini. Journal of Chemical Ecology 32:1999–2012.

Oosting, H. J. 1954. Ecological processes and vegetation of the maritime strand in the southeastern United States. Botanical Review 23:226–262.

Stalter, R. 1979. Some ecological observations on an *Ilex* forest, Sandy Hook, New Jersey. Castanea 44:202–207.

Wells, B. W. 1939. A few forest climax: the salt spray climax of Smith Island, NC. Bulletin of the Torrey Botanical Club 66:629–634.

Wells, B. W., and I. V. Shunk. 1938. Salt spray: an important factor in coastal ecology. Bulletin of the Torrey Botanical Club 65:485–492.

Wood, V. S. 1995. Live oaking: southern timber for tall ships. Northeastern University Press, Boston.

Inlets Come and Go, and So Do Islands

Anonymous. ND. Horseshoe Island management plan. New Jersey Division of Fish and Wildlife and U.S. Fish and Wildlife Service.

Baldassarre, G. 2014. Ducks, geese, and swans of North America. Vol. 2. Johns Hopkins University Press, Baltimore.

Boyle, W. J., Jr. 2002. A guide to bird finding in New Jersey, revised and updated. Rutgers University Press, New Brunswick, NJ. [See p. 275 regarding birds at Barnegat Inlet.]

Klebold, F. F. 2013. Building the north jetty on Island Beach Barnegat Inlet, 1937–1940. Friends of Island Beach State Park, Seaside Park, NJ. [The project required 78,000 tons of 5- to 10-ton boulders, smaller rocks of 15 to 250 pounds, and a lot of infrastructure, including a temporary railroad.]

MacClintock, P. 1943. Topography of the Cape May Formation. Journal of Geology 51:458–472.

Mountford, K. 2002. Closed sea, from the Manasquan to the Mullica: a history of Barnegat Bay. Down the Shore Publishing, West Creek, NJ. [See chaps. 3 and 4 concerning, respectively, Tucker's Island and Cranberry Inlet.]

Nelson, W. A. 1924. Reelfoot—an earthquake lake. National Geographic 45:94–114.

Pover, T. 2022. A new island for birds emerges along the New Jersey coast. News release, April 15, 2022, Conserve Wildlife Foundation of New Jersey, Princeton.

Sanders, F. J., M. C. Handmaker, A. S. Johnson, and N. R. Senner. 2021. Nocturnal roost on South Carolina coast support nearly half of the Atlantic coast population of Hudsonian whimbrel *Numenius hudsonicus* during northward migration. Wader Study 128:117–124.

Barrier Beaches on the Move

Deaton, C. D., C. J. Hein, and M. L. Kirwan. 2017. Barrier island migration dominates ecogeomorphic feedbacks and drives salt marsh loss along the Virginia Atlantic coast, USA. Geology 45:123–126.

Leatherman, S. P. 1979. Migration of Assateague Island, Maryland, by inlet and overwash processes. Geology 7:104–107.

———. 1983. Barrier dynamics and landward migration with Holocene sea-level rise. Nature 301:415–417.

———. 1988. Barrier island handbook. Laboratory for Coastal Research, University of Maryland, Baltimore.

Trouble Offshore

Anonymous. ND. 2015–2015 bottlenose dolphin unusual mortality event in the mid-Atlantic. National Oceanic and Atmospheric Administration, New England and Mid-Atlantic Region, Gloucester, MA. [See for state-by-state stranding data.]

Leu, S. T., P. Sah, E. Krzyszczyk, A.-M. Jacoby, J. Mann, and S. Bansal. 2020. Sex, synchrony, and skin contact: integrating multiple behaviors to assess pathogen transmission risk. Behavioral Ecology 31:651–660.

Morris, S. E., J. L. Zelner, D. A. Fauquier, T. K. Rowles, P. E. Rosel, F. Gulland, and B. T. Grenfell. 2015. Partially observed epidemics in wildlife hosts: modelling an outbreak of dolphin morbillivirus in the northwestern Atlantic 2013–2014. Journal Royal Society Interface 12:20150676. http://dx.doi.org/10.1098/rsif.2015.

Shore Note 2.1. The Blues Are Running!

Bemis, W. E., A. Giuliano, and B. McGuire. 2005. Structure, attachment, replacement and growth of teeth in bluefish, *Pomatomus saltatrix* (Linneus, 1766), a teleost with deeply socketed teeth. Zoology 108:317–327.

Fahay, M. P., P. L. Berrien, D. L. Johnson, and W. W. Morse. 1999. Bluefish, *Pomatomus saltatrix*, life history and habitat characteristics. NOAA technical memorandum NMFS-NE-144. U.S. Department of Commerce, Washington, DC.

Graves, J. E., J. R. McDowell, A. M. Beardsley, and D. R. Scales. 1992. Stock structure of the bluefish *Pomatomus saltatrix* along the mid-Atlantic coast. Fishery Bulletin 90:703–710. [See for genetic analysis.]

Hersey, J. 1987. Blues. Knopf, New York. [Best-selling literary treatment of bluefish and bluefishing at Martha's Vineyard.]

Scharf, F. S., J. P. Manderson, M. C. Fabrizio, et al. 2004. Seasonal and interannual patterns of distribution and diet of bluefish within a middle Atlantic Bight estuary in relation to abiotic and biotic factors. Estuaries 27:426–436. [See for dietary importance of menhaden.]

Shore Note 2.2. A Tale of Two Wrecks

Buchholz, M. T. 2004. New Jersey shipwrecks—350 years in the graveyard of the Atlantic. Down the Shore Publications, West Creek, NJ. [The foremost history on the topic.]

Coyle, G. F., and D. C. Whitcraft. 2012. Inferno at sea: stories of death and survival aboard the Morro Castle. Down the Shore Publishing, West Creek, NJ.

Hicks, B. 2006. When the dancing stopped: the real story of the Morro Castle disaster and its deadly wake. Free Press, New York.

Jahn, R. 1980. Down Barnegat Bay: a nor'easter midnight reader. Beachcomber Press, Mantoloking, NJ. [See pp. 83–85 concerning the *Minturn* wreck).

Noble, D. L. 1976. A legacy—the United States Life-Saving Service. Historian's Office, US Coast Guard, Washington, DC.

Veasey, D. 2000. Guarding New Jersey's shore—lighthouses and life-saving stations. Arcadia Publishing, Charleston, SC. [Between 1887 and 1911, 1,257 ships wrecked on the New Jersey coastline, whereas 916 did so in North Carolina during the same period.]

Shore Note 2.3. Jaws 1916 Style

Capuzzo, M. 2001. Close to shore: a true story of terror in an age of innocence. Broadway Books, New York.

Castro, J. I. 2000. The sharks of North American waters. Texas A&M Press, College Station.

Fernicola, R. G., Jr. 2001. Twelve days of terror: a definitive investigation of the 1916 New Jersey shark attacks. Lyons Press, Guilford, CT.

Handwerk, B. 2002. Great whites may be taking the rap for bull shark attacks. National Geographic News, August 2.

Shore Note 2.4. Coastal Furies: Hurricanes and Nor'easters

Chaplin, J. E. 2006. The first scientific American: Benjamin Franklin and the pursuit of genius. Basic Books, New York. [See p. 122 for Franklin's insights about nor'easters.]

Davis, R. E., and R. Dolan. 1993. Nor'easters. American Scientist 81:428–439. [A primary source of information.]

Dolan, R., and R. E. Davis. 1992. Rating northeasters. Mariners Weather Log 36(1):4–11.

Greening, H., P. Doering, and C. Corbett. 2006. Hurricane impacts on coastal ecosystems. Estuaries and Coasts 29:877–879.

Pover, T. 2022. Holgate—record breaking site for piping plovers. Conserve Wildlife Blog, July 8. Conserve Wildlife Foundation of New Jersey.

Rachlin, J. W., R. Stalter, D. Kincaid, and B. W. Warkentine. 2017. The effect of Superstorm Sandy on salt marsh vascular flora in the New York Bight. Journal of the Torrey Botanical Club 144:40–46.

Savadove, L., M. T. Buchholz, and S. Mazzella. 2019. Great storms of the Jersey Shore. 2nd ed. Down the Shore Publishing, West Creek, NJ.

3

Tidal Salt Marshes

Grasslands Like No Others

A salt marsh sanctions space and a rooted integrity.
—JOHN HAY, *THE WAY TO THE SALT MARSH*

TIDAL SALT MARSHES edge the eastern coast of North America save for the rocky shorelines of northern New England and Canada. Unlike the precipitous drop in the sea floor along the perimeter of the Pacific coast, the continental shelf on the Atlantic shoreline extends gradually seaward for miles before giving way to the dark depths below. In the shallows near the shore, tidal marshes mark the frontier between land and sea, and the New Jersey coast boasts a full share of these bewitching gardens. For the most part, they develop on the mainland where barrier beaches shelter the coastline, whereas others rim the protected landward edges of the same formations (described in chapter 2). The physical presence of barrier beaches limits the impact of wave action that would otherwise prevent sediments for coalescing into a substrate on which marsh vegetation can gain a foothold (i.e., except in rare instances, wave action itself does not significantly damage marsh vegetation).

Two forces effectively limit the diversity of the vegetation capable of surviving in tidal wetlands. First, water completely inundates the lower parts of the plants for several hours about twice a day, each followed by an equal period when they lie exposed to deal with temporary desiccation—in all, nature's own brand of water torture. Second, salt infuses soil and water alike, which presents insurmountable osmotic problems as well as toxic overdoses for most vascular plants. These harsh conditions essentially eliminate competition from potential invaders, leaving those that can cope—halophytes—in a position to assume dominance in often large, monotypic stands.

Tidal salt marshes offer visitors more than a visually pleasing panorama—they also generate one of nature's more distinctive scents. For some, the odor adds another sensory dimension to the appeal of wetland vegetation, whereas to less charitable noses it just plain "stinks." The origin of the odor lies a few inches below the marsh floor in oxygen-starved mud. True, the burrows of organisms channel some oxygen belowground at low tide, but in general anaerobic conditions prevail under the thin veneer of aerated mud. This harsh environment becomes the realm of anaerobic bacteria whose metabolic functions produce a by-product known as hydrogen sulfide, which famously emits the pungent smell of rotten eggs. Under normal circumstances, the odor does not indicate a polluted environment but instead represents a natural function within a tidal marsh, specifically the anaerobic digestion of organic matter. Hydrogen sulfide also reacts with iron in the sediments, which accounts for the mud's black color. Stinky or not, the smell remains an enduring legacy of tidal marshes.

The profile of a typical salt marsh, beginning at its landward edge, slopes downward toward open water. Because the upper marsh is older, its higher elevation results from a longer period for the accumulation of sediments and peat sod in a process known as vertical accretion. Tidal inundation, of course, becomes less frequent as the elevation increases, and results in a distinctive profile of communities. However, because of the gradual gradient, tidal creeks follow meandering courses as they cross the marshes.

Marshes High and Low

By far, two closely related grasses dominate New Jersey's tidal marshes; both produce their flowers and seeds aligned along one side of the culm, the jointed hollow stalk common to all true grasses. Salt hay, at about two feet in height and the shorter of the two species, develops in meadows above the tidal zone, although storms or unusually high tides occasionally inundate these sites. Ecologists recognize these meadows as "high marsh" because of their position at the upper, landward edge of tidal wetlands. The ecotone—the formal designation for a transition area—between high marsh and upland vegetation lies beyond all but the most

Shore Note 3.1 About Grasses and Graminoids

Just two species of plants—smooth cordgrass and marsh hay—dominate the natural vegetation in New Jersey's coastal marshes, and a third—*Phragmites*—represents an aggressive invader, each being a true grass as opposed to lookalikes collectively known as graminoids. Botanists separate grasses from graminoids (and other plants) on the basis of their hollow stems (culms) that are plugged at intervals known as nodes, which often gives a culm a jointed appearance that is particularly obvious in bamboo. Grasses also feature leaves with a basal sheath that wraps around the culm somewhat like a split tube and long narrow blades with parallel veins. Grass leaves emerge alternately in two ranks from the culms. A membranous flap-like structure, often fringed, known as a ligule develops where the basal sheath and culm join. Rather uniquely, the growing points of grasses lie at the surface or just below ground level, which represents an evolutionary adaption to cope with frequent grazing (or mowing) as well as fire. In either case, grasses normally survive and rapidly regrow.

Grass flowers are small, complex structures of bracts, scales, and florlets arranged in spikelets. These in turn form larger inflorescences such as panicles, spikes, and racemes. Grasses rely on wind for pollination, hence their flowers lack color, scent, or nectar to attract pollinators. The fruit, each technically known as a caryopsis but to most known simply as a "grain," is dispersed commonly by wind but also by hitchhiking on the fur of animals or by surviving in their droppings. Many grasses, in particular those growing in dry locations, develop extensive root networks that not only reach water but also anchor the soil, including the sands in coastal dunes.

Grasses have coevolved with bison and other grazers with digestive systems adapted to deal with tough fibers. Even some dinosaurs ate grasses. Today grasses occur on every continent, including as one of the two species of vascular plants in Antarctica. Because carnivores depend on herbivores, grasses often form the foundation of terrestrial food chains, a relationship recognized millennia ago when a biblical prophet proclaimed that "all flesh is grass" (Isaiah 40:6). Not incidentally, the domestication of rice, corn, and wheat—all grasses—founded economies and civilizations. Agrostology, the study of grasses, represents the only branch of botany devoted to a single family, Poaceae, which includes some 12,000 species.

Sedges, bulrushes, spike rushes, and rushes typify common graminoids, but some nonetheless bear misleading names such as the rush known as blackgrass. The reverse may also occur, as is the case of Barnegat Bay's "sedge islands," which in fact are vegetated with smooth cordgrass, the same true grass that dominates the large marshes along the shoreline. Bulrushes separate into three forms, those with only triangular stems, others with triangular stems bearing leaves, and those leafless species with round, whip-like stems. All of these groups produce small nut-like seeds. Many graminoids provide excellent food and cover for wildlife. Three-square bulrush, for example, offers excellent habitat for muskrats, and some sedges produce large quantities of seeds prized by waterfowl. Pennsylvania sedge forms a grasslike ground cover in the Pine Barrens. Equally confusing, not a single species of seagrass—eelgrass and widgeongrass, for example—represents a true grass, and the eleven species of seagrasses in North America are divided among five other families of plants.

extreme instances of flooding and thereby remains relatively free from the powerful influence of salinity. Here salt hay forms a border mixed with blackgrass (also known as saltmeadow rush), salt grass, and two shrubs, groundsel and marsh elder, which remain in place on the upper fringe of the high marsh unless conditions change dramatically (see following). Seaside goldenrod adds a touch of color to the scene. Blackgrass often forms sizable clumps that develop as their rhizomes spread outward. Many of these plants become infested with reddish galls formed by jumping plant lice, relatives of aphids and similar in appearance to miniature cicadas. The larvae—known as nymphs—of these parasitic insects lodge on the plants where they secrete substances that stimulate abnormal vegetative growth. The swellings enclose the larvae in a protective habitat where they safely feed on the plant's juices, and in the process the galls become a distinctive feature on the stems of blackgrass. Other species of jumping plant lice parasitize just one or a specific group of plants (e.g., hackberry and holly) but seldom damage their hosts.

Below the upland border, the high marsh develops primarily as a monotypic community of salt hay distinctively highlighted by matted swirls or "cowlicks" (fig. 3.1, right). In bygone days, the meadows were cut for forage made attractive by abundant yields from a maintenance-free environment and a mineral content that precluded any need for providing livestock with additional salt. Initially cut by hand, salt hay was later mowed by teams of draft animals that were often covered as protection against biting insects (fig. 3.2, top); where necessary, the teams were also outfitted with snowshoe-like "mud boots" that kept the animals from bogging down in soft ground. Today, aided by modern harvesting equipment, only one farm still mows salt hay meadows for forage (fig. 3.2, bottom). Salt hay also became a staple for making paper, some of which served as newsprint for a Philadelphia daily, but most provided the fiber for the wrapping known as butcher's paper, browned by the iron content of the water. One mill produced almost a ton of paper daily. The industry, initiated in 1832 at Harrisville, faded into history about 60 years later, leaving behind a ghost town as the only memory of a once prosperous community.

Smooth cordgrass reaches heights of six or more feet and occupies the regularly flooded "low marsh" immediately seaward of its smaller relative (fig. 3.1, left). Stands of these plants grow at their tallest near the outer edge of the marsh, where they protect the shoreline by dissipating wave energy; they likewise trap and accumulate sediments and thereby expand the marsh by accretion. Snow geese winter-

FIGURE 3.1. A zone known as "low marsh" (at left) develops where tides daily inundate smooth cordgrass, whereas tides only occasionally reach the "high marsh" zone (at right) dominated by salt hay. Few other plants occur in either zone. Note the characteristic swirls ("cowlicks") in the salt hay meadow; also note the stand of *Phragmites* (upper right) bordering the transition from marsh to upland vegetation. Photo credit: Bob Cunningham.

ing along the coast feed extensively on the rhizomes of smooth cordgrass, using their strong bills to uproot the vegetation; this "grubbing" behavior may cause significant damage at some locations. The plants also provide key habitat for ribbed mussels (fig. 3.3), which attach to the roots with byssal threads—a protein secretion of hairlike stands with adhesive properties unaffected by water. In turn, the mussels, which may reach densities of hundreds or more per square yard, transform their organic foods (e.g., various types of plankton) into inorganic wastes that enrich the soil and supply the plants with important nutrients. Indeed, experiments reveal that smooth cordgrass grown in the absence of ribbed mussels lacks the

FIGURE 3.2. In days long gone, livestock forage was widely cropped in New Jersey from salt hay meadows using horse-drawn equipment; note the protection against biting insects (top). Today, with mechanized equipment, only one farm in the state still harvests salt hay (bottom). Photo credits: Courtesy of Special Collections and University Archives, Rutgers University Libraries (top); Pat and Clay Sutton (bottom).

FIGURE 3.3. Ribbed mussels play a key role in the ecology of the low marshes, including the stabilization of mucky soils subject to erosion. Photo credit: Christine Angelini.

vigorous growth of those grown with mussels. The relationship—habitat from the plant, nutrition from the animal—offers an example of symbiosis known as facultative mutualism in which each organism benefits from its association with the other but nonetheless can survive alone. Ribbed mussels also provide an ecological service by helping stabilize the outer edges of marshes against erosion, hence contributing to the concept of a living shoreline as an alternate to bulkheads and other artificial structures designed to retard erosion. The mussels, in fact, often contribute to the accretion of salt marshes in a process known as biodeposition. While edible, ribbed mussels do not compare favorably with prized table fare of blue mussels, and because they retain their toxic wastes when closed, those taken for human

FIGURE 3.4. Aptly named fiddler crabs abound in low marsh, where they scurry about at low tide in search of algae. During high tides, however, they retreat into burrows, which they seal with mud plugs until the water recedes. Note the female, which lacks a "fiddle," at the bottom of the photo. Photo credit: Pat and Clay Sutton.

consumption should be harvested only at high tide (i.e., when their shells open to eliminate the wastes). Akin to tree rings, these mussels can be aged by counting the namesake ribs on their shells; most survive for 10 to 15 years, but some live longer.

Fiddler crabs—more precisely mud fiddler crabs—likewise influence the growth of smooth cordgrass, in this case because their burrows improve the drainage, oxidation rates, and decomposition below the marsh surface (fig. 3.4). In turn, the root systems provide structural support for the burrows, not unlike timbers in a mine shaft, thereby enabling the crabs to occupy sites where the burrows might otherwise collapse. Elsewhere, notably at the upper and older edges of the zone, heavy accumulations of peat lessen burrowing activities. Wherever they occur, however, the burrows of fiddler crabs service the marsh floor with ventilation at low tide and irrigation at high tide. Male fiddler crabs are widely known for their enlarged claws that, when waved, attract females but also serve as weapons used to defend their burrows from other males—and size counts in both cases. Based on studies of a closely related species on the Gulf Coast, the large claw of the mud fiddler crab also dissipates heat, hence their thermoregulatory function allows males to spend more time above ground feeding and displaying before it becomes necessary to retreat to their burrows.

The marsh community includes scatterings of other plants. In late summer, the flowers of sea lavender adds a purple haze to the high marsh (fig. 3.5, left). The flower-bearing stalks arise from a basal clump of oval leaves and reach heights of 12 to 24 inches. They are long-lived perennials that may take up to nine years to mature. Stems bearing a corolla of colorful sepals, when dried, have commercial value in floral arrangements, but the flower's tiny white petals do not persist. Natives of the Pine Barrens, proudly calling themselves Pineys, once collected and sold sea lavender—locally known as sea statice—to florists in Philadelphia and New York City. The cottage industry dates to the late 1800s but ended abruptly in the early 1990s when government entities assumed jurisdiction of the salt marshes and formed the New Jersey Pineland National Reserve. Elsewhere, however, sea lavender may be threatened by overharvesting; given their slow maturity, many plants are removed before they can produce seeds. Saltmarsh mallow, with its large showy flowers atop stems three to five feet tall, stands out unlike any other wildflower in New Jersey's salt marshes (fig. 3.5, right). Although shorter, marsh pink likewise colors the verdant marshes (fig. 3.5, bottom). At times, it flourishes in abundance and turns sizable areas of salt marsh into a pink swath.

Common cane—typically identified by its generic name, *Phragmites*—often invades both fresh and saltwater marshes. It is by far the dominant species in the Hackensack Meadowlands and familiar to all because of its large leaves and feathery tassels and looking somewhat like corn but with a slender, finger-thick stalk. *Phragmites* forms dense, monotypic stands that spread undeterred across large areas of wetlands to the exclusion of virtually all other vegetation (fig. 3.6). It tolerates a wide range of salinities and can survive on dry to moderately flooded landscapes as well as in a broad range of temperatures. Fire has no lasting effect on *Phragmites*

FIGURE 3.5. Sea lavender (left), saltmarsh mallow (right), and marsh pink (bottom) add touches of color to the green expanse of salt marshes. Photo credits: Bob Cunningham (left, right); Pat and Clay Sutton (bottom).

FIGURE 3.6. The invasion of *Phragmites* across a salt marsh to the edge of a tidal creek stands out even in the somber cloak of winter, as shown here on the shore of Barnegat Bay near Bayville. Dense, monotypic stands of this aggressive grass occupy ever larger areas of salt marsh but offer little value as food or cover for wildlife. Photo credit: Patricia Dixon.

communities, and the plants succumb only when their roots freeze. The plants reproduce from seeds, but new growth more commonly sprouts from long runners and rhizomes. Given these abilities, *Phragmites* has gained lasting footholds in virtually all of the saltwater marshes in New Jersey (see also shore note 6.1).

Unlike their terrestrial counterparts—the plains and prairies of the North American interior—tidal marshes normally escape the influences of herbivory produced by hoofed mammals, gophers, prairie dogs, grasshoppers, and a host of other herbivorous insects (but see below for an exception). This is an important distinction, as it means that huge amounts of biomass escape direct consumption and instead provide a renewable medium for decomposition and a steady flow of recycled nutrients. Energy from the dead foliage flows not only through the marsh, but also into ecosystems elsewhere, including those offshore, although the export of surplus nutrients is not as great as once believed. Nonetheless, large areas of vegetation that otherwise contribute little food value as forage become a crucial first step in marine food chains via decomposition. (On the Pacific coast, where salt marshes occupy much smaller areas, upwellings enriched by detritus from the sea floor carry abundant nutrients to coastal and marine communities.) The supply of nutrients from decomposing marsh plants, in part, gave rise to the slogan "No salt marshes, no sea food," a battle cry for stemming the loss of coastal environments to development, drainage and pollution. Note, too, that the bulky root systems of saltmarsh vegetation form thick layers of peat under both high and low salt marshes, including those on the landward side of barrier beaches, as noted in chapter 2. Unfortunately, salt hay and smooth cordgrass were introduced in some areas on the Pacific coast (e.g., San Francisco Bay), where both soon became pests. Smooth cordgrass, in particular, invaded mud flats and thus ruined crucial feeding areas where shorebirds could probe for invertebrates.

Because of an unnatural predator-prey imbalance, herbivory recently emerged as a significant ecological force in New England, where its severity kills smooth cordgrass and thereby transforms areas of once-verdant low marsh into barren mud flats. The setting began with the overharvest of blue crabs, striped bass, and other predators that allowed a surge in the numbers of marsh crabs, small herbivores that normally exert little influence on marsh vegetation. However, with their inflated numbers, the crabs consumed so much plant material—stems, roots, and rhizomes— that the cordgrass could not survive and the marshes died. This relationship offers an example of an ecological death spiral known as a top-down trophic cascade and underscores the importance of maintaining healthy predator populations in natural communities. Moreover, given that these same species occur in New Jersey, a similar fate might well befall the salt marshes bordering much of the Jersey Shore. Hence, it might be wise to monitor marsh crab populations at a few key areas (e.g., The Wetlands Institute) to detect any changes in their abundance.

Shore Note 3.2 The Wetlands Institute: Conservation for All Ages

Founded in 1969 by Herbert Mills, former executive director of the World Wildlife Fund, the non-profit institute focuses on a mission dedicated to the appreciation, understanding, and steward-ship of coastal and wetland ecosystems with programs in research, conservation, and education. The facilities include research labs, a dormitory for undergraduate students and visiting scientists, specimen collections, exhibits of wetland habitats and other coastal environments, a gift shop, and a lecture hall located on 6,000 acres of undisturbed wetlands in Cape May County. An aquarium building houses a tank for hands-on learning experiences, a hatchery for rearing horseshoe crabs, a plankton lab, and exhibits featuring diamondback terrapins, all with a focus on local marine life and its conservation. Visitors gain access to the wetlands along a marsh trail and elevated walkway; a lookout tower and observation decks provide additional viewing and photographic opportunities. Several live web cameras offer views of the marsh, including close-ups of a platform with an osprey nest. Guided tours include walks to natural areas and back-bay boat trips; kayaks and paddle boards are also available. In all, The Wetlands Institute provides an excellent opportunity to discover the dynamics of intertidal wetlands.

Public programs include two annual festivals, one features the spectacle of horseshoe crabs spawning concurrently with the arrival of migrant shorebirds (see chapter 6), the other highlights the fall migration of birds, dragonflies, and butterflies through the Cape May Peninsula (see chapter 5). Both festivals provide participants with hands-on experiences and demonstrations (e.g., banding birds).

The Wetlands Institute's conservation efforts focus on a variety of key marsh and beach-dependent species. Aided by volunteers, the reTurn the Favor program rescues horseshoe crabs stranded on the beaches at Delaware Bay. Institute staff and volunteers also patrol roadways to protect and rescue diamondback terrapins seeking nesting areas. Another project deals with unwanted monofilament fishing line that, if carelessly discarded, might entangle wildlife. Collection stations at local marinas provide sites where the line can be safely deposited and later recycled into plastic products (e. g., park benches and tackle boxes). Similarly, another conservation project locates and removes derelict crab traps ("ghost traps") that kill diamondback terrapins, as described elsewhere in this chapter. The staff also developed and distributes bycatch-reduction devices that lessen the chances of terrapins entering crab traps without reducing the crab harvest. The Wetlands Institute assists with the management of Stone Harbor Bird Sanctuary—a protected area of old-growth forest—with biological inventories and the removal and control of invasive plants.

Education ranks high in The Wetlands Institute's priorities, with an agenda that ranges from field-based ecology courses in association with several universities to summer nature and home-school programs that target children between the ages of 5 and 13. More than 12,000 students from more than 150 local schools annually visit the institute, along with nearly 17,000 other visitors. The Wetlands Institute is open to the public seven days a week, but check ahead of time for seasonal changes in visiting hours and the availability of escorted tours and lectures.

The staff conducts research dealing with conservation biology of wetland and coastal species and welcomes the additional involvement of visiting scientists and graduate students. A summer internship program for undergraduates has been a key activity for more than 20 years. To date, students from nearly 200 academic institutions have participated with research activities under the aegis of The Wetlands Institute's mission.

Few species of vertebrates live exclusively in the relatively narrow strip of salt marsh bordering New Jersey and other states on the Atlantic coast. Nonetheless, two truly endemic species deserve mention. Diamondback terrapins, so named for the distinctive pattern of the scutes forming their carapace (upper shell), can also be identified by black flecking on their legs, necks, and heads; the faces of some also sport a prominent black "moustache" (fig. 3.7). As might be expected, their feet are broad and webbed, but not modified into flippers as is the case for sea turtles. Females are noticeably larger than males (carapace lengths of 6–9 vs. 4–5.5 inches), a relationship known as reverse sexual dimorphism, which shows up in a few other groups of vertebrates (e.g., hawks and owls). Among their adaptations to saltmarsh environments, the terrapins secrete excess salt from lachrymal glands, which enables them to drink brackish water, whereas they avoid drinking full-strength salt water; after rains, they also drink from a thin film of fresh water lying atop the heavier salt water. In winter, diamondback terrapins settle into the muddy

FIGURE 3.7. Diamondback terrapins are closely associated with coastal marshes. The species, although no longer exploited for food, today remains distressed as bycatch in crab traps and as roadkill. Some individuals, often males, show a dark "moustache" along their upper jaw line. Photo credit: Kevin Knutsen.

bottoms of tidal creeks where they enter into a state of brumation, a condition specific to reptiles and amphibians in which respiration and digestion slow to a point of "suspended animation," akin to hibernation. When active, they feed on crabs, marine worms, and snails (but with the notable exception of mud snails, as noted later). The terrapins' own tasty meat once led to their heavy exploitation as table fare in chic restaurants, with prices reaching $125 per dozen in the marketplace—big money for pockets in the early 1900s. Such pressure soon diminished their numbers, and most coastal states eventually provided some degree of legal protection, but in New Jersey their current status as a "species of concern" does not grant as much security as might be desired.

However, threats continue, not only from degraded marsh habitat but also because the terrapins often enter and drown in crab traps; the small males more easily fit through the entrances, resulting in a population skewed toward females. Abandoned or lost crab traps—so-called ghost traps—continue drowning terrapins for years. In Georgia, for example, two abandoned traps contain the remains of 133 terrapins, mostly males based on carapace measurements of the accumulated shells. New designs for crab traps feature devices that help exclude the terrapins yet still catch and retain crabs; the excluder devices are mandatory in New Jersey. In places, roadkills of females seeking nesting sites also become severe enough to alter the structure of local populations. Sandy, unvegetated roadsides in fact may attract female terrapins, especially where more natural nesting habitat is no longer accessible. To help, "Turtle Xing" signs alert motorists on roadways near salt marshes and, at areas where the terrapins may be especially vulnerable to traffic, roadside fences reduce the losses. Several conservation organizations in New Jersey, including Earthwatch, The Wetlands Institute, and the Great Bay Terrapin Project, actively protect diamondback terrapins.

In 1998, ornithologists separated what was then known as the sharp-tailed sparrow into two species, one subsequently known as the Nelson's sparrow, which nests inland on northern Great Plains and the edges of Hudson Bay but retreats to eastern salt marshes for the winter. The other, now recognized as the saltmarsh sparrow, indeed remains year-round in the salt marshes bordering the Atlantic coast—and the second of the two endemic vertebrates in our discussion. They forage on the marsh floor but when disturbed fly weakly for short distances before dropping back to the ground. Insects, aquatic invertebrates, for which they sometimes probe, and a few seeds form the bulk of their diet.

Saltmarsh sparrows nest rather precariously slightly above the normal high-tide line that separates the zones of high and low marsh. The females build and attach their cup-like nests to the bases of marsh-edge vegetation just two to six inches aboveground. The birds seemingly time their nesting activities to fall between two successive spring tides (so named not for the season but because the water "springs" to high levels twice each month when the moon is either full or new). Still, nests at these sites remain at risk of flooding from storms or unusually high tides and many initial efforts fail, and most of the annual production accordingly arises from a second nesting effort following the loss of the first nest. Females alone care for the broods, and in fact both sexes are promiscuous and forgo bonding as pairs.

Virtually any changes befalling a salt marsh jeopardize these sparrows, whose populations have indeed dropped rapidly in recent years coincident with coastal developments. The encroachment of *Phragmites* also claims prime habitat—birds and most other marsh creatures simply cannot coexist with the choking growth of this invasive grass. Moreover, the growing prospect of rising sea levels adds further concern for the future of saltmarsh sparrows.

Pannes and Halophytes

Abrupt zonation represents a hallmark of salt marsh vegetation. The ecotones between stands of one species to another are not gradual as is normal elsewhere but instead are sharply delineated. These knife-edged ecotones result from slight changes in elevation and their effect on soil salinity (i.e., salts accumulate in greater concentrations in lower sites in comparison with higher ground with better drainage). For example, clumps of less tolerant vegetation often dot the high marsh at sites just a few inches above the surrounding area. However, zonation is nowhere better illustrated than at pannes—shallow, often circular depressions formed in high marsh. These originate when storms cast layers of wrack into the marsh above the normal high tide mark, which in turn smothers the buried vegetation. Without soil-binding roots, the site erodes and forms a depression; ice scours also may produce similar disturbances that form pannes.

Storms or exceptionally high tides irregularly fill the pannes with salt water, as opposed to the relatively permanent water levels in pools that develop in areas of low marsh (see following). As the trapped water evaporates from a panne, it leaves behind a gradient of soil salinity, with the greatest concentration at the center of the depression. Thus, at its rim, the panne supports vegetation tolerant of modest levels of salinity, whereas zones of ever more tolerant plants develop inward. Only the most salt-tolerant halophytes survive at or near the center of a dried panne, where the surface in fact may sometimes be encrusted with salt; in extreme cases, the center may be devoid of all vegetation. Overall, the zonation surrounding a circular panne forms in rings in a pattern not unlike a target. Many pannes, however, may be irregularly shaped, but the vegetation in these nonetheless displays distinctive zonation.

Glasswort, also known as pickleweed, characteristically thrives in the saltier, inner zones of pannes. The low-growing succulent stems and branches of the plants extend upward for 4 to 20 inches and bear scale-like leaves. The plants gradually turn from green to bright red in the fall as the plants mature and accumulate salt (fig. 3.8). Their tissues contain sodium carbonate ("soda ash") that was at one time processed for making glass. The taxonomy of glasswort remains cloudy at best; the flora of New Jersey's salt marshes apparently includes at least three and maybe four species. The mature plants are edible and sometimes pickled or served as garnishes. In some places, one or the other of several closely related species of glasswort provide food for the larvae of certain butterflies. Other zones in pannes may include salt grass, sea blite, orache, and marsh fleabane.

Seaside arrowgrass, which occurs along the northern Atlantic coastline south to New Jersey, plays a special role in pannes where saline and exceptionally waterlogged soils preclude the presence of other vegetation. These plants, which are not true grasses, develop as tall (three feet high) basal clusters of linear leaves from which a central stalk emerges bearing a spike-like inflorescence. In response to waterlogging, their roots spread outward and form hummocks that cover small areas of otherwise inhospitable soil. The inner shoots die as the hummocks expand, leaving a ring of living vegetation in which the center fills with "high and dry" accumulations of dead leaves—elevated sites that provide a suitable substrate for plants previously excluded from the panne community (e.g., sea plantain and pink sea thrift). Ecologists thus regard seaside arrowgrass as "ecosystem engineers," organisms capable of altering a community's composition, structure, and diversity.

Pannes also develop along the upper edges of low marsh where spring tides potentially reflood the depressions twice each month. As the pannes dry, the salinity of the enclosed water increases to a level about one-third greater than seawater.

FIGURE 3.8. Glasswort tolerates extremely high levels of salinity and thereby occupies sites where other salt marsh vegetation cannot survive. Green at first, glasswort turns brilliant red by the end of summer. Photo credit: Kevin Knutsen.

In between the floods, eastern saltmarsh mosquitos lay their eggs on the temporarily dry surface; these hatch when water again fills the pannes. The last batch of eggs overwinter in diapause, a dormant period of arrested development. Eastern saltmarsh mosquitos serve as vectors for equine encephalitis and dog heartworm.

Saltmarsh Pools and Tidal Creeks

Relatively permanent pools develop in salt marshes, most commonly in low marsh at sites where poor drainage leads to waterlogging and low productivity, which results in patches devoid of vegetation that slowly meet and merge into pools (fig. 3.9, bottom). Thereafter saltmarsh pools expand until their edges eventually

FIGURE 3.9. Tidal creeks meander through salt marshes where they provide corridors for aquatic fauna such as minnow-like mummichogs (inset) to move "in and out" with the changing tides (top). Note the taller growth of smooth cordgrass along the creek edges in comparison with stands of the same species in the background. Salt marsh pools also harbor mummichogs as well as widgeongrass and other submerged aquatic vegetation (bottom). Photo credits: Pat and Clay Sutton (top); Jeffery Merrell (inset); Kathleen Strakosch Walz, New Jersey Department of Environmental Protection (bottom).

connect with a tidal creek, after which sedimentation gradually fills the shallow basins to the point where smooth cordgrass can reclaim these sites. Start to finish, this cycle may take up to 100 years; overall, however, the dynamics do not incur a net loss of marsh area as the pools come and go.

Tides regularly replenish the water, and with the exception of unusually dry summers, most of the ponds maintain their depth and a constant level of salinity—requirements for a sustainable aquatic community that includes fishes and aquatic plants. One of these is the mummichog, a small (three to four inches) and abundant species of killifish—and not a true minnow—that lives in both pools and tidal creeks (fig. 3.9, inset). The quaint name stems from a Native American word meaning "going in crowds," which reflects their gregarious association with others of their own kind. "Mummies" tolerate a broad spectrum of environmental conditions, including salinity (up to three times the concentration of seawater), temperature, dissolved oxygen, and even pollution—all traits leading to their use in research, not the least of which was as the first fish to travel in space. They also serve as "canaries" that indicate the health of salt marshes. For these and other reasons (see following) marine biologist Kenneth Able recognizes mummichogs as "the most important fish" in New Jersey's salt marshes.

Mummichogs eat small crustaceans (e.g., amphipods and copepods), fly larvae, especially those of mosquitos, marine worms known as polychaetes, fish eggs, carrion, and algae, but detritus, although ingested at times, provides no nutritional benefits. They spawn clutches of up to 300 eggs at spring tide in empty mussel shells or on other surfaces that might be available. When the tide recedes, however, the spawning sites lie above the water level and remain so as the embryos develop and, with nature's own brand of remarkable synchrony, the eggs hatch when the next spring tide again inundates the vegetation.

Although small, mummichogs serve as important links in the complex structure of a saltmarsh ecosystem. For example, they represent a major food for fish-eating birds (e.g., herons) and larger fishes of several kinds, including eels. Mummichogs are themselves significant predators of mosquito larvae, with some estimates suggesting that a single fish might consume 2,000 "wigglers" per day. Moreover, mummichogs often suffer heavy infestations of gill parasites—trematode larvae freshly released from snails. The infected fish rise to the surface (presumably to gasp for air), where they behave in conspicuous jerking movements. These circumstances directly benefit the parasite. To wit, herons notice and ingest the infected fish and, in doing so, continue the trematode's complex life history that requires a three-stage cycle of hosts consisting of fish-eating birds, snails, and mummichogs to produce a new generation.

Striped killifish, a close relative of mummichogs and a dweller of salt marshes and shallow coastal waters, participate in cleaning symbiosis, a behavior more commonly associated with tropical reef fishes. Cleaning symbiosis typically involves two species: a "client" seeking a "cleaner" to remove its ectoparasites (e.g., trematodes and fish lice). As a client, striped killifish solicit the cleaning services of a sheepshead minnow, a tubby beer-bellied fish that can survive in shallow water and gulp air at the surface. A parasite-laden striped killifish invites the cleaner by assuming a face-down vertical position and twisting its body into an S-shaped curve. In response, a sheepshead minnow picks off a parasite, after which the client may briefly move away before returning and again assuming the same body position as before to incite removal of another parasite—a process that may recur five or six times and ends when either the client or cleaner swims off. Inextricably, mummichogs do not participate in cleaning symbiosis despite serving as hosts for the same ectoparasites as those infecting striped killifish.

Widgeongrass, sago pondweed, horned pondweed, and filamentous algae typically thrive in saltmarsh pools, which often attract waterfowl and other waterbirds seeking small bodies of open water. In particular, the quiet waters in the pools serve as optimal habitat for widgeongrass, which is sensitive to wave action and currents; the plants' thread-like leaves provide a staple in the winter diet of black ducks. Likewise, the foliage of this and other submersed aquatic vegetation harbors numerous species of invertebrates that form an important part of the food webs at these sites. In winter, the relatively warm water in saltmarsh pools provides a thermal refuge for mummichogs.

Saltmarsh pools also offer sites where seaside dragonlets, the only truly marine odonate (dragonflies and damselflies), can deposit their eggs. Pairs of these relatively small dragonflies "hook up" in tandem when breeding, and the pairs skim over the pools in search of suitable sites for oviposition. The latter commonly occurs on mats of algae growing on the surface of the water. After hatching, the nymphs can cope with salinities reaching concentrations 2.6 times greater than that of seawater (91 ppt vs. 35 ppt), hence they continue maturing even as the salinity increases as the water slowly evaporates. The adults are weak fliers and spend most of the time perched on the culms of smooth cordgrass two to four inches above the marsh surface. These traits may minimize the risk of predation, including attacks by birds and larger species of dragonflies, although they remain particularly vulnerable to entrapment in spider webs. A blue-black thorax and abdomen, along with unmarked wings, identifies the males, whereas females may develop in three distinct forms, most notably those with brown-spotted wings and a yellow thorax with black stripes. The other two forms lack wing spots but differ in the coloration of their bodies (both, however, eventually become all black and indistinguishable from one another). An ovipositor under the tips of their abdomens clearly differentiates the females, regardless of their coloration.

Tidal creeks (fig. 3.9, top) fall broadly into two categories. Some originate inland and thus bring fresh water into the salt marsh, but these also may carry several types of anthropogenic pollution, including fecal contamination, industrial wastes, and fertilizers. Because of their toxicity and extreme persistence, heavy metals represent serious contaminants, whereas the relatively short-lived nitrogen and phosphates in fertilizers accelerate eutrophication (e.g., abnormal algal blooms). Other tidal creeks extend only to the inner edges of the marsh, flush with each tidal cycle, and, except for precipitation, receive virtually no input of fresh water. Upstream, they grade into progressively smaller channels known as rivulets that drain the marsh floor. Compared to the marsh proper, rivulets flood earlier on a rising tide and remain inundated longer than the surrounding marsh on a falling tide.

The network of creeks and their rivulets provides corridors for the dispersal of aquatic organisms deep into the marsh for food and cover. In fact, as the tide rises, three times as many fish travel in the rivulets when compared to those that swim across flooded creek banks. Still, the rivulets occupy only a small area—just 3 percent in one study—so, overall, greater numbers of fish spread into the marsh over the creek banks. The diversity of fish populations increases in the upper reaches of tidal creeks where the composition of the larval forms and juveniles changes during the course of the year. Conversely, populations, typically of older individuals, near the mouths of the same creeks maintain greater permanence.

The borders of tidal creeks sometimes develop natural levees two to six inches high and several feet wide. These form from sediments carried by rising tides that overflow the creek banks and deposit relatively more sediments near the edge and less as the overflow spreads out across the marsh surface. The levees commonly nourish taller stands of smooth cordgrass in comparison to the shorter stature of the same species elsewhere in the marsh.

Skinny as a Rail

Six species of rails seasonally or occasionally visit New Jersey's coastal marshes, but a few maintain year-round residence. The bodies of all are laterally compressed, an adaptation for moving nimbly through marsh vegetation and the basis for the common metaphor for thin humans. Some, such as the diminutive black rail, are exceptionally secretive and rarely seen, whereas others are somewhat more likely encountered either audibly or visibly. Of these, Witmer Stone considered the clapper rail as the "most characteristic bird of the great salt meadows which line the New Jersey coast" (fig. 3.10). A complex of several subspecies occurs in the coastal marshlands from southern New England to Texas as well as in two isolated populations in the western United States—an example of a discontinuous distribution. As shown by band recoveries, those in the northern part of their range, including New Jersey, migrate southward along the coast to overwinter between North Carolina and Georgia, although some reach the Florida Panhandle. Fieldwork at Tuckerton indicated that many birds leave the area during the last week of

FIGURE 3.10. The clattering "kek, kek, kek, kek" of clapper rails, also known as marsh hens, resonates in the still of a salt marsh. Rails provide sporting challenges for a small but dedicated cadre of hunters. Photo credit: Kevin Knutsen.

August. Thus, when Hurricane Hugo hit the coast of South Carolina in late September 1989, the devastation claimed so many clapper rails that it markedly reduced the breeding population returning to New Jersey the following spring. Conversely, after Hurricane Belle traveled up the eastern coast in mid-August 1976, surveys of the drift line in New Jersey indicated that the storm killed an estimated 20,000 young and adult clapper rails before they headed south. Such losses amply illustrate the importance of catastrophic events to the welfare of a migratory species anywhere within their yearly range.

Clapper rails nest in low marsh, often within 50 feet of tidal creeks or pool edges where males construct platforms, some topped with grassy domes and outfitted with access ramps. The taller stands of smooth cordgrass, which generally occur along the creek margins, provide prime nesting cover. According to ornithologist Alexander Wilson (1766–1813), the nests in New Jersey were so abundant early in the nineteenth century that a single egger could harvest 100 dozen eggs in one day (i.e., representing about 135 nests). Both sexes incubate clutches of 8 to 10 eggs, with the female generally sitting during the day and the male at night. Unusually high tides account for most nest failures, but the birds compensate for such losses with as many as five renesting attempts; overall, nesting success usually tops 80 percent. About one week after the eggs hatch, the parents divide and separately care for about half of the brood, which includes carrying the chicks on their backs during high water.

The birds are opportunistic feeders, taking a wide variety of animal foods (e.g., snails, grasshoppers, and small clams), supplemented in winter with seeds and other plant materials. However, crustaceans, primarily fiddler crabs, form much of their diet; these become prime targets at low tide. When feeding on fiddler crabs, the birds—no doubt with wisdom gained by experience—first remove the single large claw of their male victims before swallowing the crab whole; female crabs go down without the precaution of such treatment. Equipped with long, slightly decurved bills, clapper rails nonetheless seldom probe deeply into the marsh floor in search of food and instead forage on mudflats ("crabbing") or fish in shallow water. Because many of their foods have hardened exteriors, clapper rails regurgitate pellets consisting of fragments of exoskeletons and shells, which accumulate at concealed sites where the birds hide after feeding.

Hunting today claims only an insignificant percentage of the rail population, and the statewide harvest seldom exceeds 1,000 birds of all species. In the past,

Shore Note 3.3 Protecting Precious Marshes: Edwin B. Forsythe National Wildlife Refuge

More than 47,000 acres along the southern New Jersey coast remain secure in one of the largest national wildlife refuges in the eastern United States. Originally two separate refuges—Brigantine established in 1939 and Barnegat in 1967—and later combined and renamed for New Jersey congressman Edwin B. Forsythe (1916–1984), the habitat consists largely (78 percent) of salt marsh interspersed with shallow bays, which are supplemented by impounded freshwater and brackish wetlands along with nearly 5,000 acres of woodlands and fields. About 6,000 acres of pristine barrier beaches in the refuge's Holgate Unit at the southern tip of Long Beach Island are recognized as a National Wilderness Area, which provide undisturbed nesting habitat for piping plovers—birds listed federally as a threatened species and endangered by New Jersey. The refuge also includes a satellite area in Brick Township that features a wildlife trail named in honor of William "Willie" deCamp, founder of the conservation organization Save Barnegat Bay.

The refuge lies on a major pathway for migratory birds within the Atlantic Flyway, hence the habitat meets the needs of waterfowl such as Atlantic brant and black ducks (Fig. 3.11). Indeed, some 45 percent of all black ducks in North America overwinter in New Jersey, with many of these accommodated by habitat within the refuge. A few black ducks nest on the refuge, but most breed elsewhere in freshwater wetlands farther north (e.g., Canada's Maritime provinces). Their numbers have faltered in recent decades, hence the refuge directs much of its management efforts to improving conditions for black ducks.

The impounded wetlands, which occupy nearly 1,500 acres, were developed to provide habitat for a greater variety of wildlife than occurs in saltmarsh communities. Water levels in these impoundments are managed using a technique known as "drawdown." Early in the growing season, water is removed to stimulate greater growth of vegetation beneficial to waterfowl. The drawdown also exposes mudflats where migrant shorebirds forage for a rich variety of small invertebrates. Later in the year, the impoundments are reflooded to coincide with the arrival of fall migrants. All told, at least 322 species of birds seasonally visit or reside year-round on the refuge.

An eight-mile Wildlife Drive travels through the marshes, including one of the diked impoundments, and woodlands, which together provide visitors with year-round and up-close views of birdlife. Two observation towers and boardwalks equipped with spotting scopes highlight birding opportunities along the drive. Several walking trails add to the outdoor recreation available at the refuge. In season, visitors can also enjoy watching an active osprey nest under 24–7 surveillance with a video camera; the adults and their nestlings can be viewed on a monitor in the Information Center or online.

FIGURE 3.11. American black ducks occur widely in eastern North America, where many overwinter in salt marshes along the Atlantic coastline, including New Jersey. Despite management efforts at the Forsythe National Refuge and elsewhere, the continental population of black ducks has diminished in recent decades. Photo credit: Eric Reuter.

The refuge benefits from its association with the Friends of Forsythe, a nonprofit citizens organization that operates the gift shop, which sells books, apparel, and souvenirs. Members also greet visitors, conduct nature walks, provide environmental education programs for schoolchildren and civic groups, and raise funds in support of refuge projects.

however, market hunting took a heavy toll; in 1896, gunners in New Jersey felled tens of thousands of clapper rails in just two days. Today, as in the past, the hunts are timed to coincide with exceptionally high tides—"marsh hen tides"—that crowd the birds on higher sites in the marsh landscape. Traditionally, hunters work in pairs, taking turns poling a boat to flush the birds and shooting from the bow. Daily bag limits are generous—recently 10 clapper rails per day during a season lasting just over two months—but seldom fulfilled, and the few hunters that still hunt rails do so in what now may be as much a cultural experience as it is a sporting event. All species of rails are legally hunted, but along with sora rails, clapper rails top the list in the annual harvest.

Some Tales of Snails

Marsh periwinkles glide across the mud at low tide but ascend the stems of smooth cordgrass as the tide rises (fig. 3.12). Biologists long believed that these snails fed solely on algae and detritus on the marsh floor and merely perched on the grass stems as a defense against the arrival of crabs and other predators into the flooded marsh. More recently, however, biologists discovered that these snails also graze on the cordgrass. Moreover, the snails also function as "fungus farmers" whose husbandry begins when the snails cut into the leaves of smooth cordgrass using their rasp-like radulae. Grazing, as it turns out, is indeed less for gleaning food from the plant's tissues and more for preparing the site for fungi. This occurs when the snails fertilize the wound with their nitrogen-rich feces—an overt practice of

FIGURE 3.12. At high tide, marsh periwinkles ascend the stems of smooth cordgrass to avoid predators; when the tide recedes, they descend to graze in the detritus on the exposed soil. Photo credit: Mary Hollinger, National Oceanic and Atmospheric Administration.

"farming." The feces also contain hyphae and thus help disperse the fungi to new locations in the marsh. In return, the fungi become the preferred food for the snails in a relationship known as facultative mutualism (a beneficial but not mandatory association for both organisms). Conversely, the interacting effects of grazing and fungal infections can suppress the growth of smooth cordgrass, as shown by field experiments in which the removal of the snails significantly increased production.

A related species, the common periwinkle, crossed the Atlantic Ocean from Europe sometime in the first half of the nineteenth century, apparently hitchhiking in the ballast of merchant vessels. They arrived in Nova Scotia and thereafter steadily spread southward as far as New Jersey by 1892; they become most common in the lower reaches of the intertidal zone where they occur on both rocky and muddy substrates. Like many introduced species, common periwinkles faced no natural enemies in their new habitat that might control their numbers or distribution and soon made their presence known in the native community of coastal organisms. They became numerous enough to displace native mud snails from about 70 percent of their previously occupied habitat, but the two species maintain separate niches in locations where physical—not biological—conditions keep them apart. In particular, common periwinkles graze on the epiflora growing on the shells of eastern mud snails, which interferes with the foraging, movements, and reproductive activities of the latter, as well as preying on their egg capsules. In the absence of mud snails, the benthic substrate becomes less disturbed, which in turn may dramatically increase the presence of marine worms known as polychaetes. Common periwinkles also alter the composition of algae communities by differentially grazing on some species and not others. Fortunately, common periwinkles, though present in New Jersey, have not yet become a problem to the same extent as they have on the coast of New England.

Snails, of course, provide a protein-rich link in the food chains for several predators in salt marshes, not the least of which is the black-clawed mud crab (although some, with a different focus on anatomy, identify the species as the black-fingered mud crab). Though small (1.5 inches), these crustaceans are armed with strong, thick claws, one larger than the other and bearing a "tooth" at its base. They abound in the low marsh, where they provide an example of top-down control in which predators affect populations of organisms lower in the food chain—a relationship known as a trophic cascade. The links focus on the marsh periwinkle and smooth cordgrass, actors in a scenario noted earlier. The crabs prey heavily on the snails—no doubt why the snails climb up cordgrass at high tide—and include a greater percentage of these victims in their diet when the prey population becomes more numerous (i.e., a density-dependent relationship). The crabs construct U-shaped lairs with two entrances in the marsh floor in which empty snail shells accumulate and thereby enable biologists to determine what the crabs eat. Based on this method, marsh periwinkles make up nearly 66 percent of the prey captured by black-clawed mud crabs. Moreover, if unchecked by the crabs, the periwinkles reach densities of 600 to 1,000 per square yard and wield enough grazing pressure to destroy a stand of cordgrass in about a year. All told, the crabs stand as a key player in regulating the health of a tidal salt marsh and offer one more example to illustrate the importance of predators in marine as well as terrestrial ecosystems. Stated in the words of Henry David Thoreau, without predators, an otherwise balanced ecosystem resembles "a tribe of Indians that had lost all its warriors."

Eastern mud snails, mentioned earlier, form clusters of immense numbers, sometimes in the hundreds of thousands, which often consist of separate age groups. They scavenge on detritus and carrion and leave slime trails that provide a chemical path followed by others. Curiously, however, the slime trail of sick or injured mud snails no longer appeals to would-be followers and is soon abandoned. Some vertebrates, among them clapper rails, feed on mud snails, but despite their considerable abundance, they rarely occur in the diet of diamondback terrapins that otherwise prey on snails of similar size. Laboratory tests revealed the apparent reason: the shells of mud snails are two to three times more resistant to crushing than the other foods terrapins readily consume (e.g., marsh periwinkles and fiddler crabs). Often, foraging animals avoid otherwise desirable foods because they have evolved a chemical or physical defense (e.g., bitter-tasting or toxic tissues, venom, spines or thorns), but in this case the high energetic cost of breaking open the snails outweighs the benefits of their easy access and food value. In short, the payoff is just too small for the effort, and the terrapins thus seek other sources of nourishment.

Of Mosquitoes and Ditches

In their larval stage, mosquito populations follow a gradient across the elevational profile of tidal salt marshes, with more species—and numbers—thriving in high marsh and diminishing as the terrain gently slopes downward into low marsh. Two reasons seem to explain the gradient. First, in the low marsh, mummichogs, along with other predators, gain greater access to mosquito larvae during daily tidal fluctuations (i.e., higher rates of predation occur in regularly flooded low marsh). Second, daily tides rarely reach the high marsh, which flood only during lunar tides or periods of heavy precipitation (e.g., storms) and thereafter often remain inundated long enough for mosquito larvae to mature. Moreover, when flooded, the thick stands of vegetation in high marsh hinder movements of predators, which increases the survival of mosquitoes in these areas. Overall, these conditions make the high marsh key habitat for the larvae of several kinds of mosquitoes and so becomes the focus of water management.

Mosquitoes accordingly remain prevalent as annoying pests as well as vectors for several diseases, and efforts to diminish their larval habitat began early in the last century, with New Jersey leading the way. Because the life cycle of all mosquitoes begins in water, the removal of surface water clearly presents an effective means of limiting their populations. Ditching began in the early 1900s, but efforts at a far larger scale did not occur until the 1930s, when the Civilian Conservation Corps and other public works of the Depression era provided the necessary manpower (fig. 3.13, left). By 1938, grids of ditches cut across almost 90 percent of the tidal marshes between Maine and Virginia.. The ditches ran straight and parallel, at intervals of 115 to 230 feet, from the upper edges of high marsh downslope to the nearest tidal creek. Some ditches were located expressly—and effectively—to drain pools in the marsh.

Leaving aside their impact on mosquitoes, the ditches impaired many components of the wetland ecosystem. Pools simply disappeared along with the communities they supported, but perhaps more damaging was the drastic reductions of the invertebrate populations that formed crucial strands in the marsh's food webs. Up to 95 percent of the mollusks and crustaceans, for example, vanished from the lower marsh. Additionally, the drained areas fostered invasions of upland plants, notably two shrubs—marsh elder and groundsel—that were previously confined to the upper edges of high marsh (fig. 3.13, right). These changes obviously reduced the value of the marshes as habitat for waterfowl, clapper rails, and other wildlife. A few species nonetheless adapted to the altered marshes. For example, willets selected nesting sites on the spoil shoulders bordering ditches in a tidal marsh near Tuckerton. The deposits were only slightly higher than the surrounding

FIGURE 3.13. Grids of mosquito ditches etch some of New Jersey's salt marshes, an effort that began in the early twentieth century (left). The altered drainage patterns created by the ditches enabled invasions into the marsh interior by woody vegetation such as marsh elder and groundsel (right). Photo credits: Cape May Mosquito Control Department (left); Bob Cunningham (right).

marsh but provided the highest terrain available and remained above water throughout the nesting season. Elevation, and not the proximity to water nor the immediate vegetation, influenced where the willets built their nests.

In a classic example of unintended consequences, spoil removed from the ditches often dammed the flow of surface water, which created shallow pools that ironically provided prime habitat for mosquito larvae—the very targets of the ditching program! In the 1960s, biologists in New Jersey pioneered a technique that would more effectively control mosquitoes while at the same time help restore the grid-ditched marshes as wildlife habitat and eliminate or reduce pesticide applications. The technique—open marsh water management (OMWM)—manipulates the hydrology of small areas of larval habitat to enhance their access to predators (e.g., mummichogs and sheepshead minnows). Some natural depressions are deepened, from which relatively deep (as compared with earlier ditches) trenches radiate. The deeper water in these ditches sustains predator populations throughout the mosquitoes' breeding season, and where the terrain permits, the ditches direct their flow to natural pools instead of draining into tidal creeks. Spoil removed from the new ditches fills other depressions or is spread thinly throughout the marsh in ways that do not affect the surface hydrology (i.e., avoids pooling). The OMWM program was widely adopted and remains the standard for mosquito control in New Jersey's coastal marshes as well as in other states. Conversely, the technique may be adding to the effects of rising sea levels on ponding in salt marshes (i.e., more open water and less vegetation).

Bites to Remember

Whereas mosquitoes generally top the list of pests associated with salt marshes, greenhead flies deserve a special place in the hall of fame for painful bites. Greenheads, named not for the color of their heads but for their bulging emerald-green eyes, belong to a family that includes horse and deer flies (fig. 3.14). In preference to other vegetation, females lay their eggs on the shorter stems—those about two feet tall—of smooth cordgrass. After hatching, the larvae drop to the marsh sod below and prey on invertebrates, including larvae of their own species. The developing flies remain in the larval stage throughout the winter, then briefly undergo pupation the following spring before hatching as adults with a life span lasting three to four weeks.

As adults, both males and females rely on flower nectar as a source of energy, but the females require blood meals to extend their breeding cycle. Initially, the carryover of fat deposits in the larvae to adult females nourishes the first batch of eggs without the necessity of blood meals. This ensures production of at least one generation of offspring in an environment where large mammals are uncommon. Thereafter, however, blood meals become necessary for the development of addi-

FIGURE 3.14. Greenhead flies have justly earned a notorious reputation for their stinging bite, which torments birders and others visiting salt marshes in late summer. Photo credit: E. Hoopes.

tional eggs, and the females quickly become aggressive in their quest for sources. This sequence of events likely explains why greenheads become increasingly more annoying for humans as the summer progresses.

As might be expected, the mouth parts of females differ significantly from those of males. Their scissor-like mandibles gouge an ever-deepening wound into which blood pools from capillaries slashed by the laceration, whereas males completely lack mandibles. (In contrast, female mosquitoes skillfully pierce their victims with a needle-like proboscis that withdraws blood without causing tissue damage.) Despite the nature of the injury, however, the pain from a greenhead bite results from the host's reaction to the saliva that the females secrete as an anticoagulant.

An open duct from the salivary glands empties near the tip of the hypopharynx—a tongue-like mouth structure—from which the secretion enters the wound, whereas in males the saliva duct remains closed, each being another anatomical adaptation that correlates with their respective diets. In days gone by, horses drawing wagons loaded with salt hay suffered from the relentless attacks of greenheads, often to an extent that some farmers, taking pity, outfitted their teams with protective covers.

Locales such as Brigantine—dubbed by some as the "greenhead capital" of New Jersey–deploy traps as a means to depress the population of annoying flies. These are deceptively simple contraptions that employ a one-way entrance inside a box about 16 by 32 inches in size with an open bottom and screened top. Each box, painted black and erected on posts two feet above ground, services about a quarter acre. The flies enter from the bottom and, attracted by the light above, pass through the narrow entrance where they become entrapped in the upper chamber and soon weaken and die. The females, obsessively driven in their search for blood, mistake the traps for four-legged, warm-blooded animals—deer, cows, and other livestock, which in life would be attacked on their soft undersides. Some operators suspend plastic milk jugs or large soft drink bottles—also painted black—beneath the traps, where their swinging motion furthers the deception of a living animal. The traps indeed remove large numbers of greenheads, sometimes thousands per day, but the fly population nonetheless persists because each trapped female has already laid up to 200 eggs *before* searching for a blood meal. Hence, to fully preclude reproduction, a control method must necessarily remove female greenheads as soon as they hatch.

Readings and References

General

Able, K. W. 2020. Beneath the surface: understanding nature in the Mullica Valley. Rutgers University Press, New Brunswick, NJ. [A comprehensive overview of the salt marshes and associated environments in one of the least disturbed and cleanest watersheds in the megalopolis between Boston and Washington, DC.]

Merrill, C. (ed.). 1998. The way to the salt marsh: a John Hay reader. University Press of New England, Hanover, NH.

Teal, J., and M. Teal. 1969. Life and death of the salt marsh. Little, Brown, Boston.

Marshes High and Low

Avissar, N. G. 2006. Changes in population structure of diamondback terrapins (*Malaclemys terrapin*) in a previously surveyed creek in New Jersey. Chelonian Conservation and Biology 5:154–159.

Baltzer, J. L., E. G. Reekie, H. L. Hewlin, et al. 2002. Impact of flower harvesting on the saltmarsh plant *Limonium carolinianum*. Canadian Journal of Botany 80:841–851.

Bayard, T. S., and C. S. Elphick. 2011. Planning for sea-level rise: quantifying patterns of saltmarsh sparrow (*Ammodramus caudacutus*) nest-flooding under current sea-level conditions. Auk 128:393–403.

Bertness, M. D. 1984. Ribbed mussels and *Spartina alterniflora* production in a New England salt marsh. Ecology 65:1794–1807.

———. 1985. Fiddler crab regulation of *Spartina alterniflora* production on a New England salt marsh. Ecology 66:1042–1055.

———. 1991. Zonation of *Spartina patens* and *Spartina alterniflora* in a New England salt marsh. Ecology 72:138–148.

Bertness, M. D., C. P. Brisson, M. C. Bevil, and S. M. Crotty. 2014. Herbivory drives spread of salt marsh die-off. PLOS ONE 9(3):e92916. https://doi.org/10.1371/journal pone 0092916.

Bertness, M. D., C. P. Brisson, T. C. Coverdale, et al. 2014. Experimental predator removal causes rapid salt marsh die-off. Ecology Letters 17:830–835.

Bertness, M. D., and E. Grosholz. 1985. The population dynamics of the ribbed mussel, *Geukensia demissa*: the costs and benefits of an aggregated distribution. Oecologia 67:192–204.

Brennessel, B. 2021. Diamonds in the marsh, a natural history of the diamondback terrapin. 2nd ed. Brandeis University Press, Waltham, MA.

Calloway, J. C., and M. N. Josselyn. 1992. The introduction and spread of smooth cordgrass (*Spartina alterniflora*) in south San Francisco Bay. Estuaries 15:218–226.

Darnell, M. Z., and P. Munguia. 2011. Thermoregulation as an alternate function of the sexually dimorphic fiddler crab claw. American Naturalist 178:419–428.

Davenport, J., and E. A. Macedo. 1990. Behavioral osmotic control in the euryhaline diamondback terrapin: response to low salinity and rainfall. Journal of Zoology 220:487–496.

DiQuinzio, D. A., P. W. C. Paton, and E. R. Eddleman. 2002. Nesting ecology of saltmarsh sharp-tailed sparrows in a tidally restricted salt marsh. Wetlands 22:179–185.

Dorcas, M. E., J. D. Willson, and J. W. Gibbons. 2007. Crab trapping cause population decline and demographic changes in diamondback terrapins over two decades. Biological Conservation 137:334–340.

Estes, J. A., J. Terborgh, J. S. Brashares, et al. 2011. Tropic downgrading of planet Earth. Science 333:301–306. [An overview of trophic cascades and their effects on various types of ecosystems.]

Fogel, B. N., C. M. Crain, and M. D. Bertness. 2004. Community level engineering effects of *Triglochin maritima* (seaside arrowgrass) in a salt marsh in northern New England. Journal of Ecology 92:589–597.

Franz, D. R. 2001. Recruitment, survivorship, and age structure of a New York ribbed mussel population *Geukensia demissa* in relation to shore level—a nine year study. Estuaries 24:319–327.

Grimes, B. H., M. T. Huish, J. H. Kerby, and D. Moran. 1989. Atlantic fiddler crab. Species profiles: life histories and environmental requirements of coastal fishes and invertebrates (Mid-Atlantic). Biological report 82(11.114). U.S. Fish and Wildlife Service, Slidell, LA. TR EL-82-4, Army Corps of Engineers, Vicksburg, MS.

Grosse, A. M., J. C. Maerz, J. Hepinstall-Cymeerman, and M. E. Dorcus. 2011. Effects of roads and crabbing pressures on diamondback terrapin populations in coastal Georgia. Journal of Wildlife Management 75:762–770.

Grosse, A. M., J. D. van Dijk, K. L. Holcomb, and J. C. Maerz. 2009. Diamondback terrapin mortality in crab traps in a Georgia tidal marsh. Chelonian Conservation and Biology 8:98–100. [Reports 133 drownings—83 percent of which were males—in two abandoned traps.]

Haines, E. B. 1977. The origins of detritus in Georgia salt marsh estuaries. Oikos 29:254–260. [By the same author, see also Interactions between Georgia salt marshes and coastal waters: a changing paradigm. 1979. Pp. 35–46 in Ecological processes in coastal and marine systems (R. J. Livingston, ed.). Plenum, New York.]

Hodkinson, I. D., and J. Bird. 2000. Sedge and rush-feeding phyllids of the subfamily Liviinae (Insecta: Hemiptera: Psylloidae): a review. Zoological Journal of the Linnean Society 128:1–49.

Jordan, T. E., and I. Valiela. 1982. A nitrogen budget of the ribbed mussel, *Geukensia demissa,* and its significance in nitrogen flow in a New England salt marsh. Limnology and Oceanography 27:75–90.

Kemp, P. F., S. Y. Newall, and C. Krambeck. 1990. Effects of filter-feeding by the ribbed mussel *Geukensia demissa* on the water-column microbiota of *Spartina alterniflora* saltmarshes. Marine Ecology Progress Series 50:119–131.

Lewis, W. J. 2021. New Jersey's lost Piney culture. History Press, Arcadia Publishing, Mount Pleasant, SC.

Newcomb, C. E. 1996. Salt marsh flowers of southern New Jersey. Plexus, Medford, NJ.

Nixon, S. W. 1982. The ecology of New England high salt marshes: a community profile. FWS/OBS- 81-55. U.S. Fish and Wildlife Service, Office of Biological Services, Washington, DC.

Roosenburg, W. M., and J. P. Green. 2000. Impact of a bycatch reduction device on diamondback terrapin and blue crab capture in crab pots. Ecological Applications 10:882–889.

Shriver, W. G., T. P. Hodgman, J. P. Gibbs, and P. D. Vickery. 2010. Home range sizes and habitat use of Nelson's and saltmarsh sparrows. Wilson Journal of Ornithology 122:340–345.

Smith, J. M., and R. W. Frey. 1985. Biodeposition by the ribbed mussel *Geukensia demissa* in a salt marsh, Sapelo Island, Georgia. Journal of Sedimentary Research 55:817–828.

Szerlag, S., and S. P. McRobert. 2006. Road occurrence and mortality of the northern diamondback terrapin. Applied Herpetology 3:27–37.

Talbot, C. W., and K. W. Able. 1984. Composition and distribution of larval fishes in New Jersey high marshes. Estuaries 7:434–443.

Teal, J. 1962. Energy flow in the salt marsh ecosystem of Georgia. Ecology 43:614–624. [A seminal study heralding the productivity of salt marshes and their role as exporters of nutrients to other coastal environments. Later research (Haines 1977) modified the magnitude of these original estimates.]

Weiss, H. B., and G. M. Weiss. 1965. Some early industries of New Jersey (cedar mining, tar, pitch, turpentine, salt hay). New Jersey Agricultural Society, Trenton.

Pannes and Halophytes

Miller, W. R., and F. E. Egler. 1950. Vegetation of the Wequetequock-Pawatuck tidal marshes, Connecticut. Ecological Monographs 20:143–171. [See for details about salt pannes.]

Saltmarsh Pools and Tidal Creeks

Able, K. W. 1976. Cleaning behavior in the cyprinodontid fishes: *Fundulus majalis*, *Cyprinodon variegatus*, and *Lucania parva*. Chesapeake Science 17:35–39.

Abraham, B. J. 1985. Species profiles: life histories and environmental requirements of coastal fishes and invertebrates (mid-Atlantic)—mummichogs and striped killifish. U.S. Fish and Wildlife Service Biological Report 82(11.40). U.S. Army Corps of Engineers TR EL-82-4.

Campbell, B. C., and R. F. Denno. 1978. The structure of the aquatic insect community associated with intertidal pools in a New Jersey salt marsh. Ecological Entomology 3:181–187.

Dunson, W. A. 1980. Adaptations of nymphs of a marine dragonfly, *Erythrodiplax berenice*, to wide variations in salinity. Physiological Zoology 53:445–452.

Hackney, C. T., W. D. Buranck, and O. P. Hackney. 1976. Biological and physical
  dynamics of a Georgia tidal creek. Chesapeake Science 17:271–280.
Kneib, R. T. 1986. The role of *Fundulus heteroclitus* in salt marsh trophic dynamics.
  American Zoologist 26:259–269.
Mallin, M. A., and A. J. Lewitus. 2004. The importance of tidal creek ecosystems.
  Journal of Experimental Marine Biology and Ecology 298:145–149.
Rozas, L. P., C. C. McIvor, and W. E. Odum. 1988. Intertidal rivulets and creekbanks:
  corridors between tidal creeks and marshes. Marine Ecology Progress Series
  47:303–307.
Santiago Bass, C., and J. S. Weis. 2009. Conspicuous behavior of *Fundulus heteroclitus*
  associated with high digenean metacercariae gill abundances. Journal of Fish
  Biology 74:763–772. [Infections of flatworm larvae increase predation.]
Shenker, J. M., and J. M. Dean. 1997. The utilization of an intertidal salt marsh creek by
  larval and juvenile fishes: abundance, diversity, and temporal variation. Estuaries
  2:154–163.
Smith, J., and L. Niles. 2016. Are salt marsh pools suitable sites for restoration? Wetland
  Science & Practice (December):101–109. [See for the dynamics and ecological values
  of these habitats.]
Smith, K. J., and K. W. Able. 1994. Salt-marsh tide pools as winter refuges for the
  mummichog, *Fundulus heteroclitus*, in New Jersey. Estuaries 17:226–234.
Taylor, M. H. 1999. A suite of adaptations for intertidal spawns. American Zoologist
  39:313–320.
Von Baumgarten, R. J., R. C. Simmonds, J. F. Boyd, and O. K. Garriott. 1975. Effects of
  prolonged weightlessness on the swimming pattern of fish aboard Skylab 3. Aviation,
  Space, and Environmental Medicine 46:902–906.
Wilson, W. H., Jr. 2008. The behavior of the seaside dragonlet, *Erythrodiplax berenice*
  (Odonata: Libellulidae), in a Maine salt marsh. Northeastern Naturalist 15:465–468.
Wiltse, W. I., K. H. Foreman, J. M. Teal, and I. Valiela. 1984. Effects of predators and
  food resources on the macrobenthos of salt marsh creeks. Journal of Marine
  Research 42:9233–942.

Skinny as a Rail

Eddleman, W. R., and C. J. Conway. 1994. Clapper rail. Pp. 167–179 in Migratory
  shore and upland game bird management in North America (T. C. Tacha and
  C. E. Braun, eds.). International Association of Fish and Wildlife Agencies, Washington, DC.
———. 1998. Clapper rail (*Rallus longirostris*). No. 340 in The birds of North America
  (A. Poole and F. Gill, eds.). The Birds of North America, Inc., Philadelphia. [Source
  for the two-day tally of rails killed in New Jersey by market hunters.]

Kozicky, E. L., and F. V. Schmidt. 1949. Nesting habits of the clapper rail in New Jersey. Auk 66:355–364. [Includes observations of Alexander Wilson.]

Meanley, B. 1985. The marsh hen: a natural history of the clapper rail of the Atlantic coast salt marsh. Tidewater Publishers, Centreville, MD.

Schmidt, F. V., and P. A. McLain. 1951. The clapper rail in New Jersey. Proceedings of the Northeastern Fish and Wildlife Conference 7:164–172.

Stewart, R. E. 1951. Rail populations of the Middle Atlantic states. Transactions of the North American Wildlife Conference 16:421–430.

Some Tales of Snails

Bertness, M. D. 1984. Habitat and community modification by an introduced herbivorous snail. Ecology 65:370–381.

Brenchley, G. A. 1982. Predation on encapsulated larvae by adults: effects of introduced species on the gastropod *Ilyanassa obsoleta*. Marine Ecology Progress Series 9:255–262.

Brenchley, G. A., and J. T. Carlson. 1983. Competitive displacement of native mud snails by introduced periwinkles in the New England intertidal zone. Biological Bulletin 165:543–558.

Shepard, O. (ed.). The heart of Thoreau's journals. 1961. Dover, New York. [See entry for March 23, 1856, on p. 157 regarding the absence of warriors as akin to an ecosystem lacking predators.]

Silliman, B. R., and M. D. Bertness. 2002. A trophic cascade regulates salt marsh primary production. Proceedings of the National Academy of Sciences 99:10500–10505.

Silliman, B. R., C. A. Layman, K. Geyer, and J. C. Zieman. 2004. Predation by the black-clawed mud crab, *Panopeus herbstii*, in mid-Atlantic salt marshes: further evidence of top-down control of marsh grass production. Estuaries 27:188–196.

Silliman, B. R., and S. Y. Newell. 2003. Fungal farming in a snail. Proceedings of the National Academy of Sciences 100:15643–15648.

Tucker, A. D., S. R. Yeomans, and J. W. Gibbons. 1997. Shell strength of mud snails (*Ilyanassa obsoleta*) may deter foraging by diamondback terrapins (*Malaclemys terrapin*). American Midland Naturalist 138:224–229.

Of Mosquitoes and Ditches

Bourn, W. S., and C. Cottam. 1950. Some biological effects of ditching tidewater marshes. Research Report 19. U.S. Fish and Wildlife Service, Washington, DC. [Some results of the damage reported in this widely cited study were later challenged.]

Burger, J., and J. K. Shisler. 1978. Nest-site selection of willets in a New Jersey salt marsh. Wilson Bulletin 90:599–607.

Crans, W. J. 1977. The status of *Aedes sollicitans* as an epidemic vector of eastern equine encephalitis in New Jersey. Mosquito News 37:85–89. [Establishes the importance of the eastern saltmarsh mosquito in the transmission of EEE to humans.]

Erwin, R. M., J. S. Hatfield, M. A. Howe, and S. S. Klugman. 1994. Waterbird use of saltmarsh ponds created for open marsh water management. Journal of Wildlife Management 58:516–524.

Ferrigno, F., and D. M. Jobbins. 1968. Open marsh water management. Proceedings of the New Jersey Mosquito Extermination Association 55:104–115. [Presents a method, still in use, for ditching marshes without dire ecological consequences.]

Shisler, J. K., Jr., F. H. Lesser, and T. L. Schulze. 1975. Reevaluation of some effects of water management on the Mispillion Marsh, Kent County, Delaware. Proceedings of the New Jersey Mosquito Extermination Association 62:276–278. [Indicates that the impacts of ditching were less than reported—and thereafter widely cited—in the work of Bourn and Cottam (1950).]

Smith, J. B. 1907. The New Jersey salt marsh and its improvement. Bulletin 207. New Jersey Agricultural Experiment Station, New Brunswick, NJ. [Reports the first effort to control mosquitoes with ditches.]

Talbot, C. W., K. W. Able, and J. K. Shisler. 1986. Fish species composition in New Jersey salt marshes: effects of marsh alterations for mosquito control. Transactions of the American Fisheries Society 115:269–278.

Wolfe, R. J. 1996. Effects of open marsh water management on selected tidal marsh resources: a review. Journal of the American Mosquito Control Association 12:701–712.

Bites to Remember

Bosler, E. M., and E. J. Hansens. 1974. Natural feeding behavior of adult saltmarsh greenheads, and its relation to oogenesis. Annals of the Entomological Society of America 67:321–324.

Rockel, E. G., and E. J. Hansens. 1970. Distribution of larval horse flies and deer flies (Diptera: Tabanidae) of a New Jersey salt marsh. Annals of the Entomological Society of America 63:681–684.

Stoffolano, J. G., Jr., and L. R. S. Yin. 1983. Comparative study of the mouthparts and associated sensilla of adult male and female *Tabanus nigrovittatus* (Diptera: Tabanidae). Journal of Medical Entomology 20:11–32.

Shore Note 3.1. About Grasses and Graminoids

Barkworth, M. E., L. K. Anderson, K. M. Capels, et al. (eds.). 2007. Manual of grasses
 for North America north of Mexico. Utah State University Press, Logan.
Gibson, D. J. 2009. Grasses and grassland ecology. Oxford University Press, New York.
Piperno, D. R., and H. D. Sues. 2005. Dinosaurs dined on grasses. Science
 310(5751):1126–1128.

4

Barnegat Bay

The Face of the Jersey Shore

All is sands and flowing tides,
meadows and salt hay,
a narrow strip of land divides
the ocean from the bay.
It is a gunman's favorite site
with snipe and ducks galore,
in the bay the weakfish bite
and the bluefish swim near shore

—CAPT. BUNK, "CHADWICK," FROM *DOWN BARNEGAT BAY:*
A NOR'EASTER MIDNIGHT READER, ED. ROBERT JAHN

BARNEGAT BAY and two contiguous bays to the south represent a 43-mile-long continuum of coastal lagoons along New Jersey's coastline. Manahawkin Bay lies immediately to the south of the Route 72 causeway that connects the mainland with Long Beach Island; the causeway, rather than a landform, marks the boundary between the two bays. Still farther to the south, Little Egg Harbor continues until terminating at the Tuckerton Peninsula, a 5,000-acre wetland complex included in the Jacques Cousteau Estuarine Research Reserve. The three-bay estuary system is enclosed on its seaward border by Island Beach and Long Beach Island. The shallow bays average about five feet in depth, but large areas of flats occur along their eastern edges (i.e., on the protected, landward side of the barrier beaches). Because of the enclosed nature and shallowness of the system, winds outweigh tidal forces as the primary influence on circulation patterns. Seawater today enters the system only from two locations, at Barnegat Inlet near its middle and from Little Egg Inlet at its southern end. Other connections have come and gone, notably Cranberry Inlet (see chapter 2).

A third source of seawater emerged when a canal linked the northern end of Barnegat Bay with the Manasquan River, as described later

A 668-square-mile watershed in the Pine Barrens supplies the estuary with freshwater, most of which flows into the northern part of Barnegat Bay from three sources: the Metedeconk River, Toms River, and Cedar Creek. Considerably less freshwater enters Manahawkin Bay and Little Egg Harbor, which thus are naturally somewhat more saline than Barnegat Bay. A mosaic of sand, silt, clay, shells, and organic matter covers the bottom of the estuary. For example, sandy mud predominates near the mouth of the rivers, whereas silt and clay occur in coves and other areas with reduced water circulation.

Extensive beds of eelgrass cover much of the estuary, with widgeongrass occurring less widely (fig. 4.1). Stands of wild celery, horned pondweed, and sago pondweed develop where the influence of freshwater moderates the salinity. Some 165 islands of varying sizes dot the estuary. Most of these, known locally as sedge islands, formed naturally from thick accumulations of peat and sediments; some provide major nesting areas for gulls and other waterbirds. The islands' "sedges," however, are actually stands of smooth cordgrass. Others—spoil islands—were created from deposits of dredged materials, and these, too, at times may provide suitable habitat for certain birds.

Barnegat Bay lies at the narrowing of the Atlantic Flyway, one of four avian pathways crossing North American on a north-south axis that were delineated from the seasonal travels of banded waterfowl (fig. 4.2). Whereas the Atlantic Flyway extends over an area packed with one-third of the nation's human population, it also includes a rich tapestry of ecosystems ranging from Arctic tundra, deciduous forests, salt marshes, estuaries, bays, and sounds to the verdant warmth of the Everglades and the Caribbean Islands. At its wide northern terminus, the flyway forms a branch paralleling the eastern coastline through New England into Labrador and beyond; another traverses Hudson Bay—routes followed by the flyway's signature species: American black duck and Atlantic brant. Still another arm extends deeply into the continent's interior grasslands and features redheads and canvasbacks.

In 1987, Congress added an initiative known as the National Estuary Program (NEP) to the mission of the Environmental Protection Agency. NEP identifies nationally significant estuaries threatened by pollution, development, or overuse.

FIGURE 4.1. Dense beds of eelgrass, known as meadows, support a rich community of animal life—from scallops to finfish—but also include velvet-like coatings of epiphytes that thrive on eelgrass leaves and, as shown here, tiny polychaete worms that construct white tubes on the leaf blades. Photo credit: Virginia Institute of Marine Science.

Its goals are to protect and restore the health of these estuaries while concurrently enhancing their living resources and supporting economic and recreational activities. Barnegat Bay National Estuary Program officially became part of NEP in 1995 but was renamed as the Barnegat Bay Partnership in 2010. The new name better reflects the alliance of more than 30 municipal, state, federal, academic, business, and private organizations working together to conserve the natural resources of the bay and its watershed.

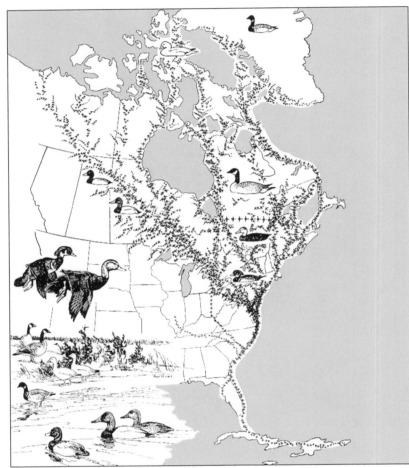

U.S. Fish & Wildlife Service

Atlantic Flyway

FIGURE 4.2. Barnegat Bay lies at the confluence of several aerial routes that collectively form the Atlantic Flyway. These arise from breeding grounds with habitat as varied as Arctic tundra, coastal wetlands, and ponds and lakes, including some in the distant northern prairies. Map courtesy of the U.S. Fish and Wildlife Service.

Eelgrass: Underwater Meadows in Barnegat Bay

At times, a thick green strip of vegetation edges the shores of Barnegat Bay. This is a wrack line dominated by eelgrass torn from the bay's muddy floor by a violent storm and piled onshore by wind-driven waves. Unlike *Sargassum*, an algae that accumulates on the beachfront after a far-off storm, eelgrass is a vascular plant whose tissues share artery-like pipelines in which nutrients commute between root and leaf tip. Whereas its linear leaves resemble bright green ribbons, eelgrass nonetheless is not a true grass of lawn or prairie but instead is one several species collectively known as seagrasses, eleven of which occur in North America. It bears

FIGURE 4.3. As shown here, Atlantic brant commonly forage on sea lettuce, an aptly named leafy macroalga that the birds added to their diet when eelgrass suddenly died off in Barnegat Bay and elsewhere along the Jersey Shore in the 1930s. Photo credit: Taylor Finger.

tiny flowers, which in turn produce seldom-seen seeds, but eelgrass more often spreads by a network of creeping rhizomes that establish dense beds—"meadows"—in protected bays and estuaries along coastlines in the Northern Hemisphere. In North America, huge communities of eelgrass dominate coastal waters as far north as Alaska (Izembeck Lagoon) and south to Baja California (Laugna Ojo de Liebe) on the Pacific coast, but along the Atlantic coast eelgrass flourishes—at least in the past—as much as anywhere in Barnegat Bay and its southern appendage, Little Egg Harbor. If there is a marine counterpart to the famed vegetables of the Garden State, it is surely eelgrass.

Any story about the eelgrass in Barnegat Bay might well begin with Atlantic brant, a small relative of the familiar Canada goose (fig. 4.3). The birds nest on the shores of Greenland, Spitzbergen, Ellesmere, Baffin, and other islands in the

High Arctic. There, for a brief period each summer, the brant reproduce during a narrow window of opportunity. Any earlier and the tail end of the previous winter strikes hard at the onset of nesting, any later and the cold of the forthcoming winter threatens the survival of the year's crop of youngsters—a temporal pattern analogous to a bed "just right" for Goldilocks.

Nesting over, the birds leave the Arctic in late summer—some in early August—and strike south, resting and concentrating en route at a few staging areas. They fly in long, undulating skeins, sputtering along with rapid wingbeats, often low above the water. At times, the long lines of brant, which shun the traditional V formations of other geese, suddenly ball up into an amoeba-like mass, then once more string out into sinuous skeins. The flocks swing widely around points of land, staying well out over water instead of taking a shortcut across a threatening landscape on the shoreline. Brant can be noisy on the wing, not with the majestic honking of geese but with a guttural "car-rrhup" or some derivatives—"rr-r-rup" and "ruk-ruk," for example—that Alexander Wilson likened to baying hounds. The last birds arrive in early November, and by then nearly 80 percent of all Atlantic brant find winter quarters along the coastal margins of New Jersey. Of the remainder, most favor Long Island Sound, but others reach Chesapeake Bay and Back Bay in Virginia, and Currituck and Pamlico sounds in North Carolina. But wherever brant may overwinter, there was eelgrass, always eelgrass.

Matters changed drastically in the 1930s, when eelgrass rather suddenly disappeared from all but a few locations along the Eastern Seaboard (see following). The lush, undulating meadows vanished wholesale, including those in the heartland of the brant's wintering grounds in New Jersey. Some estimates posit that at least 90 percent of the biomass of eelgrass was gone by the time the birds returned in the autumn of 1931, and most of the remainder had disappeared by the following year. The rapidity with which eelgrass melted away lacks precedence in botanical history. By comparison, it took years for disease to virtually eliminate American chestnut from the deciduous forests east of the Mississippi that have yet to recover.

As must be obvious by now, eelgrass was the dietary mainstay of brant. The birds prize the nutrient-rich rhizomes but more often graze at low tide on the long ribbons of leaves. Indeed, the gizzards biologists examined sometimes contained folded leaves more than 30 inches in length. Studies indeed revealed that eelgrass once represented fully 85 percent of the birds' winter diet yet represented just 9 percent after 1932. As stated by the era's leading authority on waterfowl food habits, Clarence Cottam, "Of all American waterfowl, the sea brant is perhaps the most specialized and least adaptable as to food and feeding habits." In other words, the birds apparently lacked much wiggle room to eat anything other than eelgrass. Just as pandas must have their bamboo, so do brant depend on eelgrass— or so it seemed.

Initially, the end of the eelgrass produced a holocaust for the brant population that, according to Cottam's estimates, plummeted to 10 percent of its former size. By 1933–1934, the winter census at some key locations along the coast revealed only 2 percent of their former numbers. Nor did eelgrass rebound. In 1937, Charles E. Renn was unable to find living plants north of Barnegat Inlet, and for "about half a mile south of the inlet, below Barnegat City [now Barnegat Light] there were a few scattered plants, not more than a hundred in all." The situation was hardly better along the western shore of Barnegat Bay, where only seven leaves of eelgrass were discovered—and these were a garnish inadvertently stuck on some clams plucked from Tuckerton Harbor and served in a local restaurant.

The eelgrass famine altered the feeding behavior of brant, which previously tipped up to reach the leaves waving just below the surface at high tide. At low tide, they simply walked across the flats clipping the exposed plants, grazing not unlike livestock in a pasture. Where the growth was especially thick, the birds greedily removed more than they could eat, which later floated in mats available for gleaning at high tide. When unusually high tides covered the meadows too deeply for tipping, brant grazed on fresh plants stranded in the wrack line. With the eelgrass no longer abundant, however, brant sometimes trailed behind feeding scaup and redheads—ducks that dive for their food—scrounging floating vegetation uprooted from deep water and even stole food directly from the bills of the hapless ducks. They also followed oyster dredges to glean fragments of vegetation dislodged from deep water. In short, the hungry brant had become opportunistic feeders. To cope, the starving brant necessarily switched to a new diet. Topping the list was sea lettuce, a leafy alga previously ignored, likely because of its somewhat limited nutritional qualities. Concurrently, the brant increased their intake of grit, presumably to improve the grinding power in gizzards suddenly filled with the sea lettuce, or maybe just as a means of appeasing hunger pangs. Still, sea lettuce fell short as a so-called emergency food—at least initially—and the starving birds began searching for food in unprecedented flights to nearby salt marshes. Meanwhile, the brant population wintering at Barnegat Bay dropped from about 28,000 in 1927–1928 to just 1,980 in the winter of 1932–1933. Brant hunting closed in the Atlantic Flyway in 1933 and did not again become a regular event until 1951. Today, fewer than 10,000 brant winter on the New Jersey coast, with about half of these favoring Barnegat Bay. Looking at it another way, hunters were allowed a daily bag limit of eight brant in the seasons between 1925 and 1930, whereas the current limit allows only one per day.

Despite partial recovery of the meadows, the birds no longer depend on eelgrass as the foundation of their winter diet. By the 1980s, fewer than 10 percent of the brant wintering in New Jersey still grazed on the patches of eelgrass available along the New Jersey coast—most continued foraging on sea lettuce, which remains the staple today. Moreover, smooth cordgrass, a widely occurring marsh plant, became an auxiliary in the birds' new diet. In severe winters, the brant now seek fields with cover crops of clover or rye, and some graze on lawns, including at golf courses. Enabled by the species' relatively long-lasting family bonds, the new diet became a tradition steadily ingrained in each new generation—circumstances that likely explain why the birds did not return to eelgrass.

So what malady had so suddenly destroyed the eelgrass meadows? Dubbed "wasting disease," the pathogenic agent remained unknown for many years, but the culprit was finally confirmed: an infectious slime mold, which because of its primitive structure was originally—and wrongly—thought to be a parasitic protozoan. Known only by its scientific name, *Labyrinthula zosterae* destroys the tissue structure of eelgrass, and only eelgrass, by dissolving the plant's cellular contents with potent enzymes as it spreads cell to cell. Within hours the chlorophyll-containing organelles in the infected cells begin losing their wholesome green color and fade into hues of olive or straw yellow that mark ill health. Small dark spots form on the external surface of a sickened leaf; these lesions coalesce and eventually blacken the entire blade, which in death breaks off and floats away. Eventually, the rootstock itself blackens and decays. Eelgrass meadows along the entire coast of North America succumbed to the attack, which also devastated those on the shores of Europe. Some, recalling the plague that ravaged medieval Europe, characterized the eelgrass catastrophe as a botanical Black Death.

Bad as it was for brant, a host of other organisms also became victims as parts of a community whose structure rested squarely on healthy eelgrass meadows. Near the famed Woods Hole marine station in Massachusetts, for example, about one-third of the invertebrates dwelling in eelgrass meadows vanished along with the eelgrass. Only burrowing species, whose needs depend less directly on the waving grasses, remained relatively unaffected. Still, soft-shelled clams quickly diminished because the eelgrass no longer slowed the currents that kept their "seed" in the bays instead of washing away into the void of deep water. Bay scallops, another commercially important species, likewise disappeared with the eelgrass, in this case because, as juveniles, they attach and develop on the leaves and, as adults, derive up to 30 percent of their body carbon from eelgrass detritus. Indeed, the loss of eelgrass as a source of detritus—the nutritional and the energetic footing for many of the community's food chains—emerged as one of the more serious effects of the disease.

Northern pipefish represent one of the vertebrates dwelling in eelgrass communities. Like their seahorse relatives, male pipefish nurture their young—more precisely, first as eggs and later as larvae—in abdominal pouches, a structural and behavioral oddity that promotes the idea that "pregnant" males actually "give birth" to their offspring. In fact, female pipefish produce and deposit their eggs in their mate's pouch and thereafter forsake any further parental duties, leaving the male in full charge of incubating and protecting the brood. Pipefish blend well in eelgrass, where they remain hidden by sharing the same color and linear shape as well as by adapting a vertical posture—head up, tail down—that fits right in with the foliage. Eelgrass also provides a feeding platform for pipefish that, lacking teeth, simply suck up small crustaceans from the leaf surfaces using their small mouths and tubular snouts as vacuum cleaners (see below). Some small, free-swimming prey may suffer the same fate if they pass carelessly near the feeding end of a vertical pipefish. In winter, pipefish leave the bays and head for deeper water where they become torpid and lie essentially motionless and often partially buried on the bottom. Some curl snugly around sand dollars, although it remains unclear if this happenstance represents some sort of an ecological relationship. Temperatures at these wintering locations remain warmer than the bays yet rise enough in spring to arouse the fish from their torpid state (i.e., a temperature-defined zone occurring not far offshore).

The surfaces of eelgrass leaves, when healthy, support a felt-like coating of algae, bacteria, and other microorganisms important to the welfare of other marine life. Some of these epiphytic organisms tap the leaves for food, whereas others simply use the leaf surfaces as a convenient substrate on which to conduct their daily affairs. Unlike *Labyrinthula*, however, these epiphytes seldom harm eelgrass despite being so abundant that their biomass may exceed that of a leaf blade itself. At times, the rich blanket of epiphytes may impair photosynthesis, but the plants normally replace older leaves with new growth as often as six times per year and thereby cope with such burdens. A long list of species forms the epiphytic community. Worldwide, the foliage of eelgrass collectively bears 120 species of large algae and 91 species of microalgae that in turn directly or indirectly nourishes a zoo of minute animals as well as the juvenile stages of some larger species. These consist of grazers and their predators, which together number a hefty 124 species. Because eelgrass leaves grow from the base of the plants, the uppermost leaf surfaces are older and thus support larger and more mature epiphytic communities than occur on the lower part of the same blade.

Clearly, the fortunes of many species depend heavily on eelgrass, but none more so than did a limpet now forever at rest in the graveyard of extinction. An insignificant loss? Perhaps, but speak of such things to the ghosts of passenger pigeons. Numerous species of limpet occur worldwide, but these are not a separate family of mollusks and instead evolved within several groups of more typical snails. The shells of limpets, although coiled, are much compressed and, in profile, resemble miniature Chinese hats—the "coolie" hats of laborers—under which the soft-bodied animals cling to some sort of substrate, often a hard surface. In this case, however, the eelgrass limpet, true to its name, attached itself exclusively to eelgrass—a classic obligate relationship since no other plant sufficed as the limpet's source of nourishment. Nature adapted the radula—the rasping, tongue-like structure snails use for feeding—of this species solely for grazing on the epithelial cells of eelgrass leaves. Like brant, the limpets experienced a major famine in the 1930s, but unlike either eelgrass or the birds, the limpets did not recover.

James Carlton and his colleagues stitched together the story behind the extinction of eelgrass limpets. Namely, with the recovery of eelgrass, why not also the unfortunate limpets? The riddle hinges on different tolerances to salinity. Eelgrass survives within a broader range, from full-strength seawater in the bays to the brackish waters in the upper reaches of estuaries. Not so for limpets or *Labyrinthula*, neither of which can survive reduced salinities. Thus, of the three organisms, only eelgrass could survive in low salinity refugia in the estuaries. In the saltier bays, however, *Labyrinthula* rapidly wiped out the plants, which in turn brought an end to the limpets. Later, after the epidemic had run its course, eelgrass reoc-cupied its former habitat in the bays where it again flourishes albeit without the small mollusks. For the first time in recorded history, extinction had claimed a species of marine invertebrate when one of nature's small lights simply winked out forever—a loss triggered, as it happened, by a virulent plant disease.

Eelgrass, although largely recovered in Barnegat Bay, remains rare elsewhere on New Jersey's southern coastline. Outbreaks of wasting disease still occur periodi-cally along the Atlantic coast, although these fortunately have so far fallen short of the devastation wreaked in the 1930s. Currently another threat arises from algal blooms—"brown tides"—whose extreme densities can exceed a million cells in just a few drops of water; the resulting coffee-colored water effectively blocks sunlight from reaching the plants and other components of the benthic commu-nity (e.g., bay scallops). Initial efforts to transplant eelgrass produced spotty results, in part because of the unknown genetic diversity in the stock used in the plantings. In particular, stock obtained from sites where a genetic bottleneck once occurred may not survive in the environmental conditions prevailing at other locations (genetic bottlenecks form when once-large populations decline in size and there-fore carry forward a diminished gene pool). As a result, the diminished genetic diversity in the eelgrass transplanted from these sources likely handicapped the initial restoration efforts. Greater success occurred thereafter when the trans-planted stock was screened for genetic diversity. Nonetheless, physical factors such as ice scour and winter storms may at times lessen the survival of the newly established beds. In contrast, the harmful effects of brown tide may be mitigated by planting eelgrass in the fall, which affords the plants several months of growth—a vegetative "leg up"—before algal blooms develop in the following summer. In all, experimental evidence indicates that with careful site selection and optimal tim-ing eelgrass and its ecological functions can be successfully restored in waters where it once flourished.

For all of its ecological importance, eelgrass does have something of a downside. Revelers of summertime on the Jersey Shore understandably detest mosquitoes, which some visitors waggishly regard as the top guns of the New Jersey Air Force. But even mosquitoes fall short of the torment of stable flies, small insects with

Shore Note 4.1 Estuaries and Their Troubles

Coastal features known as estuaries partially enclose areas where fresh and salt water mix and create a transition zone of brackish water. River valleys drowned by rising sea levels form a common type of estuary represented in New Jersey by Delaware Bay and Raritan Bay. In contrast, Barnegat Bay represents a lagoon type of estuary where barrier beaches partially enclose a system fed by freshwater streams, in this case by Toms River and Cedar Creek, among several others. Seawater enters with the tidal flow through Barnegat Inlet and Little Egg Inlet and, since 1925, the Manasquan (Point Pleasant) Canal. Because of the comparatively small tidal flow through these connections with the ocean, a relatively long period is required to completely exchange the volume of water in Barnegat Bay—96 tidal cycles, with one cycle occurring about every 13 hours. The tidal amplitude itself varies from three feet at Barnegat Inlet and thereafter progressively diminishes to about six inches north and south of the inlet.

Several features distinguish estuaries. First, the influx of nutrients carried in river sediments endows estuaries with almost unparalleled productivity, as shown by their immense biomass of vegetation, shellfish, and finfish. Such productivity supports important recreational and commercial fisheries, which were too often exploited by unsustainable harvests. Barnegat Bay, however, lacks the outflow from a large river and instead depends on detritus as its major source of nutrients. In some estuaries, notably in drowned valleys of large rivers, the profile shows a wedge-shaped lens of fresh water lying over the heavier salt water. In such areas, a marine fauna typically thrives on the bottom of the estuary beneath a layer of fresh water. The leading edge of the lens tapers as it extends seaward until it completely gives way to salt water. However, in a shallow lagoon estuary like Barnegat Bay, wind so thoroughly mixes fresh and salt water that this stratification develops only in relatively small areas near the mouths of a few small rivers (where it may in fact disappear when drought diminishes the flow of fresh water).

big bites that find windrows of beached eelgrass among their choicest locations to reproduce. These pests, often called beach flies, resemble the common house fly and indeed belong to the same family. Unlike house flies, however, stable flies come with bayonet-like mouthparts with which both males and females painfully extract blood from their victims. They bite viciously and relentlessly, especially around the ankles and other places where human skin seems thin and tender, in all making scantily clad bathers easy targets.

Female stable flies lay their eggs in decaying vegetation, hence eelgrass wrack presents an ideal nursery. The larvae, small but rather stocky white maggots, thrive

Unfortunately, estuaries today commonly suffer from serious pollution, including contamination by heavy metals, sewage, and agricultural chemicals. Pollution originates from specific points such as an industrial site or sewage facility as well as from non-point sources such as runoff from agricultural fields and paved surfaces. Point-source pollution is more easily identified and corrected, but remedies for non-point pollution remains far more difficult. For example, recent work has shown that the runoff from fertilized lawns contributes a much larger portion of the nutrient load in Barnegat Bay than previously believed. In short, the continuing expansion of commercial and residential developments in coastal areas continues to impair the water quality in estuaries.

Acceleration of a natural process known as eutrophication—the nourishment of an aquatic system—from overloads of nitrogen and phosphorus troubles virtually all levels within estuarine ecosystems. These include algal blooms that limit the penetration of sunlight, which in turn impairs the survival of submerged aquatic vegetation and its dependent food chains. Decomposition of algae also depletes the dissolved oxygen available to aerobic organisms and in some cases creates a "dead zone."

In Barnegat Bay, the excessive eutrophication likely contributed to an explosion of jellyfish with an unwelcome sting. Additionally, docks and bulkheads along the bay's edges provide the polyps—an early stage in the life cycle of bay nettles—with an ideal surface on which to attach and produce numerous buds. Each bud develops into a medusa—the familiar bell-shaped adult stage of jellyfish—with the result that the hundreds of polyps attached to a single dock may produce thousands of adult bay nettles. Control of the adult population seems impossible, but the polyps may be curtailed. To that end, the New Jersey Department of Environmental Protections organized the Barnegat Bay Bulkhead Blitz, which encourages the owners of waterfront properties to scrub away the polyps infesting their docks and bulkheads (see also Sting Like a Bee in this chapter).

on microbes and the warmth of the decomposing plants. These populations may be large. Traps at one site on Barnegat Bay caught an average of 370 flies per bushel of eelgrass wrack. Eelgrass washed ashore only a day or two earlier becomes suitable as breeding habitat, and a new generation of flies reaches maturity two to four weeks later. As might be expected, the fly populations jump soon after storms or unusually high tides replenish the wrack line with fresh deposits of eelgrass. Attacks may occur just about any place on the Jersey Shore, but they seem larger and more common on the strand forming the eastern edge of Barnegat Bay. Winds from the west carry stable flies across the bay and dunes to the beachfront in just

15 minutes, but the invasion ends just as abruptly when the wind changes direction. Still, the pesky flies emptied the beaches to the extent that resorts allegedly suffered "severe economic losses," which brought pressure for ending this scourge to sunbathers. In response, staff at the New Jersey Agricultural Experiment Station recommended spraying eelgrass wrack with a broth that included DDT, an insecticide widely applied at the time (1951). Such treatments, the agency suggested, would surely end the loss of both blood and income and thereby save tourism. Others, more cynical, thought that the spraying operations were more likely triggered by the discomfort the flies brought to those in residence at the governor's summer home at Island Beach. DDT was later banned in the wake of *Silent Spring*, a seminal work by Rachel Carson that spearheaded a public awakening about environmental health and, eventually, creation of the Environmental Protection Agency, the Endangered Species Act, and other regulatory measures.

Long ago, a few folks along the Jersey Shore maintained a commercial interest in eelgrass. One was William S. Sword, whose artist father had resourcefully converted Life Saving Station No. 14 on Island Beach into a summer cottage and studio. In 1899, the elder Sword applied horse and winch to relocate the sea-weathered building across the dunes from the beachfront to someplace, now unknown, on Barnegat's eastern shore; William took over the dwelling when his father died in 1915. William had several callings, including professional photographer, antique dealer, and decorator for the Rosenbach Galleries in Philadelphia and, at least for part of the year, as a seaweed entrepreneur on Barnegat Bay.

The "seaweed" of course was eelgrass, and William Sword harvested enough of the leafy plants to employ six men from March to November. The hardy crew pitch-forked tons of eelgrass from the wrack line onto horse-drawn hay wagons. Processing the crop was simple but back-breaking labor and likely included regular visits by stable flies. Once inland, the green and still wet eelgrass was again tossed by pitch fork, this time onto drying racks constructed of chicken wire for curing in the sun and fresh air. When dry, the strong "rotten-egg" odor—hydrogen sulfide—dissipated, leaving the eelgrass ready to compress into 200-pound bales, which Sword's Seaweed Industry shipped by rail from South Seaside Park to Philadelphia.

What were the commercial uses of eelgrass? Quite a few, as it turns out. The dried leaves made fine packing material for pottery and provided excellent insulation when wrapped around various types of pipe, stuffed in walls, or even in ovens. Because they also absorb sound, eelgrass leaves were quilted into rolls and applied to the walls of hotels and other buildings, including conservatories of music where, it seems, the food of brant could also muffle the outpourings of a brass band. In Boston, the firm of Samuel Cabot Inc. pioneered the development of seagrass quilts, which were manufactured by stitching dried eelgrass leaves between layers of Kraft paper. Cabot's Insulating and Deafening Quilt gained wide recognition, so much so that Rudyard Kipling requested a cost estimate for an order of 200 square feet. The famous author advised Cabot that he had "found the Quilt invaluable as a deadener of noise" and now wished to test its resistance to weather. By 1930, Cabot's quilts were quieting the ruckus in apartment buildings throughout the New York City area, but the business later failed when wasting disease abruptly ended the supply of eelgrass. William Sword's enterprise at Barnegat Bay ended at about the same time and for the same reason.

Other industrious souls developed and patented a process for transforming eelgrass into paper, some of which was considered of high grade, but others thought it less so. Eelgrass also found eternal rest as stuffing inside the quilted linings of caskets. Old timers along the Jersey Shore claimed that eelgrass also filled the mattresses in the beds of those intrepid immigrants who crossed the Atlantic cramped into Cunard's steerage. Once the ships docked, the mattresses were replaced, perhaps with those freshly packed with stock from William Sword's operation at Island Beach. Another legend stitched into local history indicates that eelgrass once caught the attention of Henry Ford. In 1905, before he hit it big time, Ford raced a car on the beach at Cape May—he finished last—where he later bought land on which he intended to build a factory and racetrack. These never materialized, but the story goes that Ford learned of eelgrass's leafy abundance along the Jersey coast and, for a time, used the material in the seat cushions of his Tin Lizzies after they went into production in 1908. Regrettably, the story remains unconfirmed, and some other stuffing perhaps softened the bumps for those braving the ruts that passed for the roads of the day. But just maybe, somewhere in a neglected corner, a dusty seat cushion filled with eelgrass awaits discovery, which would add another page to the history of aquatic meadows in Barnegat Bay.

Float Like a Butterfly, Sting Like a Bee

With apologies to Muhammad Ali, this is about Barnegat Bay and its jellyfish, not his boxing prowess. A small species with a medusa—the gelatinous bell-shaped dome—averaging about three inches in diameter and now known as the bay nettle has a long been a part of the bay's fauna.[1] Recently, however, the population of bay nettles has exploded to the point of disrupting the food web in the bay. Additionally, the species' stings, although not lethal, produce an uncomfortable rash on the skin of swimmers and others enjoying the water.

Bay nettles come in two varieties: some show white markings. whereas reddish brown markings distinguish others. All are otherwise transparent. About 24 thread-like tentacles dangle from the medusa, each equipped with stinging cells known as cnidocytes (jellyfish belong to the phylum Cnidaria, which reflects the presence of these structures). Each of these specialized cells contains a coiled stinger, which is released on contact and injects a toxin into either a predator or prey. Bay nettles feed on at least 23 taxa, among others including polychaete worms, barnacle larvae, fishes and their eggs and larvae, shrimp, gastropods, mosquito larvae, and zooplankton.

Two reasons largely account for the increased numbers of bay nettles. First, they tolerate low-quality water—now commonplace in Barnegat Bay—produced by runoff laden with nitrogen and other nutrients. The nutrients, particularly during the summer months, stimulate eutrophication (excessive enrichment) that leads to blooms of phytoplankton. The blooms produce undesirable changes in the water's content of dissolved oxygen, which harms fish and other aquatic organisms but not bay nettles. The second reason involves polyps, another stage in the life cycle of bay nettles (and other jellyfish). These cylinder-shaped structures attach to hard surfaces where they clone and release ephyrae (early-stage adults)

---

[1] The species in Barnegat Bay was previously known as the sea nettle. In 2017, however, a taxonomic study revealed that the DNA signatures of the nettles in Chesapeake Bay and nearby shorelines were different enough to recognize two species (see Bayha, Collins, and Gaffney 2017). Populations differentiated by one of the signatures matched the DNA in the jellyfish in Barnegat Bay, and along with those in Chesapeake Bay, these were thereafter formally recognized as a separate species, the bay nettle. Hence, literature published before 2017 about sea nettles in Barnegat Bay actually concerns bay nettles. Note, however, that both species have similar life cycles. The other and larger species, still known as the sea nettle, more commonly occurs in the open ocean.

that rapidly develop into medusae. Given the substantial development of Barnegat Bay's shoreline, which includes docks, bulkheads, and pilings, the availability of these hard surfaces offers more sites where polyps can attach. Indeed, a single dock can provide habitat for thousands of polyps, which can give rise to overwhelming numbers of jellyfish. Additionally, the bay's rising water temperatures accelerate the rates at which the jellyfish grow and mature, thereby increasing the number of generations produced per year.

In 2016, a small but dangerous jellyfish with a medusa about the size of a quarter turned up in Barnegat Bay. Known as "clinging jellyfish"—so named because they grasp surfaces such as eelgrass and leafy algae with their specially modified tentacles—this invader generally occurs in shallow water at the northern end of Barnegat Bay where submerged aquatic vegetation prevails. Their transparent medusae feature a single cross-like "X," which often turns red, orange, or yellow when individuals get ready to reproduce. The species, now common along the coast from Maine to New Jersey, originates from the northern Pacific Ocean where two variants occur, one highly venomous, the other less so. Unfortunately, the more virulent variant reached New Jersey and packs a sting that may hospitalize humans.

Comb jellies, while somewhat similar to jellyfish, also occur in Barnegat Bay but represent an altogether different phylum, Ctenophora, which lack stinging cells. One of these, known as a sea walnut, emits tiny green flashes of light at night (i.e., an example of bioluminescence). Comb jellies are voracious predators that may consume 10 times their body weight each day feeding on fish eggs and larvae, zooplankton, and, alas, oyster larvae. However, comb jellies themselves are prey for bay nettles, a relationship that keeps bay nettle populations in check, which not only may be an important relationship in the bay's food chain but also may help restore oysters.

An effort known as Stop the Sting hopes to diminish the burgeoning jellyfish population by scrubbing polyps from bulkheads, docks, and other hard surfaces. Preliminary results, as reported by marine biologist Paul Bologna, indicate that ephyrae—the stage in the life cycle between polyp and medusa—declined at some of the research sites where polyps were removed. The study will continue, but the data currently at hand nonetheless provide a hint about the efficacy of scrubbing hard surfaces as a means of curbing local jellyfish populations in Barnegat Bay.

Coastal Colonies

Colonial waterbirds nesting along the Jersey Shore include long-legged waders nesting in trees and shrubs (primarily herons and egrets) and ground nesters (gulls, terns, and black skimmers). Most have been extensively studied, often in Barnegat Bay, resulting in a large volume of literature, but limitations of space dictate only an overview of a few species. Nonetheless, it remains important to emphasize the diversity of this avifauna as well as the difficulties these birds encounter from human activities and, in recent years, from growing numbers of nest predators, notably herring and great black-backed gulls. Many colonies of ground-nesting species have in fact abandoned their favored locations on sandy beaches and moved into salt marshes, especially to marshy islands rimmed with sandy shores. Still, even these face the continuing threat from rising sea levels. In an earlier time, feather hunters and eggers depleted the populations of these birds, which slowly recovered after these practices were outlawed.[2] Gulls were further aided by food supplements available at landfills. Today, many of the species face serious limitations related to the quality and quantity of their breeding habitat.

Colonies of two or more species nesting together in trees and shrubs, commonly known as rookeries or heronries, warrant further note because they provide a textbook example of resource partitioning. Based on body size, each species locates its nests at a different height in the vegetation, which lessens interspecific competition. The nests of a large species such as the great egret typically occupy the upper level at rookeries at Barnegat Bay, with progressively smaller species nesting in the lower levels. Cattle egrets, the only exception, nest higher than expected based on size, which may be associated with their relatively new arrival in North America (i.e., shoehorning into a vertical profile long occupied by other species; see below).

---

[2] To expose the pervasive exploitation of birds by the millinery trade, banker-turned-ornithologist Frank M. Chapman (1864–1945) surveyed the hats worn by women shopping in Upper Manhattan in 1886: of 700 hats, 542 were adorned with whole birds or their parts, which represented 40 native species, including 21 outfitted with the feathers of common terns. His survey triggered a crusade that eventually led to the Lacey Act (in 1900), which in part curbed plumage trafficking, the first national wildlife refuge (in 1903), and the Migratory Bird Treaty Act (in 1918).

FIGURE 4.4. Well named, black skimmers sweep across surface waters in search of food, snapping shut their extended lower bills on contact with small fish (left). Laughing gulls nest in marsh vegetation, adding more material as needed when faced with rising water levels (right). Both species nest in colonies. Photo credit: Kevin Knutsen (left); Henry J. Hipp (right).

Black skimmers, though related to gulls and terns, have evolved some distinctive features unlike those of their kin. Foremost among these is their unique bill shape and feeding behavior. True to their name, these sleek black and white birds—some liken their plumage to tuxedos—gracefully glide, bills agape, just above the water in search of small fish (fig. 4.4, left). Their elongated lower mandibles slice the surface, snapping shut when they encounter a victim. At hatching, the upper and lower mandibles are of equal length, which enables the chicks to pick up the food their parents drop on the ground before their ever-hungry young; the distinctive asymmetrical bill shape appears by the time the young birds fledge (i.e., when about 25 days old). Less obvious, however, is their unique ability to constrict their pupils in bright light, from round to a catlike vertical slit, an adaptation that facilitates coping with reflections from water and sand. Because the birds also forage at night, the elliptical shape may be helpful but not essential in the dim light, given that they tactically, not visually, locate and capture their prey. When nesting, skimmers, more so than gulls and terns, divert intruders with well-developed distraction displays. The performance employs belly flops, fake collapses, struggling hops, and flapping wings, all designed to lure predators away from nests and chicks. Black skimmers do not swim, and both sexes issue doglike barks, especially when disturbed.

Black skimmers typically nest on sandy beaches where they lay three or four eggs in shallow scrapes. They return year after year to beaches where they successfully nested in the past. The birds favor sites where common and least terns also nest, a strategy that provides the skimmers with both an alarm system and a vigorous mobbing defense against predators. However, with the advance of development, the colonies at many beaches experience human disturbances, and the birds frequently abandon these locations and move to sites less traveled, commonly to accumulations of wrack in salt marshes. Heavy losses to predators also result in colony abandonment. In New Jersey, herring and laughing gulls prey on skimmer eggs and chicks; indeed, one observer witnessed laughing gulls seize 18 chicks in a four-hour period. Because of these issues, New Jersey lists the black skimmer as an endangered species.

Laughing gulls, by far the most numerous species of the gulls seen in summer on the Jersey Shore, nest in colonies, often with hundreds, even thousands, of pairs. Ideal locations lack predators, human disturbances, and tidal flooding, a description fitting the higher islands in salt marshes, where they build their nests in stands of smooth cordgrass. The birds maintain their nests in ways to keep their eggs and chicks above flood tides, primarily by attaching nests to adjacent stems or adding more material as a means to elevate the nests (fig. 4.4, right).

Laughing gull colonies grew in size and number, nearly doubling the breeding population in New Jersey during the 1960s and 1970s. However, because of the increase of the birds in both New Jersey and Jamaica Bay in nearby New York, the birds became a hazard for aircraft at a major airport and some 50,000 were shot beginning in 1991. As a result, the nesting population at Barnegat Bay plunged. Meanwhile herring gulls expanded their breeding range southward into New Jersey, and laughing gulls thereafter faced a new and abundant predator of their eggs and chicks—a situation made even worse when great black-backed gulls also extended their breeding range southward. In response, laughing gulls moved from their traditional nesting sites to lower islands where flooding often destroys their nests. Selection of colony sites thus becomes a compromise between nesting on low islands to avoid mammalian predators or on islands high enough to lessen the risk of flooding but more susceptible to interactions with the two larger gulls.

The more aggressive herring gulls also outcompete laughing gulls when they forage together at sanitary landfills (garbage dumps), which provide a year-round and dependable source of food for scavenging birds.

Cattle egrets represent a rare example of a vertebrate that successfully settled in the New World without direct or indirect help from humans.[3] Most likely aided by trade winds, the birds crossed the Atlantic Ocean from Africa and successfully established colonies along the northern coast of South America, then spread northward through the Caribbean and on to Florida in 1942. Thereafter they steadily expanded their range to the west and northeast, reaching New Jersey in 1951. For the most part, cattle egrets seemingly fit in rather well into the nesting rookeries of native species in North America (fig. 4.5, left). Competition for nest sites and materials remains low in the southern United States (e.g., Alabama), where cattle egrets breed later in the season than the other species sharing the same rookery (e.g., snowy egrets). However, in northern rookeries (e.g., New Jersey) the birds nest concurrently with the other species, which results in more competition and aggressive interactions between cattle egrets and their neighbors. Nonetheless, the diet of cattle egrets, unlike those of other herons and egrets, seldom includes aquatic foods. Instead, they forage on insects in fields, along highway edges, on lawns, and in pastures where, in keeping with their name, cattle stir up grasshoppers, beetles, other invertebrates, and occasionally small vertebrates, especially frogs; in doing so, the cattle (and sometimes farm equipment) fulfill the role played by numerous species of African grazers (fig. 4.5, right). Their relationship with cattle rewards the birds with three times more efficiency than if they foraged alone. In return, the birds sometimes perch on cattle to remove external parasites. Cattle egrets also respond to smoke in search of insects fleeing from fires.

In New Jersey, cattle egrets nest in rookeries along the coast from Cape May to Barnegat Bay, with a small colony at Arthur Kill, and in winter migrate to Florida, the Caribbean, and South America. Recently, the population has diminished, and while the reason remains unclear, it likely involves the steady loss of agricultural

---

[3] Glossy ibises also reached the New World from Africa, presumably traveling a route followed more than a century later by cattle egrets; the species was first recorded in the United States in 1817 at Great Egg Harbor, New Jersey. As reported by George Ord (1781–1866), a Mr. Oram shot the bird, which he found so unusual that he gave it to Thomas Say (1787–1834), a prominent naturalist often regarded as the "father" of American entomology. Ord published the original descriptions of several species, including the tundra swan and grizzly bear (see also shore note 5.1).

FIGURE 4.5. Following their arrival to North America, cattle egrets fit into the vertical structure of established rookeries (left), which in New Jersey and other northern areas in their breeding range leads to aggressive interactions with native species (e.g., snowy egrets). Close monitoring of their feeding behavior revealed that cattle egrets capture far more prey per minute when foraging near a cow's head, as opposed to a cow's side or rear (right). Photo credits: James F. Parnell.

lands to development. In 2012, New Jersey listed the cattle egret as a threatened species.

Final mention goes to the least tern, the smallest of its kind in North America and another waterbird once exploited for its feathers. Like other terns, it plunge dives for small fish, aided by its ability to hover when searching for promising targets. Least terns nest on barren beaches, including those formed by washovers or on deposits of dredged materials. However, encroaching vegetation at these sites will induce the birds to move and establish colonies elsewhere. Each pair may scrape out several shallow depressions before selecting one in which the female lays two or three sand-colored eggs. The chicks, also protectively colored, often join others in large groups guarded by a few adults. Although diminutive, least terns fearlessly dive-bomb intruders that threaten their nests. Nonetheless, predators destroy many nests, especially in the larger mainland colonies, as does coastal flooding. The least tern appears on the state list of endangered species.

In sum, colonial waterbirds nesting in large colonies, and particularly those nesting at ground or close to water level, face ever more difficulties finding sites where human disturbances, predation, and flooding will not impair their breeding success. All of the many species, including those nesting in rookeries, clearly require rigorous action from conservation agencies and organizations to protect, enhance, or even create new nesting habitat. Lacking such, the populations of several of these species may again diminish just as they once did during a bygone era of exploitation.

Old Barney: Beacon of the Jersey Shore

Of the dozens of lighthouses on the Atlantic coast, the Barnegat Light stands with perhaps three others as the dominant icon of a "candle in the wind," once a lonely sentinel for mariners and now a must-see landmark for tourists (fig. 4.6). The tower stands 162 feet tall and requires scaling 217 steps to reach the light; in daytime, mariners easily identified its pattern of contrasting colors: half red (top), half white (bottom). Fondly known as Old Barney, the structure was commissioned on January 1, 1859, and remained in service until deactivated in 1944, in part because a lightship anchored offshore in 1927 lessened its necessity. Both Old Barney and its short-lived predecessor (1835–1857) were built in response to the considerable loss of ships along the New Jersey coast, which triggered the nametag Graveyard of the Atlantic, a designation later associated with the coast of North Carolina. In 1971, the National Register of Historic Places formally recognized Old Barney, whose light was ceremoniously illuminated again in 2009, 150 years to the day after it first beamed across the waves.

The history of Old Barney includes more than its former role as a guiding light for ships at sea. One of these concerns its designer, then a lieutenant and later the victorious general at Gettysburg, a battle widely acknowledged as the turning point in the Civil War. George Meade (1815–1872) graduated from West Point in 1831 but remained in the army only briefly—just long enough to engage in the Seminole Uprising—before resigning to work as a civil engineer for the War Department. In 1842, he rejoined the army as a second lieutenant in the Corps of

FIGURE 4.6. Affectionately known as Old Barney, the lighthouse at Barnegat Inlet has long served as a beacon for mariners and, incidentally, helped form what is today the U.S. Fish and Wildlife Service (see text). Photo credit: Pernille Ruhalter.

Topographical Engineers, serving gallantly in the Mexican-American War. After the war, he designed and built lighthouses and breakwaters, including the lights at Absecon and Cape May. His innovative designs included one known as a screwpile, which twisted the tower's corkscrew-like supports into unstable bottoms, and another in which a cylindrical inner tube was surrounded by a thick cone-shaped wall.

Less well-known is the role Old Barney played in the history of wildlife conservation. In 1789, in one of its first acts, Congress assumed jurisdiction over the 12 lighthouses operated by the colonies and authorized construction of others—clear recognition of the economic importance of shipping to the new nation. For birds, however, the unblinking beams proved fatal; first lured, then blinded, thousands collided each year into the thick glass surrounding the lantern, especially during migration periods. The toll did not go unnoticed by naturalists, including famed artist John James Audubon (1785–1851), who wrote in his *Ornithological Biography* that during snowstorms Canada geese sometimes "fly against beacons and lighthouses, dashing their heads against the walls in the middle of the day. In the night they are attracted by the light of these buildings and now and then a whole flock is caught on such occasions." Similarly, village crank and literary giant Henry David Thoreau reported birds dead from "broken necks" littering the ground at the base of a lighthouse at Cape Cod. Thoreau erred, however, in his postmortem diagnosis: more than a century later, X-rays revealed that most birds colliding with windows die from head injuries, not broken necks.

Still, it was C. (for Clinton) Hart Merriam (1855–1942), then an undergraduate at Yale and not yet 22, who brought lighthouse-bird collisions to center stage in 1877 with a 165-page study of the birds of Connecticut, a paper that established his reputation as a naturalist with a bright future. He wrote, "Hundreds of thousands of birds [die each year during migration] by flying against lighthouse towers." One of his sources, a keeper at the Faulkner Island Light, reported finding 200 to 300 dead birds at the foot of the tower on a May morning in 1877; that same night, about the same number collided with the light at the entrance of New Haven Bay. Whereas Merriam lamented the loss of the birds, which included rare as well as common species, he recognized that the toll represented a unique source of biological information, notably including species-specific migration schedules. The dead birds indeed had a story to tell.

In New Jersey, bird collisions began almost immediately after Old Barney went into operation. In February 1859, the keeper reported damage caused by waterfowl, to which the district responded by ordering wire netting placed about the lamp house. Unfortunately, the fate befalling most of Old Barney's log books remains uncertain; some may eventually turn up, long buried in archives or forgotten in dusty attics, whereas fires perhaps destroyed others. Nonetheless, we can deduce that the wire screen provided little help, as an entry for April 1925 in the logbook at the Barnegat Light Museum reports that gulls flew into the lantern and broke three panes of glass, leaving 60 dead gulls at the site. In October of the same year, a far larger toll occurred when birds ranging in size from cormorants to warblers were killed; as cited by Witmer Stone, no fewer than 500 birds of 30 species littered the ground near the foot of Old Barney at a density of 25 per square yard. Waterfowl, because of their large size and abundance, often caused the most damage at this and other lighthouses, and it is with some degree of irony that the 1991 New Jersey Waterfowl Stamp, a purchase required by all of the state's waterfowl hunters more than 16 years old, featured a flock of Atlantic brant flying safely past Old Barney's colorful tower (fig. 4.7). Similarly, the 1996 federal duck stamp displayed a pair of surf scoters flying by Old Barney.

Merriam went on to medical school but ended his successful practice after just six years, which he exchanged for a career dedicated to natural history, just at the time ornithology was gaining a wide following in scientific circles. Indeed, in 1873, a group of prominent ornithologists, Merriam included, met in New York and founded what is now known as the American Ornithological Society (AOS). Although one of the younger attendees, Merriam was elected secretary of the new organization and named chairman of the important Committee on Bird Migration. As part of his efforts to determine some characteristics of migration, he again enlisted the help of lighthouse keepers as a source of useful information and specimens. Lighthouse collisions, unlike other observations, recorded nighttime movements and, with the dead birds in hand, provided Merriam with a means to confirm the identifications made by the keepers.

The strategy worked and produced a flood of responses (in the process making the keepers rather good at identifying birds and even taxidermy). Merriam, in fact, could not handle the volume of data and advised his colleagues at the 1884 AOS meeting that he needed help. In response, the organization authorized Merriam to ask Congress to establish a Division of Economic Ornithology in the Depart-

FIGURE 4.7. The 1991 New Jersey duck stamp featured two hallmarks of Barnegat Bay—its iconic lighthouse and flocks of brant. Besides a valid hunting license, waterfowl hunters in New Jersey each year must purchase both state and federal duck stamps, which are also collected by philatelists. Photo credit: Dale Lockwood.

ment of Agriculture. The effort was approved in the Senate, but the House insisted that the work be conducted within the existing Division of Entomology, and in 1885 Merriam was appointed to direct the work. A year later, Merriam's unit gained independent status as the Division of Economic Ornithology and Mammalogy. Much of the work strayed from the control of predators and pests or the economic importance of birds and mammals—the rationale for the unit's existence—and little came of the lighthouse data. Instead, the focus centered on surveys of mammals and their taxonomic status. For Merriam, minute differences in the skulls of brown bears became a consuming interest, and he split the bears into dozens of species and subspecies, most of which are no longer recognized.

In 1895, the agency became the Division of Biological Survey and was again renamed in 1905 as the Bureau of Biological Survey. Merriam, after 25 years at the helm, left the bureau in 1910 and pivoted his interests to Indian cultures, particularly for tribes in California. In 1940, the bureau was combined with the Fish

Commission in the Department of Commerce and transferred to the Department of the Interior as the U.S. Fish and Wildlife Service, which remains today as the federal government's lead agency for the management and conservation of wildlife resources.

All told, a path that began when nineteenth-century lighthouse keepers swamped a young physician with their tallies of dead birds led to an agency whose responsibilities today include wildlife refuges, fish hatcheries, endangered species, waterfowl and other migratory birds, and legions of other national and international management and regulatory activities. And Old Barney, standing tall in one of the major migration routes for North American birds, played a role never imagined by its talented designer-engineer, then a junior officer who would later become a national hero on a battlefield in Pennsylvania.

The Manasquan Canal

Canals sometimes produce unintended consequences along with the economic benefits for which they were carved into the land. The Suez Canal, entirely at sea level, allowed fishes from the Red Sea access to the eastern Mediterranean, a movement known as Lessepsian migration, named after the canal's builder, Ferdinand de Lesseps (1805–1894). Strangely, the migration seldom included movements in the other direction, and the composition of the fish fauna changed little in the Red Sea. In 1932, expansion of the Welland Canal, which skirts the natural barrier of Niagara Falls, enabled an invasion of sea lampreys into the upper Great Lakes, where they soon decimated a fishery dependent on lake trout.

Although hardly on the same scale, completion of the Manasquan Canal—some prefer Point Pleasant Canal—in 1926 nonetheless caused an inflow of salt water into the northern reaches of Barnegat Bay where the water was more fresh than saline (fig. 4.8). The impact of this perturbation went unrecorded by scientists of the day and thus lacks contemporary documentation. Today such a project would require an environmental impact statement brimming with surveys and potential threats as determined by squads of specialists. Still, the changes did not evade those laymen of the day who maintained close contact with the bay, in part because of its importance to their livelihood. Indeed, oysters, which once survived in the upper bay, now were no longer protected from a major predator, the Atlantic

FIGURE 4.8. Completion of the Manasquan (or Point Pleasant) Canal in 1926 allowed sea-strength salt water to enter and overwhelm the freshwater environment at the north end of Barnegat Bay. Photo credit: Pernille Ruhalter.

oyster drill, a snail that requires a full dose of salinity to survive. Years later, experiments disclosed that these destroyers of oysters, notably including the thin-shelled immature form known as spats, cannot tolerate salinities of less than 15 parts per thousand (seawater, by comparison, hovers at about 35 ppt, or 3.5 percent salt). One experiment revealed that salinities of 10 ppt killed the drills in seven days. Hence, a powerful bar to the presence of oyster drills was removed when the canal connected Barnegat Bay with the Manasquan River near its mouth to the ocean. The ravaged oyster population in the upper bay steadily ebbed as the drills reduced the breeders and, even more critically, the nursery stock for their replacement.

Oyster drills rely on a keen sense of smell to locate their prey, which are typically sessile (i.e., immobile and permanently attached to a substrate), hence even these slow-moving predators can steadily close in for the kill. As implied, an oyster drill bores a single circular hole, as if punctured by a pin, through the shells of their prey, which also include mussels and other mollusks. They bore using a radula equipped with thousands of minute teeth arranged in rows not unlike a rasp. Although aided by an acidic secretion to soften their victim's shell, the drilling proceeds slowly but eventually reaches and destroys the soft body tissues inside. A tubular proboscis encasing the radula then sucks up the meaty scraps. When the wounded oyster can no longer close its shells, crabs and fishes often devour the exposed remains before the drill has finished its meal.

Before completion of the canal, bass, yellow perch, bluegill, and other game fishes thrived in the Metedeconk River, which flowed into the upper end of Barnegat Bay and offered excellent fishing in what radio newsman and columnist Fred Van Deventer called a freshwater paradise. When the digging ended, however, the southern end of the canal entered the bay near the river's mouth, forever ending this paradise—and the fishing—when the water in the upper bay turned salty and tides for the first time influenced the local biota. Stands of wild celery and other freshwater plants once flourished in the same area and attracted several kinds of ducks, including redheads, American wigeon, and canvasbacks. But these too—vegetation and waterfowl alike—disappeared when salt water overwhelmed the system. The types of decoys produced in the area also reflect these changes, albeit inferentially. Carvers producing decoys prior to completion of the canal regularly included redhead decoys in their repertoire of species, but they thereafter dropped these after the once-common birds went elsewhere; those redhead decoys still in use were repainted to mimic scaup or even black ducks, both of which commonly overwinter in saline waters.

Mallards and Coastal Developments

The post–World War II period brought a boom of development to the shores of Barnegat Bay, virtually all of which preceded by two decades the watchful eyes of state and federal agencies later dedicated to monitoring environmental protection. Suburban lagoons, in particular, were dredged from the bay's marshes as sites for water-access homes perched along the edges of bulkheaded channels (fig. 4.9).

Shore Note 4.2 Seagulls They're Not

The beaches, bays, and marshes along the Jersey Shore teem with several species of gregarious, mostly white birds. To many enjoying the sun and water, these are simply "seagulls," a convenient but none too accurate collective terms for gulls and terns. True, both groups share a common family—Laridae—but each nonetheless differs from the other in enough ways to be assigned to separate subfamilies. Depending on the season, at least six species of gulls commonly occur along the Jersey Shore, as do five species of terns; other species of both groups occur irregularly or in lessor numbers.

Gulls (Larinae), in comparison with terns (Sterninae), are bulky and broad winged, with square or rounded tails. They skim for floating food as well as patrol shorelines on foot to scavenge on just about any sort of morsel they can find and swallow (and sometimes fight among themselves over those they cannot). Dumps attract large numbers of gulls, which also kill and eat the chicks of other birds as well as prey on newly hatched turtles. Their bills are robust and slightly hooked. Gulls also commonly land and swim on water, which terns rarely, if ever, do. Some species soar with the wind. In their summer breeding plumage, laughing gulls have black heads, whereas the heads of others commonly seen in summertime New Jersey are entirely white. Immature birds of the larger species take at least two years to attain their adult plumage.

Terns, sleek-bodied and narrow winged, have forked tails, a feature that varies in its extent by species. They fly more gracefully than gulls, usually with their slender bills pointing downward toward the water. When foraging, terns often hover briefly before plunge diving for small fish; dumps do not attract terns. In breeding plumage, most species have black caps, which are crested in two species occurring along the Atlantic coast, but in winter the front of the cap (i.e., forehead) turns white. Terns develop their adult plumage within a year after hatching.

A prominent red spot tips the otherwise yellow lower bill of several species of gulls. The sight of it triggers begging behavior in hungry chicks, to which the parent birds (of either sex) respond by disgorging food into the mouths of their young. Niko Tinbergen (1907–1988), who studied this relationship in herring gulls, identified the red spot as a releaser for a type of innate behavior known as a fixed action pattern. For this and other behavioral research, Tinbergen shared a Nobel Prize in 1973 for medicine or physiology (oddly, the awards include no prize for biology). A challenge for some aspects of his work with gulls later arose, but his concept of a releaser—the red spot in this case—remains widely accepted.

Great black-backed gulls, with their five-foot wingspan, outsize all other species of larids and indeed is the largest gull in the world. Once shot for their plumage, the birds slowly regained their former numbers and, aided by food-rich dumps, extended their northern breeding range southward to New Jersey and beyond. Herring gulls likewise have extended their breeding range southward to include New Jersey. Other commonly seen species in New Jersey include laughing and ring-billed gulls and common and least terns. New Jersey lists the latter as endangered because of poor reproduction (i.e., they nest on sandy beaches subject to human disturbances, flooding, and predation). Uniquely, gull-billed terns regularly feed in marshes where they forage on insects instead of diving for fish. In the early 1800s, Alexander Wilson observed gull-billed terns darting after large black spiders in the marshes at Cape May. The stomachs of several birds he examined were "crammed with a mass of these spiders alone," but their identity remains a mystery.[1] Herring gulls have learned to crack open shellfish simply by dropping them on hard surfaces. This behavior, passed on from one generation to the next, presumably originated when a careless gull accidently dropped a clam or mussel and discovered an easy way to access a tasty meal; it was later bolstered when roads and other hard surfaces appeared on the coastal landscape. Young gulls lack the foraging prowess of adults but, in keeping with this and other learned behaviors, become more proficient as they mature. Roadways, typically near tidal creeks, littered with broken shells provide telltale evidence of gull-dropped shellfish (flat tires at these drop zones provide indirect evidence). Ribbed mussels are exposed and readily accessible at low tide, but just how herring gulls extract clams buried in mud remains unclear. Somewhat strangely, only herring gulls have adopted this behavior in New Jersey despite the presence of other species (e.g., laughing gulls).

Gulls have also learned to grab French fries and other finger foods from people otherwise enjoying the Jersey Shore, most notably at Ocean City, where a particularly brazen gull once pitched headlong into a stroller on the boardwalk to seize a slice of pizza from a startled toddler. Indeed, the birds' summer diet at these locations may be dominated by food stolen from unsuspecting beachgoers instead of those naturally available in marshes, wrack lines, and swash zones. The aggressive gulls have thus become a nuisance in search of a humane remedy. The answer: daily flights of hawks and falcons trained for the ancient art of falconry; by their intimidating presence, the raptors disperse the gulls but, being well fed by their handlers, seldom make a kill. Known as abatement falconry, the practice, which requires a federal permit, offers an effective but bloodless control of troublesome birds. It also returns the gulls to their natural diet and feeding behavior, including the removal of smelly refuse from beachfronts.

------

[1] The scientific community does not teem with spider experts, and neither of the two I located could reliably pinpoint a candidate to support Wilson's observations. However, I am indebted to one of these authorities, Michael L. Draney, who suggested that the arthropod in question might not be a spider at all but a crab. His insight led me to single out marsh crabs, creatures about 1.5 inches in size, purplish black (both sexes), and common in eastern salt marshes as a good match for the mysterious "spider." Still, I find it hard to imagine that Wilson could mistake a crab for a spider, given that crabs have hardened exoskeletons, stalked eyes, and clawed appendages, which are especially obvious in male fiddler crabs. Nonetheless, Wilson's description seems more consistent with a marsh crab than with any spider currently known and may reflect his limited knowledge of certain invertebrates. Some modern accounts of the foods eaten by gull-billed terns indeed list the unmistakable fiddler crab, and a study conducted in Texas recorded three unidentified spiders that were fed to nestlings. In general, however, I think it probable that virtually all references to spiders as a staple in the diet of gull-billed terns originated in the literature when one source cited another, thereby collectively perpetuating a single, and perhaps mistaken, identification made in a Cape May salt marsh of two centuries past.

FIGURE 4.9. Large areas of Barnegat Bay's shoreline were developed with lagoons and homes before environmental laws protected these and other wetlands. The lagoons attract mallards that readily adapt to the highly altered habitat. Photo credit: Pernille Ruhalter.

Only narrow strips of marsh vegetation survive along the bulkheads in what are otherwise highly manicured environments with little resemblance to waterfowl habitat. Mallards, the most ubiquitous and adaptable of waterfowl, nonetheless cope—and persist—in these conditions, nesting and rearing their broods in a man-made world well infused with human traffic. Nesting sites include ornamental shrubs, wood piles, turned-over boats, and flower gardens. Moreover, some mallards migrating from their northern breeding grounds found the lagoons satisfactory as winter quarters.

Unlike their "wild" counterparts, however, the urban mallards face challenges that include a new suite of threats. Not the least of these are house cats and herring gulls that prey heavily on the ducklings around the clock, a situation made worse by the lack of protective cover. Some structures, notably storm sewers, claim entire broods when the ducklings fall through the grillwork as they trail behind their mothers down the streets, leaving frantic hens pacing helplessly on the pavement above. According to one study, 72 percent of the ducklings hatching in these urbanized environments are lost before fledging, and 40 percent of these include the loss of the entire brood, in all almost twice the mortality rate for ducklings hatched in marshes. The scarcity of invertebrate foods—the foundation in the diet of mallard ducklings—in the lagoons no doubt further contributes to poor survival. On the upside, the man-made environment supports few egg-eating predators (e.g., fish crows) in comparison with nesting habitat in the surrounding marshes, resulting in far greater hatching success. Accidents involving cars and phone wires claim adult mallards, and the potential for disease increases as well. Botulism, for example, flourishes in stagnate water, especially when decaying organic matter accumulates, as is the case when humans throw bread and other scraps to ducks waiting near docks.

Lagoon-dwelling mallards provide residents with year-round aesthetic values and, in season, contribute to the annual waterfowl harvest. Homeowners generally take a proprietary interest in the birds, which become relatively tame in the lagoons, although the same birds behave warily elsewhere, a flexible behavior of obvious significance. The few complaints expressed by residents focus on messy yards and the potential for contaminated water (i.e., the man-made channels hinder water circulation, which diminishes regular flushing). All told, lagoon developments along the Jersey Shore now provide well-established albeit uncharacteristic habitat for waterfowl.

Shore Note 4.3 Middens: Learning from Shell Piles

Archaeologists love middens, those piles of ancient trash that reveal much about cultures of bygone ages. These troves yield various types of information, but the most obvious revelations concern dietary preferences and, by inference, the tools and methods of securing food. For the Native Americans who once lived in southern New Jersey, Barnegat Bay was a bountiful source of provisions, not the least of which were shellfish—lots of them. To reap this bounty, people of the Middle Woodland Culture (200 B.C.E. to 500 C.E.) traveled seasonally to the shore from their permanent villages farther inland. At the end of the harvest, they carefully piled the shells at locations that remained in use for generations.

Today, the best-known shell midden in New Jersey appears as a prominent mound in a marsh near Tuckerton; many others disappeared when they were mined to provide flux for the iron furnaces in the Pine Barrens. Because of its higher elevation, the Tuckerton mound supports a clump of red cedars, giving the midden an island-like presence in a sea of marshland. Nineteenth-century farmers mined the shell heap as a source of lime for their fields, but the midden still presents an impressive structure of about 100 feet in length, 50 feet in width, and rising about 12 feet above the marsh; and it may extend as much as 14 feet belowground. As such, it once served as a landmark for mariners sailing along the adjacent coastline. The midden developed at the edge of a bay, but rising sea levels later transformed the surrounding area into the marshland present today.

The shells of the clam also known as the northern quahog form most of the midden, but a few oyster and whelk shells also occur. Quahogs still remain plentiful in the region and elsewhere along the Atlantic coastline. To preserve this food, Native Americans likely cured the meat on drying racks erected over a fire, hence charcoal often occurs at shell middens. After a day's drying, the meat assumed the consistency of beef jerky and remained edible for weeks and months. Larger clams—those more than three inches in length and known today as "chowders"—were preferred, from which the meat from 12 would represent an average serving.

So far, virtually no artifacts, including any evidence of stone tools designed to open the clams, have turned up in the Tuckerton midden. Instead, fresh clams were most likely opened with another clam, which was accomplished by striking the stout "beak" or umbo, a knobby projection near the hinge, of the unopened hammer clam against the shells of other clams. Based on simulations, a shell used in this way could open 20 to 30 clams before the tool itself broke. Replacements, of course, were immediately at hand. Large numbers of shells in the Tuckerton midden showed evidence that suggested they were opened in just such a fashion, whereas the beaks of others had been shattered. Carbon dating of one shell tool indicated the midden was active some 1,530 years ago. Given the lack of stones at the site, some of the broken shells likely provided material for knives, scrapers, and projectile points.

Another midden, this one located near the mouth of Oyster Creek, consists of eastern oyster shells. Many of these grew to lengths of 8 to 10 inches, far larger than the 3- to 4-inch oysters of the present time. Few of the ancient shells bear the telltale borings of oyster drills, a predatory snail that centuries later would devastate local and regional oyster populations. A midden in Cape May County reflects changes associated with rising sea levels. Oyster shells dominate the oldest deposits, but as the water deepened, oysters became steadily less available for harvest. Over time, the composition of the midden gradually changed until the upper, younger strata consisted only of quahog shells, thereby indicating a dietary change necessitated by rising sea levels.

These cultural sites also exert ecological influences. Shell middens on the Delmarva Peninsula, for example, support a distinctive flora that includes species seldom found elsewhere in the region. In a greatly dissimilar habitat—the temperate rainforests on the coast of British Columbia— western red cedars growing on shell middens grew taller, produced more radial growth, and suffered less top die-back than trees of the same species growing adjacent to the middens. The vegetation growing on shell middens may also be of greater diversity and provide more cover. These effects result from enriching the soil with the persistent release of calcium and phosphorous as well as by improving both the drainage and soil pH.

A School for Decoys and Their Carvers

In 1924, the earliest known duck decoys were discovered in a dusty cave near a marsh in Nevada, left there at least 1,000 years earlier by a now vanished Indian civilization known as Tule Eaters. These relics, 11 in number, were crafted from reeds and decorated with feathers, some of which were remarkably lifelike replicas of canvasbacks. The Tule Eaters, and no doubt other Native Americans, clearly understood the gregarious nature of waterfowl and used replicas to lure wary birds into range of their weapons, just as duck hunters do today. They also unknowingly established what centuries later became a unique and highly collectable form of American folk art (fig. 4.10).

At Barnegat Bay, two ecological settings forged a culture of waterfowl hunters, some of whom were also skilled craftsman. The first of these, of course, concerns the combination of abundant wetland habitat and equally abundant waterfowl of several species, including brant, black ducks, greater scaup, and, at one time,

FIGURE 4.10. Wooden decoys, originally produced for waterfowl hunting ("working decoys"), today represent a form of American folk art highly desired by collectors. Those carved by Harry V. Shourds (1861–1920) represent a style associated with Barnegat Bay, as shown here by an Atlantic brant (top), common goldeneye (middle), and American black duck (bottom) on display at the Tuckerton Seaport, a project of the Barnegat Bay Decoy and Baymen's Museum Inc. Photo credits: Pernille Ruhalter.

redheads and canvasbacks, among others. The second was the local availability of wood admirably suited for decoys—Atlantic white cedar, whose straight-grained, rot-resistant wood was also easy to carve (see chapter 7). The same wood likewise was favored by Barnegat's boat builders, who concurrently developed a lightweight, low-profile craft—the sneakbox—expressly designed for duck hunting. Not only did sneakboxes provide hunters with transportation to their favorite hunting areas, but a single man could also haul the craft into dense marsh vegetation for concealment, thereby forgoing any need for constructing a fixed blind. Other hunters took advantage of the sneakbox's low profile and anchored their craft in open water near or within a spread of decoys. Meanwhile, in their barns and workshops carvers were producing decoys, each in their own form and style, yet with features in common with other carvers in the area. Thus was born a "school" not unlike those of landscape painters (e.g., the Hudson River School), of which the Tuckerton School became the best known of those associated with Barnegat Bay. Other locations (e.g., Chesapeake Bay, MD, and Currituck Sound, NC) likewise produced their own schools whose distinctive regional patterns later became touchstones for avid decoy collectors.

Decoys carved in the tradition of Barnegat Bay are hollow (as opposed to the solid bodies typical of decoys carved at, say, Chesapeake Bay) and fashioned from two pieces of well-seasoned Atlantic white cedar. Oddly, the planks are not of the same thickness, with the thinner of the two located at the bottom. The planks were joined temporarily to shape the body with a draw knife and rasp, then separated and hollowed out by hand, often with a small adz-like gouge specifically developed for this purpose and known as a dugout tool. Consequently, the decoys themselves are sometimes cited as "dugouts." Experienced carvers could chip out these hollows so that the walls were just three-eighths to a half inch thick. That done, the head and neck—often carved from pine—were attached with nails driven through to the upper section and the halves permanently united with white lead paste and nails. The fully assembled decoys were then sanded and painted, with the latter often reflecting the individual style of each carver.

Because they were hollow, the decoys rode high in the water, which increased their visibility to passing waterfowl, and their light weight allowed more to be carried in sneakboxes. For ballast, most Barnegat decoys have rounded bottoms weighted with pads of lead that are attached with nails or screws, but some carvers in Tuckerton and Manahawkin instead poured hot lead into rectangular recesses cut into the wood to maintain the clean lines of their decoys. Detailed carving appears only around the bill and consisted of nostrils, nail tip, and curved groves that separate the mandibles from the rest of the head; otherwise, the bodies typically lack any carved features. Some claim that the heads of Barnegat decoys are larger than normal, but, if so, the slight difference fails as a reliable criterion for their identification. The decoys representing most species bear distinctive blade-like tails set midway on the vertical axis of the body, but high tails distinguish those of geese and brant. Another regional feature concerns the leather loops attached to the bottom front of the decoys to which the anchor lines were tied; these connections often remain on decoys still in their original condition.

These decoys were seldom signed—carvers elsewhere commonly branded their initials into the undersides of their productions—but, for practiced eyes, the above distinctions signal those originating from Barnegat Bay. The design reached its ultimate form around 1880, with the hollow construction apparently representing the final development in the transition from earlier styles.

A number of carvers in the area were known for their skills, but Harry V. Shourds (1861–1920) of the Tuckerton School reigns foremost among the lot. A house painter by trade, he also spent considerable time as a bayman, but decoy carving filled much of his time, and remarkably his lifetime production numbered in the thousands. The story goes that Shourds would go to the barbershop with a sawed-out blank and pocketknife, sit down, and carve away under the barber's apron to produce a flawless decoy head by the time his haircut was finished. His particular style featured high-domed heads and a short lateral groove near the bill tip to indicate the mandibles. Shourds sold his decoys for $6 per dozen, but collectors today pay tens of thousands—or more—for just one in the best of condition. Shourds established a lineage of decoy carvers—all with the same first name—beginning with his son, Harry M. Shourds (1890–1943), and later his grandson, Harry V. Shourds II (1930–2017). Decoy collectors also prize the distinctive decoys of Harry Grant (1860–1924) and Taylor Johnson (1863–1924), among others, as representative of Barnegat Bay.

Regrettably, Barnegat Bay did not escape the stain of market hunting that came to the fore in the late 1800s coincident with the flush of decoy carvers. Railroad access to the coast opened markets for perishable goods and the rapid growth of urban centers hungry for fresh meat (e.g., Philadelphia, which increased its population elevenfold between 1850 and 1900) together spurred the commercial exploitation of wildlife. The story is part of a larger and certainly grim chapter in conservation history often highlighted by the unyielding slaughter of bison and passenger pigeons. At Barnegat Bay, waterfowl of course were the primary targets, and dozens were killed with a single shot from so-called punt guns—effectively small cannons—some with bores nearly two inches in diameter. Some punt guns weighed more than the men pulling the triggers—and some models were double barreled. These massive firearms were charged with large doses of powder and one to two pounds of shot, and commonly fired before dawn at rafts of sleeping ducks. The punt guns rested on chocks mounted on low-riding boats, which were often painted white to lessen their visibility on the water's surface—a shrewd means of camouflage that enabled gunners to hide in the path of the moon's reflection as they approached their unsuspecting quarry. Shorebirds—sandpipers and plovers, among others—were also targets for market hunters, and they too were lured into gunning range with decoys. The wanton harvest at Barnegat Bay ended up in the dining rooms at fashionable hotels, particularly in Philadelphia.

Few records survive to fully document the extent of market hunting at Barnegat Bay, but in 1899, a hunter operating out of Barnegat Village killed 115 ducks in one day's shooting, not counting escaped cripples, and lamented that the toll would have been higher had he not run out of powder. Another reports that a shipment of 800 brant left Tuckerton bound for the Philadelphia market on a Saturday night in 1901. Similar situations prevailed elsewhere. At Chesapeake Bay, for example, market hunters operated perhaps 100 punt guns, and the blasts from several of these reportedly killed more than 400 ducks at a time and, overall, might bag as many as 15,000 ducks in a single day—by any measure, unsustainable plundering of a wildlife resource. Similarly, a group of market hunters in Iowa shot an average of 1,000 ducks per week. Thankfully, all of this ended in 1918 when Congress enacted the Migratory Bird Treaty Act, which established the framework for waterfowl hunting seasons and bag limits as well as ending all hunting for most species of shorebirds, songbirds, and, yes, whooping cranes (fig. 4.11).

FIGURE 4.11. Staggering numbers of waterfowl were shot without limit before enactment of the Migratory Bird Treaty Act in 1918. The toll at Barnegat Bay included birds shot expressly for sale at markets in nearby Philadelphia and New York City. The bag often included shorebirds as well as waterfowl. Photo from the collection of Wayne Capooth.

Readings and References

General

Jahn, R. 2000. Down Barnegat Bay: a nor'easter midnight reader. Plexus, Medford, NJ. [See p. 60 for the full poem, written in 1899 by "Capt. Bunk," from which the epigraph was excerpted.]

Kennish, M. J. 2001. Physical description of Barnegat Bay–Little Egg Harbor estuarine system. Journal of Coastal Research Special Issue 32:13–27.

Kennish, M. J., and R. A. Lutz (eds.). 1984. Ecology of Barnegat Bay, New Jersey. Springer-Verlag, New York.

Lincoln, F. C. 1935. Waterfowl flyways of North America. U.S. Department of Agriculture Circular 342, Washington, DC. [By the same author, see also The migrations of American birds. 1939. Doubleday, Doran, & Company, New York.]

Lloyd, J. B. 1990. Six miles at sea—a pictorial history of Long Beach Island, New Jersey. Down the Shore Publishing, Harvey Cedars, NJ.

Mountford, K. 2002. Closed sea: from Manasquan to the Mullica—a history of Barnegat Bay. Down the Shore Publishing, West Creek, NJ.

Eelgrass: Underwater Meadows in Barnegat Bay

Barry, T. W. 1962. Effect of late seasons on Atlantic brant reproduction. Journal of Wildlife Management 26:19–26.

Bologna, P. A. X., and M. S. Sinnema. 2012. Restoration of seagrass habitat in New Jersey, United States. Journal of Coastal Research 28:99–104.

Campanella, J. J., P. A. X. Bologna, J. V. Smalley, et al. 2013. An analysis of the population genetics of restored *Zostera marina* plantings in Barnegat Bay, New Jersey. Population Ecology 55:121–133.

Campanella, J. J., P. A. X. Bologna, S. M. Smith, et al. 2010. *Zostera marina* population genetics in Barnegat Bay, New Jersey, and implications for grass bed restoration. Population Ecology 52:181–190.

Campbell, B. C., and K. W. Able. 1998. Life history characteristics of the northern pipefish, *Syngnathus fuscus*, in southern New Jersey. Estuaries 21:470–475.

Carlton, J. T., G. J. Vermeij, D. R. Lindberg, et al. 1991. The first historical extinction of a marine invertebrate in an ocean basin: the demise of the eelgrass limpet *Lottia alveus*. Biological Bulletin 180:72–80.

Carson, R. 1962. Silent spring. Houghton Mifflin, Boston.

Cottam, C. 1934. Eelgrass disappearance has serious effects on waterfowl and industry. Pp. 191–193 in Yearbook of agriculture. U.S. Department of Agriculture, Washington, DC. [See for the commercial uses of eelgrass.]

Cottam, C., J. J. Lynch, and A. L. Nelson. 1944. Food habits and management of American sea brant. Journal of Wildlife Management 8:36–56. [The classic account for the crash of brant populations following the catastrophic loss of eelgrass in the early 1930s. See Kirby and Obrecht (1982) for a challenge to the size of the brant population prior to the eelgrass die-off.]

Dennison, W. C., G. J. Marshall, and C. Wigand. 1989. Effect of "brown tide" shading eelgrass (*Zostera marina* L.) distributions. Pp. 675–692 in Novel phystoplankton blooms: causes and impacts of recurrent brown tides (E. M. Cosper, V. M. Bricelj, and E. J. Carpenter, eds.). Springer-Verlag, Berlin.

Dexter, R. W. 1944. Ecological significance of the disappearance of eelgrass at Cape Ann, Massachusetts. Journal of Wildlife Management 8:173–176.

———. 1947. The marine communities of a tidal inlet at Cape Ann, Massachusetts: a study in bio-ecology. Ecological Monographs 17:261–294.

Fonesca, M. S., J. J. Fisher, J. C. Zieman, and G. W. Thayer. 1982. Influence of the seagrass, *Zostera marina* L., on current flow. Estuarine, Coastal, and Shelf Science 15:351–364.

Gastrich, M. D., R. Lathrop, S. Haag, et al. 2004. Assessment of brown tide blooms, caused by *Aureococcus anophagefferens*, and contributing factors in New Jersey coastal bays: 2000–2002. Harmful Algae 3:305–320.

Hansens, E. J. 1951. The stable fly and its effect on seashore recreational areas in New Jersey. Journal of Economic Entomology 44:482–487.

Kirby, R., and F. Ferrigno. 1980. Winter, waterfowl, and the saltmarsh. New Jersey Outdoors 7 (Nov.–Dec.):10–13.

Kirby, R. E. and H. H. Obrecht III. 1980. Atlantic brant-human commensalism on eelgrass in New Jersey. Wildfowl 31:158–160.

———. 1982. Recent changes in the North American distribution and abundance of wintering Atlantic brant. Journal of Field Ornithology 53:333–341.

Lewis, H. 1932. The eelgrass situation on the Atlantic coast. Transactions of the American Game Conference 19:411–423.

McRoy, C. P., and C. Helfferich. 1980. Applied aspects of seagrasses. Pp. 297–343 in Handbook of seagrass biology: an ecosystem perspective (R. C. Phillips and C. P. McRoy, eds.). Garland STPM Press, New York.

Milne, L. J., and M. J. Milne. 1951. The eelgrass catastrophe. Scientific American 184(1):52–55.

Muehlstein, L. K., D. Porter, and F. T. Short. 1991. *Labyrinthula zostere* sp. nov., the causative agent of wasting disease of eelgrass. Mycologia 83:180–191. [Provides conclusive evidence, some sixty years after the event, that a previously unknown species of slime mold caused the massive die-off.]

Renn, C. E. 1937. The eelgrass situation along the middle Atlantic coast. Ecology 18:323–325.

Sand-Jensen, K. 1977. Effects of epiphytes on eelgrass photosynthesis. Aquatic Botany 3:55–63.

Short, F. T., L. K. Muehlstein, and D. Porter. 1987. Eelgrass wasting disease: cause and recurrence of a marine epidemic. Biological Bulletin 173:557–562.

Smith, L. M., L. D. Vangilder, and R. A. Kennamer. 1985. Foods of wintering brant in eastern North America. Journal of Field Ornithology 56:286–289.

Stauffer, R. C. 1937. Changes in the invertebrate community of a lagoon after disappearance of the eelgrass. Ecology 18:437–431.

Thayer, G. W., W. J. Kenworthy, and M. S. Fonseca. 1984. The ecology of eelgrass meadows of the Atlantic coast: a community profile. FWS/OBS-84/02. U.S. Fish and Wildlife Service, Washington, DC.

Vaughn, D. E. 1982. Production ecology of eelgrass (*Zostera marina* L.) and its epiphytes in Little Egg Harbor, New Jersey. PhD diss., Rutgers, the State University of New Jersey, New Brunswick.

Wicklund, R. I., S. J. Wilk, and L. Ogren. 1968. Observations on wintering locations of the northern pipefish and spotted seahorse. Underwater Naturalist 5(2):26–28.

Wyllie-Echeverria, S., and P. A. Cox. 1999. The seagrass (*Zostera marina* [Zosteraceae]) industry of Nova Scotia (1907–1960). Economic Botany 53:419–426. [Source for Kipling's quote and for Cabot's production of eelgrass quilts.]

Float Like a Butterfly, Sting Like a Bee

Bayha, K. M., A. G. Collins, and P. M. Gaffney. 2017. Multigene phylogeny of the scyphozoan jellyfish family Pelagiidae reveals that the common US sea nettle comprises two distinct species (*Chrysaora quinquecirrha* and *C. chesapeakei*). Peer Journal. https://doi.org/10.7717/peerj.3863.

Bologna, P. A. X., J. J. Gaynor, C. Castellano, and D. Restaino. 2014. Range expansion of the sea nettle (*Chrysaora quinquecirrha*) and its impact on pelagic food webs. ICES CM 2014/A:14. [The jellyfish population in this study, conducted in Barnegat Bay, is now recognized as *C. chesapeakei*.]

Gaynor, J. J., P. A. X. Bologna, D. J. Restaino, and C. Barry. 2016. First occurrence of the invasive hydrozoan *Gonionemus vertens* A. Agassiz 1862 (Cnidaria: Hydrozoa) in New Jersey, USA. BioInvasions Records 5:233–237.

Hoegler, B. 2019. Float like a butterfly, sting like a bee: 3 jellyfish in Barnegat Bay. Save Barnegat Bay, Toms River, NJ. [A primary source for information appearing herein, including pilfering parts of its title.]

Meredith, R. W., J. J. Gaynor, and P. A. X. Bologna. 2016. Diet assessment of the Atlantic sea nettle *Chrysaora quinquecirra* in Barnegat Bay, New Jersey, using next-generation sequencing. Molecular Ecology 25(24):6248–6266. [See previous citations regarding the subject species.]

Coastal Colonies

Blake, C. H. 1961. Notes on the history of the cattle egret in the New World. Chat 25(2):24–27. [Lists the arrival date of the birds in New Jersey and suggests how northeast trade winds likely assisted their dispersal across the Atlantic Ocean.]

Burger, J. 1978a. Competition between cattle egrets and native North American herons, egrets, and ibises. Condor 80:15–23.

———. 1978b. The pattern and mechanism of nesting in mixed-species heronries. Wading Birds, Research Report No. 7:45–58. National Audubon Society, New York.

———. 1979. Resource partitioning: nest site selection in mixed species colonies of herons, egrets and ibises. American Midland Naturalist 101:191–210.

———. 1981. Feeding competition between laughing gulls and herring gulls at a sanitary landfill. Condor 83:328–335.

———. 1984. Colony stability in least terns. Condor 86:6–67.

———. 1996. Laughing gull (*Larus atricilla*). No. 225 in The birds of North America (A. Poole and F. Gill, eds.). Academy of Natural Sciences, Philadelphia, and American Ornithologists' Union, Washington, DC.

Burger, J., and M. Gochfeld. 1990. The black skimmer, social dynamics of a colonial species. Columbia University Press, New York.

———. 1991. Nest site selection in least terns (*Sterna antillarum*) in New Jersey and New York. Colonial Waterbirds 13:31–40.

———. 2016. Habitat, population dynamics, and metal levels in colonial waterbirds, a food chain approach. CRC Press, Boca Raton, FL. [A trove of information, including a graph illustrating the dramatic impact of shooting laughing gulls near JFK International Airport.]

Burger, J., C. D. Jenkins Jr., F. Lesser, and M. Gochfeld. 2001. Status and trends of colonially-nesting birds in Barnegat Bay. Journal of Coastal Research 32:197–211. [Highlights declining numbers of active colonies and proposes ways to increase nesting areas.]

Burger, J., and J. Shisler. 1980. Colony and nest site selection in laughing gulls in response to tidal flooding. Condor 82:251–258.

Chapman, F. W. 1896. Birds and bonnets. Forest and Stream 26(5):84.

Dinsmore, J. J. 1973. Foraging success of cattle egrets, *Bubulcus ibis*. American Midland Naturalist 89:242–246.

Gochfeld, M., and J. Burger. 1994. Black skimmer (*Rynchops niger*). No. 108 in The birds of North America (A. Poole and F. Gill, eds.). Academy of Natural Sciences, Philadelphia, and American Ornithologists' Union, Washington, DC.

Grubb, T. C., Jr. 1976. Adaptiveness of foraging in the cattle egret. Wilson Bulletin 88:145–148.

Ord, G. 1817. An account of the American species of the genus *Tantalus* or *Ibis*. Journal of the Academy of Natural Sciences of Philadelphia 1:53–57. [See the appendix for current nomenclature for the glossy ibis.]

Patten, M. A., and G. W. Lasley. 2000. Range expansion of the glossy ibis in North America. North American Birds 54:241–247.

Safina, C., and J. Burger. 1983. Effects of human disturbance on reproductive success of the black skimmer. Condor 85:164–171.

Tattoni, D. J., E. A. Mordecai, and M. L. Stantial. 2020. Spatial and temporal changes in nesting behavior by black skimmers (*Rynchops niger*) in New Jersey, USA, from 1976–2019. Waterbirds 43:307–313.

Thompson, B. C., J. A. Jackson, J. Burger, L. A. Hill, E. M. Kirsch, and J. L. Atwood. 1997. Least tern (*Sternula antillarum*). No. 290 in The birds of North America (A. Poole, ed.). Academy of Natural Sciences, Philadelphia, and American Ornithologists' Union, Washington, DC.

Zusi, R. L., and D. Bridge. 1981. On the slit pupil of the black skimmer (*Rynchops niger*). Journal of Field Ornithology 52:338–340.

Old Barney: Beacon of the Jersey Shore

Audubon, J. J. 1835. Ornithological biography, or an account of the habits of the birds of the United States of America. Vol. 3. Adam & Charles Black, Edinburgh. [See pp. 10–11 in a facsimile published in 1985 by Abbeville Press and the National Audubon Society.]

Klem, D., Jr. 1990. Bird injuries, cause of death, and recuperation from collisions with windows. Journal of Field Ornithology 61:115–119.

Kraft, B. R. 1960. Under Barnegat's beam, light on happenings along the Jersey Shore. Privately printed, New York. [See p. 47 regarding collisions of ducks, geese, and brant.]

Merriam, C. H. 1877. A review of the birds of Connecticut, with remarks on their habits. Transactions of the Connecticut Academy of Arts and Science 4:1–165.

Nash, C. E. 1936. The lure of Long Beach. Long Beach Board of Trade. [See chap. 7 regarding the designation "Graveyard of the Atlantic" to characterize the frequent shipwrecks on Barnegat Shoals.]

Sterling, K. B. 1977. Last of the naturalists: the career of C. Hart Merriam. Rev. ed. Arno Press, New York.

Stick, D. 1952. Graveyard of the Atlantic: shipwrecks on the North Carolina coast. University of North Carolina Press, Chapel Hill. [This work largely overshadowed New Jersey's earlier claim as the Atlantic's "graveyard." See Nash (1936). As it happens, Stick (1919–2009) was a native of the Garden State.]

Thoreau, H. D. 1865. Cape Cod. [See p. 168 in a reprint published in 1951 by College and University Press, New Haven, CT, and arranged with notes by D. C. Hunt.]

The Manasquan Canal

Bence, J. R., R. A. Bergstedt, G. C. Christie, et al. 2003. Sea lamprey (*Petromyzon marinus*) parasite-host interactions in the Great Lakes. Journal of Great Lakes Research 29:253–282.

Galtsoff, P. S., H. F. Prytherch, and J. B. Engle. 1937. Natural history and methods for controlling the common oyster drills (*Urosalpinx cinerea* Say and *Eupleura caudate*

Say). Fishery Circular 25. Bureau of Fisheries, Washington, DC. [One of the first studies addressing the predators devastating oyster harvests on the Atlantic coast.]

Golani, D. 1998. Impact of Red Sea fish migrants through the Suez Canal on the aquatic environments of the eastern Mediterranean. Pp. 375–387 in Transformation of middle eastern natural environments: legacies and lessons (J. Albert, M. Bernhards-son, and R. Kenna, eds.). Yale Forestry and Environmental Studies Bulletin 103, New Haven, CT.

Gosner, K. L. 1985. Working decoys of the Jersey Coast and Delaware Valley. Art Alliance Press, Cranbury, NJ. [See pp. 22–25 regarding the ducks and vegetation present before completion of the Manasquan Canal. By letter, the author noted the response of the carvers when redheads later became scarce.]

Van Deventer, F. 1964. Cruising New Jersey Tidewater, a boating and touring guide. Rutgers University Press, New Brunswick, NJ. [See p. 179 regarding the freshwater "paradise" in upper Barnegat Bay.]

Mallards and Coastal Developments

Figley, W. K., and L. W. VanDruff. 1982. The ecology of urban mallards. Wildlife Monograph 81:3–40.

A School for Decoys and Their Carvers

Barber, J. 1954. Wild fowl decoys. Reprint. Dover, New York. [See p. 20 regarding market hunting at Barnegat Bay.]

Bonnell, S. 1947. Barnegat Bay. Pp. 105–112 in Duck shooting along the Atlantic Tide-water (E. V. Connett, ed.). William Morrow, New York.

Burke, P. B. 1985. Barnegat Bay decoys and gunning clubs. Ocean County Historical Society, Toms River, NJ.

Fleckenstein, H. A., Jr. 1979. Decoys of the mid-Atlantic region. Schiffer, Exton, PA.
———. 1983. New Jersey decoys. Schiffer Publishing, Exton, PA.

Gosner, K. L. 1985. Working decoys of the Jersey Coast and Delaware Valley. Cornwall Books and Art Alliance Press, Cranberry, NJ. [The best of its genre for the state.]

Grinnell, G. B. 1901. American duck shooting. Forest and Stream Publishing, New York. [By a noted conservationist and trailblazer for initiating the National Audu-bon Society; see p. 596 for the daily kill at Chesapeake Bay by market hunters.]

Kimball, D., and J. Kimball. 1969. The market hunter. Dillion Press, Minneapolis, MN.

Lloyd, J. B. 1994. Golden age of gunning. Pp. 26, 28–29 in Old Time Barnegat Bay Decoy and Gunning Show [Program notes].

Musgrove, J. W. 1949. Iowa. Pp. 193–223 in Wildfowling in the Mississippi Flyway (E. V. Connett, ed.). Van Nostrand, New York.

Starr, G. R., Jr. 1974. Decoys of the Atlantic Flyway. Winchester Press, Tulsa, OK.

Walsh, H. M. 1971. The outlaw gunner. Tidewater Publications, Centreville, MD.

Shore Note 4.1. Estuaries and Their Troubles

Baker, R. J., C. M. Wieben, R. G. Lathrop, and R. S. Nicholson. 2014. Concentrations, loads, and yields of total nitrogen and total phosphorous in the Barnegat Bay–Little Egg Harbor watershed, New Jersey. Scientific Investigations Report 2014–5072. U.S. Geological Survey, Lawrenceville, NJ.

Chizmadia, P. A., M. J. Kennish, and V. L. Ohori. 1984. Physical description of Barnegat Bay. Pp. 1–28 in Ecology of Barnegat Bay, New Jersey (M. J. Kinnish, ed.). Springer-Verlag, New York.

Kennish, M. J. 2001. Physical description of the Barnegat Bay–Little Egg Harbor estuarine system. Journal of Coastal Research (Special Issue) 32:13–27.

———. 2009. Eutrophication of Mid-Atlantic coastal bays. Bulletin of the New Jersey Academy of Science 54:1–8.

Shore Note 4.2. Seagulls They're Not

Able, K. W. 2020. Beneath the surface: understanding nature in the Mullica Valley estuary. Rutgers University Press, New Brunswick, NJ. [See pp. 130–133 for more about herring gulls dropping shellfish.]

Bent, A. C. 1921. Life histories of North American gulls and terns. U.S. Natural History Museum Bulletin 113, Washington, DC. [A standard reference, this work probably was the first in the modern era of ornithology to cite Wilson's observations. If so, it likely established a precedent for including spiders in later publications that listed the foods of gull-billed terns.]

Brewer, T. M. 1840. Wilson's American ornithology. 1970 reprint. Arno Press & the New York Times, New York. [See pp. 631–630 concerning gull-billed terns foraging on spiders.]

Burger, J. 1977. Nesting behavior of herring gulls: invasion into Spartina salt marsh areas of New Jersey. Condor 79:162–169.

———. 1978. Great black-backed gulls breeding in salt marsh in New Jersey. Auk 90:304–305.

———. 1989. Least terns populations in coastal New Jersey: monitoring and managing of a regionally endangered species. Journal of Coastal Research 5:801–811.

Cristol, D. A., J. G. Akst, M. K. Curatola, E. G. Dunlavey, K. A. Fisk, and
   K. E. Moody. 2017. Age-related differences in foraging ability among clam-dropping
   herring gulls (*Larus argentatus*). Wilson Journal of Ornithology 129:301–310.

Erwin, R. M., T. B. Tyler, J. S. Hatfield, and S. McGary. 1998. Diets of nesting gull-
   billed terns in coastal Virginia. Colonial Waterbirds 21:323–327. [Cites fiddler crabs
   as an important food.]

Lewis, A. S. 2022. Angry birds. New York Times Magazine, June 26: 36–45. [Describes
   how falconry controls nuisance gulls at Ocean City, NJ.]

Peterson, R. T. 2010. Peterson field guide to birds of eastern and central North America.
   6th ed. Houghton Mifflin Harcourt, Boston. [See for differences between gulls and
   terns as well as species-specific features.]

Quinn, J. S., and D. A. Wiggins. 1990. Differences in prey delivered to chicks by individual gull-billed terns. Colonial Waterbirds 13:67–69. [Mentions spiders as food.]

Ten Cate, C. 2009. Niko Tinbergen and the red patch on the herring gull's beak.
   Animal Behaviour 77:785–794. [A challenge to Tinbergen's research.]

Tinbergen, N. 1961. The herring gulls world. Rev. ed. Basic Books, New York.

Shore Note 4.3. Middens: Learning from Shell Piles

Christenson, A. L. 1985. The identification and study of Indian shell middens in eastern
   North America: 1643–1861. North American Anthropologist 6:227–243.

Cook-Patton, S. C., D. Weller, T. C. Rick, and J. D. Parker. 2014. Ancient experiments:
   forest biodiversity and soil nutrients enhanced by Native American middens.
   Landscape Ecology 29:979–987.

McAvoy, W. A., and J. W. Harrison. 2012. Plant community classification and the flora
   of Native American shell-middens on the Delmarva Peninsula. Maryland Naturalist
   52:1–34.

Mounier, R. A. 1997. Archaeological data recovery: Avalon Gulf Resort and Country
   Club, Middle Township, Cape May County, New Jersey. Bulletin of the Archaeology Society of New Jersey 52:1–23. [See for changes associated with rising sea levels.]

———. 2003. Looking beneath the surface, the story of archaeology in New Jersey.
   Rutgers University Press, New Brunswick, NJ. [See pp. 141–145 concerning shell
   middens.]

Stanzeski, A. J. 1981. Quahog "shell tools." Bulletin of the Archaeological Society of
   New Jersey 37:15–18.

———. 2001. The Tuckerton shell mound. Bulletin of the Archaeological Society of
   New Jersey 59:47–50.

Trant, A. J., W. Nijland, K. M. Hoffman, et al. 2016. Intertidal resource use over
   millennia enhances forest productivity. Nature Communications 7:Article 12491.

5

Cape May

A Gateway South

Waves of migratory birds funnel through Cape May, washing over the Cape as steadily as the waves of the mighty Atlantic wash its shores.

—CLAY AND PAT SUTTON, *BIRDS AND BIRDING AT CAPE MAY*

THINK BIG for a moment and visualize the Cape May Peninsula as a giant funnel that each fall directs an astonishing collection of migrating birds and insects southward. For most of these southbound travelers, the tip of Cape May presents their first encounter with a large water barrier that interrupts their continued passage over land—and a prelude to another at Cape Charles at the tip of the Delmarva Peninsula. For shorebirds and strong fliers such as ospreys and peregrine falcons, crossing the mouth of Delaware Bay is "just another day at the office," but for many others the trip presents a challenge. At its northern end, the funnel's wide mouth gathers and concentrates the winged horde not only from New Jersey but also from a swath of eastern North America that extends through New York, Pennsylvania, and New England into eastern Canada. The funnel only concentrates migrants moving southward in the fall, whereas in the spring the same birds return north unrestricted by the narrow peninsula and indeed, most remain over the mainland to avoid crossing Delaware Bay.

Besides its physical geography, the biogeography of Cape May deserves brief mention. The peninsula juts southward far enough to mark the end of the distribution for some northern species and the beginning for others more closely associated with a warmer climate. The length of the growing season offers a useful comparison. About 225 frost-free days—a span that defines the growing season—occur each year at the peninsula's southern tip, but these diminish in number to 158 days long at its northern end. Cape May thus lies at a latitude that offers the first hint of change between north and south in the biogeography of eastern North America. For example, swamp chestnut oak, pond pine, and loblolly pine—all southern species—extend their ranges northward to Cape May but not beyond. Delaware Bay also marks the northern boundary for black needlerush, which occurs in large, dense stands along the coastline in Delaware but does extend into New Jersey. The ranges of the closely related bayberry and wax myrtle overlap on the peninsula but gradually separate, so that bayberry dominates to the north and wax myrtle takes over to the south.

Some Real Snow Birds

Some 15 species of hawks migrate though Cape May, an event well known to ornithologists but also, as we shall see, to others much less inclined to let the thousands of accipiters, falcons, and buteos pass by unharmed. Large numbers of other birds follow the same route, a part of the larger Atlantic Flyway, among them species representing groups as diverse as owls, swallows, night herons, woodpeckers, warblers, and woodcock. The impressive migrations occur only in the fall, established in part by records of bird strikes at the Cape May Light as well as by the fieldwork of generations of keen observers.

As first described in 1936, northwest winds do much to channel the birds into the funnel—an event known as "wind drift." Normally, migrants travel across New Jersey on a diagonal swath whose southern edge extends across the state's waistline between Raritan Bay on the northeast and Camden on the southwest, which among other things largely conforms to an ancient coastline and avoids the Pine Barrens. The Appalachians, similarly aligned, form the northern edge of the swath, and many hawks, especially buteos and accipiters, follow these ridges across the state each fall. However, when a northwest wind blows across this swath, it deflects the flightpath of the birds to the coast where, facing the open sea, they fly south and accumulate at Cape May (fig. 5.1). These movements, including those of songbirds, generally occur just after a cold front passes through the region. Based on a census conducted for several years, an annual average of 45,500 hawks passed through Cape May, dominated by two accipiters, sharp-shined (fig. 5.2) and

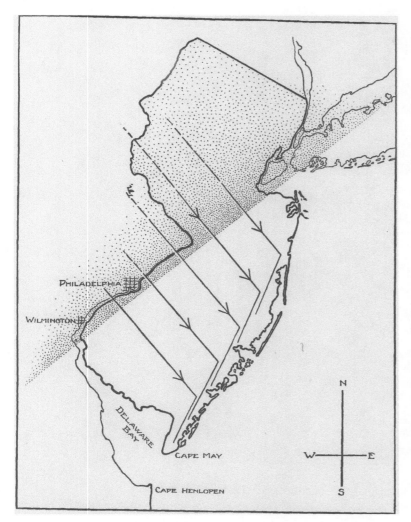

FIGURE 5.1. The shaded area, which corresponds with the diagonal orientation of New Jersey's physiographical features (see Fig. 1.2), indicates the broad path normally followed each fall by migrating birds. Northwest winds, however, deflect segments of these flights to the coast, where, temporarily halted by Delaware Bay, the birds concentrate at Cape May before continuing their southbound journey. Based on Allen and Peterson (1936) and used with permission of the American Ornithologists' Union.

Cooper's hawks, and a small falcon, the American kestrel. The flights south also include lesser numbers of ospreys, broad-winged hawks, red-tailed hawks, merlins, peregrine falcons, and a scattering of other species.

The same northwest wind deters the hawks, as well as other migrants, from crossing Delaware Bay—a flight likely to end tragically by the wind displacing the birds too far out to sea. To return to land under such circumstances would require that the birds fly a considerable distance directly *into* the wind to reach the Delaware shoreline, an effort almost sure to fail. Instead, they move west across the tip of the peninsula, then head north up its western shore where they disperse to forage and rest in habitat matching their species-specific preferences

FIGURE 5.2. Sharp-shinned hawks top the list of raptors in the fall migration at Cape May, most of which are juveniles (right) instead of adults (left). Other prominent species include Cooper's hawks, American kestrels, ospreys, and barn owls. Photo credits: Ed Sharron, National Park Service (right); Alan Schmierer, Creative Commons (left).

(e.g., woodlands for accipiters and fields for kestrels). Thus, for key sites like Cape May, preservation of a landscape endowed with a mosaic of habitat types becomes an obvious conservation goal.

When refueled, many birds cross a narrower part of the upper estuary to reach the mainland, although specific "jumping off" locations for these movements have never become apparent. Some species, notably those that soar with the aid of thermals, generally avoid crossing open water, where they would be forced to rely on their own power to meet the challenge. Wind direction and strength, of course, play important roles in whether or not a bird of any species elects to cross the bay. Some idea of which raptors are more likely to cross the expanse of Delaware Bay relates to the relationship between the wing length and width of each species. This information forms the basis of what is known as an aspect ratio—the square of the wingspan divided by wing area—which affects drag and thus the energetic cost of powered flight. An analysis of the aspect ratio for raptors, including the migrants at Cape May, revealed that birds with high aspect ratios—those with relatively long, often pointed wings—tend to cross the bay more often than those with shorter wings and lower aspect ratios. Hence, northern harriers, ospreys, and peregrine falcons commonly cross the bay, whereas turkey vultures and red-tailed hawks do so infrequently; American kestrels and sharp-shinned hawks belong to an intermediate group.

Juveniles predominate in the hawk population passing though Cape May, whereas older birds usually travel assisted by updrafts along the mountain ridges farther inland. This distinction, at least in part, may be related to the foraging abilities of the two age groups, with the older birds having greater experience hunting in forested mountains and the juveniles more inclined to forage in surroundings similar to sites where they fledged. Another idea suggests that the younger birds, more so than the adults, quickly yield to the strong winds in the mountains and drift to the coast when they encounter gaps that facilitate their eastward movements.

Cape May and its migrants today represent one of the nation's premier centers for ecotourism. Thousands of birders, some from other lands, spend millions enjoying one of nature's grander spectacles. But it was not always so. Cape May and Hawk Mountain in Pennsylvania, another major bottleneck along the eastern route, once were shooting galleries where migrating hawks were legally slaughtered. In both cases, the rather predictable arrival of the birds and their concentrated numbers provided shooters with unparalleled opportunities to kill scores on a daily basis. Both New Jersey and Pennsylvania were among the states that offered bounties on hawks in the late 1800s, but the rewards (25–50 cents per bird) ended when, along with a greater-than-expected pinch on the state treasuries, farmers complained that their fields were overrun with rodents. Protection thus was afforded to red-tailed hawks and other buteos, but those species that foraged on birds—namely sharp-shinned and Cooper's hawks—remained legal targets.

Predictably, the slaughter produced an outcry from conservationists, some of whom monitored the situation at Cape May in person. During the course of such a visit—and much to his chagrin—field guide pioneer Roger Tory Peterson

Shore Note 5.1 Cape May's Own Warbler (Well, Actually Not So Much)

In May 1812, Philadelphia naturalist George Ord (1781–1866) collected a handsome, brightly colored warbler in a maple swamp somewhere in Cape May County. Not recognizing the bird, he presented the specimen to his companion, Alexander Wilson (1766–1813), later acknowledged as the "father" of American ornithology. Wilson too was unfamiliar with the bird, which he described, painted, and named in his landmark work, *American Ornithology*, serially published between 1809 and 1814, the last installment completed by Ord after Wilson's death (fig. 5.3). The "new" species, however, was not as new as then believed, as English naturalist George Edwards (1694–1773), in his case, by coincidence, the "father" of British Ornithology, had already painted and described the species in the

FIGURE 5.3. While visiting Cape May early in the nineteenth century, famed ornithologist Alexander Wilson described what seemed to be a new species of warbler, which had in fact already been discovered by another ornithologist. Although named for the area, Cape May warblers appear only infrequently among the host of other songbirds migrating through Cape May. Photo credit: James Parnell.

West Indies well before 1812. Because of the rule of priority in such matters, Wilson lost his rights as the bird's discoverer along with rejection of the Latin name he proposed for the species. Nonetheless, Wilson's popular designation for the bird—Cape May warbler—remains accepted to this day. The bird Ord collected was the last of its kind recorded at Cape May for more than a century, although these circumstances may reflect a lack of observers more than the lack of birds.

A female was not described until 1835, the effort of Charles L. Bonaparte (1803–1857), an accomplished naturalist and a nephew of Emperor Napoleon. While on an extended visit to the United States, Bonaparte collected the bird at Bordentown, New Jersey, on the Delaware River, about 76 air miles due north of Cape May. Among his many other contributions, he is remembered for updating Wilson's volumes and honored in the name of Bonaparte's gull.

In breeding plumage, male Cape May warblers are distinctively marked with chestnut cheeks, large white wing patches, an olive back, and a yellow breast of warblers with black "tiger" stripes. Both males and the duller-colored females have yellow rumps. They breed in the spruce-fir forests of northern New England and eastern Canada west to Alberta and build their nests near the tops of the taller trees. When visiting their nests, the wary females fly to the lower part of the tree, then work their way upward concealed by the outer branches, retracing these movements when leaving.

On their breeding grounds, Cape May warblers feed on insects, particularly favoring the caterpillars of the spruce budworm, a moth whose populations unpredictably irrupt in some years.[1] Such swings in the abundance of the caterpillars influence the size of the warbler population, which expands with the budworm irruptions or becomes locally scarce or absent in the intervals between these bonanzas. In comparison with their relatives, Cape May warblers produce clutches of unusual size—up to nine eggs—which likely represents an adaption designed to increase their productivity in years when the caterpillars abound. The birds overwinter in the Caribbean, where they forgo insects and instead forage on nectar and the juice of grapes and other fruits, a diet facilitated by another adaptation—their curled, semitubular tongues.

An interesting biography for a warbler, albeit that its association with Cape May remains little more than a fleeting stopover during migration and, at that, only for a limited number of individuals. Still, George Ord's chance encounter provided an enduring name for a small bird and a feathery thread in the storied fabric of the Jersey Shore.

---

[1] Aldo Leopold established the term "irrupt" to distinguish a population explosion from other usages such as the "eruption" of a volcano, the sudden appearance of a skin disease, or the spontaneous outburst from an audience. The best-known irruptions include those of lemmings in the Far North and the locusts that plagued biblical Egypt. In 1961, *Webster's Third New International Dictionary* formally recognized the term, which thereafter appeared in other dictionaries. See Flader (1981).

(1908–1996) innocently sat down to a home-cooked meal of broiled sharp-shinned hawks. He felt like a spy dining with the enemy but admitted that the birds nonetheless proved good eating! Indeed, most of the gunners carried basketfuls of their victims home for food, whereas others shot the hawks simply as practice for the forthcoming hunting season. Fortunately, the killings diminished somewhat when the Witmer Stone Wildlife Sanctuary was established in 1935 at the very spot where the shooting was particularly devastating. (A year earlier, hawks migrating at Hawk Mountain in Pennsylvania were similarly protected, thereby becoming the world's first preserve specifically established for raptor conservation.) Still, not until 1959 did state law protect all species of hawks in New Jersey.

Others on the Move

Whereas hawks remain the centerpiece of fall migration at Cape May, at least a score of other species of birds also regularly funnel into the peninsula each year. Indeed, compared with more than a century of interest in other raptors, owls came to the fore of research at Cape May only in recent decades, as have studies of American woodcock, a somewhat elusive game bird.

Three species account for nearly all of the owl population passing though Cape May; based on their capture for banding, northern saw-whet owls predominate (61 percent), with long-eared (20 percent) and barn owls (17 percent) next in abundance. Four other species combined represent the balance (3 percent), which primarily consisted of eastern screech owls. These data, however, conflict with visual counts, in which barn owls occur most commonly (73 percent), followed by northern saw-whet (9 percent) and long-eared owls (8 percent), thus reflecting biases in one or both of the methods used to determine the relative abundance of each species in the population. Nonetheless, both agree on the three principal species that accumulate during the fall at Cape May. Unlike the sharp-shined and other hawks passing through the area, the age structure of the owl population includes far more adults than juveniles, but an explanation remains elusive.

Owls, as might be expected, migrate at night, which poses difficulties in tracking their movements, but a night-vision scope, moonlight, and even the beam from the Cape May Light enable useful observations. By such means, the flight path charted for barn owls heads west-southwest from the tip of Cape May (i.e., across the mouth of Delaware Bay), which does not coincide with the route sometimes followed by hawks and other land birds, as described earlier. Instead, this line of flight directs the birds to locations on the Delaware coast somewhat to the north and west of Cape Henlopen. In one observation, 17 birds, likely long-eared owls, took off from different locations but coalesced into a loose group as they headed out over Delaware Bay. Nonetheless, definitive statements concerning the routes followed by owls migrating south from Cape May await studies of birds outfitted with radio transmitters.

Still, long over-water flights by owls, and particularly by barn owls, may occur more commonly than once believed. A nesting barn owl banded in central New Jersey turned up less than two years later in Bermuda, a straight-line distance of some 776 miles, nearly all over water; presumably it migrated on the same route during the intervening period. Another barn owl, this one banded as an adult in Wisconsin, landed on a ship 225 miles off the coast of Georgia. Because of its age, this likely was not the bird's first migration, which suggests its previous travels may have likewise included long flights over open water. Yet another, banded just inland from the Texas coast and recovered near Veracruz, Mexico—a straight-line distance of 610 miles—may have flown directly across the Gulf of Mexico and not, as then assumed, traveled over land between the two locations. Such travels, if representative of the capabilities of barn owls, indicate that a nonstop trip across even the widest point on Delaware Bay might be easily accomplished even in the absence of helpful winds.

Some of Cape May's owls have problems on roads. Northern saw-whet and eastern screech owls together accounted for more than 80 percent of the 250 raptors tallied in a ten-year study of road kills on the Cape May Peninsula. Most of the victims were less than one year old, hence reflecting a greater vulnerability of young owls to vehicular collisions (recall that adults outnumber juveniles in the overall owl population at Cape May). The majority of the road kills occurred at the tip of the peninsula as opposed to farther inland on the Garden State Parkway en route to Atlantic City. Because most of the saw-whet owls were killed after the fall migration suggests that Cape May might also serve as a major wintering area for the species (i.e., after arriving, large numbers remain on the peninsula for the winter).

American woodcock, affectionately known to some as "timberdoodles," also concentrate at Cape May during their fall migration (fig. 5.4). By taxonomic affiliation, woodcock are shorebirds but have gone their own way and evolved into

FIGURE 5.4. American woodcock, also known as "timberdoodles," are upland-dwelling shorebirds favoring moist woodlands and thickets where they feed almost exclusively on earthworms. Many migrate through Cape May to overwinter in states farther south, but others remain in southern New Jersey until spring. Photo credit: Jack Dermid.

denizens of moist woodlands and thickets and a diet almost exclusively of earthworms. Their range covers most of eastern North America, but the woodcock passing through Cape May represent a population largely confined east of the Appalachian Mountains. Recoveries of those banded during the fall buildup at Cape May indicate this population nests in New England and eastern Canada and winters on the coastal plains of Virginia and North Carolina, although at times some also remain on the peninsula during the winter. As with the hawks, juveniles form the vast majority of woodcock passing through Cape May.

The woodcock overwintering at Cape May risk encountering winter storms, one of which covered Cape May with snow, ice, and sleet in January 2000. To continue foraging for earthworms under such conditions, the birds seek unfrozen roadsides and parking lots, but the two-day storm still claimed large numbers of woodcock—one area alone yielded a tally of more than 400 dead or weakened birds. The body mass of the stricken birds was about half of their normal weight, with the loss likely representing at least 10 days of starvation. Many of the birds were adult males, which suggests that they were attempting to again overwinter at a more northerly latitude to gain early access to mates and the best breeding habitat the following spring (i.e., an advantage over those wintering farther south). Indeed, based on their gonadal development, many of the males were in breeding condition and thus in a state of sexual readiness for the subsequent arrival of migrating females.

Some unique physical adaptions evolved in keeping with the birds' food habits, with their long bills being the most obvious of these. Clearly designed for deep probing, the bills develop with tactile cells at their tips whose sensitivity can detect the slightest movement of an earthworm. Moreover, the bill tip can open while imbedded in the soil to grasp slippery prey, enhanced by the roughened surfaces of both the upper bill and tongue. The nasal openings on the bill lie well up the bill so that breathing remains unaffected when the birds probe for food. Additionally, the large eyes of woodcock are strategically located high and well back on the head, which enables a wide field of vision to better spot predators; thus displaced, the ears instead somewhat lie below and forward of their eyes. These (re)arrangements evolved concurrently with a change in the anatomy of the woodcock brain, in which the cerebellum lies below the rest of the brain and above the spinal column. Remarkably, in comparison with other birds, the brain of a woodcock is thus upside down!

Because frozen ground, as well as snow, curtails their ability to successfully probe for worms, woodcock necessarily leave their northern breeding areas before winter weather prevails. Early snows in the Northeast indeed trigger large migrations but they move singly or in loose "flights" of a few birds (i.e., woodcock lack the flocking behavior typical of most migrating shorebirds). They migrate at night and fly low, usually no more than 100 feet above ground or water. Once at Cape May, the birds forage at night in fertile locations such as recently abandoned fields and weedy pastures, and seek cover during the day in woodlands, which again indicates the importance of habitat types that match the needs of migrating birds. When ready to move on, they apparently cross the full width of Delaware Bay in a nonstop flight.

Market hunters, and later sport hunters, once heavily exploited the woodcock that concentrated at Cape May every fall. Daily bags of several hundred were not uncommon, perhaps because the shooters mistakenly believed that the temporary abundance of the birds at Cape May indicated a huge woodcock population

Shore Note 5.2 Labrador Duck: Gone Forever

One autumn day in 1875, a gunner on Long Island Sound smartly felled a smallish black and white sea duck (fig. 5.5). His shot was memorable not for its accuracy but for its finality—it proved fatal not only for the hapless bird but for a species. Gone forever were Labrador ducks, whose ghosts linger today in a handful of skins, bones, and eggs—the latter of doubtful validity—scattered and all but forgotten in a few far-flung museums. These pitiful remains represent the only species of waterfowl succumbing to extinction in the recorded history of North America.

Extinction claimed Labrador ducks before much of anything was learned about their natural history, virtually all of which concerns only their wintering ecology. Neither their nests, supposedly limited to a small area in southeastern Labrador, nor their food habits were studied by naturalists of the day. We might suppose, since they were sea ducks akin to eiders and scoters, that small mollusks and crustaceans dominated the diet, which at times perhaps included seagrasses. Such fare seems consistent with the lateral bill flaps at tips of their bills; these presumably served as sensory adaptations for the tactile detection of benthic foods. Lamellae—structures designed for straining food—fringing the edges of their bills seem disproportionately large in Labrador ducks and may have helped sort foods gleaned from sandy bottoms.

Much of what was likely always a small population of Labrador ducks overwintered near Long Island, with some venturing farther south to Chesapeake Bay and New Jersey—all locations where the birds were vulnerable to market hunting. Alexander Wilson observed a few in the Philadelphia market, and Audubon described their occurrence on the New Jersey coast as "in greater or less numbers every year." The famed artist, although having no personal experience with the species, nonetheless included a pair, which he identified as "pied ducks," in his folio of North American birds. A taxidermist in Camden, New Jersey, secured specimens in perfect plumage using fishhooks baited with mussels suspended from a trotline sunk a few feet below the surface. These observations, reported by Witmer Stone, were supplemented by records of specimens presumably from New Jersey and housed in public and private collections, but all lack supporting data. Stone concluded that these almost certainly came from "Great Egg Harbor or Cape May where Philadelphia gunners of the day did their shooting."

However, because Labrador ducks were not good table fare—some in fact spoiled awaiting buyers—they were not often targets of choice for gunners, and other causes apparently precipitated extinction of the species. More likely, severe losses occurred during the breeding season, when local people freely took both nesting birds and their eggs, thereby rapidly pushing the

COLOR PLATE LIV (Formerly Plate 78)

Adult Male

LABRADOR DUCK
Immature Male

Adult Female

FIGURE 5.5. Now extinct, Labrador ducks once overwintered along the Jersey Shore as far south as Cape May. John James Audubon illustrated a pair of these ducks in a rather unnatural pose, but, as shown here, a painting by Louis Agassiz Fuertes (1874–1927) more realistically portrays the species. Note the unusual bill flap. Photo credit: Dale Lockwood.

small population toward its fateful end. Yet despite the tragedy of the Labrador duck, an enlightened era of conservation developed early in the twentieth century, which prevented further extinctions of waterfowl in North America (e.g., at the time, wood ducks seemed destined to a similar fate, but the species today thrives in New Jersey and elsewhere in its extensive range in North America).

capable of unlimited harvesting. Finally, however, the unconscionable toll became a rallying point for conservationists, ultimately resulting in state and federal agencies protecting and managing key areas of woodcock habitat (e.g., Higbee Wildlife Management Area).

Eastern kingbirds, northern flickers, and tree swallows are among the songbirds passing through in large flocks. At the peak of their southward migration, at the end of August, as many as 5,000 kingbirds per day reach Cape May, but even larger numbers—more than 10,000—occurred in the past. Similar numbers of flickers provide a spectacle in October and quickly gain the rapt attention of hungry Cooper's hawks. Tree swallows concentrate at Cape May in even greater numbers that often reach 20,000, and on at least one occasion may have peaked at 500,000. The huge flocks—"smoky clouds" provides an apt description—roost in freshwater marshes choked with *Phragmites*. During the day, the swallows visit bayberry thickets, which led to the belief they were doing so to waterproof their feathers on the wax-laden berries, but in fact the berries provided a supplement to their insect-based diet.

The list could easily go on to include American robins, orioles, purple martins, and scores of others, but final mention here goes to yellow-rumped warblers (fig. 5.6). Although now named for their distinctive markings, they were once known as myrtle warblers (also quaintly as "butter-butts") to reflect the importance of both bayberry and wax myrtle berries in their winter diet—along with tree swallows one of the few birds able to digest the waxy fruits. In the past, "myrtle warblers" were half of a twosome of closely related species, the other being a western counterpart known as Audubon's warbler. However, taxonomists now regard the two forms, which hybridize, as subspecies. The immense numbers of yellow-rumped warblers at Cape May strain the ability to provide reliable estimates, which may run between 100,000 and 150,000 on some daily counts in October—once topping out at 1 million! Like the Cape May warbler and several others of their kind, yellow-rumped warblers nest in the northern coniferous forest but overwinter for the most part in the southern United States and Mexico instead of traveling deep into the tropics of Central and South America.

A stunning phenomenon known as the "morning flight" occurs during the fall migration at Cape May and similar locations elsewhere. Shortly after sunrise, thousands of migrant songbirds sweep westward across the tip of the peninsula, then turn *northward* up the eastern shore of Delaware Bay. Warblers make up the

FIGURE 5.6. Yellow-rumped warblers, once known as myrtle warblers because of their fondness for bayberry fruits as a winter food, are one of the more numerous species of songbirds that journey south through Cape May each autumn. Photo credit: James Parnell.

majority of neotropical birds in these flights—86 percent based on the seminal study of these events—which also include vireos, tanagers, and orioles, among others, but rarely thrushes. Virtually all of these species migrate at night, hence the morning flight represents the dawn dispersal of birds completing the previous night's journey. Several factors, likely acting in combination, seem involved. One of these—disorientation—concerns birds that overshoot the peninsula during the night and find themselves over water at sunup without visual landmarks. Thus disoriented, they reverse course and return in a northbound flight to Cape May. Similarly, birds blown offshore at night by northwest winds arrive at Cape May at dawn from the east, continue flying around the end of the peninsula, and then head north along the Bayshore. Poor weather undoubtedly contributes to disorientation of birds involved in the morning flight. In other cases, fatigue and hunger may launch local flights of migrants in search of roosting and feeding areas. Some birds in the morning flight will continue their flight all the way around Delaware Bay, but most return to Cape May and continue their southward migration across the bay toward Cape Henlopen.

Migrating with Six Legs and No Feathers

The magic of migration also includes insects. About 9 species dragonflies (of 326) in North America annually migrate long distances north and south across the continent, of which green darners dominated (95 percent) one particularly massive fall flight at Cape May with twelve-spotted skimmers and black saddlebags among those forming lesser percentages (fig. 5.7). In a stunning spectacle, this swarm, estimated at more than 400,000 strong, passed by for two hours in a band about 980 feet wide and at least 50 feet deep. These enormous flights typically occur only on a single day each year in August or September, whereas low-density migrations of solitary dragonflies take place more uniformly throughout much of the fall.

The features of dragonfly migrations remarkably parallel those of birds in terms of season, weather conditions, and routes, with the largest aggregations following the "leading lines" of ridges and shorelines, often on peninsulas. Similarly, large numbers move south in the wake of a passing cold front. At Cape May, the flights of dragonflies move west across the tip of the peninsula, then turn north to follow its western shore, thereby making virtually no attempt to cross the mouth of Delaware Bay—movements exactly as those described earlier for some species of hawks. Moreover, dragonflies, like songbirds, make ready for migration by accumulating stores of fat to fuel their long flights, which they initiate before their primary food sources—aerial insects—decline as the season changes. Green darners, each weighing but a fraction of an ounce, may fly for up to eight hours on stored fat, but again like migrating songbirds, they gradually exhaust these reserves and must stop periodically to replenish their supply of energy.

Dragonfly migrations, as especially noted for green darners, differ from those of birds in one import respect—individuals apparently migrate in one direction only. For example, biologists recently determined that the annual migration of green darners includes three generations to complete; the first travels north (e.g., New England to Minnesota) in spring after hatching in the southern United States, the second returns in fall to the south (e.g., Florida to Texas), whereas the

FIGURE 5.7. Insects as well as birds migrate through Cape May, among them dragonflies, including large numbers of green darners. Photo credit: James Parnell.

third overwinters in residence before renewing the cycle with another generation of northward-bound individuals.

Although a deplorable act in itself, the hawks shot at Cape May nonetheless provided information about their food habits during migration. As expected, the accipiters found an abundance of food in the warblers, robins, and other birds that likewise accumulated at Cape May during the fall migration. The stomachs of 189 sharp-shinned hawks, for example, contained the remains of 208 birds of 44 species and those of 22 Cooper's hawks included 30 birds of 17 species. However, the stomach contents of 41 merlins—falcons once known as pigeon hawks because of their preference for birds—revealed something of a dietary surprise: more dragonflies than anything else. As with songbirds, dragonflies provide a plentiful food supply that arrives concurrently with their predators, a synchrony that may not be mere coincidence.

Much remains unknown about the migrations of dragonflies, but high-tech approaches now offer ways of learning more about their movements. These include tiny radio transmitters attached to their bodies that enable tracking both on the ground and from airplanes. Analyses of stable isotopes in the wings from adults and cast-off skins of final-stage nymphs, when compared with the water chemistry at breeding sites, also determine the origins and travels of dragonflies, as noted earlier for green darners. Dragonflies are also marked directly on their wings, either with numbers or color codes, using a nontoxic paint pen. An international network of citizen scientists and professional biologists known as the Dragonfly Migration Partnership currently monitors the travels of dragonflies in Canada, Mexico, and the United States.

For naturalists of every age, the migration of monarch butterflies stands as one of nature's more spectacular and well-known events (fig. 5.8). As summed up by comedian George Carlin, "The caterpillars do all the work, but the butterflies get all the publicity." Their 2,200-mile northbound odyssey spans three or sometimes four generations, each of which ends when, before dying, the females lay their eggs on milkweed plants. The eggs produce vividly striped caterpillars that feed exclusively on milkweed leaves, from which they acquire the distasteful protection of cardiac glycosides that deter would-be predators—a chemical defense passed on from the caterpillars to the adults. (Adult monarchs are not similarly tied to a single source of food and feed on nectar from the flowers of various plants, including seaside goldenrod along the shoreline and the aptly named butterfly bush in urban yards.) This cycle repeats at three or even four additional stops before the last generation reaches the northern edges of the species' breeding range in southern Canada. Remarkably, the adults hatching at the last stop on the northward migration turn south and unerringly travel back (without breeding) to the same location where their ancestors overwintered at least two generations earlier. The monarchs, which are daytime migrants, employ both sun and magnetic compasses as navigational tools to guide their travels both north and south.

Differences in their migration routes and wintering grounds separate monarch butterflies into two geographically distinct populations. One, confined to the west side of the Rocky Mountains, overwinters along the coast of Southern California, the other, far larger population, remains east of the Rockies and winters

FIGURE 5.8. The fall migration at Cape May also includes monarch butterflies, as shown here clustered on groundsel; with favorable winds, they will cross Delaware Bay en route to a secluded forest in central Mexico, where illegal logging threatens their winter survival. The colorful larval stage (inset) feeds solely on milkweed, whose diminished abundance has recently emerged as another threat to the species. Photo credits: Pat and Clay Sutton; Kevin Knutsen (inset).

in just 25 square miles of forest in mountains northwest of Mexico City. Only after decades of fruitless searching was the remote location finally discovered in 1987. Less than 20 years ago the monarch population overwintering in the mountains approached one billion, but on average some 350 million today reach their mountain retreat each year, and threats continue to reduce the population (see following).

Shore Note 5.3 Conservation at Cape May

The unique role played by Cape May, especially regarding migratory birds, has not gone unnoticed by state, federal, and private conservation organizations. As a result, a mix of refuges and preserves, along with supporting research and educational efforts, protects significant sites in the region, of which a short list appears here (see also shore notes 3.2 and 3.3).

Cape May National Wildlife Refuge, established in 1989, consists of three divisions: Great Cedar Swamp, about 6,500 acres of mixed habitat featuring bogs with old-growth Atlantic white cedar; Two-Mile Beach, more than 500 acres of undisturbed barrier beaches of particular importance to piping plovers and remnant stands maritime forest; and Delaware Bay, a division of about 4,500 acres stretched along five miles of bayfront of vital significance to migrating red knots (see chapter 6). Both the Ramsar List of Wetlands of International Importance and the Western Hemisphere Shorebird Reserved Network include the refuge—a clear reflection of its importance.

Cape May Point State Park lies at the tip of the funnel collecting fall migrants. Its 235 acres include a designated natural area of 153 acres and the Cape's historic lighthouse. A viewing platform, befittingly dubbed Hawkwatch, presents a centerpiece for birders enjoying the fall migration. Invasive plants currently threaten the integrity of the park's rich native flora, but a vigorous control program now underway may turn the tide.

Cape May Bird Observatory, sponsored by the New Jersey Audubon Society, began in 1976 when Pete Dunne, later director of the observatory and founder of the World Series of Birding, hired on to census hawks, which remains a highlight of the local calendar. Today the observatory stands as

Oyamel fir growing in stands at altitudes of 9,000 to 11,000 feet serve as the winter roosts, with the hordes of butterflies draping the trees like orange blankets. The forest lies in a fog belt where the moist air protects the masses of butterflies from freezing. Similarly, the forest canopy acts like an umbrella against the rigors of all but the most severe winter storms, while also creating a microclimate up to 12 degrees Fahrenheit warmer than in open areas nearby. Thus protected, the butterflies huddle in a semistupor for most of the winter, although they briefly move about on warm days looking for water. With the coming of spring, the same monarchs that completed the long, southward migration to Mexico leave their winter home to begin the first leg in a new cycle of northbound spring migration. By late May and early June, what is usually the next-to-last brood produced in the multigenerational march north reaches New Jersey.

one of the world's most respected—and visited—institutions of its kind. The diverse programs include banding hawks and owls, monitoring butterfly populations, and, for all age groups, workshops, lectures, and field trips. The physical facilities include the Center for Research and Education in Goshen, New Jersey, which features a model backyard habitat, and the Northwood Center (visitor information, bookstore, and gift shop) at Cape May Point.

Cape May Migratory Bird Refuge, known locally as The Meadows and owned (since 1981) and managed by The Nature Conservancy, consists of about 250 acres of open meadows, dunes, open beach, and freshwater marsh. A beach-restoration project created ponds behind the dunes and further added to the structure of the habitat, and droughts create mudflats that, in season, attract large flocks of shorebirds. Once a pasture, the site has regrown into a mosaic of native vegetation, but water-control structures will be required to maximize the benefits for wildlife.

Higbee Beach, a Wildlife Management Area operated since 1978 by the New Jersey Division of Fish and Wildlife, also protects habitat for migratory birds. At about 1,160 acres, the mixed-oak forest, fields, hedgerows, and patches of shrubs also include dune forests on the shores of Delaware Bay and Cordez's Woods, a large stand of old-growth deciduous forest. In particular, the site serves the needs of migrating American woodcock, legally hunted here, and the morning arrival of other night-flying migrants, including songbirds and owls. In spring, arriving neotropical migrants commonly "fall out" in this area (i.e., large flocks of exhausted warblers, tanagers, and other songbirds literally drop into the shelter of the woody vegetation, decorating the trees like Christmas ornaments).

Based on a 13-year average, the fall migration at Cape May consists of about 3,490 monarchs each year, but the annual variation in the census ranges from just 452 to 15,751. Their numbers increase in September and continue growing until early October, after which they gradually decline. Note that dips in annual censuses do not necessarily represent a cause for alarm, as far larger numbers may occur in years shortly after these lows (but see following). The monarchs arrive at Cape May in waves, which occur at an average of seven per year and last for three days. As noted earlier for migrating birds, the butterflies accumulating at Cape May replenish their energy stores before continuing onward, in this case from nectar extracted from the local flora and heavily supplemented by butterfly bushes and other flowering ornamentals planted just for this purpose by the thoughtful residents of Cape May Point. Thus nourished, and with the help of a favorable wind, the monarchs resume their long journey to Mexico fluttering across Delaware Bay.

Habitat alteration at Cape May poses relatively few worries for monarch butterflies in comparison with the threats migrating birds face from urbanization of the regional landscape. That, however, is not the case in Mexico where logging, grazing, and clearing diminish the butterflies' vitally important winter habitat. In particular, the commercial value of oyamel fir provides a strong incentive for harvesting the trees even on areas now designated as butterfly sanctuaries. In 2000, these locations were collectively declared a Monarch Butterfly Biosphere Reserve and in 2008 were recognized as a UNESCO World Heritage Site—titles that unfortunately do not necessarily preclude continued degradation of the forest and its unique role. On the other hand, the potential of the butterflies as a source of income currently supports a budding local economy based on ecotourism, in which the proprietary interests of the residents may foster greater care for the butterflies' winter quarters.

Herbicides now seem to pose an even greater threat by removing milkweed from a vast area of North America where monarchs breed. The loss of these essential plants stems from the development of genetically modified crops that can tolerate certain types of herbicides, whereas common weeds such as milkweed cannot. One estimate indicates a 58 percent reduction in milkweeds was accompanied by an 81 percent decline in monarch production between 1999 and 2010. Countermeasures focus on promoting milkweed production in city parks, in residential gardens, and especially along roadsides. The National Wildlife Federation's Project Heroes helps children and their families develop butterfly-friendly gardens. In 2018, New Jersey enacted the Adopt a Monarch Butterfly Way Station, which establishes milkweed, nectar-rich plants, and shelter at sites on state lands, and a sister program designed for unused areas in drainage basins, Milkweed for Monarchs. A long-term study, begun in 1990, known as the Monarch Monitoring Project continues each year at the Cape May Bird Observatory.

Finally, any discussion of monarch butterflies should highlight, even briefly, the coloration of both the caterpillars and adults. The caterpillars' vivid stripes no doubt advertise a warning—a red flag, so to speak—that a rather unpleasant experience awaits those avian predators seeking a meal. As noted earlier, the bitter taste passes on to the adults, thereby continuing the safeguard gained from the caterpillars' milkweed diet (although a few birds do seem able to cope with the unsavory taste).

Enter the viceroy butterfly, which is remarkably similar to the monarchs in both color and pattern but acquires no protective advantage from its diet—instead, the species gains its security simply by looking like a monarch. Biologists regard this as a classic example of Batesian mimicry, in which one of two lookalike species tastes bad, but the other does not, yet both remain secure from predators.

Readings and References

General

Burger, J., and M. Gochfeld. 2000. Twenty-five nature spectacles in New Jersey. Rutgers University Press, New Brunswick, NJ. [See chaps. 15 and 17, respectively, regarding monarch butterfly and hawk migrations at Cape May.]

Stone, W. 1937. Bird studies at Old Cape May. 2 vols. Delaware Valley Ornithological Club, Philadelphia.

Sutton, C., and P. Sutton. 2006. Birds and birding at Cape May: what to see and where to go. Stackpole Books, Mechanicsburg, PA. [A major source for information presented herein and the premier reference for naturalists visiting Cape May.]

Some Real Snow Birds

Allen, R. P. 1936. Sanctuary or slaughter pen? Nature Magazine 27(3):175–176. [See for background leading to creation of Witmer Stone Wildlife Sanctuary.]

Allen, R. P., and R. T. Peterson. 1936. The hawk migration at Cape May Point, New Jersey. Auk 53:393–404. [Proposes northwest winds deflect the birds to the coast ("wind drift"), a notion refuted by Murray (1964), which in turn was challenged by Mueller and Berger (1967).

Broun, M. 1949. Hawks aloft: the story of Hawk Mountain. Dodd, Mead, New York. [By the first warden of the first sanctuary expressly established to protect raptors. See also Hardwood, M. 1989. Giants of the past: Maurice Broun. American Birds 43:242–247.]

Burger, J., M. Gochfeld, and L. J. Niles. 1995. Ecotourism and birds in coastal New Jersey: contrasting responses of birds, tourists, and managers. Environmental Conservation 22:56–65.

Goodrich, L. J., and J. P. Smith. 2008. Raptor migration in North America. Pp. 37–150 in The state of North America's birds of prey (K. L. Bildstein, J. P. Smith, E. Ruelas Inzunza, and R. R. Veit, eds.). Series in Ornithology No. 3. Nuttall Ornithological Club and American Ornithologists' Union, Cambridge, MA, and Washington, DC.

Holthuijzen, A. M. A., L. Oosterhuis, and M. R. Fuller. 1985. Habitat use by migrating sharp-shinned hawks at Cape May Point, New Jersey, USA. Pp. 317–327 in Conservation studies of raptors (I. Newton and R. D. Chancellor, eds.). International Council for Bird Preservation Technical Publication No. 5, Cambridge, UK.

Kerlinger, P. 1985. Water-crossing behavior of raptors during migration. Wilson Bulletin 97:109–113. [See for the role of aspect ratios.]

Mueller, H. C., and D. D. Berger. 1967. Wind drift, leading lines, and diurnal migration. Wilson Bulletin 79:50–62.

Murray, B. G., Jr. 1964. A review of sharp-shinned hawk migration along the northeastern coast of the United States. Wilson Bulletin 76:257–264.

Niles, L. J., J. Burger, and K. E. Clark. 1996. The influence of weather, geography, and habitat on migrating raptors on Cape May Peninsula. Condor 98:382–394.

Peterson, R. T. 1964. Birds over America. Rev. ed. Dodd, Mead, New York. [See pp. 152–176 for hawk migrations and wanton shootings, including the author's embarrassing meal of sharp-shins.]

Wiedner, D. S., P. Kerlinger, D. Sibley, et al. 1992. Visible morning flight of Neotropical landbird migrants at Cape May, New Jersey. Auk 109:500–510. [A landmark study.]

Others on the Move

Bolen, E. G. 1978. Long-distance displacement of two southern barn owls. Bird-Banding 49:78–79.

Cobb, S. 1959. On the angle of the cerebral axis in the American woodcock. Auk 76:55–59.

Duffy, K. 1985. Fall migration of barn owls at Cape May Point, New Jersey. Pp. 193–205 in Proceedings of Hawk Migration Conference IV (M. Harwood, ed.). Hawk Migration Association of North America, Rochester, NY.

Duffy, K., and P. Kerlinger. 1992. Autumn owl migration at Cape May Point, New Jersey. Wilson Bulletin 104:312–320.

Krohn, W. B. 1973. Cape May woodcock, their migration and behavior. New Jersey Outdoors 24(3):2–7.

Krohn, W. B., J. C. Rieffenberger, and F. Ferrigno. 1977. Fall migration of woodcock at Cape May, New Jersey. Journal of Wildlife Management 41:104–111.

Loos, G., and P. Kerlinger. 1993. Road mortality of saw-whet and screech-owls on the Cape May Peninsula. Journal of Raptor Research 27:210–213.

Mueller, H. C., and D. D. Berger. 1979. Over-water flights of barn owls. Bird-Banding 50:68.

Rice, N. H., M. F. Sharp, and P. Lehman. 2003. American woodcock winter mortality in southern New Jersey. Cassinia 69:6–10.

Russell, R. W., P. Dunne, C. Sutton, and P. Kerlinger. 1991. A visual study of migrating owls at Cape May Point, New Jersey. Condor 93:55–61.

Soucy, L. J., Jr. 1985. Bermuda recovery of a common barn owl banded in New Jersey. Journal of Field Ornithology 56:274.

Migrating with Six Legs and No Feathers

Agrawal, A. A. 2017. Monarchs and milkweed: a migrating butterfly, poisonous plant, and their remarkable story of coevolution. Princeton University Press, Princeton, NJ.

———. 2018. Mechanisms behind the monarch's decline. Science 360:1294–1296.

Anderson, J. B., and L. P. Brower. 1996. Freeze-protection of overwintering monarch butterflies in Mexico: critical role of the forest as a blanket and an umbrella. Ecological Entomology 21:107–116.

Butterfly Gardner. 2012. 17(2). [Summer issue devoted exclusively to butterfly bushes.]

Flockhart, D. T., J. B. Pichancourt, D. R. Norris, and T. G. Martin. 2015. Unraveling the annual cycle in a migratory animal: breeding-season habitat loss drives population declines of monarch butterflies. Journal of Animal Ecology 84:155–165. [Argues that reductions of milkweed outweigh other threats. See Inamine et al. (2016).]

Hallworth, M. T., P. P. Marra, K. P. McFarland, et al. 2018. Tracking dragons: stable isotopes reveal the annual cycle of a long-distant migratory insect. Biology Letters 14(12):2018.0741. [Details the migration of green darners.]

Inamine, H., S. P. Ellner, J. P. Springer, and A. A. Agrawal. 2016. Linking the continental migratory cycle of the monarch butterfly to understand its population decline. Oikos 125:1081–1091. [Proposes shortages of nectar, and not of milkweed herbage, explains the plight of monarchs.]

May, M. L. 2013. A critical review of progress in studies of migration of dragonflies (Odonata: Anisoptera), with emphasis on North America. Journal of Insect Conservation 17:1–15.

Nicoletti, F. J. 1996. American kestrel and merlin migration correlated with green darner movements as Hawk Ridge. Loon 68:216–221.

Pleasants, J. M., and K. S. Oberhauser. 2013. Milkweed loss in agricultural fields because of herbicide use: effect on the monarch butterfly population. Insect Conservation and Diversity 6:135–144.

Reppert, S. M., R. J. Gegear, and C. Merlin. 2010. Navigational mechanisms of migrating monarch butterflies. Trends in Neurosciences 33:399–406.

Russell, R. W., M. L. May, K. L. Soltesz, and J. W. Fitzpatrick. 1998. Massive swarm migrations of dragonflies (Odonata) in eastern North America. American Midland Naturalist 140:325–342.

Urquhart, F. A. 1987. The monarch butterfly: international traveler. Nelson-Hall, Chicago.

Urquhart, F. A., and N. R. Urquhart. 1976. The overwintering site of the eastern population of the monarch butterfly (*Danaus plexippus*: Danaidae) in southern Mexico. Journal of the Lepidopterists' Society 30:153–158. [See also Urquhart, F. A. Found at last: the monarch's winter home. National Geographic 150(2):161–173.]

Walton, R. K., L. P. Brower, and A. K. Davis. 2005. Long-term monitoring and fall migration patterns of the monarch butterfly in Cape May, New Jersey. Annals of the Entomological Society of America 98:682–689.

Wikelski, M., D. Moskowitz, J. S. Adelman, et al. 2006. Simple rules guide dragonfly migration. Biology Letters 2:325–329.

Shore Note 5.1. Cape May's Own Warbler

Baltz, M. E., and S. C. Latta. 1998. Cape May warbler (*Dendroica tigrina*). Number 332 in Birds of North America (A. Poole and F. Gill, eds). Academy of Natural Sciences, Philadelphia and American Ornithologists' Union, Washington, DC.

Burtt, E. H., Jr., and W. E. Davis Jr. 2013. Alexander Wilson, the Scot who founded American ornithology. Harvard University Press, Cambridge, MA. [Various dates appear for Ord's collection of the specimen he gave to Wilson—1809, for example, by Witmer Stone—but 1812 seems more likely, notwithstanding Ord's insertion of "1811" in the account appearing in volume 6 of Wilson's *American Ornithology*—an effort to predate Audubon's own claim of "discovering" the species in Kentucky.]

Flader, S. L. 1981. Comment on irruption. Wildlife Society Bulletin 9:237–238.

MacArthur, R. H. 1958. Population ecology of some warblers of northeastern coniferous forests. Ecology 39:599–619.

Morse, D. H. 1978. Populations of bay-breasted and Cape May warblers during an outbreak of the spruce budworm. Wilson Bulletin 90:404–413.

Rappole, J. H. 1995. The ecology of migrant birds, a neotropical perspective. Smithsonian Institution Press, Washington, DC.

Sealy, S. P. 1989. Defense of nectar resources by migrating Cape May warblers. Journal of Field Ornithology 60:89–93.

Stroud, P. T. 2000. The emperor of nature: Charles-Lucien Bonaparte. University of Pennsylvania Press, Philadelphia.

Venier, L. A., and S. B. Holmes. 2010. A review of the interaction between forest birds and eastern spruce budworm. Environmental Reviews 18:191–207.

Shore Note 5.2. Labrador Duck: Gone Forever

Bent, A. C. 1925. Life histories of North American wild fowl. Part II. Natural History Museum Bulletin 130. Smithsonian Institution, Washington, DC.

Chilton, G. 1997. Labrador duck (*Camptorhynchus labradorius*). No. 307 in The birds of North America (A. Poole and F. Gill, eds.). Academy of Natural Sciences, Philadelphia, and American Ornithologists' Union, Washington, DC.

————. 2009. The curse of the Labrador duck, my obsessive quest to the edge of extinction. Simon & Schuster, New York. [A memoir about the author's wide-ranging struggles to examine every specimen of the extinct species.]

Chilton, G., and M. D. Sorenson. 2007. Genetic identification of eggs purportedly from the extinct Labrador duck (*Camptorhynchus labradorius*). Auk 124:962–968.

Greenway, J. C., Jr. 1958. Extinct and vanishing birds of the world. Special publication 13. American Commission for International Wildlife Protection, New York.

Stone, W. 1965. Bird studies at Old Cape May. Vol. 1. Dover, New York. [Reprint of the 1937 original.]

Shore Note 5.3. Conservation at Cape May

Sutton, C., and P. Sutton. 2006. Birds and birding at Cape May, what to see, when and where to go. Stackpole Books, Mechanicsburg, PA. [See for a full listing and description of important locations and organizations.]

Sutton, P., R. Meyer, and R. Stalter. 1990. The vascular plants of Cape May Point State Park, Cape May County, New Jersey. Bulletin of the Torrey Botanical Club 117:294–300.

6

Delaware Bay
The Other Jersey Shore

Overall, the greatest problem for Delaware Bay is the overwhelming
lack of recognition of its cultural heritage and natural resources.
—LAWRENCE NILES, JOANNA BURGER, AND AMANDA DEY,
LIFE ALONG THE DELAWARE BAY

ANOTHER COASTLINE lies along the western shore of Cape May, this
one lacking barrier beaches and large embayments yet scarcely wants
for its own ecological significance. Here the beaches form a narrow strip
along the coast of Delaware Bay and, for the most part, lack dune systems. These
are low-energy beaches that receive little impact from wave action, but they
nonetheless easily erode during storms, which expose crumbling mats of peat and
debris. Moreover, because the Bayshore lacks sand-bearing currents, eroded
beaches may require decades or even centuries to recover. In short, the supply of
sand cannot keep up with the current rate of beach erosion. However, artificial
reefs constructed from bags filled with empty mollusk shells may reduce beach
erosion and hasten the recovery of beaches already damaged. These structures, set
50 to 100 feet offshore, act as breakwaters or speedbumps that lessen the force of
incoming waves and thereby protect the shoreline and reduce the loss of sand.
They also offer a substrate where spat (oyster larvae) can settle and begin forming
a self-sustaining living reef.

A wide belt of marshland extends several miles inland behind the narrow beachfront. A few secondary roads cross these wetlands and serve as somewhat tenu-
ous links between once-busy fishing villages and inland communities. Today, rising
sea levels confront both the bleak villages and the fragile beaches. Mosquito ditches

cut through the marshes (see chapter 3), and closer to land a network of dikes mark the edges of abandoned fields where farmers once harvested salt hay. Some of the stronger dikes surrounding the abandoned fields still keep out salt water, which unfortunately creates an environment where *Phragmites* invades and eventually overwhelms these sites. Conversely, native wetland vegetation—typically in the form of low marsh—gradually returns to those fields where breached dikes no longer hold back salt water.

On a larger scale, a salinity gradient ranges from seawater (about 3.5 percent salt) at the entrance to Delaware Bay and progressively becomes less saline toward the head of the bay where the influence of freshwater from the Delaware River dominates the system. Because of its greater weight, salt water extends well into the estuary beneath the upper layer of freshwater; this wedge-shaped lens of salt water gradually diminishes upstream until it entirely disappears from the water column. The Salem, Cohansey, and Maurice rivers in New Jersey also add freshwater to the bay, as do rivers entering on the opposite shore in Delaware. As with Raritan Bay and estuaries elsewhere, these conditions increase the diversity of the biota associated with Delaware Bay. Regrettably, the bay also lies downstream from numerous industrial and petrochemical facilities located between Wilmington and Philadelphia, hence water quality presents a significant challenge for many aquatic species.

The Ancient Mariners of Delaware Bay

About 480 million years ago, a few armored jawless fishes plied the waters of ancient seas, but most marine life during the early Ordovician Period lacked vertebrae and dwelled on or near the seabed. Most of these creatures, as well as the outlines of the continents, only vaguely resemble those we know today—except one. Indeed, to an untrained eye, the ancestors of horseshoe crabs easily might pass for any of the four modern species. Three of these dwell in seas bordering Asia, with the fourth species—the American horseshoe crab—occurring only in the western Atlantic Ocean. Their body plan—a domed, helmet-like shell protecting vital organs and five pairs of legs—passed through the eons essentially unchanged (fig. 6.1). Moreover, their lineage has repeatedly survived perilous times, most notably a mass extinction ca 252 million years ago that claimed about 96 percent of all marine life.

FIGURE 6.1. Thousands of horseshoe crabs breed each year on the shores of Delaware Bay; as shown here, females lead the way ashore in the clasp of a male that will fertilize the eggs she lays on the beach (top). Sometimes two or more males form a train of suiters attached to a single female. The underside of a horseshoe crab reveals five pairs of leg-like appendages; in males, the first pair bears claws used to cling to females, but they are otherwise harmless (bottom). Photo credits: Bob Cunningham.

Horseshoe crabs stand alone in the world's menagerie; the four species compose a family with closer affinities to spiders and scorpions than with true crabs. These indeed are strange creatures. For starters, their systems flow with copper-based blue blood—instead of iron-rich red blood—endowed with the unusual property of reacting to various kinds of contaminants (see following). Horseshoe crabs also "see" with ten eyes; two large compound eyes designed to locate mates (and little else), with eight simple eyes serving as guides for their movements and sensing moonlight.[1] Two of the latter develop near the mouth on the ventral surface, whereas all of the other eyes develop on the dorsal surface, including some on the tail—a hardened spike that serves both as a rudder and as a lever for flipping an overturned individual to an upright position. Though their tails seem menacing, they are completely harmless and serve no defensive purpose, despite persistent notions that they inflict venomous stings. Native Americas, with their usual resourcefulness, tipped their spears with these durable and easily obtained appendages.

Countless millions of horseshoe crabs once crept ashore each year to breed on the shoreline between southern New England and the Gulf coast of Texas. But nowhere in this extensive range were they as numerous as those millions that arrived each spring on the shores of Delaware Bay. Such abundance hardly went unnoticed, at first by those who drove their pigs to the beach each spring to gorge on what were then known as "king crabs." Other residents enriched the soil in their croplands with the bodies of horseshoe crabs or scooped up loads of crab eggs for chicken feed. Even so, these levels of harvest posed no threat to the immense population of crabs that amassed each year on the edges of Delaware Bay. Then, almost inevitably, the ancient creatures became a commodity at an industrial scale. So began a sad chapter of exploitation, highlighted by similar tragedies befalling bison and passenger pigeons.

As recounted by writer-naturalist Deborah Cramer, an enterprising innkeeper (and state senator) in Egg Harbor by the name of Thomas Beesley bought two miles of beachfront in 1855, opened a factory, and started the first commercial fertilizer business based on horseshoe crabs. He picked a good location—just a half

---

[1] The structure and function of the two large compound eyes on the shells of horseshoe crabs proved useful for understanding the visual disorders of humans. Research involving the eyes of horseshoe crabs earned H. Keffer Hartline a share of the 1967 Nobel Prize for physiology/medicine.

FIGURE 6.2. Huge numbers of horseshoe crabs were once harvested commercially along the coast of Delaware Bay. Ground up and bagged, the crabs were turned into nutrient-rich fertilizer for farm and garden. Photo courtesy of the Delaware Public Archives.

mile of beach yielded 750,000 crabs before he stopped counting. The hapless crop was machine-thrashed, roasted, and ground into a fine powder that sold for $30 a ton, half the price of imported guano fertilizers. Similar operations soon opened for business on both sides of Delaware Bay. One of these in New Jersey even built a small railroad to haul the catch to a factory at a site then known as King Crab Landing and near the present location of Highs Beach.

Once in full swing, the fertilizer industry harvested more than a million horseshoe crabs each year for more than half a century (fig. 6.2). The first signs of trouble emerged in the late 1800s when more men, gear, and time were required to maintain a profitable catch. Still, the exploitation continued unchecked for decades even as the numbers of horseshoe crabs continued to plummet. The end came in the years following World War II when one after another fertilizer plant shut down, hastened by the development and production of other types of fertilizers. Now the diminished horseshoe population at Delaware Bay could begin rebuilding, but only for a while. New stresses would again threaten horseshoe crabs.

The American eel fishery in Delaware Bay employs traps—"eel pots"—baited with horseshoe crabs, a practice that dates at least to the 1800s. Females, sometimes cut in half, serve particularly well as bait because the pheromones they emit help lure eels to the pots. When the eel fishery expanded in the 1990s, so did the harvest of horseshoe crabs. Instead of becoming fertilizer, millions of crabs were now turned into bait, a demand that increased even more when the whelk fishery likewise expanded in Delaware Bay (e.g., surveys indicated an 88 percent decline in crab numbers during a fifteen-year period ending in 2005). In this case, a whole female or two male crabs baited the whelk pots. Like the modern eel fishery, the whelk fishery today supplies both foreign and domestic markets, and the demand for bait continues to remove millions of horseshoe crabs each year.

Horseshoe crabs are also harvested in Delaware Bay (and elsewhere) to produce Limulus amebocyte lysate (LAL), a reagent with important biomedical applications. Amebocytes, a constituent of the blue blood of horseshoe crabs, react to bacterial endotoxins and other types of contamination. LAL thus offers a means to test the purity and safe production of intravenous drugs and implanted medical devices such as pacemakers and joint replacements. To meet the demand for LAL, about 500,000 horseshoe crabs were captured and bled each year along the Atlantic coast, including those in Delaware Bay. About one-third of the blood was removed humanely from each crab in sterile laboratories, after which most were returned to the sea (some were sold for bait). Regrettably, postrelease mortality may be quite significant; for the purpose of fisheries management, 15 percent is generally accepted as the mortality rate for donor crabs, but recent research indicates a far higher rate of nearly 30 percent. New Jersey halted all harvesting of horseshoe crabs in 2008, but the other states bordering Delaware Bay have not followed suit, and the population continued to decline.

Whereas an alternative to LAL was synthesized in 1997 with the development of recombinant factor C (rFC), the pharmaceutical industry continued to rely on LAL, in large part because it was entrenched as the gold standard by the U.S.

Food and Drug Administration. Although the exploitation of horseshoe crabs continues today, Eli Lilly biologist (and avid birder) Jay Bolden pressed the industry to adopt rFC based on his detailed comparisons of the two products. Indeed, rFC was not only the equal of LAL but sometimes even better. Today, Eli Lilly has integrated rFC into its testing protocols, which will hopefully establish a new norm throughout the pharmaceutical industry. If so, and in coordination with reducing the harvest by the bait industry, the population of horseshoe crabs may experience a much-needed rebound along with the birds that depend on the abundance of their eggs (see following).

Horseshoe crabs produce immense quantities of eggs. Each female deposits up to 5,000 eggs in a six- to eight-inch-deep nest excavated near the upper limits of the high-tide line—a location that keeps the eggs beyond the reach of hungry fish. Breeding coincides with the high tides associated with a full or new moon. The same female will lay additional clutches during these periods, eventually producing a seasonal total of 80,000 to 100,000 eggs. Mating is a disorganized affair. Females drag ashore at least one of the throng of males waiting at the water's edge. A male grasps the larger-bodied female with a pair of clawed claspers, and often may be joined by a cluster of additional suitors in a shoreline parade that ends when they fertilize the clutch of pearly green eggs, each no larger than the head of pin. Some of these unpaired males, known as satellite males, actually may fertilize as many eggs as the male grasping the female. Given a breeding population of a million or so horseshoe crabs, the beaches teem with about 84,000 eggs per square yard. By the end of the season, the shores of Delaware Bay have become a sandy incubator for billions of eggs (fig. 6.3, bottom).

The eggs hatch about four weeks later when another new or full moon again produces high tides. At hatching, the larvae resemble miniature versions of adults, but without tails. They remain near shore for their first few years of life, gradually moving into deeper water as they mature. Because they have hard shells, horseshoe crabs must molt as they grow; males molt 16 times, whereas females, perhaps because of their larger size, undergo an additional molt. Molting ends when the crabs reach sexual maturity, which takes at least nine years; the final molt in males includes the modification of the first pair of leg-like appendages into claspers used to grasp females during their nuptial march up the beach. Horseshoe crabs may live for 20 years, which includes about 10 seasons of breeding activity.

FIGURE 6.3. The arrival of red knots and other migrating shorebirds coincides with breeding activities of horseshoe crabs on the shores of Delaware Bay (top), a critical event that provides the birds with enough horseshoe crab eggs to fuel the final leg of their flight to far-off nesting areas (inset). A stunning accumulation of horseshoe crab eggs at a jetty at Fortescue belies their diminished abundance (bottom); years of exploitation have reduced the population of horseshoe crabs and their eggs, which in turn has severely affected the survival of red knots. Photo credits: Bob Cunningham (top; inset); Susan Allen (bottom).

Add Birds and Mix

Sometime in the misty past, shorebirds showed up on the same bayfront beaches long favored by horseshoe crabs. Today up to 15 species of shorebirds visit Delaware Bay each year (fig. 6.3, top). Of these, ruddy turnstones, sanderlings, and especially red knots maintain a close and essential bond with the bay's springtime trove of horseshoe crab eggs. Unlike migrating songbirds that typically stop daily to rest and feed before continuing their journey, shorebirds travel long distances at a time, stopping less often and remaining longer. This is an important difference because the shorebirds necessarily rely on just a few key areas that, if degraded, break a link in a vital chain for which there is no alternative.

Some of these birds such as the red knots start their trip north from wintering areas as distant as Tierra del Fuego at the tip of South America, and nearly all of the species will continue northward until reaching their nesting grounds in the far-off Arctic tundra. In between these points, the birds may stop just three times. The marathon journey of a red knot outfitted with a half-ounce gizmo known as a geolocator included a six-day, 5,000-mile nonstop segment with a flight path that crossed both the Amazon basin in Brazil and the Atlantic Ocean before touching down on the coast of North Carolina—and the bird still had at least 1,500 miles to go. After enduring flights of this magnitude, the birds arrive emaciated and with virtually no reserves of body fat. The availability of abundant and nourishing food at these stopovers clearly assumes strategic importance for shorebirds.

Red knots have evolved a remarkable adaptation to facilitate the demands of migration. In preparation for their long flights, they reduce the size of their internal organs associated with digestion, but concurrently increase the size of those organs with a direct bearing on flight—wing and breast muscles, heart and lungs. With a synchrony honed by time, the birds reach Delaware Bay—their numbers peak in late May—just when the horseshoe crabs begin their ancient spawning ritual. On arrival, the knots will gorge on the lipid-rich crab eggs—a feeding frenzy in which the birds nearly double their weight. These gains include the rebuilding of their digestive organs, which cannot initially handle the small bivalve mollusks that served as their winter diet, but the soft crab eggs provide a perfect substitute. The bounty of crab eggs is of such a magnitude that knots need only remain at Delaware Bay for about half the time they spend at stopovers elsewhere in the world. Thus refueled, the knots and other shorebirds resume their flight to the Far North.

Timing is critical in the life cycle of shorebirds nesting in the Arctic. The birds arrive just as the grip of winter is waning but before insects—the bulk of their summer diet—abound. The fat reserves replenished at Delaware Bay not only fueled the last leg of their flight to the Arctic but now must also sustain the birds during the onset of nesting. Courtship activities demand energy, but egg production requires even more, and more yet for incubation. If the birds have not fared well at Delaware Bay, their chances for successful breeding diminish considerably. Arctic summers are short—the "window" for nesting is brief and without opportunity for a second chance. The nestlings must be fledged and gone well before winter again closes in.

Problems!

All is not well at Delaware Bay for horseshoe crabs and shorebirds alike. Because of the harvest of crabs for eel and conch bait, fewer crabs breed on the beaches, reduced to the point where their output of eggs no longer fulfills the needs of the birds. The crab harvest has seriously disrupted nature's long-standing economy of supply and demand, and the food shortage shows up on the scales. In 1997–1998, 60 to 80 percent of the red knots left Delaware Bay weighing in excess of about 6.5 ounces, whereas by 2006–2007, only 14 to 40 percent had attained the same weight. With less fat available, the underweight birds face hard times completing their migration and breeding successfully. Research has also determined that underweight knots at Delaware Bay experience greater mortality than heavier individuals. By 2007, the red knot population stopping at Delaware Bay had plummeted by more than 75 percent—down from a peak of 94,000 in 1989—and the species was listed as threatened in 2014. The trend continued, reaching a low of 6,880 birds in 2021.

An important side effect corresponds with the abundance of horseshoe crabs. When deposited, the eggs in the crab nests lie beyond the reach of red knots—their bill is far too short in length—but this limitation becomes unimportant on a beach crowded by thousands of female crabs busy with nesting. Their excavations dislodge and bring to the surface eggs from other nests. As many as 50 nests may occupy a square yard of beach, a density not unlike the same number of tea cups atop a card table—and just about as easy to disturb. Under such conditions, millions of the dislodged eggs litter the beachfront, and along the shoreline, these often accumulate in thick windrows that quite literally become cafeterias for the hungry birds. Conversely, with a diminished number of nesting females, far fewer eggs become dislodged and available to eat. Note that the birds act as salvagers of otherwise doomed eggs; if left uneaten, the exposed eggs soon dry and lose their viability, having made no contribution to a new generation of horseshoe crabs.

Other species of shorebirds stopping at Delaware Bay experienced similar consequences, among them ruddy turnstones. Although short, the sturdy slightly upturned bills of these strikingly marked shorebirds enable them to excavate deeply enough to reach crab nests. Nonetheless, the numbers of ruddy turnstones dropped 77 percent over a nine-year period ending in 2007. Somewhat lesser reductions occurred during the same period for semipalmated sandpipers, sanderlings, short-billed dowitchers, and dunlins, but in combination this group declined by 50 percent.

The vital importance of horseshoe crabs to migrating shorebirds has garnered international attention. In 1986, Delaware Bay was tapped as the first site in the Western Hemisphere Shorebird Reserve Network, which steadily expanded to include 94 other locations extending from Alaska to Tierra del Fuego. This movement recognizes areas critical to the life cycles of shorebirds and promotes science and management as tools to ensure their continued integrity as productive habitat. At the local level, New Jersey imposed a moratorium on the harvest of horseshoe crabs in 2008, and Delaware excludes females from its harvest, but other states bordering Delaware Bay continue to remove large numbers each year—but not without furthering the serious ecological consequences, as described above. In 2001, the impacts of these removals was lessened somewhat with the creation of a 1,500-square-mile sanctuary off the mouth of Delaware Bay in which trawlers cannot legally harvest horseshoe crabs. Still, the horseshoe crab population breeding at Delaware Bay currently shows only a slight increase, perhaps in part because of the long period required for these animals to reach sexual maturity.

In 2022, the Atlantic States Marine Fisheries Commission proposed to renew the harvest of female horseshoe crabs in Delaware Bay, despite the greatly reduced population of red knots stopping along its shores, as noted above. The proposal dismayed conservationists, who insisted that the commission's population estimates of 45,000 red knots were greatly inflated and thus were not a reliable justification to again harvest female horseshoe crabs, which the commission had banned

Shore Note 6.1 The Curse of *Phragmites*

Common reed, better known simply as *Phragmites*, has and continues to commandeer both coastal and inland marshes across the breath of North America. The species consists of three subspecies, one native to much of North America, another occurring along the Gulf Coast, and the last—the aggressive troublemaker—an import from Europe. In one form or another, *Phragmites* thrives on every continent except Antarctica, which hints at its broad tolerance for environmental conditions. In short, *Phragmites* is one tough, adaptable plant, often unwanted and always difficult to control.

The European subspecies apparently arrived early in the nineteenth century as seeds hitchhiking in the ballast of ships. It rapidly gained a foothold, pushing out the native subspecies with its aggressive growth and ability to colonize many types of wetlands. Uniquely, *Phragmites* completely occupies the full spectrum of plant succession—pioneer to climax—in which it crowds out virtually all other plant life, including the two native saltmarsh dominants, smooth cordgrass and marsh hay. The result is a monoculture of 12-foot-tall grasses that spreads rapidly both by seed but more efficiently by rhizomes that may grow 6 feet in length each year and eventually extend 60 feet from the mother plant. Some evidence suggests that *Phragmites* produces toxic substances that inhibit the growth of other plants. The matter remains unclear, but if true, it represents an example of allelopathy—the adverse effect on plants of one species by the chemical secretions of another species.

Phragmites modifies coastal marshes in other ways, including stemming the flow of small tidal creeks. When their rhizomes cross these arteries, they entrap sediments, forming dams that effectively curtail further movement of water into the marsh. In a similar fashion, the dense stands of *Phragmites* elevate the marsh floor, likewise altering the hydrology of the wetland and, in turn, impacting the fauna dependent on regular tidal inundation. Both of these developments curtail mummichogs as well as markedly alter the arthropod fauna. For example, entire trophic levels of herbivores and their predators (e.g., spiders) diminish, largely replaced by detritivores. Most of the

in 2013. Additionally, conservation biologists monitoring the local situation—some for decades—underscored the sharp reduction in the horseshoe crab eggs available to the birds: about 50,000 eggs per square yard in the 1990s but just 7,000 in 2022. Fortunately, the commission later rejected the proposal, at least for now thwarting further threat to both crab and bird.

Just how large a population of horseshoe crabs might be required to return the birds to their former numbers remains unclear, but harvesting females seems sure to further lessen the food resources available to the red knots stopping on

displaced arthropods represent free-living insects readily incorporated into the food web (e.g., prey for birds), whereas a single and much less accessible stem-feeding insect dominates the fauna associated with *Phragmites*.

Farms along the New Jersey Bayshore once diked off areas of salt marsh to exclude salt water and thereby create conditions suitable for growing and harvesting crops of marsh hay. Similar activities occurred along the New England coast. However, with the eventual abandonment of these farms, *Phragmites* invaded those hayfields where the dikes continued to keep out salt water. As a result, *Phragmites* covers much of the New Jersey Bayshore. Fortunately, however, both native vegetation and its associated fauna quickly return to sites where breached dikes no longer keep out salt water. Hence, for both private and public conservation agencies, returning tidal flows presents an important way to restore coastal marshes to their former composition and function. Elsewhere, herbicide treatments, coupled with prescribed burns, initiate the restoration of *Phragmites*-infested marshes.

Still, *Phragmites* may have some benefits, as recently determined by a study led by a Rutgers ecologist. The highly noxious introduced form readily traps sediments that naturally elevate marsh profiles at rates that keep pace with rising sea levels. Stands of *Phragmites*, more so than those of other marsh plants, produce greater amounts of belowground tissues, which increases the vertical growth of the marsh profile. Additionally, the dense growth above ground accumulates large amounts of dead foliage that capture and hold sediments carried by the daily tidal flow. Indeed, of the marshes sampled in the study, only two sites—both in the *Phragmites*-dominated Hackensack Meadowlands—were keeping pace with the rate of sea level rise. *Phragmites* thus may offer a biological means of defending salt marshes against sea level rise and can do so without any financial investment. Such results may be achieved simply by reducing ongoing efforts to control *Phragmites* with expensive herbicide treatments, which also would allow precious resources to be redirected to other conservation activities.

the shores of Delaware Bay. It's also obvious that two of Delaware Bay's most prominent natural resources warrant continued and close monitoring to effectively protect birds and crabs alike.

A Trio of Fishes

The Delaware watershed—a large bay and estuary fed by a major river—forms an aquatic treasure rich with fishes. Of these, three species illustrate the breadth of fish fauna in this system: two being anadromous, another catadromous; one being a bony finfish, another an ancient form with a cartilaginous skeleton, and a third resembling a snake; one a tasty sport fish, two others prized only as food. All, however, currently face hard times.

Each spring during April and May, adult American shad return to the Delaware River and its freshwater tributaries. Similar runs occur each year from Florida to the Saint Lawrence River, but all are keyed to water temperatures of 50 to 55 Fahrenheit, hence those in the South begin months earlier than those farther north. Each run consists of shad returning to the same rivers where they hatched years earlier, then left as fingerlings to mature in the ocean, and now reenter freshwater to spawn. Such a cycle occurs in a few other species—Pacific salmon perhaps being the best known example—and identifies the shad and others as anadromous fishes. Remarkably, the returning adults find the same sites where they hatched years earlier. They rely on a keen sense of smell as their primary means of locating their natal areas; some swim upstream for more than 200 miles to return "home." This ability evolved as a means of ensuring that the fish spawn where the bottom—sand and gravel in the case of shad—water velocity and other conditions provide optimal habitat.

Such a system of homing behavior precludes searching, perhaps fruitlessly, for a new spawning area. In other words, if conditions were good enough in the past (when the adults hatched), they should still be good enough to produce yet another generation. The run to specific spawning areas thus evolved as a hardwired tradition in the life history of anadromous fishes. In the modern world, however, dams and pollution too often short-circuit the value of anadromous behavior. Legend has it that George Washington encamped at Valley Forge because the shad run in the Schuylkill River, a tributary of the Delaware, would feed his troops after a winter of short rations. The tale lacks hard evidence, although Washington was indeed familiar with shad runs on the Potomac River.

Mature females each produce about 130,000 eggs, although a few may spawn several times that number. Once fertilized, the eggs drift in keeping with the current and hatch 7 to 10 days later, but many have entered the food chain as the prey of small fish and insect larvae. The tiny hatchlings ("fry") seek safety in sheltered areas and freshwater marshes where they grow into three- to five-inch-long fingerlings in readiness for their fall departure downstream. Once in the ocean, the young fish join others that hatched in rivers elsewhere along the Atlantic coast.

These, too, become an important link in food chains, this time for larger predators such as bluefish. The young shad will spend the next four to five years in the ocean where they form large schools. During this period, they will migrate north in the spring to feed on the abundant plankton in the Gulf of Maine and, especially, in the Bay of Fundy where huge tides stir up tons of nutrient-rich sediments. Indeed, some biologists claim that every shad produced on the eastern coast will visit the Bay of Fundy. In fall, the shad head south for the winter, traveling as far as North Carolina, and return north again the following spring. In all, the route forms a huge loop rather than a linear path that runs parallel to the shoreline.

Adult shad, unlike Pacific salmon, do not necessarily die after spawning. Curiously, the postspawning mortality rate varies along the Atlantic coast on a north-south gradient. Shad spawning in rivers north of Cape Hatteras, North Carolina, may survive for more than one season, whereas virtually all others die after spawning just once. About 6 percent survive in the Delaware River, with the survival rate increasing northward until it reaches about 80 percent in Canada. Those that survive will spawn again the following year.

Anglers prize American shad for their size and sporting qualities; as the largest species in the herring family, most shad weigh between three and eight pounds (females are larger than males). Moreover, shad make good table fare, which is reflected in the species name, *sapidissima*, Latin for "most savory." Adult shad lack teeth and feed almost exclusively on plankton, yet they eat nothing when on their upstream spawning runs. Mysteriously, however, some shad will bite on lures and flies, perhaps for reasons of aggression rather than hunger; most anglers use lures designed expressly for catching shad.

Shad runs in the Delaware River no longer resemble those of the past. Pollution took its toll, and while the river itself remains free of dams, they do block the runs that once spawned in its tributaries. Nonetheless, overfishing, largely from years of commercial exploitation, more likely explains why so few shad now return to the Delaware River. Today both the commercial harvest and the sport fishery remain closely regulated, so perhaps better days lie ahead for shad runs in the watershed of the Delaware River.

American eels travel upstream to mature in several New Jersey streams and rivers, of which the Delaware River is the largest. They are thus catadromous, a type of migration in which fish mature in freshwater but spawn in the ocean, and the American eel stands alone as a catadromous species in the fish fauna of North America. Eels start life in the Sargasso Sea, which, unlike other seas and oceans, has no coastlines. Instead, four major currents define its borders, of which the well-known Gulf Stream forms the western edge. The unusually clear water in the Sargasso Sea remains exceptionally calm—a windless sea once the bane of crews sailing wind-powered vessels and still feared as part of the infamous Bermuda Triangle. Large rafts of brown algae—Sargasso seaweed—float on the surface buoyed by air-filled bladders that Portuguese mariners called "sargaco," which thereafter identified this distinctive area of the Atlantic Ocean. European eels also spawn in the Sargasso Sea, but Atlantic eels have no counterpart on the Pacific coast of North America.

Female Atlantic eels each produce as many as four million eggs, which hatch into larva known as leptocephli, the first of several stages that develop on a long journey to a far-off river. At this stage, the larvae resemble flattened, transparent willow leaves with small heads and large teeth. For the next 7 to 12 months, the leptocephli will drift west and north guided by the surface currents of the Gulf Steam. After about 200 days, the larvae move closer to shore and metamorphose into glass eels, still transparent but now 2 to 3 inches long and shaped like adults. As they move into estuaries, glass eels lose their transparency and, for the next several months, start moving upstream. However, the young eels still remain sexually undifferentiated.

Glass eels then become known as yellow eels as their pigmentation continues developing. They also differentiate sexually in this stage, an event that seems influenced by environmental factors such as population density—high density favors a greater proportion of males. Maturation continues as the yellow eels metamorphose into silver eels, but their sexual organs do not fully mature until they return to the ocean years later. When they depart, the adults may be at least 10 years old and some two or even three times that age. They do not forage on their journey back to the Sargasso Sea—in fact, at this stage their digestive tracts actually wither—and they will die after spawning.

Two circumstances in this cycle produce panmixia—the widespread and thorough mixing of genes in a widely distributed population (as opposed to the evolution of races or subpopulations with specific geographical affinities). First, the spawning eels breed randomly in the Sargasso Sea, so that eggs of a female that matured in Nova Scotia might be fertilized by a male arriving from New Jersey. Second, the leptocephali disperse passively, subject only to the whims of local currents, and therefore eels do not necessarily mature in the same watersheds where their parents matured. As a result, panmixia produces a single population that lacks adaptations keyed to the features of specific habitats, hence enabling each eel to cope with a board range of environmental conditions.

Atlantic eels play a role in the life cycle and dispersal of the eastern elliptio, a common freshwater mussel in the Delaware and other watersheds in the eastern part of North America. In recent years, however, few young elliptios have turned up in those systems in which eel populations have diminished. When reproducing, the mussels eject tiny clam-like larvae called glochidia, which attach themselves to the blood-rich gills of passing fish (some liken this to a Pac-Man attack). During this phase, the larvae function as parasites but do not harm their hosts. After about 20 days, the glochidia metamorphose into juvenile mussels and drop off their hosts to begin a sedentary life on the river bottom. Although several species of fishes may serve as hosts for the glochidia, experiments revealed that American eels prove the most effective—about 90 percent of the glochidia attached to their gills transform into juvenile mussels, with each eel supplying more than 13 mussels. Elliptios provide an important ecological service; in the Delaware River they filter and cleanse the water six times before it reaches the ocean.

Atlantic eels, as noted earlier, have commercial value, especially in markets serving ethnic groups in the northeastern United States and in Europe. In Delaware Bay, the fishery catches eels in baited traps called "pots," whereas V-shaped weirs capture adult eels when they migrate downriver en route to the Sargasso Sea. However, things are not well for the Atlantic eel, and the harvest has rapidly declined because of water pollution, dams, and overfishing. The harvest includes glass eels, which have considerable value in overseas markets as stock for mariculture production—a demand that promotes illegal netting. In a creek near Absecon, for example, authorities caught three poachers with 24,000 glass eels worth $2,500 per pound on the open market. Small eels also provide anglers with a prized bait for striped bass and other game fish. Harvests peaked in the 1970s and 1980s, and then steadily lessened to the point where the stock is widely regarded as depleted. Some believe the species has reached the point of becoming endangered, a formal designation twice considered and rejected by the U.S. Fish and Wildlife Service. Additionally, a parasitic nematode from Asia now infects the swim bladders of

American eels in many areas; although apparently not fatal, it impairs the swimming abilities of adult eels and thus may curtail their spawning migrations.

The range of the anadromous Atlantic sturgeon extends from New Brunswick in southern Canada to the east coast of Florida. Those in the Delaware River belong to a distinct population segment associated with the New York Bight. Fossils of sturgeon date to the Cretaceous Period, and because the modern species resemble their early ancestors, they are regarded as "primitive fishes" or "living fossils." Atlantic sturgeon reach 15 feet in length and may weigh 800 pounds, although most are nearer half that size. Like other species of sturgeon, they have cartilaginous skeletons and smooth scaleless skins and five lateral rows of bony plates (scutes) armor their bodies.. They lack teeth and suck in food—shellfish, other bottom-dwelling organisms, and some finfish—detected by four sensitive barbels that border their mouths. Atlantic sturgeon may live for 60 years and take several years to mature (6–10 years for males and 10–20 years for females).

Atlantic sturgeon spawn in freshwater and may produce as many as three million eggs per female once every two to six years. After spawning, the adults return to the ocean, where they remain near the coastline. Meanwhile, their sticky eggs adhere to the hard bottom of the spawning area. After hatching, river currents carry the larval fish downstream to the safety of sloughs and other protected areas where they remain for a year before the free-swimming fry move into the main channel to continue their journey to the estuary. They stay in Delaware Bay for about 6 years before entering the ocean. Adult sturgeon display the odd habit of leaping, which may represent some form of communication, but much still remains unclear about this behavior.

Like other species of sturgeon, the Atlantic sturgeon is predisposed to the harmful effects of commercial exploitation. They have long been harvested for meat and their leathery skin, made into clothing and book bindings, but it was the delicacy of their roe—"black gold"—that relentlessly fueled the sturgeon fishery. A site at the mouth of Stow Creek on the New Jersey side of Delaware Bay became known as Caviar Point because of its role in the commercial harvest of sturgeon. By 1895, a train left Caviar Point daily with carloads of caviar and smoked sturgeon bound for both domestic and foreign markets.

The combination of slow maturity and the emphasis on harvesting females placed unsustainable burdens on sturgeon populations. The Delaware River once was the largest fishery for Atlantic sturgeon—some 2,535 tons were harvested in 1890—but overfishing soon took its toll and the harvest plummeted by 90 percent in the early 1900s. What was once a population estimated at 180,000 adult sturgeon today numbers between 300 and 500 breeding females. Pollution added to the woes. Moreover, the losses also include sturgeon caught as bycatch—the innocuous sounding term for nontarget species caught (and usually die) in gill nets or by trawlers. Today, sturgeon throughout the world face extinction, and the Atlantic sturgeon is no exception—those in the New York Bight were listed as endangered in 2012.

A Small Niche for a Little Bird

In 1957, ornithologists formally recognized a new subspecies of swamp sparrow (fig. 6.4). Overall, the species occupies wetlands across a large area of eastern North America. However, the new taxon—the coastal plain swamp sparrow—breeds exclusively in salt marshes bordering estuaries along the Atlantic shoreline from Chesapeake Bay to the Hudson River, a range in which Delaware Bay represents a key location. Ecologically, the birds nest in the narrow strip of shrubs, primarily groundsel and marsh elder, that marks the inland border of high marsh. In contrast, the other subspecies of swamp sparrow nest in freshwater habitats well inland from the coastline.

Several features distinguish the new subspecies. Compared with the reddish brown plumage of other swamp sparrows, the coastal birds have grayer plumage and blacker head and body markings. Such coloring presumably helps conceal the birds against the dark mud of the marsh floor where they forage. Moreover, the dark plumage also may deter a type of salt-tolerant bacteria that degrades the feathers of these birds. Coastal plain swamp sparrows also have larger bills, an adaptation for capturing and feeding on crustaceans and other invertebrates instead of eating seeds as preferred by their inland relatives. Internally, the larger kidneys of the coastal birds enable the passage of more fluids—a clear advantage for coping with a saline environment. Their life history also differs, including smaller clutches and shorter occupancy of the nesting area. Together,

Shore Note 6.2　Oysters: Reefs, Raw, and Roasted

"He was a brave man that first ate an oyster," wrote Jonathan Swift in *Gulliver's Travels*. That daring event triggered a savory feast that has continued ever since, albeit with far less trepidation. Native Americans living along the New Jersey coast ate lots of shellfish, as witnessed by the middens they left behind, and Euro-Americans described what then seemed to be endless beds of oysters in Delaware Bay as early as 1642. By the 1750s, fresh oysters from these beds were regularly shipped to markets in Philadelphia and New York. A commercial oyster trade also developed on Barnegat Bay as well as elsewhere along the Jersey Shore. Oysters are often enjoyed "as is" on the half shell, but chefs also prepare more elaborate dishes, including hardy oyster stews, turkey stuffing, and the delicacy known as Oysters Rockefeller. Other cooks simply roast oysters on a grill until they open, ready to eat after a quick dip in a tangy sauce. Some oysters include a tasty bonus—a female pea crab that invades a young oyster and, as a kleptoparasite, spends its adult life stealing food captured by the oyster's gills. George Washington, for one, considered the tiny crabs as a treat, as do gourmets today.

New Jersey's oyster industry eventually faced difficulties, the first of which was chronic over-harvesting. Regulations, accompanied by reseeding projects, attempted to deal with the issue, but the once abundant oyster population never fully recovered. Outright disaster struck in 1957 when a protozoan parasite dubbed MSX devastated the oyster population in New Jersey. The harvest in Delaware Bay, for example, plummeted from 711,000 bushels in 1956 to just 49,000 in 1960. The industry rebounded somewhat when the oysters developed a measure of resistance to MSX. However, a second blow arrived in 1990 when another parasite, the agent of a disease known as Dermo, again killed oysters wholesale, especially those planted in managed beds. But unlike with MSX, oysters have so far not evolved much resistance to Dermo. (Neither MSX nor Dermo affects humans.) Today, the industry continues on a sustainable basis in Delaware Bay, but only as a remnant of a once far larger enterprise. The Haskin Shellfish Research Laboratory operated at Bivalve by Rutgers University works closely with both the oyster industry and resource managers to enhance the stock of oysters in Delaware Bay—a cooperative effort designed to conserve both a historic industry and a way of life for the Bayshore region.

these features appear to reduce the risk of losing nests to floods from unusually high tides and storms (i.e., a shorter window of opportunity for misfortune to occur).

Still, a void remained in the profile for the new subspecies—where did these birds spend the winter? To find the answer, biologists analyzed the feathers in the reddish cap that males develop before they begin their spring migration. Impor-

Historically, an economically viable oyster fishery also existed in the Mullica River estuary, where, long before the two diseases emerged, black drum threatened the industry. Thousands of the fish, which showed up in the summer and often weighed more than 100 pounds, easily crushed oysters with their large pharyngeal (throat) teeth outfitted with prominent grinding surfaces that resemble pebbles set in concrete. The threat was confirmed years later when studies of captive black drum revealed that the fish daily consume nearly one oyster per pound of body weight (e.g., a 45-pound black drum each day might feed on 40 oysters). Faced with economic hardship, the resolute oystermen netted and even dynamited the fish, once killing some 2,000 black drum on a single day in July 1902 and, not incidentally, attracting legions of sharks seeking an easy meal. Nonetheless, the black drum population remained abundant, and the dynamiting continued to 1917, perhaps ended in part by America's entry into World War I. Today, oyster farms in the Mullica River estuary safely produce their crops in drum-proof trays or bags.

The decline in oyster numbers bears ecological as well as socioeconomic implications. A single oyster daily filters up to 50 gallons of water, which clears the water of microalgae and suspended particles and removes harmful contaminants such as bacteria, nitrates, phosphorous, and heavy metals. An oyster reef also adds 50 times more surface area to a flat bottom, which in turn provides niches for complex communities of small crustaceans, worms, mollusks, small fishes, and other marine organisms—an assemblage that usually improves recreational fishing in the immediate area.

The reefs also provide a hard substrate necessary for each new generation of oysters. Each female may produce millions of eggs and a single male may eject more than 2 billion sperm, but only one of every million fertilized eggs will survive to maturity. The larvae pass through three stages, the last of which settles on a hard surface where it will remain permanently attached (most of the other larvae perish simply because they fail to land on a suitable surface). The larvae—at this stage known as spat—will develop into mature oysters in about three years. Existing reefs, of course, offer ideal hard surface for spat. As a result, undisturbed oyster reefs steadily build into sizable structures favoring both their own kind as well as other marine life. Because of their filtering activities and the architecture they provide, oysters have earned the designation of ecosystem engineers.

tantly, the chemical composition (in the form of isotopes) of new feathers reflects the soils and water at the site where the plumage develops. In other words, a given location has its own "fingerprint" that is incorporated into new plumage (or hair, in the case of mammals). Thus, using the isotope fingerprint from feathers collected when the birds arrived on their breeding grounds, the biologists could seek a match with similar data from various geographical locations elsewhere. Based

FIGURE 6.4. A subspecies of the swamp sparrow, the coastal plain swamp sparrow, breeds exclusively in salt marshes bordering estuaries, including Delaware Bay, whereas two other subspecies breed well inland in freshwater habitats across much of eastern North America. Additionally, the head and body plumage of coastal plain subspecies is darker in comparison with the swamp sparrow shown here. Photo credit: James F. Parnell.

on this analysis, coastal plain swamp sparrows overwinter in coastal marshes stretching northward from South Carolina, across North Carolina, and barely into southern Virginia. On-the-ground searches for the birds at several locations in this region subsequently confirmed the analysis.

Somewhat curiously, the distance between the breeding and wintering areas is not extensive. Why this is the case likely concerns the feeding ecology of these birds. Because they probe for food in the mud, the birds need to migrate south only just far enough to avoid frozen ground. Not surprisingly, therefore, temperatures cold enough to harden the marsh floor indeed seldom occur in their wintering areas.

Along the Bayshore

Of the larger rivers flowing into Delaware Bay from New Jersey Bayshore, the Maurice River stands out both ecologically and historically. The 50-mile-long Maurice—locally pronounced as "Morris"—drains much of the southern Pine Barrens and discharges its tea-colored water into an extensive area of salt marshes. One of the largest stands of wild rice in New Jersey grows along the river (fig. 6.5). The species grows abundantly in the Great Lakes area, where it has a long cultural

FIGURE 6.5. Wild rice grows along the shores of the Maurice River, part of which is included in the national registry of Wild and Scenic Rivers in recognition of its natural, cultural, and historical significance. Photo credit: Pat and Clay Sutton.

history as a staple in the diet of Native Americans, but it is not closely related to the rice associated with oriental cuisines or southern plantations.

A remarkable migration of raptors is associated with the drainages of the Maurice and Cohansey rivers. A tally at the mouth of the Maurice River alone included some 12,000 raptors of 17 species. The composition of migrating raptors in this area differs somewhat when compared with the fall flight a few miles to the south at Cape May, in part because of species-specific tendencies to cross expanses of open water (see chapter 5). Red-tailed hawks, for example, occur more commonly along the Bayshore, whereas ospreys and falcons are less prevalent. Moreover, a diverse assemblage of raptors also overwinters in drainages of the two rivers and the adjacent Bayshore. Significant numbers of waterfowl also occur along the Maurice River; a 25-year census recorded 35 species of ducks and geese, but the tally sadly noted an 85 percent decline in wintering black ducks (see below for more about the status of the species). In all, the Delaware Bayshore serves as a critically important area from both migrating *and* wintering raptors, a dual function not known to occur elsewhere and more than enough reason for protecting this special area of New Jersey.

In 1993, the National Park Service added about 34 miles of the Maurice River to its Wild and Scenic River program, in part because of the area's history. The New Jersey side of Delaware Bay once supported a major oyster fishery that, at its peak, represented the largest of its kind entirely within the jurisdiction of a single state. Nonetheless, New Jersey enacted restrictions on the oyster harvest as early as 1719, but these were scarcely obeyed or enforced. The harvest continued essentially unchecked, leading to the emergence of Bivalve—as aptly named as a town can be—on the west shore of the Maurice River near its mouth. Bivalve was a hive of industry, all associated with oysters. By 1876, the railroad arrived and within 10 years carried away 10 railcars of oysters each week. The oyster harvest diminished in the 1930s, but the coup de grâce arrived about 1957 with the arrival of a protozoan disease known as MSX. The oyster fishery collapsed as the harvest plummeted by 98 percent within two years, made all the worse by another disease, Dermo, that turned up a few years later—the industry never recovered, and only a small, highly regulated harvest continues. Nor does much remain of Bivalve, although rather fittingly it is the site of the Haskin Shellfish Research Laboratory operated by Rutgers University. Its mission concerns the pathology, ecology, genetics, and populations of marine shellfish in New Jersey. Also in the area is

Shore Note 6.3 Barn Owls: Monkey-Faced Hunters

Barn owls, famous for their heart-shaped faces, stand apart from other owls (fig. 6.6). Their distinctive facial disk, nature's own form of a parabolic dish, collects, amplifies, and directs sound to their ears, which lie behind their eyes but within the disk. Their ears are particularly sensitive to the high-frequency sounds emitted by small mammals, the mainstay of their diet. Additionally, the ear openings differ in shape and location, with one (the left) higher than the other; the left ear also points slightly downward, the right slightly upward. The orientations of the feathers forming the ruff edging the facial disk also differ—slightly downward on the left, slightly upward on the right, thereby matching the corresponding ear. Because of these arrangements, sounds reach the ears differentially, which provides the owls with a means for precisely locating their prey without visual contact. Moreover, barn owls learn and memorize different sounds and thereby can separate noises made by prey from those originating from non-prey and other sources (e.g., wind-rustled grass).

Barn owls hunt with eerie silence. This ability lessens the chance of being heard by their potential victims while also improving their ability to locate prey with their sensitive hearing. Three adaptations reduce the flight noise of owls. A stiff, comb-like fringe bordering the leading edges of the primary flight feathers promotes laminar air flow and reduces noise. Modifications also occur on feathers at the trailing edge of the wing, where a soft, hairlike fringe reduces the turbulence where the air meets after flowing across the top and bottom of the wings during flight. Finally, the downy upper surfaces of the wing feathers lessen the noise produced when these feathers move over each other with each wing beat (the "down" forms from extensions of feather structures known as barbules). Because of the large surface area of their wings in relation to their body mass, barn owls can fly slowly and turn abruptly without stalling—a benefit for cruising in search of prey.

The diet of barn owls consists mainly of small rodents, but they also eat bats, lizards, and, at times, birds. The latter may become more prevalent during periods when rodent populations suddenly crash. Like other raptors, barn owls regurgitate pellets containing bones, hair, and other indigestible materials that reflect their food habits. The pellets pile up beneath roosts or in nests and, when regularly collected and examined, reveal dietary shifts associated with the changing seasons or the abundance of prey populations.

Barn owls mate for life. They nest in tree cavities and buildings that offer easy access, but they sometimes excavate burrows in stream banks. They breed once per year, but quickly respond to a food surplus by producing a second clutch. A typical clutch consists of five to seven eggs, although food shortages reduce the clutch size. The eggs are usually laid at two- to three-day intervals. Incubation, however, begins with the first egg, thus the owlets hatch in a staggered sequence over a period in excess of 10 days. This mechanism, common among raptors, helps ensure the survival of at least part of the brood. The oldest and therefore largest nestlings outcompete their younger

FIGURE 6.6. As elsewhere, barn owls readily accept nest boxes erected in the meadows and farmlands bordering the Bayshore, where the loss of abandoned buildings has reduced the availability of adequate nesting sites. The nest boxes sit atop poles eight feet above ground level. Owlets shown here are about four weeks old (inset). Photo credits: Barn Owl Box Company.

and smaller nest mates for food. Hence only the oldest owlets survive when food is scarce, whereas most or all of the brood survive in good times. Otherwise, if all hatched at the same time, a food shortage would almost certainly lead to the loss of the entire brood.

The remaining meadows of salt hay along the Bayshore offer prime hunting habitat for barn owls, which will range up to two miles from their nests to these areas in search of meadow voles, their preferred food. For now, barn owl numbers along the Bayshore remain reasonably stable, but they swing in keeping with the abundance of their prey. However, the foraging habitat continues to diminish as development steadily claims agricultural lands and rising sea levels alter the cordgrass meadows. Suitable nesting sites likewise disappear, but nest boxes represent a successful substitution for the loss of farm buildings and tree cavities. Between 2009 and 2014, barn owls used up to 80 percent of the nest boxes available in southern New Jersey, which currently lists the birds as a species of special concern because of their vulnerability to environmental threats.

the Bayshore Center, housed in restored century-old oyster sheds and dedicated to preserving the region's history, culture, and environment.

Heislerville Game Management Area, owned by the New Jersey Division of Fish and Wildlife, protects about 7,200 acres of salt marsh, mudflats, diked hay impoundments, and oak-pine uplands. The area borders, in part, the Maurice River and fronts on Delaware Bay. The historic East Point Lighthouse, built in 1849, stands on the property. In fall, migrating butterflies and dragonflies add to the thousands of birds stopping at Heislerville. Bald eagles nest in the area and contribute to the eagle population currently rebuilding in New Jersey.

Two nearby beaches, Thompson's and Moore's, once were small communities of summer homes and a few year-round residents, but a series of storms severely damaged the buildings and access roads, which were subsequently abandoned. Most of the sand also disappeared, revealing an underlying layer of rubble and debris that had served as a makeshift effort to reduce shore erosion but rendered the beachfront useless for horseshoe crabs and shorebirds. Today, thanks to a coalition of agencies and organizations, the beaches have largely been restored and again serve as valuable shorefront habitat for wildlife.

Supawna National Wildlife Refuge lies farther up the Bayshore, where it was established in 1974 as part of the Cape May NWR complex. The refuge includes more than 2,200 acres, of which 70 percent consists of brackish tidal marsh that offers winter habitat for waterfowl, especially for the American black duck, an icon of the Atlantic Flyway. Black ducks experienced a significant reduction in numbers—estimated as 84 percent—between 1964 and 2014, and while the population has now stabilized, their winter habitat remains a crucial concern. Unlike the winter diet of other dabbling ducks, black ducks forage on snails, crustaceans, and other invertebrate foods they encounter in coastal salt marshes. Hence, any loss or modification of these marshes has a direct bearing on black ducks, and restoration of those ditched for mosquito control remains a priority (see chapter 3). Hybridization with mallards also poses problems for black ducks, both for the genetic integrity of the species as well as for their numbers. Male mallards, because of their aggressive courtship, mate with female black ducks, resulting in "genetic swamping" that produces mallard-like hybrids and fewer black ducks. Because black ducks favor salt marshes as winter habitat and mallards do not, the availability of adequate saltmarsh habitat helps keep the two species apart at the onset of pairing.

Thousands of herons and egrets representing nine species also forage in the wetlands at Supawna National Wildlife Refuge. These wading birds nest on nearby Pea Patch Island in a rookery second in size only to some large colonies in Florida; the island lies within the borders of Delaware, where it is part of the state park system. Muskrats and northern river otters also dwell in the brackish marshes, as do diamondback terrapins. Recognized as a Wetland of International Importance, Supawna National Wildlife Refuge is also part of the Western Hemisphere Shorebird Reserve Network. Mannington Meadow, protected by New Jersey Audubon, borders the Salem River near the refuge.

Snow Geese: Too Much of a Good Thing

Each year flocks of greater snow geese travel the Atlantic Flyway between their summer nesting grounds in the Arctic and wintering areas in southern New Jersey and beyond. They, along with their far more numerous "lesser" relatives in the western flyways, nest in large colonies that dot the shorelines of wetlands across a broad swath of northern tundra. Early in the past century, estimates suggested a small continental population of just 3,000 birds, which slowly increased to about 40,000 by 1960, thanks to additional refuge areas and a closed hunting season in the United States beginning in 1931. Thereafter, the greater snow goose population expanded to about 100,000 birds and remained relatively stable until 1975, when hunting resumed. Then, unexpectedly, snow goose populations of both subspecies increased exponentially, reaching a point where their numbers exceeded the carrying capacity of their breeding areas. The birds were outstripping the available food supply and, in the process, destroying for decades to come the tundra wetlands where they forage. Some colonies moved to new areas but with the same inevitable outcome. An ecological disaster loomed, which would not only include a massive collapse of the goose populations from starvation and disease but also leave behind a barren wasteland unsuitable for the needs of both the geese and other wildlife (e.g., several species of tundra-nesting shorebirds).

Marshes on the Atlantic side of New Jersey, primarily those at Forsythe National Wildlife Refuge, have long served as winter habitat for greater snow geese (fig. 6.7). As happened elsewhere, the snow goose population overwintering at the refuge jumped significantly, in this case from about 2,000 in the late 1960s to a high of 60,000 in some years during the 1970s. The burgeoning population likewise stressed

FIGURE 6.7. Edwin B. Forsythe National Wildlife Refuge protects coastal habitat for many species of wildlife, including wintering flocks of snow geese, although much of this population has now moved to the shores of Delaware Bay. Note the proximity of the refuge to the urban skyline of Atlantic City—a reflection of New Jersey's contrasting environments. Photo credit: Kevin Knutsen.

the carrying capacity of these areas, just as they had in the Far North, albeit with a difference—on their wintering grounds the hungry geese could supplement their needs by foraging in nearby farmlands. Indeed, the continental explosion of snow geese was fueled by expanding agricultural production and America's drive to feed a hungry world. On their wintering areas, the birds quickly exploited the abundance of winter wheat, barley, and rye as well as waste grains in stubble fields, all of which provided a catalyst for rapid population growth—improved nutrition that increased both winter survival and breeding success the following spring. In some nesting areas, greater snow geese also improve their reproductive output by locating their nests near those of snowy owls, whose ferocity fends off would-be predators from the surrounding area. Although a striking example of learned behavior, this advantage nonetheless benefits relatively few geese, hence it can scarcely explain the exploding population.

When foraging, snow geese "grub" on marsh vegetation using their exceptionally robust bills, which feature "grinning patches" whose edges—formally known as tomia—provide a vice-like grip on the plants they seek. Grubbing, as described by one authority, tears out tubers, rhizomes, and other underground parts of plants until the entire plant has been torn from the ground, sometimes to the point of creating barren "eat outs," just as occurred in the tundra wetlands. This behavior severely impacted about 1,700 acres—some 20 percent—of the marshes in and around Forsythe NWR, a part of which was entirely denuded. The intensity of the destruction ruptured wetland food chains and destroyed nesting habitat for clapper rails and, of course, further limited the natural food supply for the geese, a shortage that did not go unnoticed by the birds.

In the wake of these events, snow goose numbers increased along the Bayshore, especially in Cumberland County, where much larger areas of marsh were better able to withstand heavy foraging. Prior to 1983, fewer than 5,000 snow geese wintered in the area, but the population vaulted in the following years, reaching almost 80,000 in 1986. Productive farms along the Bayshore provided the birds with additional sources of high-energy food, whereas the once widespread farmlands on the Atlantic shore had steadily yielded to housing developments and shopping malls. Hence, much of the winter population of greater snow geese shifted from one side of the New Jersey coastline to the other in search of adequate food. In extremely cold winters, however, many birds leave the region to journey farther south to locations such as refuges and farmlands in coastal North Carolina. The Bayshore marshes also serve as a staging area during the spring migration when as many as 175,000 snow geese may linger en route north, but overall the birds impact only about 2 percent of the vegetation along this shoreline.

What might be done about a soaring population with a 9 percent growth rate that could double itself every eight years? Solutions included increasing bag limits and season lengths, which were initiated in 1999 in Canada but delayed in the United States by legal challenges until 2009. Additionally, hunting was authorized at specified locations during spring migration—a step that required modifying long-standing prohibitions embodied in legislation arising from the Migratory Bird Treaty (1916). Repeating shotguns, previously plugged to hold no more than three shells, could now be loaded with up to seven shells, and baiting and electronic calls were legalized to better attract the wary birds into gunning range. Although not anticipated, disturbances from hunting pressure during the spring migration provided a bonus—the birds consumed less food, which diminished their body condition and reduced their breeding success (e.g., smaller than normal clutch sizes).

Eventually the liberalized regulations stabilized the population of greater snow geese, albeit still at levels somewhat higher than desired. Significantly, damage to the overtaxed tundra wetlands lessened. Likewise, the degraded areas of coastal marshes in New Jersey, while slow to recover, no longer expanded, fostered in part by special hunts on some refuges, including Forsythe NWR. Currently, the winter population of snow geese at the refuge varies between 5,000 and 7,000 birds and, based on Audubon Christmas Bird Counts, ranges between 30,000 and 50,000 in Cumberland County. Thus, rather ironically, wildlife managers once concerned with protecting snow geese now deal with too many geese in what has been called "an embarrassment of riches."

Major League Mud

A tributary of the Delaware River somewhere in Burlington County provides Major League Baseball (MLB) teams with a substance whose properties help pitchers get a better grip on new baseballs—"rubbing mud," uniquely from New Jersey. The name of the stream remains a closely guarded secret (but is rumored to be Pennsauken Creek); so, too, is the exact site, thought be restricted to a short stretch in the freshwater tidal zone along the creek's marshy shores. The consistency of the mud, characterized as "fine, like chocolate pudding," removes the gloss and roughens the ball's surface, and unlike pine tar and other sticky stuff, MLB sanctions its use. Equipment managers rub it, often with a dab of spit, on a supply of new balls before each game.

Just what makes the mud so special remains unclear, but an analysis by a geology professor at Princeton University revealed that it contains an exceptionally large amount of finely ground quartz that was likely pulverized by ice during the Pleistocene Epoch. Others think a clay known as kaolinite might be involved, although the Princeton analysis indicated that the samples contained surprisingly little clay. The black mud does not stain the balls, as might a pitcher's clandestine application of chewing tobacco or shoe polish. The daily tidal flow supposedly refreshes the mud with its mysterious qualities; only the top inch of the mucky soil is scooped up at low tide. Moreover, one or more secret ingredients may be added when the mud is processed, further adding to the mystique. As further testimony to the mud's uniqueness, a major sports equipment company tried but failed to produce a synthetic alternative. Whatever the secrets may be, baseball teams in the major, minor, independent, and collegiate leagues now stock up each season on 32-ounce cans of the Jersey mud. Only one company offers this rather special item for sale, and it's not telling anyone anything about the mud.

The story is rooted in the death of batter Ray Chapman, an infielder for the Cleveland Indians who died in 1920 from an errant pitch—the first and only death of this kind in the history of MLB. As a remedy for wild pitches and the safety of batters, baseballs at the time were rubbed with mud made from water and infield dirt to improve a pitcher's grip and control. Fast forward to 1938 when third base coach Russell "Lena" Blackburne of the Philadelphia Athletics listened to the complaint of an umpire about baseballs treated with infield mud, which lessened the gloss but softened the covers to the point where they could be manipulated by pitchers seeking the advantage of a wobbly, hard-to-hit delivery. In response, Blackburne recalled the creamy black mud from a creek near his boyhood home in South Jersey that he thought might solve the problem. And it did—the mud deadened the glazed finish on a new baseball yet did not soften its cover. Thus began the business of selling what became officially known as Lena Blackburne Baseball Mud, which was quickly adopted by the American League and, in 1950, by teams in the National League as well.

Before his death in 1968, Blackburn passed on the business—and its secrets—to a friend, who in turn passed it on to a succession of family members, in whose possession it remains today, filling a niche mandated by MLB Rule 4.01C that baseballs shall "be properly rubbed so that the gloss is removed." Yet, after more than eighty years of use, much about a special mud from a creek somewhere along New Jersey's Other Shore remains a "dirty little secret."

Readings and References

General

Benoit, L. K., and R. A. Askins. 1999. Impact of the spread of *Phragmites* on the distribution of birds in Connecticut tidal marshes. Wetlands 19:194–208.

Burger, J., and M. Gochfeld. 2000. Spawning horseshoe crabs on Delaware Bay. Pp. 49–59 in Twenty-five nature spectacles in New Jersey. Rutgers University Press, New Brunswick, NJ. [See also pp. 61–71, Migrant shorebirds at Delaware Bay.]

Cramer, D. 2015. The narrow edge: a tiny bird, an ancient crab, and an epic journey. Yale University Press, New Haven, CT.

Dunne, P. 2010. Bay shore summer: finding Eden in a most unlikely place. Mariner Books, Boston.

Kiviat, E. 2013. Ecosystem services of *Phragmites* in North America with emphasis on habitat functions. AoB Plants 5. https://doi.org/10.1039/aobpla/plt008. [See for the benefits to wildlife.]

Niles, L., J. Burger, and A. Dey. 2012. Life along the Delaware Bay. Rutgers University Press, New Brunswick, NJ. [Stunning photos illustrate an informative text.]

Sutton, C. C., J. C. O'Herron II, and R. T. Zappalorti. 1996. The scientific characterization of the Delaware estuary. Delaware Estuary Program (DRBC Project No. 321; HA File No. 93.21).

The Ancient Mariners of Delaware Bay

Benton, M. J. 2015. When life nearly died: the greatest mass extinction of all time. Rev. ed. Thames & Hudson, New York. [An account of the Permian Extinction.]

Bolden, J. S. 2020. Application of recombinant factor C reagent for the detection of bacterial endotoxins in pharmaceutical products and comparability to Limulus amebocyte lysate. USP Pharmacopeial Forum 46(3).

Bolden, J. S., and K. R. Smith. 2017. Application of recombinant factor C reagent for the detection of bacterial endotoxins in pharmaceutical products. PDA Journal of Pharmaceutical Science and Technology 71:405–414.

Botton, M. L., C. N. Shuster Jr., and J. A. Keinath. 2003. Horseshoe crabs in a food web: who eats whom. Pp. 133–150 in The American horseshoe crab (C. N. Shuster Jr., R. B. Barlow, and H. J. Brockmann, eds.). Harvard University Press, Cambridge, MA.

Brockmann, H. J., C. Nguyen, and W. Potts. 2000. Paternity in horseshoe crabs when spawning in multiple-male groups. Animal Behaviour 60:837–849.

Cramer, D. 2018. New hope for an ancient animal. Audubon 120(2):18.

Kreamer, G., and S. Michels. 2009. History of horseshoe crab harvest on Delaware Bay. Pp. 299–313 in Biology and conservation of horseshoe crabs (J. T. Tanacredi, M. L. Botton, and D. R. Smith, eds.). Springer Science, New York.

Leschen, A. S., and S. J. Correia. 2010. Mortality in female horseshoe crabs (*Limulus polyphemus*) from biomedical bleeding and handling: implications for fisheries management. Marine and Freshwater Behavior and Physiology 43:135–147.

Maloney, T., R. Phelan, and N. Simmons. 2018. Saving the horseshoe crab: a synthetic alternative to horseshoe crab blood for endotoxin detection. PLOS Biology 16(10):e2006607.

Rudkin, D. M., G. A. Young, and G. S. Nowlan. 2008. The oldest horseshoe crab: a new xiphosurid from later Ordovician Konservat-Lagerstatten deposits, Manitoba, Canada. Palaeontology 51:1–9. [See Van Roy et al. (2015) for a more recent discovery.]

Shuster, C. N., Jr. 2003. King crab fertilizer: a once thriving Delaware Bay industry. Pp. 341–347 in The American horseshoe crab (C. N. Shuster Jr., R. B. Barlow, and H. J. Brockmann, eds.). Harvard University Press, Cambridge, MA.

Shuster, C. N., Jr., and K. Sekiguchi. 2003. Growing up takes about ten years and eighteen stages. Pp. 103–132 in The American horseshoe crab (C. N. Shuster Jr., R. B. Barlow, and H. J. Brockmann, eds.). Harvard University Press, Cambridge, MA.

Swan, B. L. 2001. A unique biomedical product (LAL) from the horseshoe crab and monitoring the Delaware horseshoe crab population. Pp. 53–62 in Limulus in the limelight (J. T. Tanacredi, ed.). Kluwer Academic / Plenum, New York.

Van Roy, P., D. E. G. Briggs, and R. R. Gaines. 2015. The Fezouata fossils of Morocco: an extraordinary record of marine life in the Early Ordovician. Journal of the Geological Society 172:541–549. [Extends the history of horseshoe crabs back another 30 million years in the fossil record.]

Add Birds and Mix

Atkinson, P. W., A. J. Baker, K. A. Bennett, et al. 2007. Rates of mass gain and energy deposition in red knot on their final spring staging site is time-and condition-dependent. Journal of Applied Ecology 44:885–895.

Haramis, G. M., W. A. Link, P. C. Osenton, et al. 2007. Stable isotope and pen feeding trial studies confirm the value of horseshoe crab, Limulus polyphemus, eggs to spring migrant shorebirds in Delaware Bay. Journal of Avian Biology 38:367–376.

Karpanty, S. M., J. D. Fraser, J. Berkson, et al. 2006. Horseshoe crab eggs determine red knot distribution in Delaware Bay. Journal of Wildlife Management 70:1704–1710.

Morrison, R. I. G., and K. A. Hobson. 2004. Use of body stores in shorebirds after arrival on high-Arctic breeding grounds. Auk 121:333–344.

Myers, J. P. 1986. Sex and gluttony on Delaware Bay. Natural History 95(5): 68–77.

Niles, L. J., H. P. Sitters, A. D. Dey, et al. 2008. Status of the red knot, Calidris canutus rufa, in the Western Hemisphere. Studies in Avian Biology 36:1–185.

Piersma, T., G. A. Gudmundsson, and K. Lilliendahl. 1999. Rapid changes in the size of different functional organ and muscle groups during refueling in a long-distant migrant shorebird. Physiological and Biochemical Zoology 72:405–415.

Tsipoura, N., and J. Burger. 1999. Shorebird diet during spring migration stopover on Delaware Bay. Condor 101:633–644.

Problems!

Baker, A. J., P. M. Gonzalez, T. Piersma, et al. 2004. Rapid population decline in red knot: fitness consequences of decreased refueling rates and late arrival in Delaware Bay. Proceedings of the Royal Society B 25:125–129.

Morrison, R. I. G., R. K. Ross, and L. J. Niles. 2004. Declines in wintering populations of red knots in southern South America. Condor 106:60–70.

Niles, L. J., J. Bart, H. P. Sitters, et al. 2009. Effects of horseshoe crab harvest in Delaware Bay on red knots: are harvest regulations working? BioScience 59:153–164. [A major source.]

Smith, D. R. 2007. Effect of horseshoe crab spawning density on nest disturbance and exhumation of eggs: a simulation study. Estuaries and Coasts 30:287–295.

A Trio of Fishes

Chittenden, M. E., Jr. 1975. Dynamics of American shad, *Alosa sapidissima*, runs in the Delaware River. Fisheries Bulletin 73:487–494.

Dodson, J. J., and W. C. Leggett. 1974. Role of olfaction and vision in the behavior of American shad (*Alosa sapidissima*) homing to the Connecticut River from Long Island Sound. Journal of the Fisheries Research Board of Canada 31:1607–1619.

Dunton, K. J., A. Jordaan, D. O. Conover, et al. 2015. Marine distribution and habitat use of Atlantic sturgeon in New York lead to fisheries interactions and bycatch. Marine and Coastal Fisheries: Dynamics, Management, and Ecosystem Science 7:18–32.

Haro, A., W. Richkus, A. Hoar, et al. 2000. Population decline of the American eel: implications for research and management. Fisheries 25:7–16.

Hein, J. L., I. de Buron, W. A. Roumillat, et al. 2016. Infection of newly recruited American eels (*Anguilla rostrata*) by the invasive swimbladder parasite *Anguillicoloides crassus* in a US Atlantic tidal creek. ICES Journal of Marine Science 73:14–21.

Hitt, N. P., S. Eyler, and J. E. B. Wofford. 2012. Dam removal increases American eel abundance in distant headwater streams. Transactions of the American Fisheries Society 141:1171–1179.

Krueger, W. H., and K. Oliveira. 1999. Evidence for environmental sex determination in the American eel, *Anguilla rostrata*. Environmental Biology of Fishes 55:381–389.

Leggett, W. C., and R. R. Whitney. 1972. Water temperature and the migrations of American shad. Fisheries Bulletin 70:659–670.

Lellis, W. A., B. S. J. White, J. C. Cole, et al. 2013. Newly documented host fishes for the eastern elliptio mussel *Elliptio complanata*. Journal of Fish and Wildlife Management 4:75–85. [See for effectiveness of Atlantic eels as hosts.]

Machut, L. S., and K. E. Limburg. 2008. *Anguillicola crassus* infection in *Anguilla rostrata* from small tributaries of the Hudson River watershed, New York, USA. Diseases of Aquatic Organisms 79:37–45.

MacKenzie, C., L. S. Weiss-Glanz, and J. R. Moring. 1985. Species profiles: life histories and environmental requirements of coastal fishes and invertebrates (mid-Atlantic)—American shad. U.S. Fish and Wildlife Service Biological Report 82(11.37). U.S. Army Corps of Engineers TR EL-82-4.

McPhee, J. 2002. The founding fish. Farrar, Straus and Giroux, New York. [A shad-themed memoir well blended with natural history and history, including Washington's choice for camping at Valley Forge.]

Neves, R. J., and L. Depres. 1979. The oceanic migration of American shad, *Alosa sapidissima*, along the Atlantic coast. Fisheries Bulletin 77:199–212.

Ogden, J. C. 1970. Relative abundance, food habits, and age of the American eel, *Anguilla rostrate* (LeSueur), in certain New Jersey streams. Transactions of the American Fisheries Society 99:54–59.

Oliveira, K. 1999. Life history characteristics and strategies of the American eel, *Anguilla rostrata*. Canadian Journal of Fisheries and Aquatic Sciences 56:795–802.

Palstra, A. P., D. F. M. Heppener, V. J. T. van Ginneken, et al. 2007. Swimming performance of silver eels is severely impaired by the swim-bladder parasite, *Anguillicola crassus*. Journal of Experimental Marine Biology and Ecology 353:244–256.

Prosek, J. 2010. Eels: an exploration, from New Zealand to the Sargasso, of the world's most mysterious fish. HarperCollins, New York. [Includes the life history and cultural associations of several species.]

Pujolar, J. M. 2013. Conclusive evidence for panmixia in the American eel. Molecular Ecology 22:1761–1762.

Shepard, S. L. 2015. American eel biological species report. U.S. Fish and Wildlife Service, Hadley, MA.

Sulak, K. J., R. E. Edwards, G. W. Hill, and M. T. Randall. 2002. Why do sturgeon jump? Insights from acoustic investigations of the Gulf Sturgeon in the Suwannee River, Florida, USA. Journal of Applied Ichthyology 18:617–620.

A Small Niche for a Little Bird

Beadell, J., R. Greenberg, S. Droege, and J. A. Royle. 2003. Distribution, abundance, and habitat affinities of the coastal plain swamp sparrow. Wilson Bulletin 115:38–44.

Bond, G. M., and R. E. Stewart. 1951. A new swamp sparrow from the Maryland coastal plain. Wilson Bulletin 63:38–40.

Greenberg, R., and S. Droege. 1990. Adaptations to tidal marshes in breeding populations of the swamp sparrow. Condor 92:393–404.

Greenberg, R., P. P. Marra, and M. J. Wooller. 2007. Stable-isotope (C, N, H) analyses help locate the winter range of the coastal plain swamp sparrow (*Melospiza georgiana nigrescens*). Auk 124:1137–1148.

Peele, A. M., E. H. Burtt Jr., M. R. Schroeder, and R. S. Greenberg. 2009. Dark color of the coastal plain swamp sparrow (*Melospiza georgiana nigrescens*) may be an evolutionary response to occurrence and abundance of salt-tolerant feather-degrading bacilli in its plumage. Auk 126:531–535.

Along the Bayshore

Ankney, C. D., D. G. Dennis, and R. C. Bailey. 1987. Increasing mallards, decreasing American black ducks: coincidence or cause and effect? Journal of Wildlife Management 51:523–529.

Kirby, R. E., G. A. Sargeant, and D. Shutler. 2004. Haldane's rule and American black duck x mallard hybridization. Canadian Journal of Zoology 82:1827–1831.

Mank, J. E., J. E. Carlson, and M. C. Brittingham. 2004. A century of hybridization: declining genetic distance between American black ducks and mallards. Conservation Genetics 5:395–403.

Sutton, C., and J. Dowdell. 2012. Raptors, waterfowl, and shorebirds on the Maurice River, Cumberland County, NJ: a twenty-five year summary of observed status and trends—1987–2012. Citizens United to Protect the Maurice River and Its Tributaries, Inc., Millville, NJ.

Sutton, C., and P. Kerlinger. 1997. The Delaware Bayshore of New Jersey: a raptor migration and wintering site of hemispheric significance. Journal of Raptor Research 31:54–58.

Snow Geese

Ankney, C. D. 1996. An embarrassment of riches: too many geese. Journal of Wildlife Management 60:217–227. [A call for action using methods theretofore unacceptable for regulating waterfowl populations.]

Bolen, E. G., and M. K. Rylander. 1978. Feeding adaptations in the lesser snow goose (*Anser caerulescens*). Southwestern Naturalist 23:158–161.

Giroux, J.-F., G. Gauthier, G. Costanzo, and A. Reed. 1998. Impact of geese on natural habitats. Pp. 32–57 in The greater snow goose: report of the Arctic Goose Habitat

Working Group (B. D. J. Batt, ed.). Arctic Goose Joint Venture Special Publication. U.S. Fish and Wildlife Service, Washington, DC and Canadian Wildlife Service, Ottawa, Canada. [A major source of information regarding "too many geese."]

Glazener, W. C. 1946. Food habits of wild geese on the Gulf Coast of Texas. Journal of Wildlife Management 10:322–329. [See for description of "grubbing."]

Lefebvre, J., G. Gauthier, J.-F. Giroux, et al. 2017. The greater snow goose *Anser caerulescens atlanticus:* managing an overabundant population. Ambio 46(suppl. 2):262–274. [See for background, results, and continuing challenges.]

Smith, T. J., III, and W. E. Odum. 1981. The effects of grazing by snow geese on coastal salt marshes. Ecology 62:98–106.

Sutton, C. C., J. C. O'Herron, and R. T. Zappalorti. 1996. The scientific characterization of the Delaware estuary. The Delaware Estuary Program (DRBC Project No. 321; HA File No. 93.21). [See for census showing buildup of snow geese between 1977 to 1986.]

Tremblay, J.-P., G. Gauthier, D. Lepage, and A. Desrochers. 1997. Factors affecting nesting success in greater snow geese: effects of habitat and association with snow owls. Wilson Bulletin 109:449–461.

Major League Mud

Anonymous. 1982. Ah, now for some joy in Mudville. New York Times, April 6: C7.

Baccellieri, E. 2019. Mud maker: the man behind MLB's essential secret sauce. Sports Illustrated (July 29) 130(20/21):42–46.

Francis, B. ND. Lena Blackburne rubbing mud a secret of the game. http://www.baseballhall.org/discover/lena-blackburne-rubbing-mud-a-secret-of-the-game. [Baseball History Series, National Baseball Hall of Fame and Museum.]

Scahill, E. 2020. Monopoly and monopsony power in a market for mud. Journal of Economics Teaching 5:30–36.

Shore Note 6.1. The Curse of Phragmites

Able, K. W., and S. M. Hagan. 2003. Impact of common reed, *Phragmites australis*, on essential fish habitat: influence on reproduction, embryological development and larval abundance of mummichog (*Fundulus heteroclitus*). Estuaries 26:4050.

Bains, G., A. S. Kumar, T. Rudrappa, et al. 2009. Native plant and microbial contributions to a negative plant-plant interaction. Plant Physiology 151:2145–2151.

Chambers, R. M., L. A. Meyerson, and K. Saltonstall. 1999. Expansion of *Phragmites australis* into the tidal marshes of North America. Aquatic Botany 64:261–273.

Gratton, C., and R. F. Denno. 2005. Restoration of arthropod assemblages in a *Spartina* salt marsh following removal of the invasive plant *Phragmites australis*. Restoration Ecology 13:358–372.

Roman, C. T., W. A. Niering, and R. S. Warren. 1984. Salt marsh vegetation changes in response to tidal restriction. Environmental Management 8:141–149.

Saltonstall, K. 2002. Cryptic invasion by a non-native genotype of the common reed, *Phragmites australis*, into North America. Proceedings of the National Academy of Sciences of the United States of America 99:2445–2449.

Sebold, K. R. 2005. From marsh to farm: the landscape transformation of coastal New Jersey. ParkNet, National Park Service, Washington, DC. [See chaps. 3 and 5 regarding diking marshes for marsh hay production.]

Uddin, M. N., R. W. Robinson, A. Buultjens, at el. 2017. Role of allelopathy of *Phragmites australis* in its invasion processes. Journal of Experimental Marine Biology and Ecology 486:237–244.

Weinstein, M. P., J. M. Teal, J. H. Balletto, et al. 2001. Restoration principles emerging from one of the world's largest tidal marsh restoration projects. Wetlands Ecology and Management 9:387–407. [Deals with *Phragmites*-dominated marshes and diked salt hay farms on Delaware Bay.]

Weis, J. S., E. B. Watson, B. Ravit, C. Harman, and M. Yepsen. 2021. The status and future of tidal marshes in New Jersey faced with sea level rise. Anthropocene Coasts 4:168–192. [See for the role of *Phragmites* as a defense against rising sea levels.]

Weishar, L., and J. M. Teal. 1998. Adaptive restoration of degraded diked salt hay farm wetlands. Pp. 356–361 in Proceedings of the Wetlands Engineering and River Restoration Conference (D. F. Hayes, ed.). American Society of Civil Engineers, Reston, VA.

Shore Note 6.2. Oysters: Reefs, Raw, and Roasted

Able, K. W. 2020. Beneath the surface: understanding nature in the Mullica Valley estuary. Rutgers University Press, New Brunswick, NJ. [See pp. 152–153 for more about black drum and oysters.]

Burrell, V. G. 1986. Species profiles; life histories and environmental requirements of coastal fishes and invertebrates (south Atlantic): American oyster. U.S. Fish and Wildlife Service Biological Report 82(11.570).

Christensen, A. M., and J. J. McDermott. 1958. Life history and biology of the oyster crab, *Pinnotheres ostreum* Say. Biological Bulletin 114:146–179.

Cressman, K. A., M. H. Posey, M. A. Mallin, et al. 2003. Effects of oyster reefs on water quality in a tidal creek estuary. Journal of Shellfish Research 22:753–762.

Davidson, A. 1979. North Atlantic seafood. Viking, New York. [See p. 206 regarding Washington's taste for pea crabs.]

Ford, S. E., and D. Bushek. 2012. Development of resistance to an introduced marine pathogen by a native host. Journal of Marine Research 70:205–223.

Grabowski, J. H., and C. H. Peterson. 2007. Restoring oyster reefs to recover ecosystems services. Pp. 281–298 in Ecosystem engineers: plants to protists (K. Cuddington, J. Beyers, W. Wilson, and A. Hastings, eds.). Academic Press, Burlington, MA.

Sutter, F. C., R. S. Waller, and T. D. McIlwain. 1986. Species profiles: life histories and environmental requirements of coastal fishes and invertebrates (Gulf of Mexico)—black drum. U.S. Fish and Wildlife Service Biological Report 82(11.51). U.S. Army Corps of Engineers TR EL-82-4. [Reports the fish's daily consumption of oysters.]

Shore Note 6.3. Barn Owls: Monkey-Faced Hunters

Colvin, B. A. 2017. Annual report on the New Jersey study area, 2016. Barn Owl Foundation, San Antonio, TX.

Graham, R. R. 1934. The silent flight of owls. Journal of the Royal Aeronautical Society 38:837–843.

Knudsen, E. I., and M. Konishi. 1979. Mechanisms of sound localization in the barn owl (*Tyto alba*). Journal of Comparative Physiology 133:1–11.

Konishi, M. 1973. How the barn owl tracks its prey. American Scientist 61:414–424.

Konishi, M., and A. A. Kenuk. 1975. Discrimination of noise spectra by memory in the barn owl. Journal of Comparative Physiology 97:55–58.

Marti, C. D., P. W. Wagner, and K. W. Denne. 1979. Nest boxes for the management of barn owls. Wildlife Society Bulletin 7:145–148.

Millsap, B. A., and P. A. Millsap. 1987. Burrow nesting by common barn owls in north central Colorado. Condor 89:668–670.

Taylor, I. 1994. Barn owls: predator-prey relationships and conservation. Cambridge University Press, New York. [A comprehensive, global account of the species.]

Watson, E., K. Szura, C. Wigand, et al. 2016. Sea level rise, drought, and the decline of *Spartina patens* in New England marshes. Biological Conservation 196:173–181. [Reflects conditions along the New Jersey Bayshore.]

FIGURE 7.1. Though rarely traveled, sandy tracks persist in otherwise remote areas in the Pine Barrens. The roadways echo a time when self-reliant people once lived off the land in isolated homesteads. Photo credit: Kevin Knutsen.

7

The Pine Barrens

Imposing Solitude

The water in the Pine Barrens is soft and pure, and there is so much
of it that, like the forest above it, it is an incongruity in place and time.
—JOHN MCPHEE, *THE PINE BARRENS*

BEAUTY, THEY SAY, lies in the eyes of the beholder. For naturalists, the
cactus-rich deserts of the American Southwest and the green ocean of a
prairie become scenic landscapes—silent places at once as sublime as
they are remote. And so it is for the New Jersey Pine Barrens, a less-traveled and
somewhat mysterious environment surrounded by the busy life of an urban state
(fig. 7.1).

Any understanding of the Pine Barrens necessarily begins with the sandy soil
that defines the region. Throughout eons of time, what is now the Atlantic Coastal
Plain developed from sediments periodically washed into what was then the sea
floor. A series of events repeatedly inundated then exposed the sea floor, which
gained additional strata each time the sea again covered the coastal plain. A Mio-
cene deposit known as Cohansey Sand was the last major layer formed in this
fashion, although rivers crossing the plains during the Pleistocene deposited additional sediments, some in the form of gravel bars. Cohansey Sand consists of
coarse grains of quartz that resist weathering and thereby inhibits the breakdown
of the sands into smaller soil particles such as clay.

The porous texture enables rainwater to move rapidly downward through the
soil profile, carrying with it organic matter and minerals and leaving behind arid,
highly leached surface soils with little fertility. All told, sandy soils function more

like a sieve than a sponge. These conditions, coupled with the natural acidity of sandy soils, limit the kinds of vegetation that can develop in the Pine Barrens. They also govern the presence and activities of certain animals. The Pine Barrens lack earthworms, for example, which cannot cope with either the aridity or the acidity of the sandy soils. In contrast, ants thrive and take over the role played by earthworms in mixing mineral soil and ground litter, a process formally known as bioturbation.

On a positive note, rainwater falling on the Pine Barrens collects in large aquifers that provide reliable supplies of municipal water for much of the region. With virtually no runoff, streams in the Pine Barrens arise from groundwater instead of more typical watersheds where surface waters feed the streambeds. Because of the eastward slope of the terrain, the groundwater also flows to the coast, where, after mixing with salt water, it develops and nurtures large areas of coastal marsh (see chapter 3). Significantly, the limitations of the sandy soils preclude most types of agricultural development and thus became a natural—and powerful—check against clearing large areas of the Pine Barrens for farms and pastures.

Pine Barrens Forests, Tall and Short

Pitch and shortleaf pines, together with blackjack and a variety of other oaks, dominate most of the Pine Barrens. In other places, where the water table lies near ground level, lowland forests—"cedar swamps"—replace the upland pine and oak communities.

An upland forest of pitch pines covers about half of the Pine Barrens and represents the largest continuous stand of the species in North America. Shortleaf pines commonly intermingle with the pitch pine, but oaks become more prevalent in the prolonged absence of fire. The result is a mosaic consisting of oak-pine forests where various oaks, among them blackjack, southern red, scarlet, and black, dominate the composition or pine-oak forests in which pitch and shortleaf pines outnumber blackjack and other oaks. The needles of pitch and shortleaf pine are similar in length—three to five inches—but these occur in fascicles of three in pitch pine and unusually just two in shortleaf pine. The cones of both species are similar in length (two to three inches) and shape (oval), and both have black, scaly bark on young trees that flattens into lighter colored plates as the trees age. In the uplands, both species may reach heights exceeding 40 feet, although, as noted later, the growth form of pitch pine can be remarkably different in other locations.

Each of the dominant pines has evolved a means for dealing with fire. In frequently burned areas, the cones of pitch pine commonly stay attached to the parent tree for several years, remaining tightly closed until a fire burns off the resin that glues the scales together (cones with these features are said to be serotinous). The same fire removes the accumulation of ground litter. Once opened, the cones shed their seeds on a forest floor where they can germinate in direct contact with the soil. Pitch pine, as well as shortleaf pine and blackjack oak, also produce new growth in the form of sprouts after fires damage or destroy their aboveground structures. The sprouts usually arise from dormant buds near the root collars on burned-over stumps or, in some cases, from roots.

The varied understory includes ground-hugging shrubs, of which beach heather represents a prime example. Other, somewhat taller shrubs, especially the true heathers, include mountain laurel, leatherleaf, sand myrtle, and lambskill. Three species of huckleberry and four of blueberry grow in moist sites throughout the Pine Barrens; the two groups generally resemble each other, but they differ enough to warrant classification in separate genera. In the field, differences in leaf and fruit structure distinguish each group. Minute yellowish resin dots occur on the underside of huckleberry leaves, whereas blueberry leaves lack these features. The fruits of huckleberries each contain 10 hard nutlets (seeds) surrounded by a small amount of fleshy pulp. In blueberries, many small and soft seeds are enclosed within a relatively large amount of tasty pulp. Another true heather, bearberry, trails over the ground, often forming thick mats with its evergreen foliage.

The herbaceous vegetation includes Knieskern's beaked-rush, a threatened species endemic to the Pine Barrens where it grows in moist, disturbed areas. Historically, fires favored this species by creating openings, but because of its intolerance to competition, it gives way to the woody plants that take over these sites. Pickering's morning glory, also rare, trails vine-like across dry sandy areas and bears funnel-shaped white flowers. The showy blue flowers of the Pine-Barren gentian, a more common species, also adds color to the herbaceous understory.

The vegetation at two large areas and two smaller sites in the Pine Barrens differs sharply from the surrounding stands of tall pines and oaks. Collectively, these areas represent a Pygmy Forest—or Pine Plains—in which densely packed and

Shore Note 7.1 A Primer on Fire Ecology

Fire occurs as a natural force of nature in virtually all terrestrial communities but varies significantly in its frequency. In their natural state, grasslands burn regularly, whereas fires occur far less often in deserts because the sparse ground litter provides little fuel. On a prairie in North Dakota, for example, lightning ignited as many as 25 fires per year. In forests, core borings or cross sections often reveal fire-scarred tree rings that are separated by decades of uninterrupted growth. To the surprise of many, fires rarely kill wildlife, which escape in burrows or simply outdistance themselves from the flames. For example, even the disastrous Yellowstone fires in 1988 killed less than 1 percent of the elk herd, with most of these dying from smoke inhalation, and fewer than 20 bison, deer, and moose.

Three areas of pines persist within the Eastern Deciduous Forest, a region that otherwise features a climax of hardwoods—various mixes of oaks, maples, beech, and hickories—but only if swept by fires several times each century (and they give way to hardwoods if they are not regularly burned). One of these includes the range of jack pine, especially around the western Great Lakes. Because of fires, the new growth of jack pine within a small area in Michigan provides the sole breeding habitat for Kirtland's warblers, which locate their nests on the ground just under the tips of the lowest branches on the young trees. However, without fires, the lower branches rise above the ground as the tree matures and no longer provide the birds with nesting cover. Once numbering just 167 pairs, Kirtland's warblers were among the first species on the federal list of endangered species, but thanks in part to prescribed burns, they were delisted in 2019. Fire also maintains longleaf pine over a large crescent-shaped area running from southeastern Virginia to eastern Texas, but because of fire suppression, less than 5 percent of the original forest remains. Red-cockaded woodpeckers depend entirely on old-growth longleaf pines as nesting habitat, and the drastic reduction of such trees has endangered the birds. Finally, fires maintain the pine-dominated New Jersey Pine Barrens (see main text) and two similar but far smaller areas in New York.

twisted pitch pines, blackjack oaks, and a few scrub oaks grow no more than 10 feet tall, with a good percentage reaching only half that height (fig. 7.2). Short-leaf pine and the oaks common elsewhere are absent, save for scrub (bear) oak. Essentially all of the scraggly pines began from sprouts arising from the root crowns of trees burned a decade or two earlier, and seedlings are few and far between. Trees in the renewed growth, although only a few years old, bear mature cones, of which nearly all are serotinous. Trees surviving a fire produce tufts of sprouts directly from the sides of their trunks.

In each case, the three pines noted above have one or more adaptations—serotinous cones, for one—that facilitate their ability to survive fires, and indeed these have evolved to the point that fire has become an essential component of their environment. Conversely, fires easily damage hardwoods, which cannot cope with repeating burning (and, in general, also do not favor sandy soil). Thus, fires "arrest" further successional development of these pinelands, which persist as perpetual subclimax communities with their own unique biota of fire-adapted species.

Fires also protect native grasslands from the invasion of woody vegetation. This results from three features that differ significantly between the two types of vegetation. First, the growing point (buds) of grasses lies at or below ground level and protected from most fires, whereas the buds of shrubs and trees develop fully exposed at the tips of branches, easily damaged by fire. Second, grasses quickly regrow after a fire and soon regain their full biomass (to grasp this feature, think of how often lawns need mowing), but woody plants may take years to reach their pre-fire size. Finally, because grasses regrow so rapidly, they also quickly mature and produce seed, often less than a month after a fire and almost always in the same growing season. By comparison, trees and shrubs require several years or even decades to produce seeds, hence giving grasses a huge reproductive advantage. Fires also add nutrients to the soil and in some cases inhibit plant diseases.

Controlled (or prescribed) burning offers practical and ecological benefits as a management tool. Defined as the skillful application of fire under exacting conditions (e.g., wind speed) on a specified area for a specific purpose, controlled burning consumes accumulated fuel and thereby lessens the threat of runaway wildfires. For ranchers, controlled burning also replaces unpalatable thatch with tender, protein-rich new growth and retards the encroachment of brush. Forest ecologists likewise burn blocks of pinelands to keep out hardwoods and improve habitat for fire-adapted wildlife. Accordingly, the New Jersey Forest Fire Service annually burns part of the Pine Barrens.

Pixie moss and broom crowberry highlight the shrubby understory of the Pygmy Forest, along with many of the same species in the upland forest, including mountain laurel, black huckleberry, lowbush blueberry, bearberry, and beach heather. Note that pixie moss is actually a small shrub that lies flat on the ground where its tightly packed evergreen foliage resembles a mat; in spring, the plants produce small, star-shaped white flowers—hardly the botanical features of true mosses. The larvae of the Buchholz dart moth feed exclusively on pixie moss; so far as is known, these moths occur only in the Pine Barrens, where frequently

FIGURE 7.2. Pitch pine and scattered oaks dominate the forests in the Pine Barrens. Most trees in these forests reach heights of 30 or more feet (see Fig. 7.1), but as shown here, curious "pygmy forests" of the same species—5 to 6 feet high—occur elsewhere in the Pine Barrens. Patches of broom crowberry commonly form the groundcover in these communities. Photo credit: Jason Hafstad.

burned sites provide suitable habitat. Broom crowberry, another low-growing shrub, reaches its southern limit in the Pine Barrens, where it occurs almost exclusively in the Pygmy Forest. The species represents a leftover from the Ice Age flora that once characterized the Pine Barrens and today occurs widely in New England and Canada; New Jersey marks the southern limit of its distribution. Unfortunately, broom crowberry has declined in the Pine Barrens, primarily because ground litter has accumulated to the point where infrequent but intensely hot wildfires destroy entire communities of these plants, which otherwise thrive in a regime of frequent "cool" fires. As a remedy, New Jersey conservation agencies bulldozed one-acre scrapes to create patches of bare sand where broom crowberry plants can establish new colonies and avoid raging wildfires. Because the seeds disperse only short distances, the scrapes are located near existing populations. Ants may provide the primary means of dispersing the seeds—an activity known as myrmecochory—and, based on field studies at Cape Cod, at least eight species of ants participate in the process.

Most ecologists agree that frequent fires explain the origin and maintenance of the Pygmy Forest. Pitch pine, as noted earlier, is remarkably adapted to cope with repeated exposure to fires, which occurred historically at intervals of 5 to 20 years, perhaps with an average of about every 8 years. Nearly all of the pitch pines in the Pygmy Forest bear serotinous cones, whereas this trait occurs far less often in pitch pines growing elsewhere in the Pine Barrens, a difference no doubt reflecting the considerable influence of fire in one area compared to the other. Serotinous cones produce huge amounts of seeds, yet nearly all of the regeneration after a fire originates from sprouts coming from root collars. After a fire, thousands of sprouts of both pitch pine and blackjack oak emerge on each acre of burned-over forest, but their density decreases as competition steadily thins the new growth. Nonetheless, the density of the trees in the Pygmy Forest remains far greater than in the surrounding areas of pine forest. Mountain laurel, a major component of the understory, also sprouts prolifically after a fire. Whereas fires usually kill broom crowberry, its seeds may actually require fire to simulate germination, hence the seeds accumulating in the soil—a reserve known as a seed bank—produce a new generation of plants after the same fire destroys the previous one.

In the past, fires swept across the Pygmy Forest with enough frequency to consume the ground litter before it accumulated to the point where it could fuel infrequent but catastrophic "hot fires" that killed root systems, destroyed seed banks, and impaired regeneration. The Pygmy Forest thus developed as an ecosystem in which the numerous "cool fires" became a force of natural selection. In such a regime, the diminutive pitch pines evolved as an ecotype—a genetically modified local form unlike others of the same species. Such pines thus remain dwarfed even when experimentally transplanted into a fire-free environment. The frequent fires also maintained open spots in the Pygmy Forest in which a diverse understory of herbaceous vegetation might thrive.

Beginning about 1940, however, fire suppression, whether by passive means such as an expanding road system acting as a network of fire breaks or by the active control of firefighters, lengthened the fire-free intervals in the Pine Barrens in general and the Pygmy Forest in particular. Ecological effects at three levels—species, community, and landscape—have or will likely result from the change in fire frequency.

First, fire-adapted species and their ecotypes will become less prevalent as other forms invade and replace the historic communities in the Pine Barrens. In short, natural selection will favor species less adapted to fire instead of the reverse. Second, hardwood swamps will replace cedar swamps (see later section). Finally, the current mosaic of large patches—the result of extensive areas that burned at different times—will give way to a more homogeneous landscape. This usually lessens the richness of the biota following the maxim of "more area, more species" while also eliminating area-sensitive species that require large blocks of habitat.

Ghosts of the Pygmy Forest

The Pygmy Forest was once home to the heath hen, a now extinct subspecies of the greater prairie chicken still found in the Midwest, where tallgrass prairies persist; another subspecies, the Attwater's prairie chicken, clings on in Texas but may soon join its eastern relative in the grave of extinction. When settlers cleared the scrubby growth of the Pygmy Forest, they unknowingly provided the birds with openings for their courtship displays on communal dancing grounds known as leks. In season, heath hens found ample food in the insects—grasshoppers were a favorite—numerous kinds of berries and greenery, but the birds especially thrived on the year-round availability of acorns. The Pygmy Forest was soon dubbed the "grouse plains," and a place where the abundance and ready availability of the birds provided gunners with sport and welcome table fare. Indeed, a stage line established in 1823 featured a stop at the grouse plains expressly to accommodate hunters. Shooting went on year-round, including during the breeding season. Witmer Stone reported that shooting from a pit dug at the edge of a lek was a favorite way of bagging heath hens. Given such abuses, overhunting took its toll, including the wanton exploitation of market hunting, and by 1870 heath hens in New Jersey were only a memory.

The original range of heath hens extended from New England to the mid-Atlantic states, perhaps as far south as North Carolina. The date when the birds vanished from New Jersey remains lost to history, but the final record of a heath hen—a single and undoubtedly lonely male—occurred in 1932 on Martha's Vineyard. The fate of the last heath hens represents a classic example of an extinction vortex, a downward spiral caused by a sequence of events, any one of which might not have proved catastrophic, but when cumulative placed small populations in

Shore Note 7.2 The Comet That Streaked across the Pine Barrens

The Central Railroad of New Jersey initiated passenger service between New York City—with a ferry connection to the terminal in Jersey City—and Atlantic City in 1929, just weeks before the nation plunged into the Great Depression. More than just another train, the engine and cars of the Blue Comet were painted to reflect the Jersey Shore—a blue engine and two-tone blue cars highlighted by a wide cream-colored band served as symbols of sky, water, and sand. Likewise, blue leather seats and blue carpet dominated the interior décor of the cars, each named for a comet, including one for the best known of all—Halley's, famously enshrined in the Bayeux Tapestry as an omen of the Norman Conquest of England in 1066. Even the tickets, napkins, and china were blue. The dining car—Giacobini—served enticing meals of sirloin steak or lamb chops, topped off with apple pie, for $1.50 or less. Indeed, the Blue Comet by design offered passengers first-class accommodations at coach rates.

Each day one of three new Baldwin engines, each a 4-6-2 Pacific, powered the train on its round-trip journey. Large 79-inch drivers enabled speeds approaching 100 mph. In practice, however, the Blue Comet raced across the Pine Barrens at 70 mph, fast enough to cover the 136-mile route in three hours. In the Pine Barrens, the train stopped at Lakewood and Lakehurst, and when passing through Chatsworth an obliging conductor heaved big-city newspapers to the town's waiting readers.

The uniqueness of the Blue Comet prompted Lionel to mimic it with an electric train, which is now a valuable collector's item that commands $10,000 or more. First offered in 1930, the standard gauge initially sold for $65, a princely sum during the Great Depression. Lionel continues to produce models of the Blue Comet, albeit now in the somewhat narrower O gauge and with lesser attention to the details featured in the earlier version. For trivia enthusiasts, note that a family member was "hit" while examining a Blue Comet model in an episode of the popular TV series *The Sopranos*.

A downpour of biblical proportions—close to 14 inches according to most reports—flooded the Pine Barrens on August 19, 1939. Made worse by the overflow from nearby cranberry bogs, the surge easily washed out the sandy roadbed under the tracks, leaving the rails intact but unsupported and a disaster waiting to happen. Engineer John Thomas had been warned about the danger and accordingly eased back on the throttle, reducing the Comet's usual speed by half to 35 mph. Despite the precaution, and hampered by poor visibility, the northbound train hit a washout as it approached Chatsworth at milepost 86. The engine and tender managed to cross the weakened roadbed, but all of the five trailing cars were derailed. Rescuers, many from Chatsworth, waded through chest-high water to reach the wreck. Fortunately, only 49 passengers were on board and, of these, 32 were injured, most by the unanchored wicker chairs that hurled about inside an observation car. (Early reports claimed 100 were killed, which triggered a massive reaction from the region's first responders.) The dining car chef, however, died a day later from burns he suffered in the crash. Remarkably, crews restored about 600 feet of track at the site within 48 hours, and all but one of the cars were reconditioned and returned to service. Today, rusting rails at the unmarked site remain as just another stretch of an abandoned and overgrown roadbed deep within the Pine Barrens.

Regrettably, ticket sales steadily diminished as the economic hard times of the 1930s wore on (recall that only 49 passengers were onboard on that fateful day in 1939). In 1941, the trail of the Blue Comet came to an end. By then the blue Pacifics, now painted black, were in service on other routes; they had been unceremoniously replaced by one of the Jersey Central's workhorse 4-4-2 Camelbacks. Some of the cars survive in train museums, but one—Biela, an observation car named for a comet not seen since 1885—became part of a diner at Clinton, New Jersey, where patrons can still enjoy fine meals. The actual dining car, the only steel-clad wooden car on the train, was damaged beyond repair and ended its days as a trackside freight station.

Blue comets, although rare, really exist. In 2016, astronomers in Hawaii discovered a blue comet deep in the outer reaches of the solar system in an orbit that approaches Earth just once every 20,000 years. The blue color of this comet, officially known as C/2016R2(PanSTARRS), originates from an abundance of ionized carbon monoxide and nitrogen emitted from its core of rock and ice. Nonetheless, New Jersey can proudly claim its own Blue Comet—one that long ago streaked across the Pine Barrens as "the seashore's finest train."

severe jeopardy. At Martha's Vineyard, these events included nests destroyed by fire followed by a winter of heavy predation, then disease, increasing sterility from inbreeding, and finally a population with too few females to maintain itself. Thus bludgeoned by a succession of misfortunes, heath hens had gone the way of passenger pigeons and Labrador ducks.

Jersey Cedar

Along the upper edges of Barnegat Bay, stands of stately Atlantic white cedar—dubbed locally as Jersey cedar—also succumbed to the new regime of salinity wrought by the Manasquan Canal (see chapter 4). Cedars near Cattus Island, for example, rapidly died when salt water overwhelmed the area's freshwater wetlands, and others in the region currently suffer from saltwater intrusion associated with subsidence, rising sea levels, and storms that push salt water farther upstream and into the adjacent swamps. The species' limited tolerance to salt water ends with death and the formation of "ghost forests"—acres of still-standing, skeleton-like cedars—which may be surrounded by salt marsh that has expanded into the former forest. Moreover, the dead trees emit about one-fifth of the greenhouse gases arising from ghost forests. In addition to the gasses released from the decomposing wood, the trees also transport gasses produced in the soil into the atmosphere (i.e., the trees act as straw-like conduits). Informally known as "tree farts," these emissions play a relatively small role in climate change but nonetheless further define the global carbon budget—and they may gain additional importance as rising sea levels continue to drown coastal woodlands. In all, the cedar cemeteries offer a grim example of the ecological changes resulting from the accelerated rise in sea levels now in evidence—a haunting vision captured in a monument created by artist/designer Maya Lin: 49 dead or dying cedars removed from the Pine Barrens and displayed in 2021 at Madison Square Park in New York City.

Elsewhere in New Jersey, including the Pine Barrens, Atlantic white cedar faced additional challenges, not the least of which was relentless overharvesting that began in colonial times and continued until only a fraction of the original forest remained at sites ill-suited for logging operations. Similarly, the sizable tract of cedar lying between Manahawkin and Barnegat Bay faced the woodsman's axe for centuries. Still others were converted to cranberry bogs after the trees were cut. According to botanist-explorer Peter Kalm (1716–1779), virgin stands of cedar were gone by the mid-1700s, hence those tracts that remain today represent at least a third generation of regrowth (fig. 7.3). The wood provided a fine grade of charcoal for the gunpowder that fired muskets and cannons during the Revolutionary War, and its resistance to rot and warping proved desirable for barn floors, boats, poles, barrel staves, and especially shingles. It also became, and remains, the wood of choice for decoy carvers along the Jersey Shore (see chapter 4).

As the wetland forests of cedar diminished, enterprising loggers of a new sort began mining logs buried in wetlands where the trees had flourished for generations, their wood remaining intact in graves of peat and mud. Deft probing detected the buried trees, sometimes many feet below the surface, which were then laboriously freed from the mire for cutting and splitting. Remarkably, shingles sheared from the sunken logs, even after centuries of watery internment, subsequently provide 70 to 80 years of service. When available, lumber with finer-grained wood was sold at higher prices for the manufacture of violins. Some of these logs were ancient; 1,080 growth rings were counted on the stump end of one giant, and many

FIGURE 7.3. Atlantic white cedar forests characteristically lack understories and instead feature hummocks covered with sphagnum moss. Water periodically fills the depressions between the hummocks, providing patches of habitat for swamp pink and a limited number of other herbaceous plants. Photo credit: Bob Cunningham.

others ranged from 200 to 1,000 years old. By the late 1890s, the industry waned as the supply of sunken logs dwindled and insurance companies mandated fire-proof shingles.

Atlantic white cedar, when mature, stand tall and straight in relatively dense groves in which their canopies limit the sunlight reaching the understory. In the Pine Barrens, cedar swamps commonly occur in strips up to 1,000 feet wide along steam edges; these may extend for the entire length of the stream, from its source to tide water. Other stands develop in broad poorly drained lowlands. The trees prefer slightly elevated sites and hummocks surrounded by freshwater in an arrangement that provides a measure of protection against both wildfires and the invasion of other species. Fires present a mixed blessing for Atlantic white cedar. In the eighteenth century, the large tracts once growing in the Hackensack Meadows disappeared forever after they were burned to deprive pirates of hiding places, which provides good evidence of the trees' susceptibility to fire damage. Infrequent, low-intensity fires, however, provide some benefits by increasing the sunlight available to seedlings and thwarting competitors, especially red maple. The shallow root systems of Atlantic white cedar, coupled with the spongy substrate in the swamps, enables windfalls from strong winds, and such microhabitats become sites for greater sunlight and seedling growth.

Centuries of overharvesting abetted by modern-day saltwater intrusion have reduced an estimated 115,000 acres of Atlantic white cedar in New Jersey prior to European settlement to about 26,100 acres today. To partially mitigate this loss, a consortium of state and private organizations will plant seeds and seedlings on some 10,000 acres of land where saltwater intrusion poses less of a threat. Most of these efforts, occurring over a ten-year period, will take place on state-owned forest, park, and wildlife management areas, thanks to an allotment of $20 million from the New Jersey Forest Service. Additionally, more than 2,500 seedlings have already been planted along a stream on the campus of Stockton University.

White cedar forests characteristically lack a well-developed understory but may include shrubs such as highbush blueberry, sweet pepperbush, fetterbush, and bayberry, which occasionally form nearly impenetrable thickets. A sparse cover of herbaceous vegetation includes partridgeberry, curly grass ferns that are closely associated with the hummocks at the base of the cedars, and, as described later, pitcher plants. Bog asphodel, listed in New Jersey as a threatened species, occurs in sandy bogs where it occasionally grows in large patches; after blooming, its

FIGURE 7.4. The blooms of bog asphodel (left) and swamp pink (right) add color to the ground cover in bogs and swampy areas in the Pine Barrens. Both species are rare enough to warrant listing by federal or state agencies as either threatened or endangered. Photo credits: Kevin Knutsen.

attractive spike of bright yellow flowers develops into an equally attractive collection of reddish-brown seed capsules (fig. 7.4, left). The flora at Oceanville Bog, part of the Forsythe National Wildlife Refuge, include other rarities such as Atlantic ladies' tresses and crested yellow orchids.

The shade limits the occurrence of many understory plants, but a few species not only tolerate shade but require it, precisely because a lack of direct sunlight eliminates competitors. One of these, swamp pink, also grows on hummocks beneath the cedar canopy (fig. 7.4, right). The plants, related to the lily family, consist of a basal rosette of evergreen, lance-shaped leaves. In spring, a central stalk about three feet tall emerges from the rosette, topped by a three-inch cluster of 30 to 50 pink flowers that resemble a clover blossom writ large. Pale blue stamens protruding beyond the petals add to the appeal of the pink clusters. Unfortunately, the attractiveness of swamp pink induces poaching, made worse when the transplants fail because the thieves remove too little of root systems to sustain the plant at its new location. Conservation biologists describe an additional concern: swamp pinks grow in small, scattered populations, which limits their genetic diversity. The plants in these isolated groups, for the most part, persist with a high rate of self-fertilization, and their limited range inhibits dispersal of their water-borne seeds. Ants sometimes help with seed dispersal, but few ants thrive in swamps and the relationship remains insufficient to prevent inbreeding.

Mats of sphagnum cover many sites on the floor of cedar bogs, especially in depressions. These plants absorb huge amounts of water and rather remarkably provide a sterile environment. For these reasons, Native Americans once used sphagnum for diaper material, and during World War I the moss was collected and processed into bandages. In the past, florists and nurseries consumed large quantities of sphagnum moss, and its harvest once represented another sector in the resource-based economy of the Pine Barrens. In sum, virtually all plants growing in cedar swamps necessarily cope with soils that are acidic, anaerobic, waterlogged, and nutrient poor, hence presenting a challenging environment that excludes far more species than it favors.

Atlantic white cedar, which botanists properly recognize as a cypress, provides suitable and sometimes essential habitat for a variety of animals. These include white-tailed deer that often forage heavily on cedar to the point of suppressing growth of the younger trees (i.e., those with branches low enough to reach). In general, however, overbrowsing in the Pine Barrens in not as significant as elsewhere. In the northern parts of their extensive range, for example, deer seek winter refuge in what are known as "deer yards," some of which have been visited annually for generations. Deer face a hard choice in harsh winters—to find adequate food or to seek effective shelter. Shelter wins, and winter-stressed deer concentrate in locations protected from chilling winds and deep snow, but many of these sites lack sufficient amounts of nutritious food. Starvation often follows, but the emaciated animals nonetheless remain in these sheltered sites instead of searching for food elsewhere. Unlike other evergreens, cedar offers both cover and food, but overbrowsing remains a risk, especially when deer numbers exceed

Native Americans used wild cranberries for dyes, medications, and, of course, as food. They introduced the berries to English colonists settling in Massachusetts, who thereafter included the berries in their diet, most notably as part of their Thanksgiving feasts, an association that spread as Europeans continued settling in North America. The plants grew naturally in acidic bogs, typically where a layer of sphagnum moss protected their roots from freezing, but the popularity of the berries eventually led to cultivation and commercial production—and to altered landscapes.

The industry is founded on a domesticated variety of the American cranberry, which develops as a creeping vine-like shrub bearing evergreen leaves and dark pink flowers. The structure of the flowers seemingly resembled the neck, head, and bill of a crane and gave rise to the name "crane berry" and eventually cranberry. Cultivation in New Jersey began in the Pine Barrens sometime between 1825 and 1840, with nearly all of the current operations still located in the same region. Bogs, including many of those stripped of Atlantic white cedar, were cleared, leveled, and ditched in ways that both supplied and removed water, as needed. The layout included a main central ditch from which lateral side ditches carried water to the periphery of the bog. Another ditch running completely around the perimeter connected with the others, and the entire layout was surrounded with a dike equipped with gates for controlling water flowing to and from a nearby stream.

After removing a few inches of top soil, the bed is covered with a layer of sand, then planted with cuttings from fully grown cranberry vines. Over the next three to five years, the cuttings will produce enough shoots to spread across the bog and produce a profitable crop of berries. Interestingly, in 1816 a Revolutionary War veteran named Henry Hall noticed that sand blowing inland from the dunes on the Massachusetts coast invigorated the wild cranberry bogs nearby and prompted commercial production. Today, the application of a thin layer of sand every two to five years continues as a cultural practice for refreshing commercial bogs by promoting the growth of healthy plants. The response seems remarkably like that associated with the vitality of American beachgrass growing on coastal dunes (see chapter 2).

Cranberries grow on moist soil, not in standing water, but the bogs are flooded in the fall to facilitate harvesting the berries, which float when separated from their stems. The floating carpets of red berries make attractive photos. After the harvest, the bogs are drained to allow the continued growth of the plants, then reflooded in time to protect the root zone from freezing. Once the national leader in cranberry production, New Jersey now ranks third behind Massachusetts and Wisconsin. On August 7, 2023, cranberry juice became New Jersey's official juice, thanks to the initiatives of fourth graders and their teacher, Erin Zarzycki, at Eleanor Rush Intermediate School in Cinnaminson Township.

Cranberry bogs provide the sole habitat for bog coppers, a small butterfly named for its metallic coloration that may spend its entire life in a single bog. The larvae feed exclusively on cranberry

FIGURE 7.5. Tundra swans overwintering in New Jersey often visit facilities associated with commercial cranberry operations, as shown here at Whitesbog Village. New Jersey currently ranks third in the nation for cranberry production, virtually all of which occurs in the Pine Barrens. Photo credit: Kevin Knutsen.

foliage, hatching from eggs laid singly on the underside of leaves growing just a few inches above the surface; the eggs tolerate flooding as well as freezing temperatures. Similarly, the adults rely on nectar from cranberry flowers. However, insecticide treatments largely exclude bog coppers from commercial cranberry bogs, although they readily adopt those no longer under cultivation. They are not migratory but will colonize suitable locations up to 1.5 miles away, with sites lying beyond often remaining unoccupied in the absence of intervening patches to serve as "stepping stones." New Jersey lists bog coppers as a species of high-level concern.

Whitesbog Village near Browns Mills provides an opportunity to visit an actively farmed cranberry bog as well as learn about the cultivation of high bush blueberries (fig. 7.5). Founded in the 1870s, the village became the hub for New Jersey's largest cranberry operation in the early 1900s. The restored village lies within Brendan T. Byrne State Forest, which covers some 37,240 acres of the Pine Barrens, including the 735-acre Cedar Swamp Natural Area. Double Trouble State Park also offers an opportunity to visit a partially restored company town once dependent on cranberry farming and other early industries in the Pine Barrens.

the carrying capacity of the habitat. Biologists measure this pressure by the height of the "browse line," below which virtually no twigs or other plant foods remain available for hungry deer. Fawns, of course, become the first to starve as browse lines move steadily higher. These conditions occur rarely, if ever, in the Pine Barrens, but deer nonetheless may impair the growth of younger cedars and thwart efforts to establish plantings. In particular, overbrowsing of the young trees encourages their replacement with other species, notably pine and hardwoods such as red maple.

Atlantic white cedar bogs provide year-round habitat for southern red-backed voles, which build their nests under fallen logs and feed on a well-rounded diet of seeds, fungi, berries, lichens, nuts, and a few hapless arthropods. Well named for their rust-colored dorsal pelage, these voles become abundant in mature cedar forests, where they represent a key role as prey for several kinds of predators. However, they are far less abundant in regenerating stands, which may act as "sinks" (i.e., to maintain their numbers, vole populations in such places depend on a flow of immigrants as opposed to their own reproductive success). Some evidence, based on examination of their fecal matter, suggests that these active rodents disperse mycorrhizal fungi that may play a role in the growth and nutrition of cedars, a consideration that may be especially important for regenerating a new cedar forest on cut-over bogs.

Atlantic white cedar alone provides the larvae of the Hessel's hairstreak butterfly with food. This is an obligate relationship—these butterflies have no second choice in the matter, and without the cedars' foliage their life cycle stops short of completion. Whereas the colorful adults seek nectar from a variety of flowers (fig. 7.6, right), the larvae feed exclusively on Atlantic white cedar's scaly leaves, which they match almost perfectly in color and pattern (fig. 7.6, left). In spring, the adult males perch in treetops on the lookout for mates that later lay their eggs singly on the tips of cedar shoots. Small tails form at the corners of the rear wings of both sexes; these bear spots that, together with their thin structure, seemingly represent eyes and antennae, an adaption no doubt designed to steer predators away from the actual head of the insect. After hatching, the caterpillars feed primarily on new growth, but not to the extent of damaging the health of the host tree. Some northeastern states—among them Connecticut and Maine—consider Hessel's hairstreak butterflies as a threatened species, whereas New Jersey, a stronghold for the species, has not issued a similar designation. Threats remain, how-

FIGURE 7.6. The larvae of Hessel's hairstreak butterfly feed exclusively on the foliage of Atlantic white cedar and offer a classic example of cryptic coloration (left). Conversely, the colorful adults seek nectar from a variety of flowering plants, as shown here by one feeding upside down on a drooping blueberry flower (right). Photo credits: Bob Cunningham (right); Sara Bright, Alabama Butterfly Atlas (left).

ever, and include the unintended consequences from spraying for mosquitos and gypsy moths, along with developments or activities that destroy or alter stands of Atlantic white cedar. Saltwater intrusion into the low-lying freshwater wetlands along the coast now presents a new concern for the cedars and, in turn, the butterflies they host.

Hardwood Bogs and Red Maple

When cedar bogs were cut over, as many were, hardwoods often dominated the regrowth that followed, including blackgum and sweetbay. Red maple, however, typically emerged as the dominant species in the second growth developing in

FIGURE 7.7. Red maples produce their winged seeds—samaras—long before other trees bear their own propagules—an advantage that enables their seedlings to gain a foothold early in the growing season. Note that leaves have yet to appear on the branch. Photo credit: Kevin Knutsen.

logged cedar bogs as well as transforming many other disturbed areas in the forests of eastern North America.

Red maple responds well to human disturbances and fire suppression, both reasons for the greater presence of the species at sites where it once played a lesser role. In the case of cedar bogs, logging provided the stimulus for the expansion of red maple. Additionally, fires that once killed the thin-barked red maples now occur with much less frequency, which again favors the growth and expansion of the species.

Early seed production provides red maple with an important competitive advantage. Even before their leaves appear each spring, red maples produce clusters of red seed-bearing samaras—the familiar one-winged propagules that "whirlybird" as they fall to the ground (fig. 7.7). About 85 percent of the seeds germinate, and together with their early appearance, this gives red maple a head start by establishing seedlings well before the seeds of other trees reach maturity. Because they are shade tolerant, the seedlings can survive under the canopy of other vegetation. Moreover, red maples just 4 to 10 years old produce viable seeds and soon yield crops of 12,000 or more per year, with a fully grown tree capable of producing nearly 1 million per season. In all, as an ideal generalist red maple comes close to being a perfect species. The trees combine traits of early succession—rapid maturity, tremendous seed production, and an invader of disturbed sites—with those of a climax community such as shade tolerance and longevity.

A program currently in development at Stockton University seeks to establish a sustainable maple syrup industry in southern New Jersey, much of it in the Pine Barrens. Because the geographical range of the traditional source, sugar maple, does not include this region, red maples offers a viable alternative on which to base the enterprise. Although the sugar content of red maple sap can be somewhat less in comparison with its northern relative, red maple's greater abundance and faster growth rate nonetheless will enable development of productive "sugarbushes" in New Jersey. The fledgling industry will provide supplemental income for farmers and other segments of a rural economy. Moreover, with the increased economic importance of red maple, which has little value as timber, privately owned woodlands may gain another layer of insulation against development. In addition to involving regional communities with the collection and processing of red maple sap, the program includes an educational component designed to acquaint students and adult groups with topics such as forest ecology, tree identification (a science known as dendrology), and the sustainable use of natural resources.

Bog Life: Carnivorous Plants

About 45 species (of more than 500 globally) of carnivorous plants occur in North America, primarily in association with moist, acidic, and nutrient-deficient soils—conditions exemplified by bogs in the Pine Barrens. Their unique structure and habits evolved at a cost that eliminated their ability to compete with other plants in nutrient-rich habitats, with the result that carnivorous plants thrive in environments where poor growing conditions keep out would-be competitors. They cope by gaining nutrients, primarily nitrogen and phosphorous, not from the soil but from prey they capture and digest.

FIGURE 7.8. Purple pitcher plants (left) frequently occur at boggy sites in the Pine Barrens. Other carnivorous plants in the Pine Barrens flora include three species of sundews, including thread-leafed sundew (right). Photo credits: James F. Parnell (left); Kevin Knutsen (right).

The bog flora in the Pine Barrens includes sundews, small and rather humble plants that secrete sticky droplets to capture their prey (fig. 7.8, right). Bladderworts, another group occurring in the bogs, trap their prey in small, balloon-like bladders that suddenly open when a midge larva, water flea, or other tiny invertebrate brushes against hairs around the structure's opening. Water then rushes to fill the vacuum inside the bladder, carrying with it the prey that becomes entrapped when the opening snaps shut. Many bladderworts are fully aquatic, but other species prefer muddy depressions. Purple pitcher plants, however, with their erect, tubular pitfall traps, by far represent the most conspicuous of the carnivorous plants in the bogs (fig. 7.8, left).

The tubes of pitcher plants develop from highly modified leaves that fill with rainwater, in some cases enriched by enzymes, in which captured prey drown. Fragrant scents and the colorful tubes attract the victims that, when crawling inside the lip of the tube, encounter downward-pointing hairs that inhibit their escape. Whereas a variety of animals make up the menu, ants are particularly common and represent nearly 75 percent of the prey captured by purple pitcher plants. Surprisingly, however, only a few visitors become victims—less than 1 percent overall and about a third of that for ants. Such low efficiency may serve as a means that prevents prey from developing avoidance behavior—an adaptation that would deny the plants any success at all. Spiders at times spin their webs across the mouths of the tubes and further lessen the capture rate.

The water-filled tubes also become unique microhabitats (technically called phytotelmata) in which tiny aquatic animals (collectively known as inquilines) live as a community but neither become prey nor are affected by enzymes in the pool water. The inquilines include protozoans, rotifers, crustaceans, arachnids, and insects. For example, the larvae of three species of flies, each in a different family, feed on detritus in purple pitcher plants, but avoid competing with each other by foraging in different parts of the pool, respectively the top, middle, and bottom of the water column—an example of a strategy known as resource partitioning.

Mary Davis Treat (1830–1923) deserves mention in regard to carnivorous plants, particularly bladderworts. Her career as a naturalist encompassed entomology, ornithology, and botany, in which she trained herself when living at Vineland in the Pinelands of southern New Jersey. After long hours at a microscope, she discovered how bladderworts captured their prey, described earlier, and rejected the widely held belief that the bladders were structures primarily associated with floatation. The bladders, she wrote, were "so many stomachs, digesting and assimilating animal food." She shared these revelations in her correspondence with Charles Darwin (1809–1882), who acknowledged her contributions in his book about carnivorous plants. Until then, Darwin had lacked, much to his frustration, a satisfactory explanation for the phenomenon. Treat also described for Darwin the fly-catching abilities of sundews. In all, she published five books and 78 scientific and popular articles.

Shore Note 7.4 The Dread Monster of Jersey's Big Forest

So wrote syndicated columnist J. Elfreth Watkins in 1905 about the Jersey Devil, the frightful and mysterious denizen of the forests and cedar swamps of the Pine Barrens. The legend of the Jersey Devil, as is often the case for folklore, has various origins, but most claim it started when Deborah Smith Leeds gave birth to a deformed child, the thirteenth in a brood whose abundance undoubtedly gave cause for her local name, Mother Leeds. Arrival of such a child in 1735, an era that often enough accepted witchcraft, wizards, and the like, seemed to signify that the newborn was cursed and indeed sired by Lucifer himself. In *Poor Richard's Almanack,* Benjamin Franklin further entrenched the legend when he characterized the editor of a competing almanac, one Titan Leeds, as a descendent from a family of monsters, a rather transparent reference to the spooky offspring of Mother Leeds.

Some say the baby at first appeared normal, but on the night of its birth the child developed a serpent-like body topped by the head of a horse, cloven hooves, the wings of a bat, and, of course, the forked tail of a dragon—sure signs of devilish handiwork. Thus transformed, the monster spewed some piercing cries and flew up the chimney. Still screaming, it circled over some villages, stopping briefly to wolf down a few sleeping babies, then sought haven in the forbidding recesses of the Pine Barrens.

Encounters with the Jersey Devil soon followed, some only by sound, others by sight of red eyes glowing in the cover of darkness or the beast itself hovering over a pond in a cedar swamp. In the latter instance, blasts of its fetid breath kill scores of fish, which explains those occasions when their bloated bodies scatter the surface of local ponds. A figure no less than Joseph Bonaparte, the brother of Napoleon and ex-king of Spain, claimed to have seen the monster on a deer hunt in the Pine Barrens, as did Stephen Decatur, naval hero of the War of 1812, who came to the area to test cannon balls forged from iron extracted from local bogs (see main text). Moreover, during these tests, Decatur supposedly fired a cannon ball that passed clear through the monster without in the least slowing down its frenzied passage.

Appearances of the Jersey Devil, often highlighted by howling dogs and hooting owls, foretold disasters. The monster especially liked to dart among the dunes along the nearby shore to enjoy the destruction of floundering schooners. Even lesser events indicate its malicious presence, including milk turned sour, parched corn fields, and horses suddenly gone lame in their stalls. Clearly, the Devil's presence explains centuries of misfortunes befalling residents of the Pine Barrens. More recently, the Devil has frightened berry pickers (1930) and schoolchildren (1951) and blocked a forest ranger on a road along the Mullica River (1993). Today the bat-winged, fork-tailed monster lives on, represented just a bit less menacingly by the New Jersey Devils on the ice rinks of the National Hockey League.

Dark Waters

Water in the bogs and most streams in the Pine Barrens is acidic and stained tea-like by humic substances, notably the tannins leached from the accumulated ground litter. Almost everyone has noticed the rusty stain on a sidewalk that forms around fallen pine needles—an indication of the tannin content in these materials. Additional staining arises from the high iron content of the soils. The sands lack much buffering capacity, which means they cannot neutralize the acidity, which ranges from a pH of 3.6 to 5.2, with an average of 4.4—enough to affect some forms of aquatic life. For example, at a pH of 5.8 or less, calcium no longer becomes available for the shells of snails and bivalves, resulting in a limited molluscan fauna in the Pine Barrens. Similarly, crustaceans also remain scarce where the pH drops below 6.0. Insects such as mayflies also are rare or absent, whereas the larvae of dragonflies and damselflies survive in abundance.

Whirligig beetles—a curious lot indeed—also cope well in the acidic waters of the Pine Barrens. Groups of these sleek-bodied insects swirl about on the surface like so-many miniature bumper cars, but separate parts of their compound eyes provide each beetle with simultaneous vision above and below water. They also can dive and remain underwater breathing from air trapped under their elytra, the hardened forewings that protectively cover the softer hindwings on virtually all species of beetles. When disturbed, males move to the periphery of the congregations, females to the center, a pattern that may lessen the risk of predation for the smaller, less armored, and slower-swimming females. Whirligig beetles also produce a foul-smelling and unsavory secretion that helps repel predators. Hunger likewise segregates the beetles into groups, with satiated individuals of either sex gathering at the center of the swarm and those still hungry at the periphery. Note, however, that the swarms are not associated with courtship behavior, but whatever the reason might be, whirligig beetles entertain all who stop, even for a moment, to wonder at their erratic dancing on a quiet pool.

The acidity limits the fish fauna by thwarting the development of eggs and larvae of some species, or more indirectly by affecting the invertebrates in the food chains of others. Common fishes such as yellow perch and bluegill seldom reproduce successfully below a pH of 4.9. Algae and many forms of microscopic life crucial to food chains are either specialized or absent. Low turbidity, sluggishness, and poor nutrient content also characterize the waters in the Pine Barrens, with the latter contributing to their diminished productivity. In the days long gone, sea captains along the East Coast filled the casks on their sailing ships with the tea-colored water, which remained "sweet" far longer than water from other sources that would otherwise seem more palatable (e.g., springs and wells).

Dense beds of aquatic plants such as water milfoil, alga pondweed, and bladderworts as well as fragrant waterlilies and pickerelweed provide cover for fishes in the streams and impounded waters in Pine Barrens. Several species of fishes characterize the Pine Barrens, although none of these are endemic and occur elsewhere in New Jersey. These include three related sunfishes, foremost of which is the blackbanded sunfish that can survive pH levels as low as 3.7 to 4.0. They prefer living in dense vegetation, which no doubt accounts for the protective pattern of their vertical black markings. These small fish average about 2.5 inches in length, reaching a maximum of 4 inches, and feed on crustaceans and insects, especially midge larvae. Just how blackbanded sunfish deal with acidity is not understood, but their tolerance may isolate them from predators or competitors unable to cope with such conditions. In some parts of its range, the species may be heavily harvested as aquarium stock, but it is not similarly threatened in New Jersey, where pollution from agricultural chemicals instead poses a greater concern. The related banded (or sphagnum) and bluespotted sunfishes also occur in the region as well as elsewhere in New Jersey, but neither is as characteristic of the Pine Barrens as blackbanded sunfish.

Other fishes occurring in the acidic "tea water" of the Pine Barrens include mud sunfish, yellow bullhead, pirate perch, and swamp darter. Yellow bullheads largely replace the more widely distributed brown bullhead in the Pine Barrens, which in part may be the result of competitive exclusion or because yellow bullheads better tolerate acidity whereas brown bullheads better cope with pollution.

Chain pickerel, common throughout New Jersey, represents the only native game fish in the Pine Barrens, and attempts to introduce smallmouth bass, rainbow trout, and other game fishes failed to establish sustainable populations. A smaller relative, the redfin (or grass) pickerel, also occurs in the Pine Barrens. The absence of other fish-eating species may be related to the lack of some common foods, as chain pickerel in the Pine Barrens prey on species they largely ignore elsewhere in their range. For example, in the Pine Barrens chain pickerel feed heavily on creek chubsuckers, but despite the abundance of this forage fish elsewhere (e.g., lakes in northern New Jersey) chain pickerel in those locations typically forage on other species.

In all, the fish fauna in the Pine Barrens includes 24 species (of about 70 in New Jersey), and excluding introduced and peripheral species, the number drops to just 16 species—a clear reflection of habitat conditions where relatively few fishes can survive.

The Mullica River, named for Erkki (Eric) Palsson Mullica (1636–1704), a Swede of Finnish descent, is the largest drainage in the Pine Barrens and lies entirely within its confines. Upstream the waters, stained and acidic as described above, support a limited community of freshwater fishes, but saltwater species enter the tidal sections as the river approaches its mouth in Great Bay. Forsythe National Wildlife Refuge protects the extensive salt marshes on the southern bank of the river's mouth. In winter, the river serves as a route followed by tundra swans visiting cranberry bogs in the Pine Barrens, after which they return to the coastal marshes. Bald eagles also overwinter in the Mullica's watershed, as do black ducks and other waterfowl.

The Mullica's major tributaries include the Wading, Batsto, Atsion, and Bass rivers. Shad once spawned in this system, but their annual upstream runs ended decades ago. Striped bass, however, still spawn in the Mullica, as do blueback herring, which presumably benefit from a fish ladder installed at a dam otherwise blocking their route up the Batsto River.

The Pine Barrens lack natural lakes, and those so named (e.g., Harrisville Lake and Atsion Lake) were created to power long-gone lumber, grist, and paper mills as well as forges and glass works. However, beaver ponds and ephemeral (seasonal) ponds represent natural bodies of surface water in the Pine Barrens (fig. 7.9). The latter, colloquially known as "spungs" from the Scottish word for purse, develop in shallow depressions where the water table lies close to the surface for part of the year. Water fills these ponds in the fall, winter, and spring to depths of about 10 to 20 inches, after which they slowly dry during the summer when the water table sinks deeper into the soil profile. As with the streams in the region, the water is acidic—typical pH values range between 3.8 and 4.5; leatherleaf thickets and mats of sphagnum moss characteristically develop at many of these wetlands. Spungs offer prime habitat for a variety of plants and animals, including some rare species. Some species of frogs and salamanders in the Pine Barrens indeed depend solely on spungs for breeding habitat; in the absence of fish, the eggs and

FIGURE 7.9. In summer, the eye-catching white flowers of fragrant waterlilies often dot the surface of ephemeral ponds ("spungs") tucked away in the Pine Barrens. Photo credit: Kevin Knutsen.

larvae of amphibians can mature in a largely predator-free environment. One of the obligate species, the eastern tiger salamander, is the largest of its kind in New Jersey and appears on the state list of endangered species. Spungs may face an uncertain future (as do their dependent fauna) because of the impacts of climate change on their hydrology.

Herps in the Pines

Amphibians and reptiles—collectively known as herptiles, or "herps" for short—are well represented in the Pine Barrens. Three of these represent keynote species because of their interesting life histories.

FIGURE 7.10. Pine Barrens tree frogs occur only in cedar bogs and other wetlands in the Pine Barrens and in similar habitat in the Carolinas and Florida Panhandle. Photo credit: Kevin Knutsen.

The aptly named Pine Barrens treefrog is one of the more colorful frogs in North America (fig. 7.10). Lavender white-bordered stripes run laterally along their emerald green bodies, with orange highlighting the undersides of their legs and thighs. The coloring of their front limbs gives the impression that the frogs are wearing gloves; both their front and hind feet feature well-developed toe pads equipped with sticky surfaces. They have white bellies, and males display purplish-gray throats. Females grow larger than males.

Pine Barrens treefrogs offer a textbook example of a discontinuous distribution. They occur in three widely separated populations, one each in New Jersey (the northern limit of their range), one in North and South Carolina, and another in the Florida Panhandle, including a small area of southern Alabama (the southern end of their range). Their preferred habitat consists of spring-fed seepage bogs, cedar swamps, pitch pine lowlands and pine forests adjacent to wetlands. The tadpoles display a tolerance for the brown, acidic waters at these sites. New Jersey lists the Pine Barrens treefrog as a threatened species.

In the Pine Barrens, the treefrogs breed in bogs, swamps, and especially vernal ponds, as described above. In spring, individual males announce their readiness to mate with vocalizations best described as honking—"quonk-quonk, quonk-quonk" repeated 15 to 25 times in 20 seconds, but large numbers of males in full chorus produce a loud "a-quonk-a-quonk-a-quonk." Inflated, balloon-like vocal pouches on the throats of males produce these distinctive calls. When a female responds, the pair engages in amplexus, a sexual posture in which the male grasps the back of the female with his front legs and fertilizes each of 500 to 1,000 eggs one at a time as they are laid.

Depending on water temperature, the eggs hatch 7 to 14 days later, with the tadpoles feeding on microscopic invertebrates and equally small plant matter. They grow rapidly and 80 to 100 days later emerge from the water as froglets that hide during the day in sphagnum moss or other moist cover and venture out at night in search of insects and spiders. Sexual maturity occurs two years later for males, three years for females.

Based on laboratory experiments, the acid tolerance of Pine Barrens treefrogs seems not to affect their breeding success by inhibiting competition from other, less tolerant species, including a close relative. In other words, the restriction of Pine Barrens treefrogs to acidic wetlands does not result from an adaptation that influences competition between species. This research, however, considered only larvae—tadpoles—and it may be that competitors remain absent because their eggs cannot develop in highly acidic water. Additionally, Pine Barrens treefrogs may persist where they do because the acidic water provides a barrier for some of their predators.

Another aptly named herptile, the northern pine snake, also reaches the northern limit of its range in the Pine Barrens, where they remain isolated from other populations in Virginia, Tennessee, Kentucky, and North Carolina. They favor pine-oak communities on sandy uplands but also forage along the edges of cedar swamps and pitch pine wetlands. These large and powerful constrictors normally reach 48 to 66 inches in length but may attain a maximum of 83 inches. Large dark blotches overlie a dusky white background on their dorsal surface, whereas their underside is strikingly white with black flecks, sometimes tinged with orange or pink (fig. 7.11, left). The snouts of pine snakes feature a large, pointed shield-like rostral scale used for digging.

FIGURE 7.11. Northern pine snakes in the Pine Barrens remain far removed from populations elsewhere (e.g., Virginia), and because of the risks associated with geographic isolation, New Jersey lists the species as threatened (left). Northern pine snakes excavate nesting burrows, an unusual habit that contributes to their secretive behavior (right). Note the mound of excavated sand and the track. Photo credits: Robert Zappalorti, Herpetological Associates.

Pine snakes overwinter in underground dens known as hibernacula, commonly in the company of other species such as hognose, black rat, and corn snakes as well as with others of their own kind. In the north, most pine snakes hibernate in deep burrows abandoned by mammals or in the stump holes of fallen trees. Because of their ability to dig, however, they sometimes excavate their own winter dens, usually at the base of decaying stumps where they follow root pathways downward for at least three feet—safely beyond the depth reached by frost—before enlarging a hibernation chamber. But like most species, pine snakes commonly return to the same hibernacula each winter, an example of behavior known as philopatry.

After emerging from their winter dens, usually in mid-April, pine snakes forage and bask during the day and seek shelter in hollow logs or stump holes at night. In May, after shedding, female pine snakes leave scent trails marked with pheromones—skin lipids that attract males. About a month after mating, a gravid female seeks an open, sunny location in the upland forest. Such sites meet rather specific criteria, including a minimum of plant cover and sandy soils that, like the fabled beds in Goldilocks, are neither too firm nor too soft—"just right" for digging. The reduced plant cover, particularly woody vegetation, lessens encounters with hefty roots that may require the snakes to change the direction of their excavations (i.e., turns in the tunnels, some by as much as 150 degrees). Conversely, some herbaceous ground cover—particularly grasses and Pennsylvania sedge—remains desirable; their fibrous roots help stabilize the soil above the tunnel and nest chamber and prevent cave-ins. Many pine snake nests are located in clearings near winter dens.

Females initially test the suitability of the soil, first by making small "pretest" depressions, then with exploratory "test holes," and finally by excavating four- to five-foot long tunnels that end in a chamber enlarged to hold their eggs. Clutches average about 9 eggs, with a range of 3 to 16 that varies proportionately with the snout-to-vent length of each female. The tunnels typically lie horizontally below the surface but briefly dip downward near the midpoint, then return to their previous depth before reaching the egg chamber—likely a precaution designed to trap rainwater entering the tunnel and prevent flooding the eggs. On average, nest chambers lie about 6.5 inches underground, a relatively shallow depth that may ensure adequate solar heat for hatching (i.e., although the snakes dig deeper when constructing hibernacula, they do not when excavating their nest chambers).

Northern pine snakes use their strong neck muscles to power their digging activities, a process that begins when they force their heads into soil loosened with the large rostral scale at the tip of their snouts. Next the snakes crook their heads against their necks, forming a "scoop" to drag out the loosened soil each time they back out of the excavation; the work takes two to four days to complete, given that they avoid digging during the midday heat. Digging accumulates dump piles of sand on one side of the entrance, telltale evidence of these efforts (fig. 7.11, right). Often a second and rarely as many as four other females may use the same nest, but each digs a separate egg chamber off the main tunnel. Females do not return to the nest after laying their eggs. Red foxes, coyotes, raccoons, and striped skunks dig up about 25 percent of the nests in search for food, and human poachers illegally collect both eggs and nesting females for the pet trade.

Rattlesnakes represent one of the more unappreciated and certainly misunderstood group of reptiles in the United States—most humans summarily kill all they encounter. In New Jersey, timber rattlesnakes persist in two geographical areas, each with its own ecological characteristics (fig. 7.12). In northern New Jersey, along the Kittatinny Mountain Ridge, a relatively pristine remnant of the Eastern Deciduous Forest cloaks the steep, rocky terrain, and the climate includes long harsh winters. In contrast, the Pine Barrens of southern New Jersey features a flat landscape of sandy soil, pine-dominated forests, and numerous bogs in a region with a more moderate climate.

The regional differences, above, dictate the hibernation sites selected by each of the two rattlesnake populations in New Jersey. In mountainous areas, the snakes seek winter dens in rocky crevices or ledges with southern exposures, often sharing these quarters with other species of snakes. But in the Pine Barrens, timber rattlesnakes typically den on stream edges bordering cedar bogs or intermittent sponges where they overwinter in rodent burrows or the natural spaces associated with the root systems of large trees, primarily Atlantic white cedar, red maple, or sweet gum. Thick mats of sphagnum moss and the roots of other vegetation help insulate the snakes from freezing in their winter dens. Additionally, rattlers hibernating in the bogs often rest in shallow, slow-moving water crossing the floor of their dens. This trait, which helps maintain a constant body temperature above freezing, may represent a feature unique of the rattlesnake population in the Pine Barrens.

Clearings in the Pine Barrens provide gravid females with basking sites where the sun-warmed sandy soil contributes to the internal incubation of their embryos. Such sites include miles of sand roads cutting through the Pine Barrens, but basking along road edges unfortunately exposes the snakes to adverse encounters with humans. As a result, a specific and essential component of the population—gravid females—experiences disproportionally larger losses from human activities (e.g., road kills, accidental or otherwise, as well as wanton killing and illegal collecting). Conversely, rattlers in rocky mountainsides of northern New Jersey largely escape these regrettable circumstances.

Whether in mountains or the Pine Barrens, timber rattlers prefer hunting—always by ambush—coiled next to logs or at the base of trees where rodents and other prey may travel or seek cover. Masked shrews, southern red-backed voles,

FIGURE 7.12. Timber rattlesnakes today are rarely encountered in the Pine Barrens. Unlike those in northern New Jersey, they commonly overwinter in dens under large trees or stumps, at a depth below the frost line and often adjoining the water table from nearby streams. Photo credit: Robert T. Zappalorti, Herpetological Associates.

red squirrels, and white-footed mice top the list of their victims in the Pine Barrens, but the menu includes many other small mammals and occasionally birds.

Timber rattlers do not reproduce rapidly. They require 9 to 11 years to attain sexual maturity, bear young at intervals of two to four years, and may breed only three to five times in their lifetimes. When gravid, the females gestate for two years, giving birth to an average of nine live young in protected sites such as hollow logs or abandoned mammal burrows. The young arrive individually wrapped in membranous sacs—the remnants of eggshells in which they developed—that they open with an "egg tooth" temporarily tipping their snouts. Instead of a full rattle, the young snakes bear only the first segment or "button," but acquire another segment each time they shed their skin.

Both pine snakes and timber rattlesnakes face threats from altered habitat, illegal collecting, and, especially in the case of rattlers, senseless killing. In response, the New Jersey Division of Fish and Wildlife lists pine snakes as threatened and timber rattlesnakes as endangered. Artificial hibernacula offer a means for improving habitat for pine snakes as well as other rare species. These well-designed and sturdy underground structures provide the snakes with reliable winter quarters and year-round escape cover. In the long run, however, a public educated and appreciative of snakes as components of viable ecosystems remains foremost for ensuring these and other herptiles maintain their rightful place in nature.

The Blueberry Queen of Whitesbog

Elizabeth C. White—Miss Lizzie to her friends and neighbors—introduced the first cultivated blueberries to the nation in 1916. Born into a Quaker family in 1871, she grew up on a large cranberry farm in Burlington County at the northern edge of the Pine Barrens; the site, a village known as Whitesbog, is now restored and part of Brendan T. Byrne State Forest. She learned the cranberry business at the side of her father and worked daily on the farm in various capacities. One task concerned dealing with a katydid that had a much-too-healthy appetite for cranberry foliage, which was resolved when she and the state entomologist discovered and burned each year the grasses on which the pesky insects laid their eggs.

Blueberries, although commonly wild in many areas, had never been cultivated. Just as it had for generations, the harvest of wild berries continued as a cottage industry for residents of the Pine Barrens. But if the native highbush blueberry could be tamed, it would extend Whitesbog's growing season with another cash crop—blueberries in summer, cranberries in the fall—but the challenge remained unresolved. Then, in 1910, Miss Lizzie read a bulletin written by Frederick V. Coville, chief botanist with the U.S. Department of Agriculture, in which he described his efforts to culture blueberries in New Hampshire. She asked Coville to continue his research at Whitesbog, in which she would assist. He accepted, thus beginning a partnership that produced a commercial blueberry six years later.

The Pine Barrens was rich with the raw materials necessary for cultivating hybrids. Highbush blueberries were the best choice for the project, and Miss Lizzie flew into action to acquire stock for Coville's experiments. She enlisted local pickers to find the best bushes and furnished each with a simple gauge on which to judge their candidates—only those berries that could not pass through the larger holes in the gauge would yield the finder a reward of $1 to $3. The pickers tagged the bushes and later returned to the site with Miss Lizzie in a horse and buggy. Cuttings from the best bushes—each named for its finder—were rooted at Whitesbog, and the best of these were later sent to greenhouses in Washington, where Coville conducted his hybridization trials. After further winnowing, the best of these were returned to grow at Whitesbog, where Miss Lizzie regularly checked them for size, color, and, of course, taste. Most were rejected, but some made the cut and became the stock for commercial production. Miss Lizzie also pioneered packing the berries in clear cellophane to show off the fruit it protected. By no coincidence, New Jersey soon emerged as a national leader in blueberry production, and in 2004 the highbush blueberry became the official state fruit.

Miss Lizzie had other interests that emphasized her love for the Pine Barrens. She established a garden consisting only of native plants at Whitesbog, where it provided a showcase for the then-novel concept to visitors. In 1943, she published "Plants of the New Jersey Pine Barrens," in which she described goldencrest, a striking plant and one of her favorites. True to its name, goldencrest produces delicate yellow-orange flowers, made all the more attractive because they stand out against whitish mats of soft wool that cover the upper parts of the plants. Their seed heads, also white, maintain the plants' ornamental qualities into the fall months, after which the first hard freeze turns the entire plant ghostly white. Goldencrest grows in native cranberry bogs and other wet areas in the Pine Barrens.

Miss Lizzie also established Holly Haven, a commercial nursery dedicated to the conservation of American holly and other acid-loving plants. Holly Haven has now faded into obscurity, but Miss Lizzie's legacy persists in the mission of the Holly Society of America, of which she was a founding member. She died at Whitesbog in 1954 after a life well marked by achievement and recognition.

Whitesbog continues to produce cranberries, but it also serves as a preserve for lakes, forests, and natural bogs rich with plants and wildlife. In particular, several hundred tundra swans visit the wetlands every winter, usually in January and February, before they return in March to their far-off nesting grounds in northern Canada. When visiting the bogs, the swans seldom feed directly on cranberries and instead seek the stolons and rhizomes of redroot. In doing so, however, the birds uproot the cranberry plants and pockmark the bottom in ways that interfere with the operation of farming machinery. Attempts to disperse the swans with noise-making cannons generally fail as the birds soon become habituated to the blasts. The growers also crisscross their bogs with cord to dissuade the birds from landing on the water. Still, swans provide an added attraction for tourists. The Whitesbog Preservation Trust operates the site, which offers visitors a view into the early history of cranberry and blueberry cultivation in New Jersey—and a chance to see where Miss Lizzie lived and worked.

Bog Iron: Kettles and Cannons

A fledgling industry of iron production began in the Pine Barrens in time to supply arms for the Revolutionary War, reaching its zenith after the War of 1812, before declining about three decades thereafter. Iron ore occurred widely in the Pine Barrens wherever the water table lies at or near the surface, notably in the numerous bogs scattered throughout the region but also in the beds of sluggish streams. This form of iron ore, known as limonite or bog ore, forms when iron dissolves in the acidic water, aided by so-called iron bacteria, and precipitates as iron oxide into irregularly shaped lumps mixed with sand and gravel.

Besides providing the ore, the Pine Barrens also offered vast supplies of wood for making the charcoal that fueled blast furnaces and forges as well as power derived from water impounded on the region's streams. Waterwheels powered large bellows that raised the temperatures in the furnaces to 2,000 degrees Fahrenheit.

Shore Note 7.5 Mexico's Fallen Eagle: Emilio Carranza (1905–1928)

Deep in the New Jersey pinelands stands a lonely monument marking the violent end of a dashing young pilot, Emilio Carranza, the Lindbergh of Mexico (fig. 7.13). In 1928, after a short but distinguished career in the air, Carranza had flown from Mexico City to New York by way of Washington, D.C., in the *Mexico Excelsior*, a close copy of Lucky Lindy's much heralded *Spirit of St. Louis*. Carranza was on a goodwill mission to the United States as a follow-up to Lindbergh's similar flight to Mexico the year before. Months earlier, Carranza, a captain in the Mexican Army, had picked up the *Excelsior* in San Diego, California, and flown the new plane to Mexico City on what was then the third longest nonstop flight (1,875 miles) in the record books as well as the longest such flight for a Mexican pilot. His countrymen proudly hailed the dashing young pilot as "el aguila solitaria"—the lone eagle.

His inbound trip to the United States included an unplanned stop in North Carolina, but this interruption hardly dampened the enthusiasm of his arrival in Washington, where he was greeted at the airport by the secretary of state, the Mexican ambassador, and a throng of admirers; the next day he had lunch with President Calvin Coolidge. In New York, he received the key to the city from Mayor Jimmy Walker and reviewed the ranks at West Point, an honor seldom awarded to someone with the rank of captain. A banquet in his honor featured headliners such as the comedic movie star Charlie Chaplin and former heavyweight boxer Jack Dempsey, as well as the mayor and president.

Carranza's return flight was to be nonstop and yet another triumph for Carranza. Thunderstorms—it was July and hot—postponed his departure for three days, a delay encouraged with the seasoned advice of Lindbergh. Here the story gets muddled, for legend has it that Carranza received a telegram from Joaquín Amaro, Mexico's war minister, admonishing the pilot to "return immediately or your manhood will be in doubt." Whether this tale is true or not—no telegram was ever discovered—the popular aviator took off into stormy weather on the night of July 12, 1928, on what was to be his last flight and cover barely 50 miles of the long route to his homeland. He was five months shy of his 23rd birthday.

The wreckage, with Carranza's body close by, was found the following day by blueberry pickers. According to investigators, the plane's controls indicated that he was trying to land, a circumstance supported in death by a flashlight tightly clutched in his hand—a makeshift landing light whose beam danced in vain across the unbroken carpet of treetops. President Coolidge offered to

FIGURE 7.13. A monument deep within the Pine Barrens silently marks the remote location where Mexico's famed pilot Emilio Carranza crashed in 1928. Note the upside-down image that symbolizes the fall of Mexico's "Lone Eagle." Photo credit: Kevin Knutsen.

return Carranza's remains to Mexico aboard the U.S.S. *Florida*, but the Mexican government instead opted for the ceremonial significance of a funeral train.

Today, the pines still whisper where the storm-tossed plane came to ground in a remote New Jersey forest. A 12-foot-high obelisk-like memorial made of stones from Mexico, one from each of the country's 31 states, marks the location. The coins of Mexican schoolchildren paid for the monument, on which one face bears the symbolic carving of a falling Aztec eagle. On the anniversary of the crash, the American Legion Post in Mount Holly conducts an on-site memorial ceremony—but for the rest of the year, the pines whisper alone.

Clam and oyster shells available from middens along the adjacent coast provided a flux for the smelting process (see shore note 4.3). To extract the iron, the erect furnaces were charged with ore, charcoal, and shells, then heated until the molten iron drained downward through the charcoal, which added carbon to the metal, and collected in a crucible at the base of the tower. From the crucible the molten iron ran through channels ending in oblong troughs called pigs, in which the metal solidified into ingots known as pig iron. In other cases, it flowed into molds formed in the sand to produce kettles, firebacks, cannonballs, and other products of the time.

The industry developed widely in the Pine Barrens but more commonly between the Mullica and Manasquan rivers where both wood and ore were particularly plentiful. The clock was ticking, however, and the death knell for bog iron sounded when a more efficient fuel, bituminous coal, and a higher grade of ore lured the industry to western Pennsylvania. Today, the bog iron industry in the Pine Barrens remains encapsulated at Batsto Historical Site within the boundaries of the Wharton State Forest.

Readings and References

General

Boyd, H. P. 1991. A field guide to the Pine Barrens of New Jersey. Plexus Publishing, Medford, NJ.

————. 1997. A Pine Barrens odyssey: a naturalist's year in the Pine Barrens of New Jersey. Plexus Publishing, Medford, NJ.

————. 2008. The ecological Pine Barrens of New Jersey: an ecosystem threatened by fragmentation. Plexus Publishing, Medford, NJ.

Burger, J. 2006. Whispers in the pines, a naturalist in the northeast. Rivergate Books, New Brunswick, NJ. [Covers the New Jersey Pine Barrens as well as similar habitat in New York, South Carolina, and Florida.]

Forman, R. T. T. (ed.). 1979. Pine barrens: ecosystem and landscape. Academic Press, New York. [The go-to source for detailed information.]

Good, R. E., and N. F. Good. 1984. The Pinelands National Preserve—an ecosystem approach to management. BioScience 34:169–173.

Harshberger, J. W. 1916. The vegetation of the New Jersey Pine-Barrens. Unabridged reprint 1970. Dover, New York.

McCormick, J. 1979. The vegetation of the New Jersey Pine Barrens. Pp. 229–243 in Pine Barrens: ecosystem and landscape (R. T. T. Forman, ed.). Academic Press, New York. [See for details concerning forest and bog plants.]

McPhee, J. 1967. The Pine Barrens. Random House, New York. [An engaging blend of local culture and natural history.]

Pine Barrens Forests, Tall and Short

Anonymous. 2019. DEP restoring habitat for pinelands plant found only in northeastern US and maritime Canada. New release, July 31, 2019, Department of Environmental Protection, Trenton, NJ. [Describes efforts to restore broom crowberry.]

Boyd, H. P. 2001. Wildflowers of the Pine Barrens of New Jersey. Plexus Publishing, Medford, NJ.

Burger, J., and M. Gochfeld. 2000. Dwarf pine plains. Pp. 215–221 in Twenty-five nature spectacles in New Jersey. Rutgers University Press, New Brunswick, NJ.

Forman, R. T. T., and R. E. Boerner. 1981. Fire frequency and the Pine Barrens of New Jersey. Bulletin of the Torrey Botanical Club 108:34–50.

Gibson, D. J., R. A. Zampella, and A. G. Windisch. 1999. New Jersey Pine Plains, the "true barrens" of the New Jersey Pine Barrens. Pp. 52–66 in Savannas, barrens, and rock outcrop plant communities of North America (R. C. Anderson, J. S. Fralish, and J. M. Baskin, eds.). Cambridge University Press, New York.

Givnish, T. J. 1981. Serotiny, geography, and fire in the Pine Barrens of New Jersey. Evolution 35:101–123.

Good, R. E., N. F. Good, and J. W. Andersen. 1979. The Pine Barren Plains. Pp. 283–295 in Pine Barrens: ecosystem and landscape (R. T. T. Forman, ed.). Academic Press, New York.

Hilley, E., and R. Thiet. 2015. Vulnerable broom crowberry (*Corema conradii*) benefits from ant seed dispersal in coastal US heathlands. Plant Ecology 216:1091–1101.

Ledig, F. T., J. C. Hom, and P. E. Smouse. 2013. The evolution of the New Jersey pine plains. American Journal of Botany 100:778-791. [Concludes the pygmy pines are fire-adapted ecotypes.]

Ledig, F. T., and S. Little. 1979. Pitch pine (*Pinus rigida* Mill.): ecology, physiology, and genetics. Pp. 347–371 in Pine Barrens: ecosystem and landscape (R. T. T. Forman, ed.). Academic Press, New York.

Peters, D. 1993. Knieskern's beaked-rush (*Rhynchospora knieskernii*) recovery plan. Northeast Regional Office, U.S. Fish and Wildlife Service, Hadley, MA. [See for detailed life-history information.]

Schweitzer, D. F., and T. L. McCabe. 2004. The taxonomy, larva, and ecology of *Agrotis buchholzi* (Noctuidae) with a new sibling species from North Carolina. Journal of the Lepidopterists' Society 58:65–74.

Ghosts of the Pygmy Forest

Bolen, E. G., and W. L. Robinson. 2003. Wildlife ecology and management. 5th ed. Prentice Hall, Upper Saddle River, NJ. [See pp. 12 and 490 concerning heath hens and their extinction.]

Connor, J. 2010. Mementos of a grouse long gone. Living Bird 29(2):36–37.

Stone, W. 1937. Bird studies at Old Cape May, an ornithology of coastal New Jersey. Vol. 1. Unabridged reprint 1965. Dover, New York. [See Heath Hen, pp. 320–322.]

Jersey Cedar

Craig, L. J., and D. S. Dobkin. 1993. Community dynamics of small mammals in mature and logged Atlantic white cedar swamps of the New Jersey Pine Barrens. New York State Museum Bulletin 487, University of the State of New York, State Education Department, Albany, NY.

Cryan, J. 1985. Hessel's hairstreak: endangered cedar swamp butterfly. Heath Hen 2:22–25.

Godt, M. W., J. L. Hamrick, and S. Bratton. 1995. Genetic diversity in a threatened species, *Helonias bullata*. Conservation Biology 9:596–604.

Johnson, K., and P. M. Borgo. 1976. Patterned perching behavior in two *Callophrys (Mitoura)* (Lycaenidae). Journal of the Lepidopterists' Society 30:169–183.

Kantor, R. A., and G. H. Pierson. 1985. Atlantic white-cedar, a valuable and historic resource. New Jersey Outdoors 12(4):26–27.

Laderman, A. D. 1989. The ecology of the Atlantic white cedar wetlands: a community profile. U.S. Fish and Wildlife Service Biological Report 85, Washington, DC.

Laidig, J. K., R. A. Zampella, and C. Popolizio. 2009. Hydrologic regimes associated with *Helonias bullata* L. (swamp pink) and the potential impact of simulated water-level reductions. Journal of the Torrey Botanical Society 136:221–232.

Little, S., and H. Somes. 1965. Atlantic white cedar being eliminated by excessive animal damage in South Jersey. U.S. Forest Service Research Note NE-33:1–4.

Martinez, M., and M. Ardon. 2021. Drivers of greenhouse gas emissions from dead trees in ghost forests. Biogeochemistry 154:471–488. [See for the relevance of "tree farts."]

Mylecraine, K. A., and G. L. Zimmermann. 2000. Atlantic white-cedar: ecology and best managements practices manual. Division of Parks and Forestry, New Jersey Forest Service, Trenton, NJ. [See for summaries of the species' abundance, distribution, ecological values, community associates, and lumbering history.]

Natural Resources Conservation Service. ND. New Jersey fact sheet: Atlantic white cedar.

Roman, C. T., R. E. Good, and S. Little. 1990. Ecology of Atlantic white cedar in the New Jersey Pinelands. Pp. 163–173 in Wetland ecology and management: case studies (D. F. Whigham, R. E. Good, and J. Kvet, eds.). Springer, Dordrecht, Netherlands.

Weiss, H. B., and G. M. Weiss. 1965. Some early industries of New Jersey (cedar mining, tar, pitch, turpentine, salt hay). New Jersey Agricultural Society, Trenton.

Zampella, R. A. 1987. Atlantic white cedar management in the New Jersey Pinelands. Pp. 295–306 in Atlantic white cedar wetlands (A. D. Laderman, ed.). Westview, Boulder, CO. [See p. 302 regarding deer.]

Hardwood Bogs and Red Maple

Abrams, M. D. 1998. What explains the widespread expansion of red maple in eastern forests? BioScience 48:355–364.

Larsen, J. A. 1959. A study of an invasion by red maple of an oak woods in southern Wisconsin. American Midland Naturalist 49:908–914.

Stoler, A., J. Vogel, and M. Olson. 2021. Developing a sustainable maple syrup industry in New Jersey through community collaboration, education, and research. Project proposal, Acer Access and Development Program, USDA Agricultural Marketing Service, Washington, D.C.

Bog Life: Carnivorous Plants

Adlassnig, W., M. Peroutka, and T. Lendl. 2011. Traps of carnivorous pitcher plants as a habitat: composition of the fluid, biodiversity, and mutualistic activities. Annals of Botany 107:181–194.

Brewer, J. S. 2002. Why don't carnivorous pitcher plants compete with non-carnivorous plants for nutrients? Ecology 84:451–462.

Caruso, L. A., and T. Kohn. 1997. Mary Lua Adelia Davis Treat, 1830–1923. Pp. 199–201 in Past and promise: lives of New Jersey women (J. N. Burstyn, ed.). Syracuse University Press, Syracuse, NY.

Cresswell, J. E. 1991. Capture rates and composition of insect prey in the pitcher plant *Sarrancenia purpurea*. American Midland Naturalist 125:1–9. [Also notes spider webs intercepting insects in pitcher plants.]

Darwin, C. 1875. Insectivorous plants. John Murry, London.

Giberson, D., and M. L. Hardwick. 1999. Pitcher plants (*Sarrancenia purpurea*) in eastern Canada, ecology and conservation of invertebrate inquilines. Pp. 401–422 in Invertebrates in freshwater wetlands of North America: ecology and management (D. P. Batzer, R. B. Rader, and S. A. Wissinger, eds.). John Wiley, New York. (Includes resource partitioning of three dipteran detritivores.)

Treat, M. D. 1875. Plants that eat animals. American Naturalist 9:658–662. [Describes how bladderworts capture their prey.]

Weiss, H. B. 1955. Mrs. Mary Treat, 1830–1923, early New Jersey naturalist. Proceedings of the New Jersey Historical Society 73:258–273.

Dark Waters

Eisner, T., and D. J. Aneshansley. 2000. Chemical defense: aquatic beetle (*Dineutes horni*) vs. fish (*Micropterus salmoides*). Proceedings of the National Academy of Sciences 97:11313–11318.

Graham, J. H., and R. W. Hastings. 1984. Distributional patterns of sunfishes on the New Jersey coastal plain. Environmental Biology of Fishes 10:137–148.

Hastings, R. W. 1979. Fish of the Pine Barrens. Pp. 489–504 in Pine barrens: ecosystem and landscape. Academic Press, New York.

———. 1984. The fishes of the Mullica River, a naturally acid water system of the New Jersey Pine Barrens. Bulletin of the New Jersey Academy of Sciences 29:9–23.

Heinrich, B., and F. D. Vogt. 1980. Aggregation and foraging behavior of whirligig beetles (Gyrinidae). Behavioral Evolution and Sociobiology 7:179–186.

Laidig, K. J., R. A. Zampella, J. F. Bunnell, C. L. Dow, and T. A. Sulikowski. 2001. Characteristics of selected Pine Barrens treefrog ponds in the New Jersey Pinelands. Pinelands Commission, New Lisbon, NJ.

Romey, W. L., and A. C. Wallace. 2007. Sex and the selfish herd: sexual segregation within nonmating whirligig groups. Behavioral Ecology 18:910–915.

Vulinec, K., and M. C. Miller. 1989. Aggregation and predation avoidance in whirligig beetles (Coleoptera: Gyrinidae). Journal of the New York Entomological Society 97:438–447.

Herps in the Pines

Burger, J., and R. T. Zappalorti. 1986. Nest site selection by pine snakes, *Pituophis melanoleucus*, in the New Jersey Pine Barrens. Copeia 1986:116–121.

———. 1991. Nesting behavior of pine snakes (*Pituophis m. melanoleucus*) in the New Jersey Pine Barrens. Journal of Herpetology 25:152–160.

———. 2011. The northern pine snake (*Pituophis m. melanoleucus*) in New Jersey: its life history, behavior, and conservation. Pp. 1–56 in Reptiles: biology, behavior, and conservation (K. J. Baker, ed.). Nova Science, Hauppauge, NY.

———. 2015. Hibernation site philopatry in northern pine snakes (*Pituophis melanoleucus*) in New Jersey. Journal of Herpetology 49:245–251.

Burger, J., R. T. Zappalorti, J. Dowdell, et al. 1992. Subterranean predation on pine snakes (*Pituophis melanoleucus*). Journal of Herpetology 26:259–263.

Hulmes, D., P. Hulmes, and R. Zappalorti. 1981. Notes on the ecology and distribution of the Pine Barrens treefrog, *Hyla andersonii*, in New Jersey. Bulletin of the New York Herpetological Society 17:2–19.

Pehek, E. L. 1995. Competition, pH, and the ecology of larval *Hyla andersonii*. Ecology 76:1786–1793. [Experiments designed to determine why Pine Barrens treefrogs occur only in highly acidic wetlands.]

Reinert, H. K., G. A. MacGregor, M. Esch, et al. 2011. Foraging ecology of timber rattlesnakes, *Crotalus horridus*. Copeia 2011:430–442.

Reinert, H. K., and R. T. Zappalorti. 1988. Timber rattlesnakes (*Crotalus horridus*) of the Pine Barrens: their movement patterns and habitat preference. Copeia 1988:964–978.

Zappalorti, R. T. 2016. Some rare reptiles and amphibians of the New Jersey Pine Barrens. Herpetological Associates' e-Book Series, vol. 1. Zappalorti Institute for Pinelands Research, Pemberton, NJ. [A guidepost in the development of this section.]

Zappalorti, R. T., J. Burger, W. D. Burkett, et al. 2014. Fidelity of northern pine snakes (*Pituophis m. melanoleucus*) to natural and artificial hibernation sites in the New Jersey Pine Barrens. Journal of Toxicology and Environmental Health, Part A 17:1285–1291.

Zappalorti, R. T., and H. K. Reinert. 1994. Artificial refugia as a habitat improvement strategy for snake conservation. Pp. 369–375 in Captive management and conservation of amphibians and reptiles (J. B. Murphy, K. Adler, and J. T. Collins, eds.). Contributions to Herpetology vol. 2. Society for the Study of Amphibians and Reptiles, Ithaca, NY.

The Blueberry Queen of Whitesbog

Buchan, P. 2016. The blueberry queen. New Jersey Monthly 41(6):42–45.

Burger, J., and M. Gochfeld. 2000. Swans at Whites Bog and coastal lakes. Pp. 249–257 in Twenty-five nature spectacles in New Jersey. Rutgers University Press, New Brunswick, NJ.

Castelli, P. M., and J. E. Applegate. 1989. Economic loss caused by tundra swans feeding in cranberry bogs. Transactions of the Northeast Section of The Wildlife Society 46:17–23.

Himber, C. P. 1998. Whitesbog's winter visitors. New Jersey Outdoors 25:18–21.

Prickett, R. 2009. Elizabeth White's refuge for the cultivation of the American holly tree. Whitesbog Preservation Trust Newsletter, Fourth Quarter:1–3.

Sheer, L., and J. Kazickas. 1997. Elizabeth Coleman White (1871–1954). Pp. 209–211 in Past and promise: lives of New Jersey women (J. N. Burstyn, ed.). Syracuse University Press, Syracuse, NY.

White, E. C. 1943. Plants of the New Jersey Pine Barrens. Bulletin of the American Rock Garden Society 1(3):53–56.

Bog Iron: Kettles and Cannons

Boucher, J. E. 1964. Of Batsto and bog iron. Batsto Citizens Committee, Egg Harbor City, NY.

Pierce, A. D. 1957. Iron in the pines. Rutgers University Press, New Brunswick, NJ. [An account of the Pine Barrens when iron was king.]

Solem, B. 2014. Batsto village—jewel of the pines. Plexus Publishing, Medford, NJ. [Chronicles the rise and fall of a prominent ironworks now restored as a historical site.]

Wacker, P. O. 1979. Human exploitation of the New Jersey Pine Barrens before 1900. Pp. 3–23 in Pine Barrens: ecosystem and landscape (R. T. T. Forman, ed.). Academic Press, New York.

Shore Note 7.1. A Primer on Fire Ecology

Cooper, C. F. 1961. The ecology of fire. Scientific American 204:150–160.

Higgins, K. F. 1984. Lightning fires in North Dakota grasslands and in pine-savannah lands of South Dakota and Montana. Journal of Range Management 37:100–103.

Singer, F. J., W. Schreier, J. Oppenheim, and E. O. Garton. 1989. Drought, fires, and large mammals, estimating the 1988 severe drought and large-scale fires. BioScience 39:716–722. [See regarding animals killed by the fires.]

Wright, H. A., and A. W. Bailey. 1982. Fire ecology: United States and southern Canada. John Wiley, New York.

Shore Note 7.2. The Comet That Streaked across the Pine Barrens

Davidson, W. A. B. 2016. Blue Comet: wonder train of 1929. Classic Trains Special Edition No. 29: great trains east: 64–69.

Grams, J. 1996. Lionel's Classic Standard Gauge Blue Comet. Classic Toy Trains 9(1):82–85.

Maltagliati, L. 2018. A blue visitor from far away. Nature Astronomy 2:852. https://doi
.org/10.1038/s41550-018-0637-3. [Notes the discovery and unusual nature of a genuine blue comet.]

Puzzilla, A. 2017. New Jersey Central's Blue Comet. Arcadia, Mount Pleasant, SC.

Shore Note 7.3. Cranberry Bogs: Producing
a Thanksgiving Tradition

Boyd, H. P. A field guide to the Pine Barrens of New Jersey. Plexus Publishing, Medford, NJ. [See pp. 33–36.]

DeMoranville, C., and H. A. Sandler. 2008. Cultural practices in cranberry production:
sanding and pruning. Pp. 16–21 in Cranberry production guide (H. A. Sandler and
C. J. DeMorganville, eds.). University of Massachusetts Extension Service Publication CP-8, Amherst, MA. [See pp. 16–21 for details about sanding.]

Wright, D. M. 1983. Life history and morphology of the immature stages of the bog
copper butterfly *Lycaena epixanthe* (Bsd. & Le C.) (Lepidoptera: Lycaenidae).
Journal of Research on the Lepidoptera 22:47–100.

Shore Note 7.4. The Dread Monster of Jersey's Big Forest

Beck, H. C. 1983. Jersey genesis, the story of the Mullica River. Rutgers University Press,
New Brunswick, NJ. [See pp. 240–250, which quotes the work of J. Elfreth Watkins.]

Cohen, D. S. 1983. The folklore and folklife of New Jersey. Rutgers University Press,
New Brunswick, NJ.

Girard, G. 2004. Tales of the Jersey Devil. Middle Atlantic Press, Moorestown, NJ.

McCloy, J. F., and R. Miller Jr. 1976. The Jersey Devil. Middle Atlantic Press, Walling-
ford, PA.

———. 1998. Phantom of the Pines: more tales of the Jersey Devil. Middle Atlantic
Press, Moorestown, NJ.

Regal, B., and F. J. Esposito. 2018. The secret history of the Jersey Devil: how Quakers,
hucksters, and Benjamin Franklin created a monster. Johns Hopkins University
Press, Baltimore.

Shore Note 7.5. Mexico's Fallen Eagle: Emilio Carranza
(1905–1928)

Barra, A. 2015. Mexico's Lindbergh. American History 50:58–63.

Pujols, R. M., and L. R. Nixon. 2011. The Mexican Lindbergh, Captain Emilio Carranza Rodriguez. Author House, Bloomington, IN.

Afterword

Never doubt that a small group of thoughtful, committed citizens can change the world; indeed, it's the only thing that has.
—WIDELY ATTRIBUTED TO MARGARET MEAD

NEW JERSEY regrettably represents a caldron simmering with a stew of environmental concerns—and the stew includes some 23 *billion* gallons of raw sewage dumped each year into the state's rivers. New Jersey harbors the most densely packed population in the nation, which demands ever more housing, malls, schools, and other urban developments as well as a supporting infrastructure of utilities and transportation. These not only consume green spaces but also increase the runoff of surface waters as the landscape steadily "hardens" under a blanket of pavement and concrete. Thus, rather ironically, urbanization reaches its zenith in what is otherwise officially known as the Garden State. Moreover, New Jersey's geopolitical location favors intense industrial development, which all too often has produced indiscriminate dumping of toxic wastes. To illustrate, in 2021 the U.S. Environmental Protection Agency recognized 114 superfund sites in New Jersey that places the state, despite its small size, at the top of the national list. By definition, the levels of contamination from hazardous materials and pollutants at these sites threaten public health (and, no doubt, wild things as well).

Finally, New Jersey's coastline provides a setting where the pace of rising sea levels poses an immediate concern not only for a spectrum of recreational and commercial interests but also for the maintenance of biological entities ranging from species to ecosystems. In sum, development, along with its attendant pollution, and a changing climate gnaw away at the Jersey Shore, touching virtually all of the natural settings described in the foregoing chapters. That said, readers by now may wonder about their role in the bond between natural history and conservation. The short answer: get involved!

Act Locally

As mentioned in chapter 1, children today spend far too little time outdoors, notably at locations where they might experience nature firsthand. Three responses come to mind. First, act to ensure the availability of parks and other green areas in local neighborhoods. Second, regularly explore these sites with children, making special efforts to stimulate naturally curious young minds about the workings of nature. These hardly need to be exotic to be effective. An anthill and its social structure, the ways vegetation varies according to differing soil and water conditions, or simply watching and comparing the foraging activities of birds provide dynamic and readily available examples. Turn over rocks, both figuratively and literally. Longer field trips, of course, to forests, fields, and wetlands spice these neighborhood experiences. Third, encourage schools to include and strengthen their science curricula with environmental subjects that cover not only basic ecological relationships (e.g., What is a food chain?) but also why a healthy environment and biodiversity remain important to all forms of life. And whenever possible, include demonstrations and hands-on experiences with these lessons. In all these things, join with children to see and explore nature's marvels. The wonderments of the natural world around us are nowhere better seen than through the eyes of children, and it becomes the responsibility of parents and teachers to instill in children an appreciation of nature, science, and environmental quality.

Citizens can serve as watchdogs for municipal pollution and other forms of environmental degradation often associated with development (e.g., urban runoff, ill-advised tree removal and erosion). To further that calling, local governments would do well to establish and support standing committees specifically charged to deal with environmental affairs, so press for their formation and participate. Similarly, membership in local chapters of state and national conservation organizations offers citizens opportunities for public service and a platform for responding to environmental threats.

Act with Sweat Equity

Citizen scientists and other types of volunteerism offer a rich variety of outdoor opportunities. Many of these concern monitoring wildlife populations or searching for rare plants, among them helping state and federal biologists catch and band migrating shorebirds as part of long-term studies of their travels and fates (fig. A.1). Others tally the location and status of coastal plants in need of protection (fig. A.2). The annual Christmas Bird Count conducted by the Audubon Society and the federally run Breeding Bird Survey rely on seasoned birders. Likewise, a cadre of volunteers aid with the hawk census and butterfly counts each fall at Cape May. Such data become the grist milled by scientists to determine long-term population trends, which may herald a warning signal for species in trouble or highlight others whose numbers indicate good or improving health. As emphasized

FIGURE A.1. Citizen scientists assist professional biologists studying shorebirds on the New Jersey side of Delaware Bay. As shown here, rockets propel a net over a large flock of red knots, ruddy turnstones, and sandpipers. Each bird is weighed, measured, and banded, then released (inset). Photo credits: Kevin Knutsen.

FIGURE A.2. Students at Raritan Valley Community College assist the NJDEP Office of Natural Lands Management with annual surveys of seabeach amaranth, a species that had vanished from the Jersey Shore for decades but suddenly reappeared in 2000. The surveys record the GPS location of each plant and its reproductive status (e.g., flowering or fruiting), condition, and threats, if any, to its future welfare. The species falls under the protection of both state and federal governments. Photo credit: Jay Kelly, Raritan Valley Community College.

by environmental journalist Mary Ellen Hannibal, "Citizen science is taking off as never before, and it is needed as never before." Indeed, it may offer the foundation for the future of large-scale field research and the best hope to protect vanishing species.

Other activities include planting milkweed for monarch butterflies, especially in agricultural landscapes where small patches of the plants harbor almost four times as many monarch eggs than occur on milkweed growing elsewhere. This suggests that cooperative projects between rural landowners and conservationists, acting alone or in groups such as garden clubs, may significantly improve the avail-

FIGURE A.3. Youngsters are among the volunteers who erect barriers designed to lessen roadkills of female diamondback terrapins crossing roadways in search of nesting areas. Halves of 10-inch drainage tubing partially buried along the edges of roads near salt marshes block the terrapins but rarely impede the movements of other wildlife. Shown here are volunteers with the Margate Terrapin Rescue Project; the Conserve Wildlife Foundation of New Jersey and The Wetlands Institute likewise install terrapin barriers along roadways. Photo credit: Kimberly Lull Wiech.

ability of prime breeding habitat for a declining species of butterfly. Likewise, citizens organize the installation of roadside fencing to prevent diamondback terrapins from crossing thoroughfares when searching for nesting areas (fig. A.3). Similar activities include planting beachgrass to restore damaged dunes, removing invasive vegetation, establishing living shorelines with bags of mollusk shells, uprighting overturned horseshoe crabs, maintaining nature trails, and the cleanup ("sweeps) of trash-ridden beaches and marshes—all of which offer rewarding opportunities for improving conditions along the Jersey Shore. A few minutes of online searching will reveal when and where to participate in these and similar projects.

Act in the Halls of Government

Action in this case concerns our willingness to bring key environmental issues to the attention of elected members of our state and federal legislative bodies. Although any list of concerns would indeed be lengthy, it undoubtedly would include such matters as attempts to weaken endangered species regulations and compromises to the ecological integrity of refuges and other sites held in public ownership (e.g., Barnegat Bay). Still, global climate change perhaps offers the best example of an issue highly charged by politics, hence it deserves further comment.

Sea levels along the Jersey Shore, as elsewhere, have fluctuated widely throughout the Pleistocene Epoch in response to a pattern of glacial and interglacial periods in which ice sheets alternately formed and melted. About 12,000 years ago an interglacial period still in effect again led to a rising sea level, which for the last 5,000 years has increased at a rate of about 0.7 mm per year, or 2.75 inches per century. By 1900, however, human influences began adding about 2.5 mm per year to the natural rate of increase, resulting in an overall rise of almost 13 inches per century—and the pace seems sure to accelerate in keeping with the rapid rate at which the polar ice sheets now succumb to melting. Indeed, the projected total rise in Delaware Bay may reach 1.3 to 4.6 feet by 2100.

An event of such magnitude has far-reaching implications, including those affecting the natural history of the Jersey Shore. Not the least of these is the ongoing retreat of the shoreline along Delaware Bay, which moved inland by 300 to 500 feet between 1930 and 2007 (and in places by as much as 800 feet). The edge of the retreating shoreline forms a bluff two to three feet high at low tide; this mini-seawall consists of soil mixed with the dense mat-like sod of marsh plants. Because wave action steadily erodes the bluff, chunks of sod break off and the edge creeps farther inland, followed by the incursion of marshland. The advancing marsh then inundates freshwater ponds and swales in the uplands and converts much of the vegetation to monotypic stands of *Phragmites*—all to the detriment of plant and animal diversity. Moreover, sand displaced from eroded beaches moves to other sites, among them the mouths of tidal creeks and offshore bars. Rising sea levels thus degrade an ecologically important shoreline where horseshoe crabs and migrant shorebirds maintain an ancient relationship (see chapter 6). In sum, concerns about rising sea levels surely warrant contact with, and responses from, our state and federal legislators.

A Final Word

Be assured that one person *can* make a difference. As prominent examples, think of environmental activists such as John Muir and his successful campaign to save the Sierra Nevada's majestic redwoods, Rachel Carson's fearless exposé of pesticide contamination, and the driving force of Marjory Stoneman Douglas that ultimately produced Everglades National Park. Legions of other naturalists might not gain similar fame, but their grassroots efforts on countless fronts—perhaps by speaking to civic groups about conservation issues or by building nest boxes for barn owls—nonetheless contribute to a better environment. So, get involved—there's much to do.

Readings and References

Anonymous. 2019. Raw sewage in New Jersey waters. NY/NJ Baykeeper, Keyport, NJ.

Hannibal, M. E. 2016. Citizen scientist: searching for heroes and hope in an age of extinction. The Experiment, New York.

Krupa, J. J. 2000. The importance of naturalists as teachers and the use of natural history as a teaching tool. American Biology Teacher 62:553–558.

Loveland, R. E., and M. L. Botton. 2015. Sea level rise in Delaware Bay, U.S.A.: adaptations of spawning horseshoe crabs (*Limulus polyphemus*) to the glacial past, and the rapidly changing shoreline of the bay. Pp. 41–63 in Changing global perspectives on horseshoe crab biology, conservation and management (R. H. Carmichael, M. L. Botton, P. K. S. Shin, and S. G. Cheung, eds.). Springer, New York.

Miller, K. G., P. J. Sugarman, J. V. Browning, et al. 2009. Sea-level rise in New Jersey over the past 500 years: implications to anthropogenic changes. Global and Planetary Change 66:10–18.

Pitman, G. M., D. T. T. Flockhart, and D. R. Norris. 2018. Patterns and causes of oviposition in monarch butterflies: implications for milkweed restoration. Biological Conservation 217:54–65.

Salant, J. D. 2021. NJ has the most superfund sites. Tax industry to clean them up, says top Dem. NJ Advance Media newsletter (politics), April 20, 2021. Iselin, NJ.

Stanford, S. D. 2012. Recent and future sea-level rise along Delaware Bay. Unearthing New Jersey 8(2):1–4.

Appendix
Nomenclature

This list presents the scientific, or Latin, names for organisms mentioned in the text. In some cases new research, often based on molecular genetics, has produced changes in long-established names. Hence, some of the names in the list may not seem familiar or agree with those appearing in literature citations. To help clarify these situations, the vacated name appears in brackets immediately following the name currently accepted. For example, the Cape May warbler, once in the genus *Dendroica*, appears here as *Setophaga* [*Dendroica*] *tigrina*. Brief annotations accompany entries where further information may be helpful. An asterisk designates an extinct species.

Plants, Including Algae and Fungi

Adam's needle, *Yucca filamentosa*
Alga pondweed, *Potamogeton confervoides*
American beachgrass, *Ammophila breviligulata*
American chestnut, *Castanea dentata*
American cranberry, *Vaccinium macrocarpon* [the genetic stock for today's commercial product]
American holly, *Ilex opaca*
American sea rocket, *Cakile edentula*
Arrowwood viburnum, *Viburnum dentatum*
Asiatic sand sedge, *Carex kobomugi*

Atlantic ladies' tresses, *Spiranthes bightensis* [a newly described species that reclassifies those plants previously recognized as *S. odorata* in coastal New Jersey and other mid-Atlantic states; the latter designation still applies to those farther south (e.g., North Carolina)]

Atlantic white cedar, *Chamaecyparis thyoides*

Bayberry, *Morella* [*Myrica*] *pensylvanica*

Beach heather, *Hudsonia tomentosa* [not a true heather]

Beach pea, *Lathyrus japonicus*

Beach plum, *Prunus maritima*

Bearberry, *Arctostaphylos uva-ursi*

Black cherry, *Prunus serotina*

Blackgrass, *Juncus gerardii* [known also as saltmarsh rush]

Black gum, *Nyssa sylvatica*

Black huckleberry, *Gaylussacia baccata*

Blackjack oak, *Quercus marilandica*

Black needlerush, *Juncus roemerianus*

Black oak, *Quercus velutina*

Bladderwort, *Utricularia* spp.

Blueberry, *Vaccinium* spp.

Blue stain fungus, *Leptographium* spp.

Bog asphodel, *Narthecium americanum*

Bog copper, *Lycaena epixanthe*

Broom crowberry, *Corema conradii*

Broomsedge, *Andropogon virginicus*

Buchholz dart moth, *Agrotis buchholzi*

Bulrush, *Schoenoplectus* spp. [*Scirpus*]

Butterfly bush, *Buddlela davidii*

Cattail, *Typha latifolia*

Common reed, *Phragmites australis* [popularly known simply as "*Phragmites*"]

Common three-square bulrush, *Schoenoplectus pungens*

Crested yellow orchid, *Plantanthera* [*Habenaria*] *critata*

Curly grass fern, *Schizaea pusilla*

Dune prickly pear, *Opuntia drummondii*

Dusty miller, *Artemisia stelleriana*

Eastern glasswort, *Lilaeopsis chinensis*

Eastern hemlock, *Tsuga canadensis*

Eastern marsh fern, *Thelypteris palustris*

Eastern prickly pear, *Opuntia humifusa*

Eastern red cedar, *Juniperus virginiana*

Eelgrass, *Zostera marina*

Elderberry, *Sambucus canadensis*

Fetterbush, *Lyonia lucida*

Fragrant ladies' tresses, *Spiranthes odorata*

Fragrant waterlily, *Nyphaea odorata*

Franklin's lost tree, *Franklinia alatamaha*

Glasswort, *Salicorniaa ambigua, S. bigelovii, S. depressa*, and possibly *S. maritima* [species designations for the group, also known as pickleweeds, remain an ever-changing taxonomic jungle]

Goldencrest, *Lophiola aurea*

Greenbrier, *Smilax* spp.

Groundsel, *Baccharis halimiflora*

Hackberry, *Celtis occidentalis* [also known sugar hackberry]

Highbush blueberry, *Vaccinium corymbosum*

Holly, *Ilex* spp.

Horned pondweed, *Zannichellia palustris*

Huckleberry, *Gaylussacia* spp.

Jack pine, *Pinus banksiana*

Japanese black pine, *Pinus thunbergii*

Japanese honeysuckle, *Lodicera japonica*

Knieskern's beaked-rush, *Rhynchospora knieskernii*

Lambskill, *Kalmia angustifolia*

Leatherleaf, *Chamaedaphne calyculata*

Live oak, *Quercus virginiana*

Lobolly pine, *Pinus taeda*

Longleaf pine, *Pinus palustris*

Lowbush blueberry, *Vaccinium vacillans*

Marsh elder, *Iva frutescens*

Marsh fern, *Thelypteris palustris*

Marsh fleabane, *Pulchea odorata*

Marsh pink, *Sabatia stellaris*

Milkweed, *Asclepias* spp. [twelve species in New Jersey, including common milkweed, *A. syriaca*]

Mountain laurel, *Kalmia latifolia*

Orache, *Atriplex patula*

Oyamel fir, *Abies religiosa*

Pacific yew, *Taxus brevifolia*

Partridgeberry, *Mitchella repens*

Pennsylvania sedge, *Carex pensylvanica*

Persimmon, *Diospyros virginiana*

Phragmites: see common reed

Pickerelweed, *Pontederia cordata*

Pickering's morning glory, *Stylisma pickeringii*

Pine-Barrens gentian, *Gentiana autumnalis*

Pine-Barrens heather, *Hudsonia ericoides* [not a true heather]

Pink sea thrift, *Armeria maritima*

Pitch pine, *Pinus rigida*

Pixie moss, *Pyxidanthera barbulata* [a vascular plant; not a true moss]

Poison ivy, *Taxicondendron radicans*

Pond pine, *Pinus serotina*

Porcelain berry, *Ampelopsis brevipedunculata*

Post oak, *Quercus stellata*

Purple pitcher plant, *Sarrancenia purpurea*

Redwood, *Sequoia, sempervirons*

Red algae, Rhodophyta, a huge taxon of many species

Red maple, *Acer rubrum*

Red root, *Lachnanthes caroliniana*

Rose mallow, *Hibiscus moscheutos*

Rush, *Juncus* spp.

Sago pondweed, *Stuckenia pectinata* [*Potamogeton pectinatus*]

Salt grass, *Distichlis spicata*

Salt hay, *Sporobolus pumilus* [*Spartina patens*; known also as saltmeadow cordgrass]

Saltmarsh fleabane, *Pluchea odorata*

Saltmarsh mallow, *Kosteletzkya pentacrpos* [*K. virginica*]

Sand myrtle, *Leiophyllum* [*Kalmia*] *buxifolium*

Sargasso seaweed, primarily *Sargassum natans* and *S. fluitans* [brown algae]

Sassafras, *Sassafras albidum*

Scarlet oak, *Quercus coccinea*

Scrub oak, *Quercus ilicifolia*

Seabeach amaranth, *Amaranthus pumilus*

Sea blite, *Suaeda maritima*

Sea lavender, *Limonium carolinianum*

Sea lettuce, *Ulva lactuca*

Sea oats, *Uniola paniculata*

Sea plantain, *Plantago maritima*

Seaside arrowgrass, *Triglochin maritima*

Seaside goldenrod, *Solidago sempervirens*

Seaside sandwort, *Honckenya peploides* var. *robusta*

Seaside spurge, *Euphorbia polygoniflora*

Sedge, *Carex* spp. and *Cyperus* spp.

Shortleaf pine, *Pinus echinata*

Slender sea purslane, *Sesuvium maritimum*

Smooth cordgrass, *Sporobolus alterniflorus* [*Spartina alterniflora*]

Smooth sumac, *Rhus glabra*

Southern red oak, *Quercus falcata*

Spike rush, *Eleocharis* spp.

Sugar maple, *Acer saccharum*

Sundew, *Drosera* spp.

Swamp chestnut oak, *Quercus michauxii*

Swamp magnolia (sweetbay magnolia), *Magnolia virginiana*

Swamp pink, *Helonias bullata*

Sweetbay, *Magnolia virginiana*

Sweet gum, *Liquidambar styracifula*

Sweet pepperbush, *Clethra alnifolia*

Sweet-scented virgin's bower, *Clematis flammula*

Thread-leaved (threadleaf) sundew, *Drosera filiformis*

Three-square bulrush, *Schoenoplectus americanus* [*Scirpus olneyi*]

Trumpet creeper, *Campsis radicans*

Virginia chain fern, *Woodwardia virginica*

Virginia creeper, *Parthenocissus quinquefolia*

Water milfoil, *Myriophyllum* spp. [New Jersey lists slender milfoil, *M. tenellum*, as endangered, whereas Eurasian milfoil, *M. spicatum*, is an invasive species]

Wax myrtle, *Morella* [*Myrica*] *cerifera*

Western red cedar, *Thuga plicata*

Widgeongrass, *Ruppia maritima*

Wild celery, *Vallisneria americana*

Wild cherry, *Prunus* spp.

Wild rice, *Zizania aquatica*

Western (Pacific) yew, *Taxus brevifolia*

Invertebrates

Atlantic sea nettle, *Chrysaora quinquecirra*

Banded bog skimmer dragonfly, *Williamsonia lintneri*

Bay nettle, *Chrysaora chesapeakei*

Bay scallop, *Argopecten irradians*

Bethany Beach firefly, *Photuris bethaniensis* [misnamed, this and other fireflies in fact are beetles]

Black-clawed mud crab, *Panopeus herbstii*

Black saddlebags, *Tramea lacerata*

Black turpentine beetle, *Dendroctonus terebrans*

Blue crab, *Callinectes sapidus*

Blue mussel, *Mytilus edulis*

Buchholz dart moth, *Agrotis buchholzi*

Chain fern borer moth, *Papaiperma stenocelis*

Chalky wave, *Scopula purata*

Clinging jellyfish, *Gonionemus vertens*

Common periwinkle, *Littorina littorea* [introduced species]

Coquina, *Donax variabilis* [some authorities recognize *D. fossor* for coquinas in New Jersey]

Damselfly, order Odonata

Digenean gill trematode, *Ascocotyle phagicola*

Dragonfly, order Odonata

Eastern elliptio, *Elliptio complanata*

Eastern mud snail, *Tritia* [*Ilyanassa*] *obsoleta*

Eastern oyster, *Crassostrea virginica*

Eastern saltmarsh mosquito, *Aedes sollicitans*

Eelgrass limpet, *Lottia alveus**

Fish lice, *Argulus* spp.

Ghost crab, *Ocypode quadrata*

Goldenrod leaf beetle, *Trirhabda canadensis*

Gooseneck barnacle, *Lepas anatifera*

Green darner, *Anax junius*

Greenhead fly, *Tabanus nigrovittatus*

Greenworm, *Scolelepis squamata*

Gypsy moth, *Lymantria dispar*

Hessel's hairstreak butterfly, *Mitoura* [*Callophrys*] *hesseli*

Horse and deer flies, family Tabanidae

Horseshoe crab, *Limulus polyphemus*

House fly, *Musca domestica*

Isopod, a crustacean in the order Isopoda [a huge group, many of which occur in aquatic and marine food chains]

Jumping plant louse, *Livia maculipennis*

Katydid (bush cricket) [the common true katydid, *Pterophylla camellifolia* is representative of this large group of insects]

Locusts, the swarming phase of certain grasshoppers in the family Acrididae

Marsh crab, *Sesarma reticulatum*

Marsh fern moth, *Fagitana littera*

Marsh periwinkle, *Littorina irrorata*

Mayflies, order Ephemeroptera

Midge, *Chironomus* spp.

Monarch butterfly, *Danaus plexippus*
Moon snail, *Euspira [Lunatia] heros*
Mosquitoes, family Culicidae [well-known genera include *Anopheles*, *Culex*, and *Aedes*]
Mud fiddler crab, *Uca pugnax*
Northeastern beach tiger beetle, *Habroscelimorpha [Cicindela] dorsalis dorsalis*
Northern rock barnacle, *Balanus balanoides*
Northern quahog, *Mercenaria mercenaria* [known also as a hard-shelled clam]
Oyster drill, *Urosalpinx cinerea*
Pea crab, *Zaops [Pinnotheres] ostreum*
Pine sawyer beetle, *Monochamus carolinensis*
Pinewood nematode, *Bursaphelenchus xylophilus*
Pipevine swallowtail, *Battus philenor*
Ribbed mussel, *Geukensia demissa*
Root-knot nematode [several species, including those in the genera, *Meloidogyne* and *Hoplolaimus*]
Sand flea, *Emerita talpoida* [known also as a mole crab]
Sea nettle, *Chrysaora quinquecirrha*
Seaside dragonlet, *Erythrodiplax berenice*
Seaside goldenrod borer, *Papaipema duovata* [a moth whose larvae do the boring]
Sea walnut, *Mnemiopsis leidyi*
Shipworm, *Teredo navalis*
Soft-scale insect, *Eriococcus carolinae*
Soft-shelled clam, *Mya arenaria*
Spicebush swallowtail, *Papilio troilus*
Spruce budworm, *Choristoneura fumiferana*
Stable fly, *Stomoxys calcitrans*
Trematodes (flukes), class Trematoda
Twelve-spotted skimmer, *Libellula pulchella*
Viceroy butterfly, *Limenitis archippus*
Water flea, order Cladocera [*Daphnia* represents a common genus]
Whelk, *Busycon* spp. [*B. carica gemelin*, the knobbed whelk, is the New Jersey state shell]
Whirligig beetle, family Gyrinidae
Yucca moth, *Tegeticula yuccasella*

Fishes

American eel, *Anguilla rostrata*
American shad, *Alosa sapidissima*
Atlantic menhaden, *Brevoortia tyrannus* [known also as mossbunker]
Atlantic silverside, *Menidia menidia*

Banded sunfish, *Enneacanthus obesus* [known also as Sphagnum sunfish]

Barracuda, *Sphyraena barracuda*

Bass, *Micropterus* spp.

Blackbanded sunfish, *Enneacanthus chaetodon*

Black drum, *Pogonias cromis*

Blueback herring, *Alosa aestivalis*

Bluefish, *Pomatomus saltatrix*

Bluegill, *Lopomis macrochirus*

Bluespotted sunfish, *Enneacanthus gloriosus*

Brown bullhead, *Ameiurus nebulosus*

Bull shark, *Carcharhinus leucas*

Chain pickerel, *Esox niger*

Creek chubsucker, *Erimyzon oblongus*

European eel, *Anguilla anguilla*

Great white shark, *Carcharodon carcharias*

Ironcolor shiner, *Notropis chalybaeus*

Lake trout, *Salvelinus namaycush*

Mud sunfish, *Acantharchus pomotis*

Mummichog, *Fundulus heteroclitus*

Northern pipefish, *Syngnathus fuscus*

Pacific salmon, *Oncorhynchus* spp.

Pacific sardine, *Sardinops sagax*

Pirate perch, *Aphredoderus sayanus*

Rainbow trout, *Oncorhynchus mykiss* [*Salmo gairdneri*]

Redfin pickerel, *Exox americanus* [known also as grass pickerel]

Seahorse [in Barnegat Bay, the northern lined seahorse, *Hippocampus erectus*].

Sea lamprey, *Petromyzon marinus*

Sheepshead minnow, *Cyprinodon variegatus*

Smallmouth bass, *Micropterus dolomieu*

Striped bass, *Morone saxatilis*

Striped killifish, *Fundulus majalis*

Swamp darter, *Etheostoma fusiforme*

Weakfish, *Cynoscion regalis* [known also as sea trout]

Yellow bullhead, *Ictalurus natalis*

Yellow perch, *Perca flavescens*

Amphibians

Atlantic coast leopard frog, *Lithobates* [*Rana*] *kauffeldi*

Eastern tiger salamander, *Ambystoma tigrinum*

Fowler's toad, *Anaxyrus fowleri*
Pine Barens treefrog, *Hyla andersoni*

Reptiles

Black rat snake, *Elaphe obsoleta*
Corn snake, *Elaphe guttata*
Diamondback terrapin, *Malaclemys terrapin*
Eastern garter snake, *Thamnophis sirtalis*
Eastern mud turtle, *Kinostgernon subrubrum*
Green sea turtle, *Chelonia mydas*
Hognose snake, *Heterodon platirhinos*
Kemp's ridley sea turtle, *Lepidochelys kempii* [known also as Atlantic ridley sea turtle]
Leatherback sea turtle, *Dermochelys coriacea*
Loggerhead sea turtle, *Caretta caretta*
Northern pine snake, *Pituophis melanoleucus*
Timber rattlesnake, *Crotalis horridus* [*horridus* refers to the species' rough scales, not to a "horrible" attitude]

Birds

American kestrel, *Falco sparverius*
American oystercatcher, *Haematopus palliatus*
American robin, *Turdus migratorius*
American wigeon, *Anas americana*
American woodcock, *Scolopax minor*
Atlantic brant, *Branta bernicla hrota*
Attwater's prairie chicken, *Tympanuchus cupido attwateri*
Bald eagle, *Haliaeetus leucocephalus*
Barnacle goose, *Branta leucopsis*
Barn owl, *Tyto alba*
Black duck, *Anas rubipes*
Black rail, *Laterallus jamaicensis*
Black skimmer, *Rhynchops niger*
Bonaparte's gull, *Chroicocephalus* [*Larus*] *philadelphia*
Broad-winged hawk, *Buteo platypterus*
Canada goose, *Branta canadensis*
Canvasback, *Aythya valisineria*
Cape May warbler, *Setophaga* [*Dendroica*] *tigrina*
Cattle egret, *Bubuilcus ibis*

Chickadee, *Poecile* [*Parus*] spp. [in New Jersey, primarily the black-capped chickadee, *P. atricapillus*]

Clapper rail, *Rallus longirostris* [commonly known as marsh hen]

Coastal plain swamp sparrow, *Melospiza georgiana nigrescens*

Common goldeneye, *Bucephala clangula*

Common tern, *Sterna hirundo*

Cooper's hawk, *Accipiter cooperii*

Dunlin, *Calidris alpina*

Eastern kingbird, *Tyrannus tyrannus*

Eastern screech owl, *Megascops* [*Otus*] *asio*

Fish crow, *Corvus ossifragus*

Glossy ibis, *Plegadis falcinellus*

Great black-backed gull, *Larus marinus*

Great blue heron, *Ardea herodias*

Great egret, *Ardea* [*Egretta, Casmerodius*] *alba*

Greater prairie chicken, *Tympanuchus cupido pinnatus*

Gull-billed tern, *Gelochelidon nilotica*

Harlequin duck, *Histrionicus hisgtrionicus*

Heath hen, *Tympanuchus cupido cupido**

Herring gull, *Larus argentatus*

Ipswich sparrow, *Passerculus sandwichensis princeps*

Kirtland's warbler, *Setophaga* [*Dendroica*] *kirtlandii*

Labrador duck, *Camptorhynchus labradorius**

Laughing gull, *Leucophaeus* [*Larus*] *atricilla*

Least tern, *Sternula antillarum*

Long-billed curlew, *Numenius americanus*

Long-eared owl, *Asio otus*

Long-tailed duck, *Clangula hyemalis* [formerly oldsquaw]

Mallard, *Anas platyrhynchos*

Marsh wren, *Cistothorus palustris* [formerly long-billed marsh wren]

Merlin, *Falco columbarius*

Nelson's sparrow, *Ammodramus nelsoni*

Northern flicker, *Colaptes auratus*

Northern harrier, *Circus hudsonius* [until recently, *C. cyaneus*, and once known as a marsh hawk.]

Northern saw-whet owl, *Aegolius acadicus*

Osprey, *Pandion haliaetus*

Passenger pigeon, *Ectopistes migratorius**

Peregrine falcon, *Falco peregrinus*

Piping plover, *Charadrius melodus*

Purple martin, *Progne subis*

Purple sandpiper, *Calidris maritima*

Red-cockaded woodpecker, *Picoides borealis*

Redhead, *Aythya americana*

Red knot, *Calidris canutus*

Red-tailed hawk, *Buteo jamaicensis*

Ring-billed gull, *Larus delawarensis*

Ruddy turnstone, *Arenaria interpres*

Saltmarsh sparrow, *Ammodramus caudacutus*

Sanderling, *Calidris alba*

Savannah sparrow, *Passerculus sandwichensis*

Scaup, *Aythya* spp. [greater, *A. marila*, and lesser scaup, *A. affinis*, both overwinter on the New Jersey coast]

Semipalmated sandpiper, *Calidris pusilla*

Sharp-shinned hawk, *Accipiter striatus*

Short-billed dowitcher, *Limnodromus griseus*

Snow goose, *Anser* [*Chen*] *caerulescens* [two subspecies: greater snow goose, *A. c. atlanticus*, and lesser snow goose, *A. c. caerulescens*]

Snowy egret, *Egretta thula*

Snowy owl, *Bubo scandiacus* [*Nyctea scandiaca*]

Sora rail, *Porzana carolina*

Surf scoter, *Melanitta perspicillata*

Swamp sparrow, *Melospiza georgiana*

Tree swallow, *Tachycineta bicolor*

Tundra swan, *Cygnus* [*Olor*] *columbianus* [formerly known as whistling swan]

Turkey vulture, *Cathartes aura*

Whimbrel, *Numenius phaeopus*

Whooping crane, *Grus americana*

Willet, *Tringa semipalmata*

Wood duck, *Aix sponsa*

Yellow-rumped warbler, *Setophaga* [*Dendroica*] *coronata* [formerly known as myrtle warbler]

Mammals

Bison, *Bison bison*

Bottlenose dolphin, *Tursiops truncatus*

Coyote, *Canis latrans*

Fin whale, *Balaenoptera physalus*

Giant panda, *Ailuropoda melanoleuca*

Grey whale, *Eschrichtius robustus*

Gray wolf, *Canis lupus*

Grizzly bear, *Ursa arctos horribilis*

Humpback whale, *Megaptera novaeangliae*

Lemming, any of several species of which the brown lemming (*Lemmus trimucronatus*) is typical of those associated with three- to four-year population cycles

Masked shrew, *Sorex cinereus*

Mastodon, *Mammut americanum**

Meadow jumping mouse, *Zapus hudsonicus*

Meadow vole, *Microtus pennsylvanicus*

Minke whale, *Balaenoptera acutorostrata*

Muskrat, *Ondatra zibethicus*

North Atlantic right whale, *Eubalaena gracialis*

Northern river otter, *Lontra [Lutra] canadensis*

Raccoon, *Procyon lotor*

Red fox, *Vulpes fulva*

Red squirrel, *Tamiasciurus hudsonicus*

Southern red-backed vole, *Myodes [Clethrionomys] gapperi*

Sperm whale, *Physeter macrocephalis*

Striped skunk, *Mephitis mephitis*

White-footed mouse, *Peromyscus luecopus*

White-tailed deer, *Odocoileus virginianus*

Acknowledgments

N O BOOK of this genre can be completed without considerable help from those willing to share their insights and expertise. Thus, I take great pleasure to acknowledge—with my deepest gratitude—the contributions of John C. Abbott, Kenneth W. Able, James Allen, Joseph R. Arsenault, Katherine A. Ashton-Alcox, Barbara Battelle, Keith Bildstein, Joseph J. Bilinski, Michele Blackburn, Jay S. Bolden, Paul A. X. Bologna, Mark Boriek, Peter J. Bosak, John B. Bryans, Sherrel Bunn, John F. Bunnell, Joanna Burger, David Bushek, Lawrence B. Cahoon, Paul M. Castelli, John Cecil, Mary Ann Cerra, the late Brian R. Chapman, Monica A. Chasten, Jonathan A. Coddington, Bruce A. Colvin, Kevin B. Conner, Paul Crump, Bob Cunningham, Raymond M. Danner, M. Zachery Darnell, Robert E. Davis, William "Willie" deCamp Jr., Mark Demitroff, Emile D. DeVito, Amanda D. Dey, Patricia Dixon, Robert Dolan, Michael L. Draney, Katharine E. Duffy, Pete Dunne, Carl Eben, Britta Forsberg, Michael Fritz, Joel T. Fry, William B. Gallagaher, Mendy Garron, Shane Godshell, Laurie J. Goodrich, Ilene Grossman-Bailey, Roger Gwiazdowski, Jason Hafstad, Maina Handmaker, Paul Hart, Christopher J. Harvey, Robert W. Hastings, Gregory S. Hinks, Paul Hosier, Bernard Isaacson, Tyler Keck, Jay Kelly, Rick Lathrop, Craig A. Layman, Dale, Richard, and Drew Lockwood, Joseph L. Lomax, Christine A. Lutz, Michael A. Mallin, Janet Mann, Vincent Maresca,

Joe Martucci, Daniel G. McAuley, R. Dale McCall, Scott McConnell, Brittany McLaughlin, Matthew McLean, William A. McLellan, John J. McDermott, Steven P. Minkkinen, Kelly Mooij, Thomas E. Moorman, Brian K. Moscatello, Kent Mountford, Ted Nichols, Matthew Olson, Robert Orth, Ann Pabst, Matthew C. Pace, James F. Parnell, Michael A. Patten, Joseph R. Pawlik, Matthew Pelligrine, Darin S. Penneys, Martin H. Posey, Todd Pover, Leslie Reinhardt, Virginia E. Rettig, Eric Reuter, Cindy Rovins, Peter Rowe, Chris and Pernille Ruhalter, Eric Ruhalter, Gabrielle Sakolsky, Felica Sanders, Frederick S. Scharf, Reilly Sharp, Sandra E. Shumway, Brian R. Silliman, Ronald K. Sizemore, Sue A. Slotterback, Ainsley Smith, Edward M. Sokorai, Clyde Sorenson, Scott D. Stanford, John G. Stoffolano Jr., Aaron Stoler, Lena Struwe, Clay Sutton, Erik Swanson, Martha M. Sylvia, Graceanne Taylor, Lenore Tedesco, Peter N. Thomas, Carm R. Tomas, Vincent V. Turner, Karen Walzer, John P. Wenk, Bob Whipped, Denise Willis, W. Herbet Wilson Jr., Andrew Windisch, Louise S. Wootton, Ben Wurst, Robert T. Zappalorti, Brian Zarate, George L. Zimmerman, Jordan Zimmerman, and Michael Zupko. A special shout-out goes to Clay and Pat Sutton for jump-starting my stalled progress with their encouragement and a batch of much-needed photos. I am indebted to all, but I alone remain responsible for whatever faults that may appear in the following pages.

I have for many years—and in the preparation of several books—benefited from my association with the Randall Library at UNC Wilmington. During this period, segments of the staff have come and gone, but the turnover never lessened the willingness of each cohort to pursue even the most trivial of my many requests for research materials. To a person, they responded with diligence and dedication, and I thank all for their professionalism and assistance.

I am indebted to Peter Mickulas, Daryl Brower, Kiely Schuck, Mary Belibasakis, and Isabel Holland, all at Rutgers University Press, and to Helen Wheeler at Westchester Publishing Services for their competent and thoughtful handling of the project. Along the way, they generously granted me several accommodations regarding style and format, for which I offer my profound thanks. Joseph Dahm carefully edited the manuscript, often saving me from embarrassing mistakes, and Jen Burton expertly produced a comprehensive index. In particular, I deeply appreciate the patience granted by one and all to an old timer too often dazzled by modern technology.

Kenneth Able, with the keen eyes of a seasoned scientist, deserves mention for his critical review of the entire text and shore notes. Likewise, I am grateful for the technical help of Eric Ruhalter, Drew Lockwood, and the late Brian Chapman. Mary Ann Cerra kindly kept me abreast of happenings in New Jersey as reported in the *Press of Atlantic City*, many of which were catalysts for further research.

Finally, my wife, Elizabeth, too often widowed by my reclusive retreat to write, stands as the pillar of my life. To her I offer not only my thanks, but my everlasting love.

Index

Note: *Italic* page numbers indicate illustrations.

ground nesters, 150

groundsel, 94, 120, *121*, 229

groundwater, 254

grouse plains, 260

grubbing, 240

Gulf Stream, 226

gull-billed terns, 164, 164n1

gulls, 163–164; in Barnegat Bay, 150–153, 158; collisions with lighthouses, 158; diet of, 164; species of, 163–164; vs. terns, 163. *See also specific types*

guns, punt, 172

gypsy moths, 271

hackberry, 69

Hackensack Meadowlands, 99, 223, 265

Hall, Henry, 268

Halloween Storm, 73

halophytes, 92, 107

Hannibal, Mary Ellen, 304

hardwood bogs, 260, 271–273

harlequin ducks, 75, *76*

harriers, 187

Harrisville Lake, 279

Harshberger, John, xiv, 16–18

Hartline, H. Keffer, 214n1

Harvey Cedars, 6

Haskin Shellfish Research Laboratory, 230, 234

Hawk Mountain, 187, 190

hawks: in abatement falconry, 164; hunting of, 187–190, 199; migration across Delaware Bay, 234; migration through Cape May, 184–190, 199. *See also specific types*

Hawkwatch platform, 202

Hay, John, 91

hazardous waste, 301

Heacox, Kim, 22

heathers, 255

heath hens, 14–15, 21, 260–262

Heislerville Game Management Area, 237

"Help Your Child to Wonder" (Carson), 27

hemlocks, 3

herbarium specimens, 17, 26

herbicides, 204

herons: in Delaware Bay, 238; early naturalists' study of, 13; heronries, 150; migration of, 184; in salt marshes, 110–111

herptiles (herps), in Pine Barrens, 280–287

herring, 279

herring gulls, 150, 152–153, 163–164, 166

Hessel's hairstreak butterflies, 270–271, *271*

hibernation: by mice, 65; by snakes, 16, 283–285, 287

Higbee Beach Wildlife Management Area, *63*, 203

highbush blueberries, 70, 265, 269, 288

Highlands, *2*, 2–3

Highs Beach, 215

hockey, 276

hognose snakes, 283

hollies, 60, 68–69, *69*, 289

Holly Haven, 289

Holly Society of America, 289

Homer, Winslow, 73

homing behavior, 224

honeysuckle, 70

Hopatcong, Lake, basin of, 2

horned pondweed, 111, 134

horse flies, 122

horses, *96*, 124

horseshoe crabs, 212–223; anatomy of, 212–214, *213*; commercial harvest of, 214–217, *215*, 220, 221; decline in population of, 215–223; in Delaware Bay, 212–223; eggs of, in bird diets, *218*, 219–223; life cycle of, 217; range of, 214; reproduction of, *213*, 214, 217, *218*; at The Wetlands Institute, 103

Horseshoe Island, 74

house flies, 144

How to Raise a Wild Child (Sampson), 27

huckleberries, 255, 257

Hudson, Henry, 5

Hugo, Hurricane, 114

hummingbirds, 70

humpback whales, 7

hunting: boats used in, 170; decoys in, 162, 168–172, *169*, 263; early history of, 6–7; market, 13–14, 172, 193, 194; Migratory Bird Treaty Act on, 172; plumage, 20, 150, 150n2, 163; waterfowl stamp for, 158, *159*. *See also specific species*

hurricanes, 71, 72–73, 114. *See also specific hurricanes*

hybridization, 196, 237, 288

hydrogen sulfide, 92, 146

hydroids, 37–38

Ian, Hurricane, 72

ibises, 153n3

ice ages, 3, 60

inlets, 71–75. *See also specific inlets*

Inner Coastal Plain, 3

inquilines, 275

insects: in Barnegat Bay, 143–146; biting, 122–124; in dunes, 54, 57; early naturalists' study of, 20;

About the Author

Eric G. Bolen, now retired, served as dean of the graduate school and professor in the Department of Biology and Marine Biology at the University of North Carolina Wilmington. He previously served on the faculty of Texas Tech University and as assistant director at the Welder Wildlife Foundation. He has authored or coauthored more than 200 publications, including several books about ecology, natural history, and wildlife ecology and management, most recently *An Abundance of Curiosities: The Natural History of North Carolina's Coastal Plain*. He served as editor of the *Wildlife Bulletin* and as president of the Southwestern Association of Naturalists and is a life member of six professional societies.